EDITED BY VICKIE B. SULLIVAN

The Comedy and Tragedy of Machiavelli

ESSAYS ON THE
LITERARY
WORKS

Yale University Press
New Haven &
London

Set in Sabon type by Keystone Typesetting, Inc.
Printed in the United States of America.

Library of Congress Cataloging-in-Publication Data
The comedy and tragedy of Machiavelli : essays on the literary works / edited by
Vickie B. Sullivan.
    p. cm.
Includes index.
ISBN 0-300-08258-4 (cl : alk. paper) — ISBN 0-300-08797-7 (pb : alk. paper)
    1. Machiavelli, Niccolò, 1469–1527—Criticism and interpretation.
I. Sullivan, Vickie B.
PQ4627.M2 Z655 2000
852'.3—dc21   00-026112

A catalogue record for this book is available from the British Library.

The paper in this book meets the guidelines for permanence and durability of the
Committee on Production Guidelines for Book Longevity of the Council on
Library Resources.

10 9 8 7 6 5 4 3 2 1

The Comedy and Tragedy of Machiavelli

Contents

Acknowledgments

This volume owes its origin to Robert Faulkner and Harvey C. Mansfield, who approached me with the project; I am pleased that they did. My colleague in political theory at Tufts University, Robert Devigne, provided me with wise counsel and helpful commentary.

Introduction

VICKIE B. SULLIVAN

Niccolò Machiavelli wrote not only grave, cold-blooded political tracts, but also seemingly lighthearted comedies, poems, and fables. His corpus seems to divide between subjects of the utmost seriousness and those merely frivolous and funny. On the serious side one finds, for example, the *Description of the Way Duke Valentino Killed Vitellozzo Vitelli, Oliverotto da Fermo, Signor Pagolo, and the Duke of Gravina Orsini,* a bone-chillingly terse relation of the historical incident in which Cesare Borgia tricked his armed and formidable rivals into accepting terms of friendship only to have them murdered. As dark as this work is, the final outcome for Cesare, which Machiavelli furnishes in other works, is even darker. The master dissembler, the man who capitalizes on the gullibility of others, makes his own critical error in judgment when deciding how to exercise his influence after the death of his father, Pope Alexander VI. Cesare allows Giuliano della Rovere, a man who had reason to hate and fear Cesare, to become Pope Julius II. In *The Prince,* for example, Machiavelli dispatches Cesare, his daring deeds, and his malicious cleverness with the maxim "Whoever believes that among great personages new benefits will make old injuries be forgotten deceives himself. So the duke erred in this choice and it was the cause of his ultimate ruin."[1]

On the frivolous side of the divide, one finds the same author presenting his character Nicomaco, who is hilariously thwarted in the play *Clizia* in his attempt to have his lackey marry Clizia, the girl whom he has raised as a daughter, so that Nicomaco will be permitted to carry out his lustful designs on her. Wise to his nefarious plan, Nicomaco's wife substitutes another male servant for Clizia in the wedding ceremony and in the matrimonial bed. When Nicomaco takes the place of his phony bridegroom on the wedding night, he finds himself humiliated by his own servant, who not only successfully resists his master's misplaced amorous advances throughout the course of the night, but who toward dawn takes the offensive against Nicomaco in a most offensive manner. Thus, Machiavelli presents both the darkest realities of politics and the laughter that love and lust can inspire.

Machiavelli himself draws attention to just such a dichotomy when reflecting on the character of the correspondence he had been conducting with Francesco Vettori: "Anyone who might see our letters, honorable *compare,* and see their variety, would be greatly astonished, because at first it would seem that we were serious men completely directed toward weighty matters and that no thought could cascade through our heads that did not have within it probity and magnitude. But later, upon turning the page, it would seem to the reader that we — still the very same selves — were petty, fickle, lascivious, and were directed toward chimerical matters." Far from being censured for this variety, Machiavelli continues, he and Vettori should be praised because they imitate nature itself in all its variety.[2]

Not merely his correspondence, but the corpus itself would appear to be such an imitation of nature. What are students of his work to make of the two extremes it contains? To answer that question this book turns to the literary works and offers a lavish variety of Machiavellian scholarship, for it brings together scholars from the fields of literature, political science, and history to expound on the meaning of an array of his literary works, the light as well as the dark — on *Clizia* as well as on the *Description*.

Such variety, readers of the book will find, gives rise to a fundamental controversy among its contributors that reaches to the heart of Machiavelli's literary works and ultimately to his intentions and self-understanding. This controversy concerns the meaning of the extremes found in Machiavelli's thought, finds its origin in Machiavelli's own description of himself as a writer, and, in fact, gives this book its title: the degree to which Machiavelli's works partake of the character of comedy and of tragedy. In short, which view of the world does his work offer: a comic view, in which his sometimes playful but always pointed challenges to previous authority illuminate the way to human beings' mastery of the forces that have hitherto thwarted their earthly endeavors? or a tragic view, in which human beings are always subjected to and often crushed by forces more powerful than they? If comic, Machiavelli's vision is hopeful of the place of human beings in the world; if tragic, it is such that human beings must come to grips with the eternal human condition of unexpected loss and defeat. The scholars writing here confront this controversy over Machiavelli's outlook and intention with a view to clarifying its terms and stakes. Readers of the book will come away with profound but fundamentally opposed examples of how to read and understand Machiavelli's works.

In signing a letter to Francesco Guicciardini, Machiavelli identifies himself as "Niccolò Machiavelli, historico, comico et tragico."[3] His identification of himself as a historian is not controversial: in the same year this letter was composed he presented his *Florentine Histories* to Pope Clement VII. Neither is it surprising for the author of *Mandragola* and *Clizia* to call himself a comedian. The last element, the epithet "tragico," gives pause, however, because Machiavelli is the author of no work understood in the conventional sense as a tragedy.

One facet of his thought is nevertheless given over to grave matters and calamitous events, and prominent scholars have argued that this subject matter renders tragic those works that touch upon it. Machiavelli transmits through his writings the tragedy to which his life bore witness. For example, in *The Prince,* in *Discourses on Livy,* in the *Decennials,* and in the *Florentine Histories,* Machiavelli laments the condition of Italy, which was at the time divided and ravaged by foreign armies. Indeed, at the close of the letter to Guicciardini and immediately before he identifies himself as a tragedian, Machiavelli writes, "I vent my feelings by accusing the princes who have all done everything they can to bring us to this situation."[4] In explicating this angry closing of Machiavelli, Roberto Ridolfi renders its author a tragic playwright of a kind: "The tragedy was now at its fifth act, and Italy was its subject."[5]

The tragedy of Italy adversely affected Machiavelli's own fate. As a result of the actions of the French and Spanish armies in Italy, the Florentine republic, which Machiavelli was serving as the head of the Second Chancery, collapsed, ushering in the return of Medicean rule. Cast from office, he makes sure that we hear him bemoaning his miserable fate in the great works that he wrote as a direct result of his exile from politics. He dedicates *The Prince* to Lorenzo de' Medici and hopes that it will draw the attention of the Magnificent Lorenzo to the "low places," where he will find its insightful author "undeservedly . . . endur[ing] a great and continuous malignity of fortune."[6] Moreover, in the prologue to *Mandragola* he informs anyone who might find the light fare of the play unworthy of its creator, "who wishes to seem wise and grave," that "he is trying with these vain thoughts to make his wretched time more pleasant," having "been cut off from showing with other undertakings other *virtue*."[7] In such self-portraits, we see an anguished soul, brooding about how fortune has cast him as its victim.

Machiavelli's writings show that he is not alone in this role; fortune has cast others before him as its victim. His princes of promise, such as Cesare Borgia and Castruccio Castracani, have succumbed to overwhelming events. Thus, some scholars conclude that Machiavelli learned from his personal history as well as from history in general that inscrutable forces play an insuperable role in human events. Hanna Pitkin details Machiavelli's exhortations for men to assume control of their destinies but concludes that he regards the struggle as hopeless because fortune will always have the final judgment as to the success of their ventures.[8]

The view that Machiavelli's world contains powers beyond human control grounds the conclusion that Machiavelli has an explicitly tragic view of worldly things. For instance, Wayne A. Rebhorn sees Machiavelli's literary, historical, and political works through the lens of the literary genre devoted to what he terms the "confidence man," the master of deceit and trickery common in Renaissance literature, and suggests that Machiavelli's political heroes are variants of this type. Accepting Pitkin's view of fortune as a force that can never be adequately vanquished, Rebhorn suggests that Machiavelli's princes, because they pursue lofty, unattainable goals that put them at the mercy of fortune's malevolent vagaries, achieve in consequence of their exalted but ultimately futile struggles a stature close to that of tragic heroes.[9]

Other scholars have gone further. Giorgio Barberi-Squarotti, for instance, eliminates the distance that Rebhorn wishes to maintain between Machiavelli's prince and a tragic hero: Machiavelli's prince is the stuff of tragedy.[10] Scholars have also found tragedy in Machiavelli's comedy, arguing that his *Mandragola* is a dark satire that is at base a tragedy.[11]

When scholars point to such tragic elements of Machiavelli's thought, they often associate him with an older view, whether religious or secular, that human beings are perpetually vulnerable to forces larger and more powerful than they. Neither the present nor the future holds a solution to the problems that plague human beings generally. A variant of this tragic view also associates Machiavelli with the ancients in another way. Machiavelli regards his time as vastly inferior to that of antiquity, particularly that of ancient Rome. Machiavelli is a nostalgic admirer of the ancients. He would like to see his contemporaries imitate the glorious deeds of the Romans, but he knows that any such attempt is bound to failure because of the thorough corruption of the men of his age.[12] His age is one of tragic failure in the political and military realm.

Another school of thought denies the very possibility of tragedy in Machiavelli's thought as a whole. Leo Strauss declares, "There is no tragedy in Machiavelli." Cesare Borgia's fate, according to Machiavelli's rendition, cannot be considered tragic, he continues, because Cesare made a fundamental mistake that he need not have: "As regards chance in general, it can be conquered; man is the master."[13] Thus, Strauss rejects the possibility that Machiavelli, despite his loud lamentations regarding his fate or that of Florence or that of Italy, gives in to tragic despair. Human beings when properly armed and instructed are capable of vanquishing the forces of nature or of the divine that have hitherto thwarted their designs.[14] In order to accomplish this grand design, human beings need to reorient themselves in the world; they need to reject the morality that they have inherited from Christianity and from classical philosophy by unleashing the passions in the service of unlimited—and armed—acquisition.

Machiavelli, himself a victim of fortune, will conquer that fortune by leading humanity to this end; he will achieve this result when the adherents whom he gathers through his writings overturn the Christian and classical traditions to institute the "new modes and orders," which he alone has discovered and transmitted to them.[15] In stark contrast to those scholars who ascribe to Machiavelli a tragic view of the world, then, Strauss associates him not with an older view of any sort, but rather with modernity. In fact, according to Strauss, Machiavelli is the founder of modernity. His exhortation to conquer fortune, his rejection of august authority, his appreciation for the human good that can come from the unleashing of the passions, and his hope for a future redeemed lay an early foundation for some of the familiar doctrines of the Enlightenment.

Harvey C. Mansfield, who shares Strauss's view of Machiavelli as the self-proclaimed bearer of the new, likens him to a prince of a posthumous principality.[16] Thus, Machiavelli exaggerates his despair to accentuate the magnitude of his victory. Far from bewailing his status as a mere servant who longs to minister to the rulers of his day, Machiavelli relishes his future status as the master of a new epoch he intends to found through his writings, which contain his "mind and intention."[17] For both Strauss and Mansfield, then, modernity is in an important respect his creation—he undertook this new path knowingly—and hence, his very creation offers tangible evidence of the possibility of conquering fortune.

Because Machiavelli does not recognize the invulnerability of superhuman forces that can render human life tragic and because he teaches others to scoff at high moral claims, the denial of tragedy brings a hopeful—even comedic—aspect not only to his lighter works but to his political works as well. Strauss declares that "the spirit of comedy, not to say levity, is not absent from his two most serious books."[18] In Machiavelli's work, levity enters even the gravest of domains.

How can two such fundamentally opposed understandings arise from one writer's work? In this case, it may be answered that Machiavelli seems to encourage this stark divide among scholars, as a consideration of an important chapter in the *Discourses* illustrates. An interpretation of *Discourses* 2.5 can easily mutate from a mere recapitulation of the ancient understanding of the precariousness of civilization — and hence of all human endeavor as a result of its vulnerability to the periodic recurrence of natural disasters — to an intimation of Machiavelli's gleeful confidence that an individual can become the instigator of a new epoch, and back again.

This chapter of the *Discourses* begins with the philosophic consideration of whether or not the world is eternal: "To those philosophers who would have it that the world is eternal, I believe that one could reply that if so much antiquity were true it would be reasonable that there be memory of more than five thousand years — if it were not seen how the memories of times are eliminated by diverse causes, of which part come from men, part from heaven."[19] Machiavelli's sentence offers a playful false start that seemingly challenges the ancient philosophers' claim for the eternity of the world in the name of the Christian creation, but by its end he corroborates the ancient philosophic view of the world's eternity by providing a perfectly reasonable explanation of why records of the most distant past do not exist: they were destroyed by human and natural causes.

Later in the chapter, he turns to examine those heavenly causes of the ruin of the records of antiquity. He points to natural disasters that "reduce the inhabitants of part of the world to a few," naming plague, famine, and "an inundation of waters." He affirms, "That these inundations, plagues, and famines come about I do not believe is to be doubted, because all the histories are full of them, because this effect of the oblivion of things is seen, and because it seems reasonable that it should be so."[20] Of course, Genesis gives an account of such a flood, but tales of similar disasters appear in the writings of such classical thinkers as Plato, Aristotle, and Polybius. In both scriptural and philosophic accounts, civilization is proven to be extremely fragile, no matter how human endeavor and achievement mask for a time the fundamental vulnerability to powers stronger than it.

In Plato's *Laws,* for example, the Athenian Stranger posits that "there have been cities, and human beings engaged in politics" for an "immense and immeasurable time" and that "tens of thousands of cities have come into being during that time, and . . . just as many, in the same proportions, have been destroyed." He reflects on the causes of these alterations, giving credence to those "ancient sayings" that "tell of many disasters — floods and plagues and many other things — which have destroyed human beings and left only a tiny remnant of the human race." Of these various disasters, the Athenian Stranger decides to "focus our minds on one that occurred once on account of a flood." In focusing on this disaster, he concludes that "those who then escaped the destruction would almost all be mountain herdsmen — little sparks of the human race saved on the peaks somewhere."[21]

Like the Athenian Stranger, Machiavelli, in treating these disasters, decides to concentrate on a flood and the herdsmen who would be the progenitors of a new civilization. He asserts that an inundation of waters is the "most important . . . both because it is more universal and because those who are saved are all mountain men and coarse, who, since they do not have knowledge of antiquity, cannot leave it to posterity." Although to this point Machiavelli's focus on the flood is similar to the Athenian Stranger's, here he adds an element altogether new and strange. He continues that the flood is the most important because if it should happen that among these coarse mountain men "someone is saved who has knowledge of [antiquity], to make a reputation and a name for himself he conceals it and perverts it in his mode so that what he has wished to write alone, and nothing else, remains for his successors."[22]

It is this detail that suggests Machiavelli is not merely recapitulating the ancient understanding of human vulnerability to chance events. In the Athenian Stranger's account of the flood, for example, human beings must make an entirely new beginning. In Machiavelli's version, by contrast, this unique knower is able to arrange how the new epoch is to unfold. Thus, Machiavelli's envisioned new beginning is not entirely new, but is shaped instead by the knower's understanding and assessment of the previous epoch. Because no one else possesses his knowledge or understanding, he "perverts" his knowledge in order to react to the previous epoch; it was good or bad, worthy of imitation or of repudiation, only so far as the knower wishes it to be. The epoch that is to be born arises not from the rubble, but from one human being's knowledge and understanding.

In this way, Machiavelli suggests how one person can shape history, even in the face of the fury of nature or heaven. The individual becomes even more prominent when it is considered that his motivation stems from his personal desire for fame. He perverts history in order "to make a reputation and a name for himself." This knower capitalizes on the destruction of civilization. An individual seemingly can best the forces to which human beings are subject.[23] On this reading, then, Machiavelli is not corroborating the ancient understanding of the fragility of all human things but instead pointing the way to the human manipulation of seemingly uncontrollable events.

Upon deeper consideration, however, this individual's victory seems not necessarily ephemeral but certainly impermanent. Eventually the civilization of which he is the creator will be destroyed by similar forces. Perhaps another such as he will survive that future deluge. In this fortuity, the next knower will probably be motivated by the same desire for reputation, which will require that he wipe out the name of the founder of the previous epoch to magnify his own glory as the founder of the next. From this longer perspective, then, Machiavelli, while asserting the power of some rare individuals, seems to corroborate the understanding of the ancients: all human things, no matter how glorious, are subject to decay and destruction. Despite the prospect of this ultimate ruin of his project, however, the knower must have had the gratification of contemplating both the fact that he will change the course of history and the glory that he will thereby win, whether or not his name will endure for eternity. Clearly, then, scholars can find material enough in *Discourses* 2.5 to support either portrait of Machiavelli—that of hopeful prognosticator of a new dispensation or that of thinker resigned to the perpetual limits of human ambition.

Moreover the Machiavelli of the *Discourses* does not take pity on the perplexed reader later in the work. At two places in the third book of the *Discourses* Machiavelli touches all too fleetingly on another topic related to the possibility of human beings mastering their fates. At these points, he reflects not on the succession of epochs, but on the possibility of a single regime enduring forever; he provides conflicting responses to the possibility. The initial discussion denies the potentiality that a republic can be perpetual, and the second indicates how a republic might grasp at perpetuity. Consideration of the accidents to which republics are susceptible leads Machiavelli to declare in *Discourses* 3.17, "Because one cannot give a certain remedy for such disorders that arise in republics, it follows that it is impossible to order a perpetual republic, because its ruin is caused through a thousand unexpected ways."[24] Five chapters later, however, Machiavelli considers the benefits that captains of a harsh disposition bring to a republic and concludes that these benefits are extreme indeed. Specifically, harsh captains make extraordinary demands and order extreme punishments, which, according to Machiavelli, "are useful in a republic because they return its orders toward their beginning and into its ancient virtue."[25] As he explains in *Discourses* 3.1, the fear that such extraordinary commands induce replicates the fear people felt at the beginning of the regime, when the citizens eagerly clung to the new regime for protection, hoping that they would not be punished as they had seen its enemies punished. In 3.22, Machiavelli is quite explicit as to the character of those extreme benefits that harsh captains bring to the regime: "If a republic were so happy that it often had one who with his example might renew the laws, and not only restrain it from running to ruin but pull it back, it would be perpetual."[26]

According to Machiavelli's *Discourses,* then, perpetuity on the plane of politics is both within and beyond the grasp of human beings; he extends the promise and denies its possibility. In this way, he can be said to encourage the comic *and* tragic characterizations of his thought and works. Machiavelli is comic when he optimistically extends the promise, and tragic when he denies the possibility of its fulfillment. Thus, the *Discourses* can be said to justify either characterization of Machiavelli.

What light, then, do the literary works shed on this fundamental question? Some of the essays that follow directly address either the comedy or the tragedy contained in Machiavelli's literary works. Others do not, and need not, do so directly because the question of Machiavelli's comedy and tragedy goes to the heart of Machiavelli's self-understanding, of his intention, and of his capacities. How much can he accomplish? What is the place of human beings in the world and what is his role specifically? All of the essays speak to these issues. Some portray Machiavelli as calling forth hitherto untapped reserves of human ingenuity to control destiny, others as understanding human efficacy to be circumscribed by superhuman forces or as suffering when contemplating the demands such forces place on the human actor. When he treats the devastated political landscape of Italy, some see Machiavelli exulting in his capacities as a writer, others believe he is accepting as fated the destruction of promising political redeemers.

Mansfield's essay on *Mandragola* introduces the book's attention to Machiavelli as writer of comedies as well as to the view (which Mansfield argues) that his vision of the world inclines more toward comedy than tragedy. Mansfield finds that this comic play, like Machiavelli's political works, teaches how human possibilities can be extended when actors jettison morality. Finding the key to the play in the desire of foolish old Messer Nicia to have children, Mansfield explores how this desire, combined with Nicia's wish to preserve respectability, transforms the short-term dalliance for which Callimaco longs into an extended engagement that allows Nicia to maintain appearances while producing the children he desires. Moreover, the conspiracy that brings Callimaco to Lucrezia's bed ultimately benefits all involved. Mansfield asks, Who is this Messer Nicia, who, while appearing so foolish, is able to conquer chance and to benefit others in this way? He answers that Messer Nicia shares with Machiavelli the need for successors and a plan to acquire them that makes them both cuckolds. Thus, in Mansfield's analysis, *Mandragola* is part of Machiavelli's plan to establish for himself the perpetual republic to which he alludes in *Discourses* 3.22. On Mansfield's reading, *Mandragola* in surprising ways helps to reveal Machiavelli's deepest intentions.

In interpreting Machiavelli's comic play *Clizia,* Robert Faulkner also finds that Machiavelli's comedy conveys important lessons. According to Faulkner, the play teaches cynicism and the methods by which one can satisfy one's desires. Specifically, it shows how individuals can use the desires of others to get want they want, if only they are enlightened as to their real needs and to the motivations of others. For Faulkner, too, Machiavelli's resolute skepticism about high claims of morality and about the noble types who make them combines with his teaching that failure is the product of poor management alone so that there is no room for tragedy in Machiavelli's universe. But in Faulkner's view, the world of Machiavelli's comedy is removed from and inferior to his political world. Whereas the political works teach how to acquire the highest goods, such as security and glory, the comedies are devoted to the lesser goods contained in the private world of the household.

Arlene Saxonhouse also takes comedy as her subject, exploring it through a study of Machiavelli's letters. The letters are a venue, according to her, through which Machiavelli exercises his comic imagination, concocting narratives that poke fun at himself, at others, and at the absurdity of the world. But the imagination that Machiavelli deploys in his correspondence is central to his politics. It is necessary for penetrating to the motivations of actors on the great stage of politics. Further, the imagination that the letters display reveals Machiavelli as a prince of his own realm, making others, even the flux of nature itself, submit to his commands. For Saxonhouse, the private actions narrated in the letters are political actions, and the private man who fashions these narrations is a political ruler of a type. In linking imagination to Machiavelli's politics in this way, she corrects the mistaken understanding that takes the warning found in chapter 15 of *The Prince* against "imaginary republics and principalities" to be a condemnation of imagination simply. Ultimately, Saxonhouse offers a comic Machiavelli who delights in his imaginative powers despite the deprivations to which his life was subject.

Susan Meld Shell in her interpretation of *Discourse or Dialogue Concerning Our Language* similarly depicts a Machiavelli who knowingly revels in his extraordinary literary talents. She reveals the thoroughly Machiavellian character of this rather odd work as she finds Machiavelli's familiar political and military arguments in its literary concerns. She shows that Machiavelli's attack on Dante, for which this work is notorious, is occasioned by his dislike not so much of his great predecessor's poetry, but of the political doctrines he espouses: Dante is too aristocratic and too attached to universals. As a result he ultimately works—against his own testimony regarding his intentions—to bolster the influence of papal Rome. Nevertheless, Machiavelli grants Dante status as a type of founder. In uncovering how Machiavelli opposes himself to Dante and how he decides the matter in favor of himself, Shell asks whether

Machiavelli intends to present himself as a founder of a literary empire superior to that of Dante.

Ronald Martinez's essay entitled "Tragic Machiavelli" takes us from comedy to tragedy, from hoped-for success to fated horrors. While accepting Ridolfi's interpretation of the "tragico" of Machiavelli's signature as an expression of despair at Italy's political and military subjugation, Martinez explores the additional possibility that the epithet refers to the techniques of tragedy that Machiavelli uses in his comic plays and in his political and historical writings alike. Ranging over the comedies as well as the *Florentine Histories, The Prince,* the *Decennials, The Life of Castruccio Castracani of Lucca,* and the *Description of the Way Duke Valentino Killed Vitellozzo Vitelli, Oliverotto da Fermo, Signor Pagolo, and the Duke of Gravina Orsini,* Martinez shows that the tragic aspects of Machiavelli's writing become apparent when viewed in the light not only of other written tragedies of the early cinquecento but also of classical and medieval conceptions of tragedy. Martinez's reading gives Machiavelli the leading voice in a tragic chorus issuing from his tumultuous time and place.

Michael Harvey explores, through his reading of the poem *The Ass,* the psychological demands of Machiavelli's call for a resolute masculine virtue that subdues all in its wake. Harvey finds that the poem, like Machiavelli's political works, contains an ambivalent attitude toward forceful self-assertion. At times, Machiavelli bravely maintains that human action can bring about human salvation, but he also casts doubt on the efficacy of such efforts in a hostile world. What *The Ass* brings to clarity is Machiavelli's keen awareness of the psychic price of his conception of virtue. For one moment — a moment that occurs in *The Ass* — Machiavelli offers a glimpse into a world in which love reigns and in which the male need not be the aggressor but rather the recipient of succoring understanding. As quickly as Machiavelli offers this vision, however, he revokes it. His revocation of this tantalizing offering serves to foster a haunting sense of loss when one confronts again his world of ceaseless agon and thus renders his vision even darker than before.

Franco Fido's essay "The Politician as Writer" introduces the additional concern — addressed by the remaining essays — of Machiavelli's specific abilities and intentions as a writer of history. "Historian" is the remaining epithet that Machiavelli applied to himself in his famous signature. In the hands of these contributors, the term bears on the other two and hence on the question of the comedy and tragedy in Machiavelli's thought. They explore the degree to which Machiavelli could himself exert a measure of control over events that had gone out of control. Fido surveys the expanse of Machiavelli's career as a writer, beginning with his diplomatic dispatches, through the *Description,* the

First Decennial, his writings on France and Germany, *The Art of War, Discourse on Florentine Affairs after the Death of Lorenzo, The Life of Castruccio Castracani of Lucca,* and culminating in the *Florentine Histories.* Placing these works in the context of Machiavelli's personal circumstances and of the broader historical picture, Fido reveals Machiavelli's ability to elevate historical events and political matters to address universal concerns, producing in the process works of high literary creation. He finds that as Machiavelli matured, he relinquished the hope, expressed earlier in *The Prince,* that a prince could defeat fortune and redeem Italy. The older Machiavelli, having scrutinized the bleak political landscape, is more resigned to human weakness and loss but hopeful still that the study of past mistakes can prove beneficial.

Barbara Godorecci, too, is concerned with Machiavelli's capacity as a writer of history in her essay, "Beyond Limits: Time, Space, Language in Machiavelli's *Decennali.*" She turns to Machiavelli's presentation of explicitly poetic history, of history ordered to fit the constraints of terza rima, in his *Decennials.* Here Machiavelli chronicles those disastrously dispiriting events like the French invasions of Italy and Cesare Borgia's spectacular rise to power and ignominious downfall that draw comparisons to tragedy. In treating these grand themes within the boundaries of his poetic medium, Machiavelli laments not just Italy's subjugation but his own constraints as a writer. Godorecci shows, in particular, Machiavelli's concern with limitations of space and time. Through his artistic arrangement of words he is able to mimic the actions he describes: he condenses time and narrows space. Although his language proclaims the inadequacies of himself and his art, his poetry belies those inadequacies and reveals the tremendous power of his language to overcome such limitations.

Edmund Jacobitti likewise understands Machiavelli as a historian who is primarily a literary artist and considers the artistry responsible for the *Florentine Histories.* Jacobitti, however, distinguishes ancient and modern approaches to history, arguing that Machiavelli embraces the premodern conception of history not as a record of progress but rather as a necessarily incomplete record of eternally recurring cycles. All states and civilizations undergo periods of growth and decay that eventuate in ruin. Because history brings nothing new to light, human beings can learn from the experiences of their predecessors in previous ages. The role of the historian in this understanding is to fashion symbols from the random and the particular that will resonate in other places and at other times. The historian, then, is not an impartial recorder of events, but a literary artist who molds events to a moral and artistic vision. Jacobitti examines this ancient conception of history, how it was revived in the Renaissance, and how Machiavelli worked within it. He observes Machiavelli creating in the *Florentine Histories* didactic symbols intended neither to perfect humankind nor to overcome the cycle, but to guide a state through its maturity to its decrepitude rather than allowing it to succumb to a premature death. Inevitably, though, death will come, and thus, according to Jacobitti, Machiavelli's view of history is a tragic one.

Machiavelli's literary works present readers with variety arising from the play of opposites: the light and the grave; the hopeful and the resigned. His writings induce scholars to contemplate two opposed visions of his work as a whole — the comic and the tragic. Sometimes these visions intermingle to a degree, but ultimately no complete reconciliation is offered here: either Machiavelli understands human beings as capable of vanquishing the forces that oppose their endeavors, or not. The contributors' common focus on the literary works points to their shared conviction as to the weighty matter they contain. In taking their opposed views of Machiavelli's obsessions, intentions, and capabilities, these essays enliven, enrich, and extend the debate.

The Comedy and Tragedy of Machiavelli

The Cuckold in Machiavelli's Mandragola

HARVEY C. MANSFIELD

The *Mandragola* makes for a good introduction to Machiavelli. By reading the *Mandragola* ahead of his political works one could become acquainted with his comic and his erotic aspect, his appreciation of the nonpolitical, so that one could look for it in his politics. The levity, the double meanings, even the dirty jokes and blasphemies that run rampant in the *Mandragola* are also present, less obviously, in *The Prince* and the *Discourses on Livy,* in which they reflect his desire to treat respectable political ideas and institutions "without any respect" (sanza alcuno rispetto).[1] Yet it is also true that the *Mandragola* is a heavily politicized comedy, that both its jokes and its erotic passions are managed, hence stunted, for the sake of a political end. Its plot seems at first to tell of a private sexual conquest but turns out to have a political end. Even in private enjoyments Machiavelli has his eye on the main chance.

Unerotic Love

We are not sure when the *Mandragola* was written.[2] The first production was apparently in 1518, and Machiavelli mentions it in a letter in 1520. The action of the *Mandragola* takes place at a time clearly marked for us—ten years after 1494, that is, ten years after the invasion of Charles VIII, king of France, into Italy (1.1). The erotic conquest by the hero, Callimaco, occurs under the shadow of that political conquest and is presented as an alternative employment in a time when virtue, that is, virtue in politics, has been made incapable in Italy. Callimaco, then, is not faced with making a choice between love and command in a situation that would test the relative strength of the two.[3] Politics has for the time being relaxed its hold on him, and he becomes hot with the heat he might have spent in ambition. The purity of his eros is in question. In one of the songs that Machiavelli added to the play later, he speaks of the great power ("possanza") of love, which when tested can move lovers to disobey men, gods, and even themselves. Love provides "arms with which you are armed"[4] — a political rendering of what might seem nonpolitical.

Doubtful, too, of course, is the purity of Callimaco's morality, or of any character's morality in the *Mandragola*. Indeed, the play is about morality, not about eros. It has dirty jokes galore but no scenes of attraction or arousal, and it has no speeches of love. Since Callimaco has nothing grand in view — nothing more than the pleasure of sex or the pleasure of sexual conquest — and since he does not sacrifice anything for it but his spare time, his desire cannot be said to be noble. He is not even "sexy" — a democratic notion of modern times that simultaneously promises nobility and guarantees never to deliver it. Although the action of the play results in the satisfaction of Callimaco's desire, it seems to use and hence subordinate that desire for the purpose of producing a child. The plot contains — or consists in — a trick, but the play is unlike the *beffa* plays of the time because the fun of the trick is turned to account and given a value that proves to be political.[5] In the *Mandragola* the fun makes us laugh, but not so as to enable us to see how ridiculous we are and then to become reconciled with ourselves. Rather, it is to extend our limited sense of our possibilities, and is profoundly political.

Our sense of what is possible is limited by morality. Callimaco's desire for sexual conquest is limited by the moral prohibition against adultery, as he has set his eye on a married woman. Not that the prohibition weighs heavily on him, but it gets in his way. Lucrezia is the wife of a man who with some exaggeration might be called a professor of political science: In the prologue he is called a doctor. Though "hardly astute" (prol.; 1.1), he is said to be a specialist in the philosopher Boethius (whose name, however, is got wrong). Lucrezia and her husband are childless, and both want a child. The action of the play makes their desire a means to the satisfaction of Callimaco's desire, for he uses their desire to get them to agree to his. If the *Mandragola* went only so far as this and Machiavelli were content to make the point that love does not always accord with morality, then however well he said it, he would be saying nothing new in human experience or in comparison with previous comedy. But Machiavelli does not stop here.

At the same time and increasingly as the play proceeds, it subordinates Callimaco to the childless couple and makes his desire a means to the realization of theirs. At the end both he and they get what they want. But at the beginning, Lucrezia too is prevented by the moral law against adultery from having a child by going outside her marriage for the insemination. She is persuaded that the good end of having a child excuses the evil means by which it is got. Having a child is more serious and reputable than merely making a conquest; so Callimaco's lighthearted ambition is justified by an end outside itself. The question, then, in the *Mandragola* is not whether we have the strength to hold to morality in a difficult situation, but whether we should even try to do so. In the play Machiavelli suggests that we have neither the strength nor the obligation. And instead of restating the opposition of love to morality, he offers a reconciliation between them.

Republican Chastity

The seduction of Lucrezia in the *Mandragola* recalls through the similarity of name the rape of Lucretia in Roman history, which occasioned the founding of a republic.[6] That famous rape, followed by Lucretia's suicide, is treated by Machiavelli in his *Discourses on Livy*. For it is narrated by Livy in his history and was the subject of a famous discussion by St. Augustine in the *City of God*.[7] Shakespeare's *Rape of Lucrece* showed it to be a subject for tragedy. But in Livy's narration, Lucretia's sacrifice of her life for the shame done to her chastity was considered inspiration for a republic, a form of government that puts lawfulness or morality ahead of advantage and tyrannical passion. In its respect for morality and the law, republican virtue breathes the spirit of chastity, a seemingly nonpolitical virtue of withdrawal. Chastity in its purity of will, however, sets an example of self-sacrifice that extends from private to public behavior. Moreover the honor of women stands for the principle of limits on a tyrant's will, for whether by their own consent or as other men's property, women are subjects a king cannot have or touch. And in the face of temptation it needs to be defended. Rape, then, is an especially grave violation of law, and rape by a king is tyranny made manifest. The rape of Lucretia by the son of Tarquinius Superbus was appropriately punished by the founding of the Roman republic. Later, that republic was duly revived after the lust of Appius Claudius, head of the Decemvirs, for Virginia was revealed by her father when he killed her in order to save her from the tyrant.

Machiavelli's treatment of these affairs in the *Discourses* is altogether distant from the chaste spirit of republicanism. He speaks slightingly of the "incident of Virginia."[8] He refers to Lucretia's rape as an "accident," an "error," and an "excess."[9] The accident was used by Junius Brutus to overthrow the Tarquin kings and found the republic, but it was merely a pretext. Some other incident would have served as well and would have been found. But Machiavelli also indicates that Tarquinius Superbus could have used the incident himself. He could have survived as king and he could have foiled Brutus if he had had the wit and the ruthlessness to sacrifice his son to the popular anger — qualities that Brutus himself was to show soon in condemning his sons for their misbehavior.[10] Brutus's conspiracy to found the Roman republic could have been anticipated by a counterconspiracy to save the Tarquins.[11]

Machiavelli praises Brutus's simulated craziness or stupidity in overthrowing the Tarquins, but he is also willing to advise them with hindsight as to how they could have saved themselves. He does not suffer from moral shock over the rape committed by Sextus Tarquinius, and he does not offer a tragic interpretation of Lucretia's self-sacrifice.[12] Consequently, he does not seem to care here about the difference between a republic that respects law and morality and a tyranny that does not. The tyrant could have survived if he had satisfied the people at the expense of his son, which is advice implying that the people care more about punishing immorality than about keeping the law. As to the law, a prince who does not take away the life, wife, or property of his subjects can rule them in a tyranny not essentially different from a republic.[13]

Machiavelli treats both rape and tyranny lightly, the two being connected in the incident of the Roman Lucretia. In the *Mandragola* he goes further and treats rape as a joke. He can go further because the rape is without violence; it is a persuasion or seduction. But the seduction is not altogether without force; it does not use "open force," a Machiavellian phrase that forces the reader to construct its opposite, but the concealed force of a fraud.[14] The fraud is, first, for Lucrezia a certain argument that overcomes her conscience; and second, for her husband, Messer Nicia, it is the belief in a certain magic potion, the "mandragola," or mandrake, which makes sterile women conceive. There is, perhaps, a connection, even an identity, between the argument and the potion, for the use of the potion, which kills the man who inseminates the woman after she takes it, requires the same disregard for immoral means as in the argument.

Conspiracy and Respectability

As in Machiavelli's interpretation of the Roman Lucretia, the plot of the *Mandragola* is a conspiracy: nothing else but conspiracy is in the plot. There are no chance events, no unintended consequences.[15] The object of the conspiracy is to rape Lucrezia comically, as it were, without violence. To do so the conspirators must get around the belief of Lucrezia and her husband that adultery is wrong and make them believe it is permitted to them. In the *Dis-*

course or Dialogue Concerning Our Language Machiavelli says that the "end of a comedy is to hold a mirror to a private life," and "grave and useful effects to our life" result from it.[16] Private life is the home of natural, erotic yearnings as opposed especially to public things, that is, the prevailing notions of justice, shame, and morality — the dominant values, we would say. These notions may be laughable, but not to those who hold them; public morality (in Greek, the *nomos*) is what one is not permitted to laugh at, in public. But one is permitted to laugh at private desires that may reflect respectable public ambitions. It is easier to laugh at a young man such as Callimaco hopping around in his desire for a woman than to laugh at the same young man eager to make a name for himself in politics.

Politics is the realm of gravity, a fact that Machiavelli wants to change somewhat, but only somewhat. In the prologue to the *Mandragola* he refers to the difference between levity and gravity, offering an excuse for himself "if this material is not worthy — on account of its being so light — of a man who wishes to seem wise and grave."[17] But he cannot treat private life without treating public notions either directly or by implication. Callimaco is kept from consummating his desire for Lucrezia by the public view that it is wrong, the nomos understood in the wide sense of both law and morality, enforced by sanctions both formal and informal. Callimaco's plot is a conspiracy against society's conventions, and Machiavelli's play makes us laugh at those conventions. If we reflect, it inclines us to question them.

In the *Discourses,* Machiavelli says that Junius Brutus used the rape of Lucretia for the public purpose of founding the Roman republic. But he hints that Brutus also used the rape of Lucretia for the private purpose of making himself the founder of the Roman republic.[18] (In Livy's original version of the event, Brutus's private motive is actually more explicit than in Machiavelli's account.) In the *Mandragola,* the rape of Lucrezia is used by Callimaco for the private purpose of sexual gratification. But it also has a public consequence that is necessary to the plot and that Callimaco accepts: the making of a happy family. Not only does Callimaco seduce Messer Nicia's wife with impunity and to the delight of them both, but Messer Nicia also invites him to become a member of the household, living with Messer Nicia and serving "as the staff of his old age" (one of the many dirty jokes in the *Mandragola*) for an indefinite period — perhaps until he runs dry. Callimaco's private purpose receives a public cover of respectability, and in the process it is absorbed into the public end of continuing Messer Nicia's family and keeping it respectable. This development was unintended and unexpected by Callimaco, who wanted only the conquest with no thought of the future, but he gladly consents to the extension, indeed the transformation, of his desire.

The *Mandragola* has a happy ending because respectability is preserved, but at the cost of morality. Respectability is essential to morality because morality needs the support of social conventions without which moral people are unprotected from the risks they take with their own necessities. To be moral means to stake one's happiness on one partner for life. If doing that does not produce happiness, then at least it leaves one respectable; and failing to do it robs one of respectability. But maintaining respectability can also be fatal to morality: Messer Nicia's family could not be continued without an act of adultery. Instead of maintaining respectability for the sake of morality, as Lucrezia wishes, one may be tempted, as was Messer Nicia, to sacrifice morality for the sake of respectability and the political standing it gives. In the *Mandragola*, the adultery is itself continued and even made respectable; it is brought to Messer Nicia's home, where he welcomes a situation only he is so stupid as to misunderstand. But his outstanding stupidity also permits him a certain freedom. For to be oblivious of conventional judgment is also to be free of it. Messer Nicia gets, or will have, the children or sons ("figli") he wants. Lucrezia has her conscience salved, and Callimaco gets her, for good and with impunity. These excellent results would not be possible if the appearances were not preserved, if Machiavelli did not reestablish the obedience of his characters to the law, in the wide sense of nomos, that they had violated.

The *Mandragola* ends without pain and without scandal. In *Clizia*, a companion play to the *Mandragola*, one finds that the conspiracy in the *Mandragola* was successful in producing a son for Messer Nicia and that the product was blamed on the priest.[19] The chief representative of the law (as opposed to Messer Nicia, who is learned in the law) is the one "fingered" and commonly held responsible for having violated the law. That he is a priest reminds us that morality in Machiavelli's day, far more than in ours, was Christian. Machiavelli shows us the contradictions of morality both in general and specifically in the dogmas of Christianity: one of his lessons is that, contrary to the moral philosophers of our day, morality always comes in a specific version. A theoretical morality of universal principles is never seen in fact any more than the genus tree will be found in a forest. Every morality comes bound inseparably to the arbitrary dogma of one time or another, if for no other reason than that morality needs respectability, and what is respectable varies.

The *Mandragola* presents a private conspiracy to "rape" Lucrezia that parallels and parodies Machiavelli's interpretation of the founding of the Roman republic. It explains why the overthrow of tyranny does not do away with tyranny but rather comes by means of tyranny and reinstates tyranny. Or is *tyranny* the wrong word for morality which keeps us from getting what we want? More moderately, one can say the play shows why it is necessary to overthrow an old law and its regime and to establish a new law and a new regime. It is not sufficient merely to overthrow. Machiavelli presents the case for freer sex in the *Mandragola* but emphatically not for a sexual revolution, in the current sense, that would overthrow all hypocritical notions of fidelity and shame. That is the meaning of the comic domestication of adultery in the play.

Yet the new regime is not the same as the old. Machiavelli does not merely give us a glimpse of freedom in a brief comic vacation from morality. That was the usual function of comedy: to show the limitations of morality and then to remind us why it is needed nonetheless. But in the *Mandragola,* there is a revolution in the new attitude toward trust that it portrays. The public nomos is based on trust or belief as opposed to private erotic yearnings. One can take for granted that men and women desire sexual gratification as a necessity of their nature. But whether a particular woman will consent is not in her nature but in a belief she holds, in which she trusts. It is by trust and not by nature that husbands and wives confine their sexual attentions to each other. Trust between husband and wife is established, confirmed, and sanctioned by the trust that holds society together, as we have seen in the connection between chastity and republican virtue. Public trust controls, or attempts to control, natural private desires.

Trust is the theme of the *Mandragola,* the creation and the testing of trust. The main lesson can be given here: every ordinary human trust in the *Mandragola* is betrayed. Whether it is in the relationship of husband and wife, mother and daughter, host and guest, master and servant, ruler and ruled, or confessor and confessed — all are betrayed. There is no chance for father and son to betray each other because the problem of the play is the generation of a son (which occurs through the action of a potion rather than by a miracle). But one, and only one, relationship of trust holds — an extraordinary one, the trust of coconspirators in a common crime. As Callimaco says in response to a doubt about dealing with criminals, "When a thing does good for an individual, you have to believe that when you tell him about it, he will serve you with faith" (1.1).

Since the plot of the play is a plot to change our world, let us watch it unfold and see the plotter transformed from Callimaco to Messer Nicia with Lucrezia to Messer Nicia alone.

A New Deceit

A song to be spoken by nymphs and shepherds appears at the beginning of the play before the prologue, apparently added by Machiavelli in 1526. They complain of the brevity and painfulness of life, and they warn of the deceits of the world, which perhaps offer happiness and do not deliver. They choose a solitary life of pleasure in joy and festivity, not so solitary as not to be shared with the opposite sex. Since shepherding is a real occupation, it appears that women have to go further from reality than do men to reach the life of pleasure. No natural human end is in evidence here unless it is the pleasure found away from the world. The song ends by invoking the "name of the one who governs you" and "the one who gave you" so happy a state of grace — but without specifying who they might be. Perhaps they are Francesco Guicciardini, governor of Faenza when the *Mandragola* was shown there in 1526, and Pope Clement VII, who appointed him. Or perhaps they are God, who is mentioned next as the first word of the prologue. God has two aspects as the source of goods for men and of grace, grace being required because the goods are not enough to keep men alive or to keep them from sin. The nymphs and shepherds fleeing the world do not go in the direction of God.

The prologue takes us from the deceits of the world in the initial song to comic deceits. The prologue's speaker is Machiavelli or his representative, a "composer" (componitor) said to be of no great fame. The play is about a new chance or case ("caso") with its setting in Florence, though it could be elsewhere.[20] "The fable is called Mandragola" for a cause the audience will see. Four of the characters are introduced with the setting: first, the Doctor of laws lives near the "Street of Love," opposite to which is the church, where the friar lives. So we have law, love, and the Church that mediates between them. Then we are introduced to Callimaco, whose door is on the left, and a young woman deceived by him. "I would like you to be deceived like her" (prol.), says Machiavelli, comparing the deceit practiced by the lover on the beloved to that of the comedian on the audience. Lucrezia, though deceived, was also benefited with sexual pleasure and eventually a child; perhaps the audience too can expect such benefits — a diversion and a serious lesson.

Machiavelli then lists, though not by name, the four characters who will seem comic: Callimaco, Messer Nicia, the Friar, and Ligurio. The parasite Ligurio replaces the deceived Lucrezia in the previous list. Machiavelli excuses himself for such unworthy matter, since it is so light ("leggieri") for a man who wants to appear wise and grave. But he has been precluded from "showing other virtue with other enterprises," there being no reward for his labors. The *Mandragola,* then, is one of his enterprises or part of his enterprise. His enterprise is not to live the contemplative life, which is its own reward, but it has a certain levity that reminds one of the contemplative life. High seriousness permits low comedy because both question things people are ordinarily serious about. Machiavelli, however, seeks the reward of pleasing his audience. He knows that it is prone to faultfinding because the present age has fallen so far from "ancient virtue."[21] But he has a remedy; he warns that he too can find fault — it was his "first art." Although he may play the sergeant ("sergieri") to someone who wears a better coat than his, like Callimaco, he holds no one in esteem. Machiavelli presents himself in need of employment for his virtue, but he is more resourceful. His *Mandragola* is both relief from his other weightier enterprises and part of them.

The first scene introduces us to Callimaco and Siro, master and servant. Callimaco believes that Siro must have been "marveling" at his sudden departure from Paris, a word that occurs frequently in the play. Perhaps we are supposed to think of servants who marvel at what their masters do. Siro declares himself the model servant and says that he should never inquire into his master's affairs without being told but should serve faithfully after he has been told. The master now tells the servant why they are in Florence, although they have been there nearly a month. Callimaco does not trust Siro as a servant; his profession of fidelity means nothing, as becomes clear later in the scene when we hear of servants who can be bribed. But now Callimaco is ready to make him a coconspirator in his plot to pursue Lucrezia. He needs his servant to further his pursuit of her, to whom he is a kind of servant. Callimaco had been in Paris because there were no political opportunities in Italy and because it was safer in Paris. He was having a good time until Fortune interrupted it when Cammillo Calfucci, Lucrezia's relative, came and told him of her. The scene is parallel to the one in Livy in which Sextus Tarquinius learns of Lucretia from her husband, Collatinus, except that Cammillo's praise is more pointed.

Callimaco does not need Siro yet; so why is he telling him now, as he said, without being "forced" to do so? Partly he wants to vent himself, and partly he wants Siro to prepare his own spirit to help him. A master needs to vent himself and a servant needs to get ready: these needs on both sides of the relationship complicate the trust between the parties. Callimaco mentions three difficulties in the way of getting Lucrezia: her very honest nature "alien to things of love"; her husband who is very rich and lets her govern him and who is not *that* old; and her inaccessibility, through relatives, workers, or bribable servants. From this we learn that chastity is not incompatible with the desire to rule (1.3) and the ability to inspire fear.

Against these difficulties Callimaco mentions two hopes and then adds a third. First is Messer Nicia's simplicity; second, the wish they both have for children; and, as an afterthought, the fact that Lucrezia's mother, Sostrata, is a good sport ("buona compagna," the same description given Callimaco in the prologue). Callimaco has already engaged Ligurio to help him gain his desire. He hired a man he knew to be dishonest before he told his honest servant. Siro protests that Ligurio is a sponger or a parasite ("pappatore"), a type not usually faithful, but Callimaco can trust him in this because he will be paid and because Ligurio has no scruples. In conspiracy, the unscrupulous are more trustworthy than honest servants because scruples act as inhibitions against doing what is necessary quickly. A man you can depend on is one whose dishonesty you can be sure of. Callimaco has only a very vague plan of getting Lucrezia to the public bath, where he hopes she will change her nature and time will bring an opportunity. "What do I know?" he asks somewhat plaintively. Callimaco does not give the impression of being on top of events; he is not what we would expect from a Machiavellian prince.[22] He is ready to react, as in Paris to the report of Lucrezia's beauty, and is surely not shy about taking a risk, but he does not lead. He is led by love and by those who know how to take advantage of love.

Domestic Love

Next we meet Ligurio with Messer Nicia (1.2). Messer Nicia's name suggests that of Nicias, the Athenian general who was very rich, very pious, and very lucky — until, of course, thanks to his piety, his luck ran out in the Athenian expedition to Sicily.[23] In Messer Nicia, Nicias's piety and luck are brutally translated into stupidity, and he is introduced as a real booby, a credulous fool whose first words are "I believe." A stay-at-home, he is unwilling to leave Florence in order to go to the baths, despite medical advice to do so. In his youth he once went to Pisa and Livorno, and at Livorno saw the ocean, which was much larger than the Arno and full of "water, water, water."[24] Ligurio marvels that "having pissed in so much snow," he would find difficulty going to a bath. To piss in the snow means to leave your mark, which is what Messer Nicia wants to do by having children. When Messer Nicia retorts to Ligurio, "Your mouth is full of milk," we note that, although several fluids have been mentioned in this short scene, Messer Nicia is perhaps lacking in the vital fluid not mentioned.

The third scene begins with Ligurio reflecting on the stupidity and good fortune of Messer Nicia. Being so stupid he is fortunate to have such a wife as Lucrezia — beautiful, wise, well-mannered, and fit to govern a kingdom. Ligurio cites and disagrees with the proverb concerning matrimony that says, "God makes men, and they pair themselves off." If God made perfect pairs, there would perhaps be no need for a law against adultery, and, of course, matchmakers like Ligurio would be unnecessary. His judgment that Lucrezia is fit to govern a kingdom is in tension with Callimaco's regarding her honesty or chastity, and we shall have to see what happens. Messer Nicia can be got around, it seems, because he is stupid, boastful, a stay-at-home, and lucky.

Since getting around Nicia is the same as getting around the law, it is not surprising that they share these traits.

Once Callimaco comes over to Ligurio, he offers no praise of Lucrezia but only his need for her. His love is only an expression of the lover's need, and his selfishness is made very emphatic. His need generates hope, which generates belief. Even a false hope, he says, will make him feel better. Callimaco is in an absolute tizzy; he will do anything to succeed with Lucrezia, but he doesn't know what will work. Ligurio puts him in this state by pointing out the defect in the idea of bringing Lucrezia to the baths. The scheme might work for someone else who would be attracted to Lucrezia, and whom she might prefer if he were richer or more gracious.

To pursue the point as Ligurio does not: once you give up respectability and the stability of the home and make love your principle, whether love of money, beauty, or whatever, promiscuity is the result. One who loves Lucrezia merely because she is beautiful will love the next woman who comes along who is more beautiful.[25] Or she will love a richer and more gracious man. Sensing this, Callimaco becomes as possessive as the most jealous husband. He doesn't yet realize, but he will, that the conspiracy of which he is a part must accept or reconstruct some arbitrary law in order to succeed, some limit on the principle that one should always be attracted to the best, to the beautiful, to the good. Love of beauty has no stability. One cannot match up men and women according to how they rank in yearly, or daily, beauty contests. This is what happens at the baths, or in our day at the beach. If God had made men and women into pairs in which the partners could easily find each other, then there would be no difficulty. But the pairing off of human beings is inconsistent and barely compatible with the relentless yearning of their love.

Callimaco avers, not for the last time, that he is on the edge of dying for his love. He is desperate, and he sees no "remedy." But Machiavelli always has a remedy for the human troubles or dilemmas that he points out, and he never leaves his readers and students at a loss, in an *aporia*. He is not satisfied, like Callimaco, with mere hope (1.1). Callimaco comes to Florence because he has heard of Lucrezia's beauty, but though he has seen her (1.1), as yet he has not met her. Ligurio plays with him; he makes him feel, if not see, that beauty is an unstable principle. Therefore, it is necessary to return the conspiracy to the home — the home of Messer Nicia — where limits can be imposed. In the *Mandragola,* the seduction of Lucrezia, which lifts her moral horizon, goes apace with the domestication of Callimaco, which lowers his. Ligurio's remedy does not require Callimaco to moderate his desire, much less give it up and become a moral character. He remarks to Callimaco that "your blood accords with mine," perhaps because they both have infinite desires, one for love, the other for money. On that basis they can cooperate. All Callimaco need do is to see the advantages of respectability.

Another, related reason makes it necessary to return the conspiracy to the home. The scheme at the baths depends on time for an opportunity, and things can go wrong while they wait. Infinity of desire keeps one from settling on an attainable object. Ligurio's true or altered scheme makes everyone move so that there is no time for bad luck or for second thoughts — to say nothing of repentance — to intervene. "We will lack time for doing, much less talking," says Ligurio. This reminds us of "the necessity that does not give time" (la necessità che non da tempo)[26] that Machiavelli in the *Discourses on Livy* recommends imposing on the execution of a conspiracy, if it is to be successful.[27]

Sex and Generation

In the second act we see Ligurio's plan in operation. We learn of it, and so do his coconspirators, not all at once but one stage at a time. Ligurio introduces Callimaco to Messer Nicia as a doctor who will find out why his wife is sterile. Before accepting him, Messer Nicia wants to make his own test of the presumed "Maestro's" science, which he proceeds to do. He need only test Callimaco's competence, not his motives, for the motive is the consequence of the competence. Callimaco declares to Nicia that he hasn't labored all those years in Paris (as if!) for any other reason than to help virtuous men like himself. Callimaco has an art, and so he is selfless, like Plato's artisan, who works for his customers.[28] The phony doctor Callimaco is the only character in the *Mandragola* who is presumed to have no selfish interest, but in fact, of course, he has the most of all. The question of the selflessness of art is a close concern of Machiavelli's because an adviser like himself who denies the reality of selflessness raises doubts about his own selfish interest in giving such advice and even in writing diverting comedies.

To confirm his knowledge, Maestro Callimaco gives in Latin five causes of sterility in Messer Nicia's wife, three of which refer to his own possible inadequacy. Nicia goes into rapture with this discussion of causes, calling the Maestro "the worthiest man one could hope to find." Then Callimaco says in Italian that beyond these causes, Messer Nicia might be impotent. It seems that despite having greeted the Maestro in correct Latin, Messer Nicia did not understand what he praised. He indignantly rejects the suggestion: "Oh! You make me laugh." What makes Nicia laugh makes us laugh too. The assumption of everyone in the play, except him, is that he is impotent and that he is the cause of his wife's infertility.

The Maestro says that there would be no remedy for Messer Nicia's impotence, but that there is one for his wife's sterility. Callimaco is not much good at remedies. He promises one only when pretending to be someone else, and then he has to be prompted by Ligurio, who brings up the existence of "certain potions" that infallibly make sterile women conceive. To cover his ignorance and confusion, Callimaco says that he is careful what he says to people he doesn't know, for the selfish reason that he doesn't want to be taken for a charlatan. He, like us, is learning of the potion for the first time and without any detail. The conspiracy is changed after it begins and is revealed by stages, so that it comes as a surprise to subordinate conspirators — as Callimaco is now shown to be — as well as to the object of the conspiracy. The advantage of that method is that the conspirators become committed to the conspiracy before they know it fully; then they cannot back out of it when they find it goes further than they would have intended at first. We shall see the same trick played on Brother Timothy, and it is recommended by Machiavelli in the *Discourses*.[29] What it means when carried out consistently is that, unless there is some one plotter of the whole, all conspirators are in a sense victims of the conspiracy. It does not mean that all cannot at the same time profit from the conspiracy, as happens in the *Mandragola*.

Next, Messer Nicia and Siro discuss Callimaco, with whom Nicia is very impressed. He would not be valued in Florence, of course, where people do not appreciate virtue. Nicia himself has no status ("stato") in this town; so no wonder Callimaco doesn't remain here. He would stay in France because the king of France must take him into account, Nicia supposes and Siro confirms. But Siro's only concern is that the shame in store for Nicia will bring trouble for himself and his master. Messer Nicia is a man of political responsibility; he is stupid but (and?) he is grave and responsible. His desire to have children is for the purpose not merely of perpetuating his bloodline but also of increasing his influence in politics, thus enabling him to do more good. Children, or sons, would mean heirs for a large family that would improve his status in the town. He knows that in wanting to have children he is looking for two things someone else might flee, trouble for himself and for others (2.2). But in the *Mandragola*, politics is treated lightly. This is the only political discussion that occurs, and it is between a master and a disdainful servant, hence not a serious one. It takes place while Messer Nicia is on the way to gather a urine specimen from his wife. He comes back holding a chamber pot, representing the first appearance of Lucrezia on stage. She is not a tragic figure.[30]

Maestro Callimaco examines the specimen and gives two different analyses, one in Latin, the other in Italian. If the first analysis were correct, there would be no need for the second, in which he suggests that Lucrezia might be "mal coperta" (badly covered) at night. Messer Nicia of course misunderstands. She has a good quilt, but he wonders whether she gets cold from saying paternosters on her knees for four hours before getting into bed. Here is a joking reference to the incompatibility of Christianity and generation, the remedy for which is the mandragola. Callimaco as Maestro has a sure remedy, because of which Messer Nicia should have faith in him; and if the remedy doesn't work after a year, he will give Nicia two thousand ducats. This is not the kind of offer made by Brother Timothy and other clergy when they ask for faith.

Nothing is more certain to make a woman pregnant, continues Callimaco, than a potion made of mandragola.[31] Why, if it weren't for this, the queen of France would be barren, and infinite other princesses in that state. The rub is, however, that the first man who lies with the woman after she has taken the potion dies. Nonetheless, this is the method used by the king and queen of France in order to keep their succession going. Succession is both a family and a political reason. Messer Nicia has no such reason or no such compelling reason. He compares himself to the king of France, as Lucrezia will compare herself to Lot's daughters. By the way, Nicia knows that Callimaco is prized by the king of France and that the king of France uses a stud when he wants a child, but he doesn't put two and two together.

Following Nicia's example, let us generalize. The mandrake preserves succession at the cost of its progenitor; it uses the agent and then kills him. But in general, God or nature uses individual progenitors as agents to preserve the succession of the human species and then allows them to die sooner or later, if not within eight days as the Maestro says in this case. All human beings can be likened to the unfortunate stud who keeps the succession going at his own cost. Why does he, why do we cooperate in this business? God or nature has made the immediate pleasure of sex distinct from the long-term desire for generation, so that the latter is not necessary to the former. In the play, Callimaco wants the pleasure of sex, and Lucrezia and Messer Nicia have a desire for generation. The distinctness between sex and generation is reflected in Christianity, the ruling nomos of Machiavelli's time. Christianity frowns on sexual pleasure and prizes chastity, on the one hand, and on the other, it praises generation in asking men to be fruitful and multiply. The natural law doctrine of the Church joins the two distinct desires, laying it down that sexual pleasure is lawful only for the purpose of generation. Similarly, the plot of the *Mandragola* opposes Callimaco to Lucrezia and Messer Nicia. Callimaco, who desires sex, represents pleasure and levity; Lucrezia and Messer Nicia, who desire generation, represent morality, politics, and gravity. The deception of the plot keeps them separate but also joins them and makes them complementary so that both ends are achieved by indirection, the one as the means to the other. Machiavelli by implication criticizes Christianity and uses it against itself. If sex can be used for generation, so also generation can be used for sex; thus generation is not the end of, or higher than, sex, as Christian natural law asserts. The Christian idea that sex and generation are distinct, or its recognition of that natural truth, can be used to oppose its strictures against sex without generation.

Maestro Callimaco proposes to have Lucrezia lie first with a young man who will draw off the infection from the mandrake; then the way will be clear for Messer Nicia. Fortune has so favored Nicia that he, Callimaco, just happens to have the ingredients for making the potion with him. Nicia's immediate reaction is that he doesn't want to make his wife a whore and himself a cuckold. He cares for his wife, whom he mentions first; but he doesn't care for the unfortunate young man, except that if word of this deed got out, Nicia might be reported to the Eight, the criminal tribunal. But Callimaco explains to him how they will kidnap a young idler and shove him into Lucrezia's bedroom in the dark without identifying themselves, and he reminds him that the king and lords of France do this. Messer Nicia is satisfied. If "king and princes and lords" use this method (he adds "princes" and does not mention tyrants, 2.6), then it must be right for him. He seems oblivious to the fact that the young man might actually be the father of the son he will call his own. Being cuckolded is just a matter of perception, and nobody will know except Lucrezia and himself — and every other character in the play-plot.

An Obedient Wife

Messer Nicia reminds Callimaco that it is necessary to get his wife's consent. Callimaco says loftily, "I wouldn't want to be a husband if I couldn't dispose my wife to do things my way" (2.6). He wants an obedient wife who will consent to her husband's desire that she be unfaithful. Now Ligurio has the remedy. He says they should use her confessor, and he gives five reasons why the confessor would be willing to join the conspiracy, of which the third is money. But how will they get Lucrezia to go to the confessor, given her distrust of priests? Ligurio's further remedy is to suggest that it be done through her mother, whom she trusts.

The song at the end of the second act is devoted to stupidity. The stupid man, it says, believes everything and does not feel ambition or fear. That is a condition both pitiful and laughable, but it does allow for a certain detachment from the world, while permitting the stupid man to concentrate on one thing. Messer Nicia is stupid, the song says, and his stupidity consists in his single-minded desire to have children. Why is this desire necessarily so stupid? If it were an intelligent desire, then Nicia could be intelligent. If he were, it is not clear that the plot of the *Mandragola* would be any different. If Nicia were intelligent, he would be in charge of the plot and would allow himself to be cuckolded, just like the king of France. He would have sent his relative Cammillo to Paris to entice Callimaco to return to Italy. We all need the grave people who want children, even though they may be laughable. This play puts them down more than they deserve in order to show the nature of nomos, of the nomos on which we depend.

Nicia's stupidity is that, unlike the king of France, he doesn't want his wife to be a whore. So he is precisely not single-minded. He has not forgotten everything else but his desire for children; he wants his own child — his own natural and his own nominal child. Nicia is ridiculous because he wants something impossible, the harmony of nature and nomos or respectability. Callimaco doesn't care about the law; he is in harmony with nature. He could have wanted a son instead of sexual conquest, and it would have made no difference to him whether his son were really, that is, naturally, his. Callimaco is the single-minded character in this play. Nicia, like most of us, wants both his own natural child and his own nominal child, a double desire that Machiavelli shows us to be ridiculous because it is divided against itself. If you must have a child, should you adopt (the child is not yours) or wait for your own (you may not get one)? Nicia's care for law and respectability makes *them* ridiculous. He tries to do what they try to do — join the pleasure of sex and desire for children — as if nature had not kept them distinct. The law, or the Christian law, intends that there be no difference between the natural and the legitimate child. The legitimate child is regarded as yours by the law as if the law, in making a child legitimate, could make a child. Or is Messer Nicia after all as intelligent as the king of France and does not care about being a cuckold? In that case, rather than demanding that his legitimate son be natural, he would be indifferent as to whether his son was the one or the other. He would not care about the immortality of his body as opposed to his fame or glory or soul.

Lucrezia's seduction has now come down to enticing her to her confessor, which must be done through her mother. Nicia and Ligurio discuss how to gain the consent of Lucrezia (3.2) and quickly decide that it cannot be done through her piety. They cannot use her piety to make her trust what her confessor will recommend to her because it is precisely her piety that makes her distrust the clergy. She once had an experience of what we would call sexual harassment at a local church. But she will trust her mother, who is introduced into the play speaking of the "duty of a prudent person to take the best among bad courses" (3.1). She adds the condition that the prudent course not weigh on the conscience, thus indicating that prudence and conscience are not necessarily opposed.

In the *Mandragola*, Machiavelli uses Lucrezia to represent morality, which always has its two accompanying guides, prudence and conscience, who are represented by Sostrata and Brother Timothy. Neither guide is sufficient by itself, and though they can be made compatible, each works against the other. They are shown to be compatible, clearly, on the terms of prudence rather than those of conscience; but prudence cannot simply dispense with conscience, and Brother Timothy, however corrupt in conscience, is nonetheless an essential figure in the plot. Lucrezia is closer to her natural mother, Sostrata, than to Brother Timothy, and she trusts her more. Yet Sostrata does not question the need to consult Brother Timothy and to secure from him the gross misinterpretation of Christianity that will square Lucrezia's conscience. By the way, in the conversation with Ligurio, Messer Nicia offers the only direct criticism of the Christian church to be found in the play: "It's really bad, though, that those who should be giving us good examples are like this."[32] He also utters a passing remark that, if taken seriously, would provide the basis for criticizing conscience and religion that ordinary prudence does not: "If you knew everything, you wouldn't marvel" (3.2).

The next scene in the third act is an apparent digression, a conversation between Brother Timothy and a woman unnamed. But it is an important scene because it shows us how priests operate with human will.[33] The conversation is very salacious, but it begins innocently with Brother Timothy's saying to the woman, "If you want to confess, I will do what you want." Not today, the woman says, indicating how lightly, yet how trustingly, she considers the grave duty of saving her soul. *If you want* is how Brother Timothy begins; the woman's confession is not imposed. There is no confession unless she is willing to accept God's commands. When she accepts them as her own will, then the priest specifies what they are. Priestly rule is a kind of indirect government in which the real ruler, the priest, seems to be a mere intermediary between God and man, or between God and woman, or womanly men.

Brother Timothy Duped

Next, Brother Timothy is caught up in the plot (3.4). Messer Nicia is told to pretend to be deaf so that Ligurio controls the situation. Any protests from Nicia about the money Ligurio is unexpectedly promising that Nicia will pay to Brother Timothy can be set down to Nicia's not having heard well. Deafness is also a beautiful disguise for Nicia, who can say what he will and have it explained away. One might remark, too, that deafness is the condition of an author: he speaks but does not hear what his readers say to him, unless he anticipates them.

Ligurio catches Brother Timothy by bringing up a question of abortion, which is just the opposite of Messer Nicia's case. Nicia wants a child. Ligurio pretends that Nicia wants an abortion for his nephew's daughter, who had been staying at a nunnery, and (of course) the nuns had betrayed their trust. The purpose of this dodge is to hook Brother Timothy.[34] He is committed then to one crime, an ordinary one with him, in order to use him in an extraordinary crime with the same criminals that he might not have agreed to if it had been presented to him at first. Note that under Christianity reputation favors the woman with no child over the woman with a bastard child. Christian law is not favorable to the growth of population necessary to the strength of states.

More broadly, Machiavelli shows that religion, which necessarily accompanies morality, necessarily detracts from it. To convince Brother Timothy to arrange the abortion, Ligurio mentions the worldly honor (that is, respectability) that will be saved,[35] but he stresses the alms to do God's work that Nicia's three hundred ducats will make available. Against this is merely a piece of unborn flesh, and Ligurio then delivers a beautifully succinct statement of utilitarianism: "I believe that that is good which does good to the most and by which most are contented" (3.4). Brother Timothy readily agrees to this, and why not? Any religion, but especially Christianity, makes the commands of God paramount and thus subordinates the good of this world to the next, including the numberless souls of the dead.[36] No matter that abortion is *contrary* to God's command; the mode of subordinating this world's goods to the next's will infect morality with the utilitarian habit of choosing the lesser evil. That a priest should arrange abortions is a regular consequence of Christianity and is neither the special corruption of the Renaissance Church nor the occasional evil of a priest who goes wrong. So Ligurio says to Brother Timothy at the end of the scene (3.4), "Now you appear to me that man of religion [quel religioso] that I believed you were."

Ligurio then pretends to consult with someone in the Church and returns with the happy news, of course imaginary, that Nicia's nephew's daughter has suffered a miscarriage (3.6). Nature has done God's work, or God did not need prompting, and so Brother Timothy is not needed after all. Brother Timothy wants, of course, to keep the money anyway, as perhaps God deserves to be thanked when something goes right. Brother Timothy, however, is needed for a new task that will be explained to him in the church. The church seems to be the sanctuary of conspiracy, the place where men's intentions are most hidden and best revealed.[37] Both of the grand conspiracies in Machiavelli's *Florentine Histories,* one against the Sforzas and the other against the Medici,[38] were executed in churches.

Though Ligurio promises to return, Messer Nicia is left alone outside the church. He bursts out in frustration over having to feign deafness and under-standing nothing of what Ligurio and Brother Timothy have been saying. He has to trust them, and his comic situation illustrates the meaning of trust, which is listening or being forced to listen without questioning. Forced trust is as good as or better than implicit trust. Messer Nicia would have to behave as he does whether he was stupid or not. His stupidity is the best running joke in the play, but it is not necessary to the plot of the play. Instead of being forced to trust his tormentors, while forced to pretend he is deaf, he could be pretending to be forced, all the time laughing up his sleeve and counting on the character or necessity of Ligurio and Brother Timothy to make good his trust. Messer Nicia pretends to be deaf so well that we think him as stupid as if he were deaf in fact. If he is pretending for part of the plot, why not for the whole?

Now Brother Timothy has heard what he must do, and Nicia is assured by Ligurio, shouting at him still as if he were deaf, that he will comply with the scheme. Nicia is overjoyed, exclaiming, "You recreate me completely" (3.8). He wants to know whether he will have a boy, and when assured he will, he responds that he weeps with tenderness. Unable to produce a miracle, Messer Nicia is compelled to rely on the potion to reproduce himself. But the potion is nothing but the necessity of the various characters, suitably concealed because of the necessity of maintaining their respectability.

In the next scene (3.9) Brother Timothy is alone. He now sees what has been done to him, but he does not withdraw—he cannot. And besides, he will get something for himself if he remains in the plot. He admits he has been duped but senses also that he has not, since there is profit in it for him. It is not always to one's disadvantage to be duped. He sees more easily how he was duped because he did the same thing himself in the scene in which he is confessor for the woman. What happened was that Ligurio and Messer Nicia confessed their intent to commit the crime of abortion to Brother Timothy; and they got his absolution. His absolution consisted in his connivance, and then they used that against him. In speaking alone and so frankly, Brother Timothy confesses to the audience. He has five scenes in the play in which he confesses to the audience, far more than anyone else.[39] As a priest, he has no one to confess to except another priest. Ligurio never confesses; he acts according to necessities and, so to speak, has nothing to confess. Brother Timothy has to purge his mind ("animo")—not his soul ("anima")—of the pressure put on it by God's commands. Even the adaptable priest must, for the sake of his office, feel the pressures he manipulates. He is indeed adaptable and does not trip himself up in self-righteousness. Like Ligurio, he lives off the women whom he despises and does not desire (3.4, 3.9). Adaptable priests like Brother Timothy suggest the possibility of an adaptable Christianity. In his soliloquy he goes from acknowledging he has been duped to speaking of "my wishes" as if the plot had all along been his. He who has been duped pretends not to have been duped.

Lucrezia's Morality

There follows a crucial scene between Sostrata and Lucrezia, in which Sostrata gets her daughter to go to the priest. Sostrata begins, "I believe that you believe," the only time that such a speech occurs in the play. Callimaco's first speech was "I believe," as was Messer Nicia's. Ligurio's first speech was "I do not believe." I note that this is the central scene of the *Mandragola*, the nineteenth scene. To put the point in words, it is natural to believe but the thing believed in is conventional. Men need to believe in order to trust one another, and to trust one another in order to work together, and to work together in order to survive. The first rule of Machiavellian prudence is to use your own arms and not rely on others.[40] But you must use others; you need their help in order to get into a situation in which you do *not* need their help. And for this you need a relation of trust with them. How should one make this relation? and can it be made on a Christian basis? These are questions addressed in the *Mandragola*.

Lucrezia's first speech in the play begins, "I have always feared" (3.10). What she fears is the conflict between Messer Nicia's wish ("voglia") to have children and the demands of morality. She speaks of some error he might commit, not of a sin, and the wrongs she mentions — submitting her body to this disgrace and being the cause that some man might die for disgracing her — are not specifically Christian. She concludes, "If I were the only woman left in the world and human nature had to rise again from me, I wouldn't believe that such a course would be allowed to me." Her fear arises from her belief and from her need to believe that what she does is permitted. These are weaknesses that will be used against her.

That is Lucrezia's objection. She would not do this thing to regenerate the human race, let alone to satisfy Messer Nicia's wish to have children. Her seduction is forecast in this announcement because Brother Timothy shows how it *would* be allowed to her. Lucrezia is good, and goodness or conscience consists in a sticking point. A sticking point is something one would not do regardless of the consequences. There is a little of Kant's moralism in Machiavelli's picture of morality, as Kant understood so well what morality is; but there is also something of Plato's critique of morality.

Morality is an indivisible whole. The moral person must act, therefore, as if all morality depended on his refusal to do something obviously prudent in an extreme case. One cannot divide morality into small pieces, into discrete actions, because there is always a reason to be or not to be moral in a particular case. Once you have begun to reason your way through each case, then you do the moral action for the sake of reason, which is outside morality, and not in order to be moral. Morality, or nomos, is a spurious whole that must defend itself as a whole. It must assimilate the extreme case to the ordinary cases and decide the ordinary case *as if all morality were at stake.* The easy answer to Lucrezia would be, "You're not the only woman in the world; therefore, morality doesn't depend on you. Neither the human race nor morality depends on what you do. So live a little."[41]

But that is not true. Morality does depend on Lucrezia. Morality cannot afford not to make an issue of itself. Unless you think all morality is at stake, you can always find a reason not to be moral. That is why moral people tend to be self-righteous; they sense that in acting morally, they stand up for all morality. So the moral woman is the woman who says to herself, "I wouldn't do that if he were the last man on earth." That is what Lucrezia says, and as soon as she does, Brother Timothy has her.

In the eleventh scene of this act we are shown the seduction of Lucrezia through Brother Timothy. Brother Timothy, like Messer Nicia, reads books (3.2). Scholar that he is, he has spent two hours in study and has come up with three arguments to persuade Lucrezia's conscience.[42] His first point is the general principle that one should stay with a certain good and not leave it for an uncertain evil. The certain good is that Lucrezia will become pregnant and gain a soul for the Lord; the uncertain evil is that the man who lies with her after she takes the potion may die. The application of Brother Timothy's rule of prudence is, of course, ridiculous because the good he mentions is uncertain and the evil, so far as we know before now, is certain. Perhaps Brother Timothy's thinking is affected by the fact that, according to Christianity, it is uncertain whether death is good or evil.

After this powerful beginning, Brother Timothy has a second point. The act in question is not a sin because the will ("voluntà") sins, not the body.[43] Your will would sin if you displeased your husband and pleased yourself, but you will be pleasing him and not yourself. In effect, Brother Timothy tells Lucrezia that her will should be her husband's will. Lucrezia's will is the vital point, but it is taken away from her.[44] Her will belongs to her husband, just like her body. But do they really belong to him?

In his third point Brother Timothy brings up the biblical example of Lot's daughters, who, believing themselves to be alone in the world, committed incest with their father.[45] Their intention was good; we assume it was to repopulate the world. Brother Timothy's implication is that if incest is permitted to repopulate the world, then adultery is permitted to have a child for oneself. Drawing out the analogy that Machiavelli puts in the mouth of Brother Timothy between the example of Lot and the situation of Messer Nicia, we have this: Callimaco is in the place of Lot, and Lucrezia, of Lot's daughters. Who is Messer Nicia?[46] Messer Nicia is analogous to God, as he wants a child and God wants a soul, or many souls. According to Brother Timothy's second point, Lucrezia is obliged to please Messer Nicia; according to the third, she should please God. Pleasing Nicia is pleasing God, not so much by obeying a direct command as by reasoning through analogy to what has pleased God in a similar case.[47]

In fact, this is the Bible read "sensatamente" (judiciously),[48] which means in accordance with human necessities, not with God's commands. When Lucrezia hears this interpretation, the pressure of her goodness is relieved. Goodness consists of the things one would not do even to save the human race. It therefore creates a terrific conflict with human necessities, which do pertain to saving, thriving, and acquiring. The resulting pressure needs to be relieved, and one purpose of religion is to relieve it (the other is to create it). Religion offers relief, a release from goodness or conscience. This is a natural purpose of religion, of the natural religion that Christianity is to become if it is interpreted "sensatamente." Lucrezia's belief relieves her from her goodness. God says or indicates that it is permissible to abandon morality in the extreme case, which means that it is all right to abandon morality. Lucrezia comes to trust, is forced to trust, the priest, who shows her how to obey human necessities, those of sexual pleasure and generation, as well as providing her with the disguise for those necessities. The disguise is first as God's will, and then, when she perceives God's will, as her own.

After Brother Timothy speaks, Sostrata weighs in with the voice of prudence. Don't you see, she says to Lucrezia, that a woman who has no children has no house ("casa")? She refers not to the pleasures of domesticity but to the need for protection from the world, a need that goes together with Messer Nicia's desire to advance in the world. Some commentators are disappointed that Lucrezia gives in, they think, so easily; and they add to this her later delight in the whole scheme as it turns out. Can such a woman be considered chaste? But Lucrezia is a moral person, and her failings are the failings of morality, not particular to her.[49] She is the effectual truth of the Roman Lucretia. Brother Timothy sums up the failings of morality in his three points. First, morality has trouble coming to terms with necessary evil and has to rely on prudence, which may tempt the moral person into unnecessary evil. Second, inasmuch as morality needs religion, it requires obedience to a superior will, which detracts from one's own moral will. Third, it appears that obedience to God shades into imitation of God, and the moral person begins to think himself godly. But then what God does in support of morality does not seem always to accord with morality. In Machiavelli's judicious interpretation, God seems to obey the same necessities in dealing with humans as do humans who must live with them. Any moral paragon who thinks she could live more chastely than Lucrezia is relying on innocence or good luck or on the angel Raphael, whose protection Brother Timothy invokes as he bids Lucrezia prepare herself for the "mystery" to come.[50]

At the end of act 3, Messer Nicia declares himself the most contented man in the world. The following song praises deceit and then addresses "remedy high and rare," which shows the right path to erring souls. The "holy counsels" of a human remedy or deceit replace divine precepts and commands as human guides. In personifying the remedy, Machiavelli indicates how men come to subject themselves to a being they think will bring salvation. Unlike Boethius, the favorite of Messer Nicia who wrote *On the Consolation of Philosophy,* Machiavelli produces remedies.

Brother Timothy in Disguise

At the beginning of act 4, Callimaco is alone, waiting to hear the result. By contrast to Messer Nicia, he is full of "anguish of spirit." He is tossed back and forth by his hopes and fears; the more he hopes, the more he fears his hopes will not be realized. Fortune and Nature are so balanced that you never get a good without an evil. Callimaco mentions not God or heaven but only hell. Clearly he lacks the remedy Machiavelli has just sung to. He expresses a certain manliness, but that lasts only a while and his body trembles; indeed, seven parts of his body are agitated in seven different ways. He needs to purge himself with Ligurio, who is his confessor.

Ligurio returns with the good news; everything is arranged. Callimaco thinks that Brother Timothy is responsible for persuading Lucrezia, but Ligurio gives the credit to Sostrata. Their disagreement might make us think about the relative importance of prudence (Sostrata) and "ideology" (Brother Timothy) in an enterprise like this one. Evidently Machiavelli thinks both are necessary. Somehow, despite the obviously contrived character of Brother Timothy's bogus arguments, prudence lacks the authority on its own to clear one's conscience. Even for the most unthinking human beings, some superhuman reckoning is required to show the relationship between the human and the nonhuman and thus to justify the "holy counsels" of prudence. Callimaco is now ready to die of delight, and Ligurio wonders what kind of person is ready to die now for sorrow, now for delight, no matter which. Happiness is not the guide to happiness, in Machiavelli's opinion, one is tempted to say. Men, especially men like Callimaco, are too restless to settle down in happiness. They prefer, or they need, to live in alternating moods despite the apparent irrationality of such a course.

Then Callimaco nearly has heart failure. He forgot he was to help catch the young roustabout they would use to serve Lucrezia. He was to catch this man and also to be this man. So he forgot the necessity of a disguise *as* himself as well as a disguise *of* himself. The earlier plan had not provided for this (see 2.6). Callimaco the Maestro had forgotten that he could not simply disappear in that guise. Again Callimaco lacks a remedy, and again Ligurio finds one (but he had not anticipated the difficulty). Though Brother Timothy has been dismissed, they need him once more to pretend to be Callimaco's pretense, the disguise of a disguise. The religious man is man in disguise. Religion is a disguise of human nature required by human nature, even by Callimaco in his single-minded pursuit of Lucrezia. With religion, Callimaco can be in two places doing two things at the same time, advising and enjoying. Watching others enjoy the fruits of an enterprise you have advised is some relief from the transience of enjoyment.

This scene (4.2) is very important because it marks a turn in the play against levity and in favor of morality and respectability. For the first time Ligurio mentions the possibility of return engagements for Callimaco with Lucrezia. In the previous scene, Callimaco had spoken of one experience only, and now he is taken by surprise. Ligurio tells him that Lucrezia will agree to a continuing arrangement in order to avoid scandal ("infamia"). She will want to maintain her disguise of respectability. Chastity is a disguise that hides from the virtuous the good fortune his or her virtue depends on.

Callimaco now orders Siro to carry the potion to Messer Nicia's house. He tells his servant of ten years less than what Ligurio knows. He finds himself alone again, his confidence gone. He will kill himself if something occurs to interrupt "my design," as he calls it inaccurately. Then he easily recognizes Brother Timothy in disguise. Friars are easy to recognize in disguise, being nothing but disguise. Siro is told to obey Ligurio as if he were Callimaco, and there follows a ridiculous ceremony between Brother Timothy and Callimaco, between the disguise of Callimaco as a Maestro and Callimaco as a roustabout. Brother Timothy gives another soliloquy and pronounces himself to be the little innocent. He blames Ligurio and speaks of dipping his finger in "error"[51] but says nothing of sin or conscience (4.6). Then they all see Messer Nicia in the disguise of a monk, and all except Siro laugh at him with his little sword. Siro was willing to laugh at him earlier (2.4), but now he remembers he is a servant and is more respectful.

There follows a second soliloquy by Messer Nicia (4.8). He is disguised but very full of himself.[52] He boasts that he feels bigger, younger, and leaner — as if he were endowed with the youth of the young man he is about to capture. He tells us the funny things Lucrezia said, things she could not say on stage without lowering her character. Messer Nicia is the only character in the play to report comic conversations.[53]

In the next scene all are disguised: Messer Nicia, Brother Timothy, Ligurio, and Siro (4.9). Nicia thinks the Maestro is disguised. The Maestro was known to him in the person of Callimaco, but now that he is being played by Brother Timothy, the disguised Maestro has to be disguised. We see Nicia trying to disguise his voice, like Brother Timothy, with a ball of wax that turns out to be bitter aloes.[54] The four then capture Callimaco in disguise, Messer Nicia giving instructions for the capture. Callimaco, of course, acts very much of his own accord, but for Messer Nicia's sake he pretends to be captured. But again, it is only Nicia's inhibition against being cuckolded, or his belief in his own potency, that makes the pretense necessary.

The act ends with Brother Timothy's address to the spectators. A sleepless night will be had by all, in which he will give religious offices to Our Lady at the same time that Callimaco pays his devotions to Lucrezia.[55] The song at the end of act 4 says directly that the "holy" hours of night that accompany yearning lovers are "the sole cause of making souls blessed." Then Brother Timothy has another soliloquy to begin act 5. He complains that his fellow friars no longer maintain the reputation of Our Lady, as if assiduous attention to ritual would do the trick, as if faith were no different from reputation, and as if his actions could not have contributed to the decline he complains of. The other friars are lacking in "brain" — which is what he had said earlier of all women (3.9).[56] If the friars have come to resemble women, perhaps it is because they are more concerned with maintaining the reputation of Our Lady than Brother Timothy sees. Apart from his odious sexism, his criticisms indicate a contradiction in Christianity between the femininity of its belief and the manliness necessary to maintaining the reputation of its belief. Christianity makes hypocrites of friars and has nothing to offer to men like Callimaco. In the *Mandragola* Machiavelli shows how to "capture" such men.

Messer Nicia's Family Values

The last act deals with the sequel to Lucrezia's seduction, and it would not be necessary if her seduction were the only, or even the main, point the play has to make. There remains the need to make the seduction respectable. So, the morning after, Callimaco the roustabout is sent packing and Callimaco the Maestro is introduced into Messer Nicia's household. Nicia takes charge of both tasks. Having been cuckolded, he now arranges that the insult be made perpetual. When Callimaco has been disposed of, Nicia orders Ligurio and Siro to get out of their disguises and go out early so that they don't appear to have stayed up all night (5.2). Then Nicia tells them of his encounter with Callimaco before the latter was sent to Lucrezia's bed. He had forced Callimaco to strip, and not only looked him over but felt him too (touch being the most reliable sense).[57] Nicia had previously examined Callimaco's learning and intellect as Maestro (2.2); now if only he could put body and soul together he would have examined the whole man. Callimaco had analyzed an effluence of Lucrezia (2.6), but Nicia is the only one in the play to execute a comprehensive examination. After this, Nicia goes to Sostrata, and they discuss the stupidity of Lucrezia, who should have yielded from the first.

Nicia insists that all come to the church to see Lucrezia be blessed.[58] One might think that Nicia is counting his chickens before they are hatched, but that is not so. He has found a method that does not depend on luck. Brother Timothy has overheard Nicia's command and is eager to meet them at the church, where his merchandise is worth more. On the way, Callimaco gives Ligurio his version of the night spent with Lucrezia. He made the proposal to her, prompted by Ligurio (4.2), to live with her without scandal, and she surrendered completely, he says. The reasoning he quotes from her is wonderful: "Since your astuteness, my husband's stupidity, my mother's simplicity, and my confessor's wickedness have led me to do what I never would have done by myself, I am willing to judge that it comes from a heavenly disposition which has so willed, and I don't have it in me to reject what Heaven wills that I accept." In other words: I would not have done this myself, but I did it; therefore, heaven willed it; therefore, I will it. Lucrezia wills necessity in the guise of religion. Her reasoning shows morality refuting itself because morality assumes that one can act as one wills. She also said to Callimaco, I take you for my lord, master ("patrone"), guide; you are my father ("padre"), my defender. Callimaco is to be her father, as if she were the daughter of Lot; her adultery she understands as incest. On hearing these words, Callimaco, as always, was about to die with their sweetness. He declared himself "the happiest and most contented man who ever was in the world," and if the happiness should never fail, he would be blessed. Messer Nicia had also called himself the happiest man in the world, but without the implied reference to the next world (3.12).

Lucrezia herself, whom we see next with Nicia and Sostrata (now a pair), is hardly submissive. To Nicia, who wants her "to do things in fear of God," she appears to be a rooster, and as if she were reborn (5.5). Sostrata calls her "un poco alterata" (a little angered or a little altered [for the worse]). She is more aware, more aggressive; she knows she no longer depends on one man, though she is not liberated from men altogether.[59] But she has had her consciousness raised — or lowered. So have we. We have seen morality instructed as to its own limits.

The last scene is held before the church in the presiding presence of Brother Timothy. Messer Nicia invites Callimaco to live in his house, and Lucrezia willingly agrees that he be given a key to the room on the ground floor and that he become "our godfather" (nostro compare). The man Lucrezia calls father in private is godfather in public. The happy ending requires that they keep up appearances, but for that purpose it also requires deceit. The *Mandragola* does not end with general enlightenment, as do most comedies, but with a deceit that must be continued. So Brother Timothy leads all into the church for prayers, and the play ends.

The error of many commentators on the *Mandragola* is to focus on Callimaco and his burning desire for Lucrezia. The commentators overlook or subordinate the desire of Messer Nicia, and in lesser degree of Lucrezia, to have children. Seeing that Callimaco is so often without a "remedy" and remains suggestible throughout, they seize on Ligurio as the key character in the play, the Machiavellian schemer.[60] But Ligurio is not a principal; he is an agent.[61] He has no interest in the transformation of Callimaco from lover to godfather, in the surprise ending in which Messer Nicia too gets what he wanted. Ligurio is apparently both pimp and matchmaker. These are two occupations difficult to combine in the same case, but in the *Mandragola* Ligurio achieves this feat, one beyond his understanding. For him as for us, matchmaking is respectable and pimping is not. That the two could be necessary to each other — in Machiavelli's new design for respectability — is present only in Ligurio's actions, but not in anything he says. At a certain point (4.2) Ligurio, without explanation, changes the object of the conspiracy from satisfying Callimaco once to arranging return engagements and making them respectable. This was not Callimaco's original interest, which was to decide whether Italian women were more beautiful than French. Would it not be necessary to consider other possibilities and keep his mind open? But like Ligurio, Callimaco suddenly changes direction. Why?

We are led, then, to Messer Nicia and his desire to have children, namely, sons.[62] From that standpoint, Callimaco and Ligurio are subordinate characters, means to an end beyond their end. Messer Nicia is using them, rather than they using him. What stands in the way of this thought is Messer Nicia's "stupidity." But what does that stupidity amount to, apart from Messer Nicia's earthy language and apparently unintentional suggestions? He is stupid because he is a cuckold. But why is that necessarily stupid? If it is not always stupid to commit adultery, why is it always stupid to permit it? A new, laxer attitude toward adultery might seem to require us not to laugh so hard at cuckoldry.[63] It is, after all, the method recommended by the king of France for the perpetuation of families and kingdoms.[64] Interpreters of the *Mandragola,* who do not consider themselves ignorant or coarse and who are surely superior to most audiences, nonetheless share the conventional view that cuckoldry is ridiculous — and so it never occurs to them that a cuckold could be a hero. But let us not be prisoners of convention!

Once one turns away, dissatisfied, from Callimaco and Ligurio, Messer Nicia appears as the key figure in the *Mandragola,* and the problem of the play becomes how to enable him to have sons. If Messer Nicia does not mind being a cuckold, then perhaps he doesn't mind appearing stupid. Machiavelli praised Junius Brutus for pretending to be crazy during the affair of the Roman Lucretia.[65] Perhaps Ligurio, with whom Messer Nicia had had a "close familiarity" (una stretta dimestichezza, 1.1), was his agent, not Callimaco's. Ligurio induces Callimaco to believe that the plot is intended to accomplish his desire, and spectators and readers, expecting a conventional comedy devoted to proving once again that there's no fool like an old fool, fall just as easily as Callimaco into the misdirection.[66]

Yet the *Mandragola* is not a conventional comedy that ridicules the respectable nomos and then, at the end, returns to it and accepts it. Machiavelli's levity ends in gravity, justifies gravity, but a new gravity. Human necessities, which prompt men to laugh at and otherwise assault the grave, public beliefs by which they live, force them not to abandon gravity but to change it, reform it, renew it. Messer Nicia has a succession problem in his family to which all families are subject: through chance, the bloodline of the family may not continue. The public belief in chastity, which secures the family, does nothing to continue it. Family values are not enough. The task of perpetuation is left to the natural desire for generation — to nature. But nature is subject to chance. Machiavelli's general advice — since the *Mandragola* is probably not a proposal for family reform by itself — is to find a remedy for untoward chance and not to worry if it is morally unconventional. The *Mandragola* is part of his campaign for a "perpetual republic."[67]

As such, the theme of succession goes beyond family or even republic in the usual sense. In order to accomplish his plan, or plot, Machiavelli needs followers that will carry on his work, bringing it by the "short road" to a conclusion, after his lifetime, from the point he has had to leave it.[68] He needs

Machiavellians, and so he too has a succession problem. If we look again at the *Mandragola,* we can suspect that Messer Nicia is Machiavelli reversed, and not only with respect to his initials. Messer Nicia is very stupid; Machiavelli, who rises to "grandi prudenze,"[69] is very prudent. Accordingly, Messer Nicia pretends to be potent, and Machiavelli impotent (the "great and continuous malignity" of his fortune).[70] Both need sons, and neither can be sure of generating them in the usual way. If we disbelieve in Messer Nicia's potency, we can see how he might make use of Callimaco. If we disbelieve in Machiavelli's impotence, we can see how he might use men like Callimaco. At one point in the play, Messer Nicia reflects — in the presence of Callimaco! — on the difficulty of getting a young man into the mandragola scheme (2.6). If he tells the young man he will die, he won't be willing; if he doesn't, he will be betraying him and will be reported to the public justice. Machiavelli, too, needs young men or students willing to risk their lives; how will he tell them what to do without betraying them? He must entice them into his design, relying on their subversive virtue, encouraging them at first to forget about the crime of adultery and then, once they are committed to it, gradually revealing to them just how far that crime goes. They may suffer retribution from the public authorities, but more likely, if the authorities are prudent, they will be rewarded. Machiavelli cannot generate his students; others have to do this for him. But if he doesn't mind being cuckolded, he can manage to claim them as his own.

2

Clizia *and the Enlightenment of Private Life*

ROBERT FAULKNER

The *Clizia* is a comedy about love that borders on the scandalous. As a matter of fact, it crosses the border. But the play is not the ordinary romantic farce or, what is just now more conventional, the ordinary dramatic scandal. One should not expect the ordinary from a playwright so extraordinary. *Machiavellian* may be a common byword now, but Machiavelli was a political scientist or political philosopher. *The Prince,* his most famous work, is perhaps the most notorious handbook for unscrupulous policies ever and perhaps also the most influential treatise of political philosophy ever.

I shall argue that Machiavelli's *Clizia* is itself a mix of the amusingly popular and the gravely searching. Bawdy and raucous as it may be, *Clizia* is also maliciously penetrating as to religion, morals, and love. It teaches how to get the girl, and it also teaches how to manage in the long run mating and a household. Simply put, the play applies Machiavellian arts of scoffing and of management to sex, love, and family. It thus shows the way to enlightened reform of the relations between man and woman, parent and child, master and servant. The traditional relations of love, deference, piety, and duty are ridiculed as frauds. They are replaced by transactions for mutual utility, with an art of management as midwife. *Clizia* teaches a lot about the comedy of enlightenment, if we can figure it out. Such an inquiry, which extends to the play's connections with similar themes in its sister play, *Mandragola,* is what this essay is about.[1]

A Machiavellian Play

I fear that serious talk about comedy will have the dubious appeal of explaining a joke, especially in an age when critics eulogize irony and deprecate the importance of being earnest. Yet a comic writer has to have a serious side. If you can make people laugh at the low and the foolish, you must have some inkling of the high or at least of the knowing. The more uncommon the playwright's consideration of such things, the more penetrating his drama and even his humor. *Midsummer Night's Dream* is not mere slapstick or a sitcom; Bottom the Weaver is more than a slip on a banana peel or the roast of a particular pol. Uncommon playwrights instruct. Machiavelli, the uncommon playwright here, intended to instruct. He said so. He said so precisely in *Clizia*'s prologue, which contains a serious rethinking of the comic art. A playwright must devise "expressions which excite laughter," but the spectators who eagerly attend to "enjoy themselves" will "taste afterwards the useful lesson that lay underneath."[2]

One cannot but wonder: what "useful lesson" does Machiavelli advance beneath the biting humor of *Clizia*? And how is it related to the striking political lessons of *The Prince* and the *Discourses on Livy,* his two major works? One must wonder also at the relation between underlying lesson and humorous appeal: might Machiavelli's humor be specially designed to bite into the scruples of a broad range of spectators? It seems to me that *Clizia* advances lessons in cynicism and policy, especially for lovers, women, and servants, and advances too a correspondingly scoffing and controlled humor. The combination proves to be a powerful vehicle. I shall call Machiavellian comedy a vehicle of enlightenment. It is chiefly the saucy comedies that have led some commentators to call Machiavelli the "greatest dramatist of his age," "the greatest of Italian dramatists," and a seminal influence upon important traditions of European drama, including such playwrights as Christopher Marlowe, Ben Jonson, and William Congreve.[3] Shakespeare himself, seminal in a different tradition, was famously concerned to rebut that "notorious Machevile" and his "subtle" and "politic" portrayals of love, ambition, and comedy itself.[4]

At first sighting the plot might make one doubt whether such light drama can bear such grave interpreting. Cleandro, a young Florentine, is mad with desire for the beautiful Clizia, a girl of seventeen brought up from childhood in his household. But Cleandro has to contend with his father, Nicomaco, an old geezer who also wants to bed Clizia, and with his ambitious mother, Sofronia, who regards the match as unsuitable. Indeed, in the face of his parents' diverse passions, Cleandro's efforts are reduced to a sideshow. The plot is moved by the attempts of old Nicomaco to get the girl and the counterplots of old Sofronia to protect the girl and especially to protect the household. Nicomaco would marry off Clizia to a pliable servant, Pirro, who is to make the girl available to his master. But Sofronia, who has stopped Cleandro by command, would stop Nicomaco by a countermarriage of Clizia to Eustachio—the stinky steward ("perfumed in dung") of the family farm. Nicomaco responds with a bizarre and successful drawing of lots (there are allusions to the workings of providence), by means of which his Pirro wins out over Sofronia's Eustachio for the marriage rights. But Sofronia crowns this move by substituting for the bride Clizia a disguised male servant, Siro. What Nicomaco finds in the marital bed is not what he had expected. There follows a lewdly humiliating encounter in the dark. The threat of bringing it to light is enough to bring Nicomaco to heel. At the end the unexpected arrival of the wealthy and respectable father of Clizia persuades Sofronia to allow Cleandro to marry Clizia. Through her wits and plots and some help from *fortuna,* Sofronia manages to arrange a restored family and even a new and future prosperity.

It seems simple and even the triumph of justice. But there are strange loose ends and substantive peculiarities. Why does Clizia never appear? Why does Clizia's father, Ramondo, appear out of nowhere? Why does Cleandro's friend Palamede completely disappear after his prominence in the first scene? Why the strange linkages of Nicomaco to God? And how explain the prominence or even universality of selfish motives and calculating policies? How can there be a just restoration of family ties when each and every member seems an instrument of private passion, be it sexual desire or an appetite for wealth, respectability, and security? Why the amorality or immorality in most or all of the chief characters and in their constant conspiring?

It is no doubt true that some of the loose ends correspond to the neoclassical stage conventions of the time, but it is also true that such correspondences don't prove much in this case. Machiavelli was a dramatist who broke plenty of conventions. Or so at least a recent commentator argues: Machiavelli omitted such staples of neoclassical comedy as subplots, prominent minor characters, and leisurely one-liners and was a "pioneer," an innovator who was "inventing a new mode of theater from scratch."[5] Given the possibility of radical unconventionality, one has to wonder first and foremost about Machiavelli's own plan: the comprehensive intention that permitted him to retain what he did as well as to change what he did.

In any event, the chief peculiarity of Machiavellian comedy is not literary form but substantive outlook, a comprehensive cynicism as to human motives. This is clearly intentional, for it is the chief feature of the theory of comedy that the prologue expounds. Some who deny moral or political seriousness to *Clizia,* such as the biographer Roberto Ridolfi, neglect to address this authentic explanation of Machiavelli's intent.[6]

Both *Clizia* and *Mandragola* are unconventional from the start, that is, in their self-consciously philosophic prologues. A recent commentator goes so far as to say that Machiavelli "invented the critical prologue in which the author does something never met in classical literature: he analyzes and discusses his own art."[7] Be that as it may, the prologues stand out in their mixture of the singularly self-regarding and the singularly universal. In *Clizia* the author speaks and mentions no predecessors. Yet he speaks as wise in the manner of a philosopher — as a knower of "events always the same" and hence of the nature of human things. Consider the Roman play on which the *Clizia* is modeled, Plautus's *Casina.*[8] While the *Casina* has a prologue, the actors deliver it, and they trace the play deferentially to a Greek original. In *Clizia*'s, Machiavelli alone speaks, and he tacitly sneers at traditional literary theories.

What *Clizia*'s prologue recommends is a cynical-scoffing comedy, one which ridicules morality and piety and the supposition that either is realistic. Comedies were invented to "benefit" as well as to "delight." According to Machiavelli, the benefit is consciousness-lowering (as we may call it). An author can bring out the "avarice," "passion," and "tricks" in his characters; he should bring out in general "the untrustworthiness of all men." The doubtfulness of moral claims is the theme. While the prologue displays some initial concern that the play not appear to contain "some indecency" (disonesta), by its end Machiavelli says only that if there is anything "not decent" (non onesta),[9] women will be able to listen "without blushing." Indecency there may be — but so presented that women can get over it.[10]

This thoroughgoing cynicism as to men and morals challenges the chief literary theories of the time, especially those derived from Horace's *Art of Poetry* and Aristotle's *Poetics.* The *Art of Poetry* was the leading European vehicle of classical literary theory through the so-called middle ages until it began to be supplanted, during Machiavelli's era, by the *Poetics.*[11] Both of these works make the poet a teacher of decency, not an underminer of it. The *Art of Poetry* is especially notable for its moral intention. To convey the purpose of poetry Horace recurs to the fable of Orpheus, the "holy prophet" of divine harmony among men: in primitive times the charms of rhyme and music were to make men shrink "from bloodshed and brutal living." Then poets drew lines between private and public, things sacred and things common.

They checked "vagrant union," gave rules for wedded life, helped build towns and give laws. For such civilizing contributions the archaic poets reaped honor. A Hesiod and a Homer were even worshiped as divine. Later poets, according to Horace, hymn the gods, prepare men for battle, show a way of life.[12] He prescribes accordingly. A dramatic chorus, for example, should side with the good. It should give friendly counsel, praise justice, law, and peace, and pray that a divine justice will give good fortune to the unhappy and the reverse to the proud.[13]

Aristotle's *Poetics* is less morally didactic in acknowledging the varieties of tragedy and comedy and especially in wariness as to religious theatrics and moral-religious indictments of the poets.[14] But on the point in question the *Poetics* does not differ much. The "more serious" (semnoterei) dramatists imitate the "more noble" (kalas) men and doings; the less serious, men and things that are common and base (phaulos).[15] The distinction between high and low, noble and base, is a starting point or the starting point. Seriousness about the fate of high possibilities is the measure to the point that tragedy, not comedy, seems the high or higher drama. Still, the *Poetics* also points in other directions. Near the end Aristotle defends poets against the charge that they portray things not noble. He is circumspect. One needs to consider whether the thing said or done is actually serious or base (spoudaios or phaulos), and by whom and to whom it is said or done, and whether to obtain a greater good or avoid a lesser evil.[16] Perhaps part of the poet's task is to warn against evil under the appearance of good, such as in an Iago, to show the limitations of certain understandings of nobility, such as the sexual austerity of the pious Angelo (in *Measure for Measure*), or the compassion of Miranda and the honest kindness of Gonzalo (in the *Tempest*), or to remind of goods apart from noble conduct, such as the wisdom and poetic gift of a Prospero. Still, if Aristotle's measure of poetry proceeds beyond common decency, it begins with respect for decency or at least with the common promptings of reason in knowing: "Learning things gives great pleasure not only to philosophers but also in the same way to all other men, though they share this pleasure only to a small degree."[17]

According to Machiavelli's poetics in *Clizia,* on the other hand, the starting point of comedy is ridicule of others in order to appeal to the audience's desire to be superior. The playwright gets laughs at human beings who are silly, in love, or insulted (or harmed: "iniuroso"). The laughing is a looking down on others, not for their baseness or vulgarity but out of one's desire to be above them. The playwright appeals not to intuitions of something higher (noble or fair or pious), but to the desire to rise if only by having others reduced. Machiavellian comedy supposes the audience to be self-regarding; it appeals accordingly. This supposition is a two-edged sword. From such an audience a playwright cannot himself obtain admiration, to say nothing of worship. Machiavelli knows the difficulty. The prologue of *Mandragola* tells of the reward he expects: everyone will "sneer" and "speak ill."[18] He confronts the difficulty. Machiavelli will not bother to remonstrate or to rise above the taunts. He will defend himself and indeed beat the audience at its own game. He will obtain his own superiority. The playwright too is self-regarding in Machiavelli's sense. Hence, I suspect, the prologue's peculiarly self-regarding assertions of superiority — precisely in wielding the poison pen. Machiavelli too can speak ill and better than anyone. "This was his first art," this speaking ill, and he stands in awe of no one where Italian is spoken. Such an audience extends beyond the theater. Machiavelli's art of laughter is more like a politic art of governing or at least of rising. His ridicule is not least for the sake of reducing his rivals for literary superiority, for example, the Roman playwrights or, as I will suggest, even Dante. Machiavelli proves to be "a darling of malice" like Ligurio, the mastermind of *Mandragola,* but with a far more masterly understanding of who and what are his rivals.

Although Machiavelli wrote comedies, he wrote no drama even reminding of tragedy, Leo Strauss noted, and this is owing to the absence from his thought of moral seriousness, as Strauss also noted.[19] One can have a grim or grave outlook as to the human condition, as Machiavelli indeed has, without having a tragic outlook as to the fate of good human beings. Decency is finessed in *Clizia*'s prologue and replaced in the play proper. Nobility of conduct is conspicuous by its absence. The term "noble" (nobile) appears only in a reference to old Athens, "a noble and very ancient city in Greece," and this amidst the nostalgia for ancient things that oozes from the first song and first paragraph and then more or less disappears. Cured of belief in the actuality or at least the use of admirable human types, Machiavelli need not and cannot regard their fall as the stuff of tragedy.

Instead, human failure is the stuff of bad fortune or bad management. Improving management, so that one can master fortune, is the theme that gives seriousness to Machiavelli's political thought and to his comedies too. Amusement is the bait; underneath are useful lessons. The comedies, like their prologues, are peculiarly didactic. Life according to Machiavelli is no laughing matter — and less so than for an Aristotle or a Shakespeare. While Aristotle distinguishes comedy from tragedy, Machiavelli distinguishes the comic from the grave. Life is very grave indeed to those who grasp the prevalence of necessity. Machiavelli distinguishes not the high from the low, but light necessities, which are lesser necessities, from serious necessities, which are the real necessities. Comedy is about light necessities. The grave works are the political works that show how to overcome real necessities by security, riches, and glory. The comedies play with light necessities while intimating the road to overcoming real necessities.

In comedy, Machiavelli says in the *Discourse or Dialogue Concerning Our Language,* one cannot show serious figures. Palamede seems the most serious figure in *Clizia;* he withdraws from Cleandro's love business to pursue his own business. The figure who most moves the plot is Nicomaco, and he, like Callimaco in *Mandragola,* is driven by a necessity that is partly a "fantasia." His and Callimaco's are light necessities. Nicomaco's is a lust beyond his abilities, ruinous to his establishment, and covered over with pretensions and self-deceptions. There is plenty of opportunity for an author to exhibit silliness, lovesickness, and insult. If there are prominent serious figures in the two comedies, they are of limited seriousness. The two most prominent are Ligurio and Sofronia, one a parasite looking for a living and to rise, the other a wife limited to her household. Still, both so manage domestic affairs as to provide for their security and gain. They are not nobler souls above the fray who descend out of necessity to offer guidance, such as the duke in *Measure for Measure,* or the duke and Portia in *Merchant of Venice.* They are grave figures in the fray who manage the lighter figures so as to provide for mutual necessities and thus for their own.

In Machiavelli's accounts one looks in vain for the contemplative or imitative pleasures that Aristotle described. On the contrary. In *Mandragola*'s prologue Machiavelli complains about spending time on such "light stuff" when he would rather seem "wise and grave" (saggio e grave); he is cut off from "showing with other undertakings other *virtù*."[20] How then understand the peculiarly didactic tenor of Machiavellian comedies? Why are they particularly "single-minded" in giving "textbook lessons in ingenuity"?[21]

In the *Discourse* Machiavelli indicates something of the place of comedy in his project for overturning traditional ways and something too of the literary rivals it is meant to help in overcoming. The *Discourse* might seem but philological, a combative defense of the Florentine vernacular for writers. Yet it turns to attack especially Dante, he of the *Divine Comedy,* for not acknowledging his dependence on the Florentine vernacular. Why does defense of the vernacular turn to the issue of comedy? It is because of comedy's potential power over a wide public. Vernacular speech can be idiomatic, and idioms in local speech bite more — supply the "salt" that can make comedy "popular and understood by everybody."[22] Thus comedy can convey the lessons "useful to our daily life." There come to light certain substantive implications of Machiavelli's attack on the language of the learned. He tacitly impugns a divine comedy that attends half-bemusedly to the whole human scene, as if contemplating from on high. He recommends instead useful comedy — comedy effectual in enlightening "the generality" as to what the author wants.

The *Discourse* proceeds to show something of what Machiavelli wants from comedy. It develops a special animus toward the church, which is, one might think, the worldly patron of rival and otherworldly lessons for the generality. Machiavelli criticizes Dante for using the language of the Papal Court and on grounds more political than linguistic: "I am astonished that you attach such importance to a place where nothing happens that is good or praiseworthy. Where customs are perverted language too must be perverted." The attack on the universal language conceals a more basic attack, that on churchly customs. Then the argument turns to the power of great writers even over the vernacular and the customs it carries. Dante can teach other writers "to forget the original barbarism in which their native tongue steeped them."[23] One is reminded of *The Prince*'s concluding call to liberate Italy from the barbarians. Is not Machiavelli suggesting that great writers can play a part, especially with respect to Italy's particular barbaric customs? But which great writers? The outstanding literary feature of the *Discourse* is a coerced interrogation of Dante — over whom Machiavelli wins a spectacular victory. Machiavelli compels Dante to defend by dialogue his use of the vernacular, at the end of which Dante "confessed that I was right and went away."[24] If a poet such as Dante is henceforth to confess to anyone, he is to confess according to the new faith expounded by Machiavelli. Machiavelli intended the effect he would have on the Jonsons, Congreves, and others of the modern European literary tradition. In the *Discourse* Machiavelli then himself confesses: he confesses himself not sure that he has disabused all of those who confound his native language with "filthy usages" from elsewhere. Confession is an acknowledgment of weakness. Allies are needed. Machiavelli is the political-literary prophet who calls other writers to spread secularization — to enter the fray over the wretched customs now mixed with the everyday language of men. Recall the self-proclaiming prologues of the comedies. At the start of *Mandragola* Machiavelli appears as master of "speaking ill"; at the start of *Clizia*, as enlightener as to the worldly forces beneath men's hypocrisies. Machiavelli intends to supplant divine comedy with earthy love-comedy, one particularly fitted to teach universal lessons in scoffing and management. He would make Dante go away, together with classical-Christian poetics in general.

However that may be, what is clear is that the new poetics corresponds to Machiavelli's new political-philosophic wisdom about man's exposed state in the world. Since all men are "wicked and do not observe faith [fede] with you," according to *The Prince,* you need not keep faith with them.[25] Good faith and justice in general are an unrealistic hope and guide. Another famous aphorism explains Machiavelli's divergence from "the orders" of many writers and directs more generally: "And many have imagined republics or principalities that have never been seen or known to exist in truth; for it is so far from how one lives to how one should live, that he who lets go of what is done for what should be done learns his ruin rather than his preservation."[26] But if you watch what men really do, you can preserve yourself. Undistracted by how men should live, you can provide for and against what most moves the generality of men. If you follow Machiavelli's new customs you can come close to mastering fortune.

To sum up my broad thesis: *Clizia* exemplifies the mixture of critique and construction in Machiavelli's politic poetics. Cynical scoffing is its distinctively Machiavellian delight and part of its benefit. Yet the play also and chiefly shows how human beings searching for love and security may use one another to their mutual gain. This thought controls the plot and supplies the constructive lesson. One sees how to obtain others' aid by seeing through them and attending to what they really want. In this sense the comedies indeed are "textbook examples of human ingenuity."

Admittedly, some will object to viewing Machiavelli's comedies in the dark light shed by his political arts. They have a point. How can a political outlook as grim as Machiavelli's allow room for the acrobatic wit of a *Clizia? The Prince* and the *Discourses* recommend cruelty in preference to mercy. They recommend the art of being not merely bad, a murderer, but altogether bad, a murderer of the pope and all the cardinals.[27] One can understand why one commentator would want to deny any deeper meaning to Machiavelli's comedies, especially a moral-political meaning. Art for art's sake, literature for literature's sake, and Machiavellian comedy for the sake of literary play in language.[28] But such a proposal is impossible. To save the humor it dulls the humor, for it leads the reader away from the telling thrusts at, say, priests, gentlemen, Dante, Aristotle, and providence. In any event, such arty theorizing is contrary on its face to Machiavelli's own assertions as to the benefits of comedy, in *Clizia*, and as to the corresponding subordination of humor to useful lessons, in the *Discourse*.[29]

A Renaissance Play?

While many commentators agree that *Clizia* has a message, some deny that the message is Machiavellian. The play is of the Renaissance, they say, and its instruction merely what could be expected from the recovery of Greek and Roman drama. They point to the obvious fact that *Clizia* is a variation on Plautus's *Casina,* itself a variation on a Greek comedy.[30] In *Casina* as in *Clizia* an old father competes with his son for the bed of a young ward, father and son try to marry the girl to competing servants, and the father is foiled by his wife. One could add that *Clizia* abounds with allusions to Greek things. The Florentine incident recounted in *Clizia* is compared with a like event in ancient Athens. *Sofronia* is reminiscent of the Greek word for temperance or moderation. *Doria,* the name of the female servant who laughs so at her master's fall, is reminiscent of the Dorians, the Hellenic race that ruled in Sparta and the Greek cities of the Peloponnesus. *Palamede,* the name of the wary friend of Cleandro, is reminiscent of Palamedes, a legendary Greek wise man. Nicomaco, Cleandro, and Eustachio also have Italian versions of Greek names.

Still, such surface similarities are inconclusive, if only because elsewhere Machiavelli visibly manipulates classical themes for innovative ends. *Mandragola* radically revises the legend of Lucretia's rape by the son of the Roman tyrant Tarquin, to take the most obvious example, and *Discourses on Livy* revises Livy's account of Rome. Might Machiavelli be doing something similar with Plautus's *Casina?*

Also, there is a special difficulty in supposing that Machiavelli was the product of a certain Florentine neoclassical dramatic tradition: the tradition may not have existed before Machiavelli; he may have established it. According to Richard Andrews, only in the second quarter of the 1500s did the custom of imitating Plautus and other Roman comic dramatists arise. Andrews thinks Machiavelli was the cause, not the product: later writers used "the model of Machiavelli's *Clizia.*"[31]

In short, Machiavelli is likely to have selected *Casina* for his own reasons, and the interesting question concerns his reasons, not the conditions about him. Admittedly, an adequate account must await a fuller account of his variations on his source. At this point I will speculate that *Casina* was for Machiavelli a Trojan horse suitable for a Renaissance city. It had the cachet of the old classics while lending itself to an innovative antimoralism. *Casina* paraded a sensational sex scene and exhibited the power of passion to overturn taboos of age, incest, and gender.

Plautus had been judged doubtful, after all, by the standards of classical poetics or at least by the standards of his Roman compatriot Horace. In the *Art of Poetry* Horace calls Plautus's comedies coarse ("inurbanem").[32] In the *Epistles* he faults the plays for carelessness of finish, the result, it seems, of certain flaws of character: Plautus cared too much for money and fame. He cared too little for perfected thoughtfulness.[33] But Horace also places some responsibility on the comic tradition in Rome, with its coarse jesting and crudity of consideration. This he links cryptically to a preoccupation with "expansion." Did Roman imperialism lead to crude humor and undeveloped discrimination? After indicting Plautus and Rome, Horace recommends another guide: "Use Greek models by day, use them by night." And this is not a matter merely of form. The big advantage of the Greeks for poets is Socratic philosophy. The source of good writing is wisdom about "your matter," which is to be found in "the Socratic pages."[34]

In short, Machiavelli adopts the *Casina* for the same reason that his *Discourses* builds on Livy's history of Rome's republican empire. The old books appeal to a taste for the renaissance of classical learning, and these particular old books serve to cover an attack on the utopianism of classical political philosophy. The *Discourses* attacks aristocracy, the small city, and anti-imperialism; *Clizia*, a moral and philosophic theater.

To such arguments a serious commentator has responded that *Clizia*'s devotion to classical moral virtue is visible on its face. Suppose it true that such earlier works as *The Prince,* the *Discourses,* and *Mandragola* smack of Machiavellianism. *Clizia* differs[35] because it ridicules old Nicomaco's lusts and is thus a "critique of aggressive *virtù*." It recurs to a moderation that Machiavelli elsewhere rejected, and the proof, according to this argument, is in a name. *Nicomaco* combines the author's two names, and Nicomaco's humiliation exhibits Niccolò Machiavelli's self-punishment for his earlier excesses, literary and personal (while in his fifties he had a well-known affair with an actress in her thirties).

However ingenious this argument, it runs into difficulties. Indeed, any attempt to interpret *Clizia* as a restoration of ancient morals encounters grave difficulties. *Clizia* differs in major ways from *Casina;* and the big differences go in a Machiavellian direction. The crucial point is that *Clizia* lacks the predominantly moral resolution of *Casina.* It is about effectual *virtù,* not moral virtue.

While the Roman play basically ridicules an old man's vice, *Clizia* has an additional theme: how young men can succeed in bedding young women, and an additional answer: with a view to security in the future. In Plautus's play the son never appears. In *Clizia* Cleandro's sexual hunt seems to set the play in motion, just as Callimaco's certainly does in *Mandragola*. Both of Machiavelli's plays blend young sexual desire with old heads. They thus teach how to do it reliably and with a view to more important considerations (that is, for the long haul and without sacrificing security). But passions of the old are satisfied too. In fact, for young and old security seems to be regarded as primary, while love is but a force to be satisfied at others' expense or to be otherwise managed. In Plautus's play the distinctive metaphor for love is food. In Machiavelli's, it is war.[36] In Plautus's play the mother, while thwarting her husband, sympathizes with her son's love and promotes it. In *Clizia* mother thwarts son as well as husband for her own purpose, that is, until a marriage useful to the family may be obtained. It is a mother's "ambizione" as well as a father's lust that stands in Cleandro's way (5.5; cf. 2.3, 4), and it is that passion that governs the reconciliation of the household at play's end.

Are the lessons of *Clizia* about the virtue of moderation or about realism as to motives and management? Nicomaco's passion is ridiculed as ineffectual, not as incestuous and evil. He is "a crazy, drooling, bleary-eyed, toothless old man," even in the report of a friend (5.2); his son reports a "smelly mouth," "trembling hands," "such wrinkled and stinking limbs" (4.1). Whatever the case with Machiavelli in his fifties and his reputed lover Barbera in her thirties, Father Nicomaco at seventy seems not quite the fetching love-object for a teenager — apart from the fact (on which Machiavelli neglects to dwell) that the teenager is his ward. Nor do we see in Sofronia's victory the triumph of moral principle. In Plautus's *Casina,* indeed, the finale involved merciless ridicule of the old lecher's vices. But there was no visible effect. *Clizia* ends with success, precisely by not relying upon moral indignation. It is because of Sofronia's schemes, not her morals or piety, that we find a domestic reconstitution with the knowing wife now completely in charge.

It is true that the new ruler Sofronia is understanding as to her husband's excesses, is restrained in her remedy, and seeks to keep rather secret his humiliation. But this is only the Machiavellian equivalent of moderation, anticipation of necessity.[37] Sofronia interprets Nicomaco's excesses not as vices to be condemned, but as forces to be expected, and thinks that only forces shrewdly managed will serve as remedy. Nicomaco eventually subordinates himself, indeed, but only because he has to. Sofronia somewhat subordinates herself again because she has to, because, that is, of her dependence on Nicomaco's reputation and in general on the household. She anticipates her necessities. This dependence on the household is crucial because it is a common necessity that all share and in response to which all can ally. Cleandro and Nicomaco too had feared to turn the household "bottoms-up" (2.2; cf. 4.1). Like Sofronia they need a respectable name and household (5.2). Still, only Palamede at the start and Sofronia throughout understand the priority of the household for whatever each wishes or can reasonably wish. Nicomaco's foresight recurs only after Sofronia intimidates him. Reconciled to their necessities by her management, which includes forcing him to perceive mutual necessities, the two retire to a household restored.

Actually the household is less restored than it is secured on a new basis. It is not the old household, and it will be advanced as well as secured. This too is due to Sofronia's motives and management. Treating Clizia all along as a potential asset, she opposes "throwing away" the girl on whom "they have expended so much effort" (2.3). As soon as Clizia is known to have a father rich and noble as well as accepting of Cleandro, no other questions are asked. There is no parallel in *Casina* to this concluding affirmation, in a love-comedy, of the primacy of riches and respectability. Some critics have been surprised to find in Machiavellian comedy such a bourgeois spirit. But Machiavellian anticipation of necessity amounts to the apprehensive acquisitiveness that underlies the later and more economic teachings of a John Locke. The leading characters in *Clizia* are very much about their own "business." Still, Machiavelli's political teaching is chiefly about freedom, glory, and political empire. In his case the new basis shows its bourgeois resonance chiefly in the sphere of domestic economy — Machiavelli does not plan a full-fledged political economy — and even there more in gaining by advantageous dealing than by production.

Clizia ends by showing how human necessities can be effectively managed to a certain mutual satisfaction. It eschews moral indignation because it has eschewed morality and the complications that attend any moral seriousness of love. It also eschews the playing around, the leisurely playfulness and joyful indulgence, that goes with lovable things cherished as good and delightful in themselves. Love as well as morals is to be controlled to one's advantage.

In short, *Clizia* is less a recovery of the old Greek and Roman wisdom than a corrosive satire on it. While from its first song it advertises "ancient" or "very ancient" themes, these disguise ingenious attacks on the outlook of a Renaissance audience. The play takes aim especially at Greek philosophy in its Christian version. Consider Nicomaco. He is a respectable Christian gentleman who looks up to "ancient and modern examples" for the instruction of his son (2.4). But his ancient virtue and modern religion prove no match for his passions.[38]

Lessons in Scoffing

Even the fluffy surface of *Clizia* innovates within Renaissance convention. The fluffiest of the fluff are the six songs (*Casina* had none), and they bespeak a world of force and fraud only loosely covered by conventional romance and piety. It is true that the first song features pagan nymphs and shepherds mooning nostalgically over their antique loves. And the last song eulogizes the play itself as a "wise and noble teacher" that shows what is needed for "ascending to heaven" — and then for teaching "under a veil a great deal more." But between such gauzy veils, the first sappily pagan and the last sardonically Christian or Platonic, are four songs that treat of love, youthful ardor, woman's anger at offense, and trickery. These songs alone teach a great deal more. Their teachings are not about the decency and piety that Horace had prescribed for theatrical choruses. Machiavelli's musical commentaries treat love, ardor, and the rest simply as forces, and these are the real "lords" that will overpower decency and overpower gods as well as men. Men cannot look above passions and plots but must contend with them.

Love (not grace or truth) may bring heaven's "highest worth," according to the song after act 1, and the love in question, the "great power" that men and gods dread, is said after act 2 to be in the bodies of the "ardent young." A greater force is vengeance, especially female vengeance, whatever its occasion. We are told after act 3 that woman offended, whether "wrongly or with reason," is full of pride, anger, trickery, and cruelty. Her force is more than "all mortal force." There remains a superior force that seems the supreme force: the fraud of trickery. The trick in act 4 is paid the highest tribute; at least, the successful trick is called the "remedy high and rare" that "shows the straight path to wandering souls." Is great trickery, the conspiracy that works by providing the remedies men need, Machiavelli's replacement for the eternal claims of right or of the divinity? Consider the pleasure in trickery displayed in *Mandragola* by both Ligurio the politic and Father Timoteo the priest, and in *Clizia* by the many laughers who are freed from their master. The trick is the greater if it achieves a state of real security. So Sofronia's accomplishment: by a clever conspiracy she obtains for her household the superiority that a knowing prince seeks for his state.

This orientation by real forces presupposes the philosophic critique of morals found in all of Machiavelli's major works and most visibly in chapter 15 of *The Prince*. The comedies package critical thinking for a popular audience. That, I think, is their special task. Consider again the author's role in *Clizia*'s prologue. Machiavelli appears not only as philosopher but also as abrupt director of the actors and insinuating director of the audience. He orders the actors out front and, as if speaking for the people, back offstage. While this comedy is insistent about what is put before the audience, it puts itself in the people's shoes. Machiavelli makes himself the instrument, the people's voice, for the people's desires. He thus directs to enlightened satisfaction, rather than to moral and religious duty. But this message depends on a critique of the moral spirit. Machiavelli is authoritative as to what is played, and scoffing at morals is central to his plays. To repeat, the prologue ends by defending the immorality ("disonesta") of the play for those who might find it immoral, especially women. It is the defense of immorality, not least sexual looseness, that calls forth a new theory of comedy. Machiavellian comedy ridicules especially efforts to do what one ought. *Clizia* is quiet about incest and chastity — while outraging modesty with its sensational conclusion.

In *Clizia* one sees a reductionist view of love: sexual desire accompanied by fantasy. The real thing is the sexual urge, which is itself some mixture of desire for pleasure and desire for domination. What men think they ought to love, and thus the beauty and character of the person they love, is merely fantasy. Love as distinct from sexual passion is an imagining. It is then to be dismissed by serious people. The two most serious people in the play are Palamede and Sofronia, and both dismiss it. Replying to Cleandro in heat, Palamede would avoid lovers and musicians (as well as old people). When Cleandro wails that he must be satisfied, Sofronia tells him that he can wait to be satisfied. She plans to marry him off to someone else or wait until his fantasy dissipates (5.4, cf. 5.3; 3.3).

In Cleandro and Nicomaco alike there is nothing of the lover chastened in desire by awe before the beauty of his beloved. When in Shakespeare's *Tempest* Ferdinand first sees the young Miranda, he looks up to her as a goddess. "O you wonder," he breathes. When Miranda's father warns about "th' fire ith' blood," Ferdinand says, to some skepticism from the father, that he would not "melt Mine honor into lust."[39] Love as honorable love is absent from *Clizia*. Honor, in the sense of reverence for the worthy, is absent as a motive. Neither Cleandro nor Nicomaco looks up to Clizia's goodness (to which Sofronia alone refers [2.3]). Cleandro and Pirro certainly drool over Clizia's "delicate" charms (4.1; 2.5), but this is anticipation of a delectable dish. The men show no awe before her beauty and certainly no concern for charm and seriousness of soul. The steward Eustachio even calculates that a beautiful wife can always be a source of income (3.5). The women are not much different. Sostrata jokes at Clizia's presumed scruples about lovemaking (4.10). Sofronia does refer to this "good and beautiful girl," but she treats these attributes as qualities useful for the market, that is, as adding value to a commodity which they should make the most out of. Some such considerations probably help explain why Clizia is referred to as but an imagining ("fantasia") (1.1; 2.4; 5.3). Beauty and goodness are only images of wish fulfillment, for Cleandro as well as Nicomaco.

The critique of love in *Clizia* is comprehensive, at least to the point of extending to a critique of friendship and of love of wisdom. The key example is Palamede. The Greek Palamedes was a legendary wise man who is supposed to have invented great benefactions like lighthouses and the alphabet, but to have come to a bad end because of his supposed friends. According to one version of the legend, Palamedes was induced by the wily Odysseus to join the expedition to recover Helen of Troy and then betrayed by the leaders, including Odysseus himself and perhaps King Agamemnon as well.

Some clues in *Clizia* hint at Machiavelli's improved version of the wise benefactor. This Palamede is secretive, occupied with his own business and wary of helping others (especially lovers and musicians). He will help only if necessary. He does not help except to advise temporizing in the face of superior forces. Palamede and Cleandro together comprise a little Machiavellian commentary on friendship. They are wary, hiding rather than sharing, attentive to their own. The first words of the play strike the keynote:

> *Palamede:* Why are you leaving the house so early?
> *Cleandro:* Where are you coming from so early?
> *Palamede:* From taking care of some of my business.
> *Cleandro:* Is it a matter that can be spoken of? (1.1)

Friendship strictly speaking seems not to exist between these two. Perhaps such friendship is impossible, according to Machiavelli's fundamental individualism. No one who is knowing would act knowingly for the sake of another or would love good things as if they were inherently shareable. Even one's knowledge is oriented to one's own necessities. Still, Cleandro out of necessity seeks help in his business or at least tells of his necessity in order to vent his passion, to get it off his chest (1.1; 4.1). Machiavellian friendship is trust or aid by those who hope to gain something from one another, if only appreciation of one's burden. Palamede sees no need to serve Cleandro, although he ventures an offer, and Cleandro does not know how to use Palamede. Cleandro's affairs are not put in order except by Sofronia, whose necessities encompass his and whose power and virtù are superior.

Lessons in Management

Because each is out for himself and without limits on desire except for the limits of possibility, each must fight for his satisfaction. Machiavelli has his own version of the "state of nature" that is "a state of war," albeit one without Hobbes's doctrines of natural equality and the primacy of peace. In love as in war, the key art is of war. Cleandro compares lover to soldier (1.2); Sofronia would defend Clizia from the "camps" of husband, son, and servants alike (1.3); there are sexually charged analogies with conquest and the weapons of war (1.1; 2.1, 3; 4.5, 11, 12, etc.). Actually, love is war, according to Machiavelli, except, I suppose, as its pleasures make a soft and enduring mutual relation preferable to forced submission, that is, to rape. Cleandro and Nicomaco seek the conquest of Clizia. Cleandro wants her in any way possible (1.1). Cleandro and Nicomaco are desperate, one to the point of willing death, and the other to breaking up his household and burning down his house. But there is no moral misery, that is, disgust at one's baseness or despair at losing something admirable. There is only the misery that fears failure and that spurs the search for the strategy and tactics of victory.

Victory in love as in war requires allies and so incentives. Hence the need for management. What the young Cleandro more or less lacks on his own is the ingenious stratagems, the remedies, that Nicomaco and Sofronia manage to devise. He needs fraud as well as force, for if life is a battle it is not least a battle of tricksters. *Clizia* teaches shrewd elders like Sofronia how to earn trust by showing youthful passions the road to long-term satisfaction. Ligurio does likewise in *Mandragola*. Leaders can serve themselves in managing followers.

In *Clizia* Sofronia alone exhibits the virtù of a leader. She alone of all the characters uses the word, and she also defines it in Machiavellian fashion. Virtù is "knowing how to do something" that will provide for business, the household, "or the affairs of others" and oneself (2.3). Virtù is the ability to provide — "knowing how." It amounts to self-reliance broadly construed. But Sofronia also has "industria" (1.1), the concentration on one's advancement that underlies virtù.[40] These crucial Machiavellian qualities do not revolve about "onesta," about decency or moderation. They do indeed lead to a self-limitation of one's desires, but out of ability to size up the real necessities and to master accordingly oneself and one's environment. While Sofronia's virtù may be within domestic limits, within those limits she exhibits a characteristically Machiavellian self-reliance. Even a commentator who would have Sofronia an agent of "conventional morality" had to admit that "her methods are those of manipulation and deceit" and correspond to those of Ligurio.[41]

At first Sofronia might appear to be the traditional woman that many commentators take her for: dependent upon others, moral, and pious. She retains a certain subordination to husband as well as to household; she looks for remedies from Cleandro and from God; she "would do good all the time" and goes off to mass (2.3). But from the start her churchgoing is linked with a statement that she "does not want to submit" her affairs "to anyone" (2.3). When Sofronia returns from mass she has been devising for herself rather than praying for help from without. She has been "revolving" schemes. She now threatens to expose and humiliate her husband (2.3). By play's end Sofronia is fierce in contriving her own remedies for the security of herself and her household. This mixture of spiritedness with cynicism and inventiveness *is* Machiavellian virtù.

Sofronia exhibits in her own way the mastery of fortune that is a prominent theme in *Clizia*. It is Nicomaco who believes in good fortune and would rely on a lottery (3.6). Perhaps he mixes Aristotelian reliance on nature's goodness with religious reliance on help from providence. His son Cleandro, however, thinks fortune an obstacle to be conquered (4.1; 5.5). Cleandro repeats a notorious theme of *The Prince*: fortune, like a woman, is a "friend of the young" (4.1). While *The Prince* explains that the young are less timid and thus command fortune "with more audacity," it also indicates that audacity has its limits.[42] *Clizia* shows the limitations of even a knowing Cleandro when carried away by passion and up against superior force. Like Callimaco in *Man-dragola*, Cleandro is knowing enough to submit himself to a more knowing manager. Unlike Callimaco, he is knowing enough to devise, to spy, and to temporize until "accidenti" and Sofronia's stratagems might favor his plans.

Sofronia's art of managing fortune is a domesticated art of war. She contrives forces to intimidate her husband. She contrives ingeniously, and her forces break his power and then reconstitute it for her purposes. She does not pardon her Nicomaco out of affection. Having humiliated him to the point of sobs before witnesses from the household, she keeps him humble through his fear of exposure and restricts knowledge of his humiliation to preserve their mutual respectability. We see a version of the fundamental but limited intimidation discussed in Machiavelli's political works.[43] Any society needs a periodic recurrence to its beginnings[44] — which is Machiavellian idiom for return to an original fear, indeed, to a founding terror. The foundation of society is directed terror that so sinks into selfish men as to make them obey something other than themselves: "Men will always turn out bad for you unless they have been made good by a necessity."[45] The famous Machiavellian model of well-directed terror is Cesare Borgia. Borgia laid "very good foundations" for his rule, that is, he engaged in acts of intimidation that culminated in terrifying but pointed executions. He first set up a "cruel and ready" prosecutor to destroy the robbers and murderers who had flourished under impotent lords. This instrument having pacified the land and having thus provoked his own enmities and resentments, he was found in a piazza "in two pieces" with a piece of wood and a bloody knife: "The ferocity of this spectacle left the people at once satisfied and stupefied."[46] Sofronia's management does not involve murder as spectacle — terrifying murder is not a comic theme — but she does effect a spectacular sexual humiliation that serves to destroy the old man's domestic tyranny and to unify a reformed household.

Enlightened Household, Enlightened Women

The household as alliance: this marks *Clizia*'s radical novelty as to the pretensions of fathers and masters and the dutifulness of mothers and servants.

Claims to be paterfamilias, the sacred father, seem pretentious indeed in light of a Nicomaco's motives and trickiness. Cleandro goes so far as to call his father "the foundation and cause of my harm" (3.1). Not an original sin, but the lordly power of a father, seems the root of this son's sufferings. The wife too loses whatever reverence she may have had for Nicomaco. Both lose their awe as they discern the real motives of men, fathers or no and sacred or no. But precisely this awareness without moral illusion permits the Machiavellian equivalent of moderation. Checked by enlightenment within the family and by the corresponding threat of exposure without, Nicomaco can keep himself in the harness of domestic provider. Nicomaco's prestige as head of the family is certainly not restored, as some have suggested, nor can I see that Machiavelli shows any more archetypal fear of a Sofronia than of the Lucretia in *Mandragola*. Sofronia is the real ruler of the reordered family. "Do what you like," allows the defeated husband, "I'm prepared not to go beyond the limits you set" (5.3).

Nicomaco's status as lordly master declines with his claims to be lordly father. *Clizia* is a deconstruction by ridicule of the traditional master-servant relation. One sign of the new attitudes is the servant Doria's strangely exaggerated laughter at her master's humiliation; another, her extended triumphing at this "beautiful trick" (4.8; 5.1). But the paradigmatic example is the triumph of Siro the servant, who sets upon Nicomaco in the ultimate male gestures of contempt. First Siro defends "herself." Then he goes on the offensive — very offensive. The story of Nicomaco's humiliations by Siro, sexual and otherwise, is the most sensational action of the play. All are said to laugh at this overturn of the master. The play dwells on the servants' laughter. Machiavelli may not proceed down the legalistic and economic road later taken by John Locke, who turns the hierarchical relation between master and servant into a contractual relation between employer and employee. But insofar as service and servants are to remain in the Machiavellian order, a kind of exchange will dominate. The traditional expectation of reverence and dutifulness will be subverted by hidden disdain and by the supposition of natural equality in ends and urges. Machiavelli would destroy the case for servile deference to gentlemen and replace the old relation with new "ordini" — with a managed association that appeals to mutual utility.

Both of Machiavelli's plays foster a liberation of women that is in many ways eerily contemporary. In *Mandragola* the beautiful wife Lucrezia is liberated from pedantic husband and pious modesty to take power and a lover in her household. In *Clizia* the old wife Sofronia rises from equivocal subordination before lord and master to unequivocal if indirect control of the household. The last two acts of *Clizia* are almost "entirely in the control of women,"[47] as Ronald Martinez notes, including not only Sofronia but also the servant Doria and the offstage Clizia.

Still, for Machiavelli liberation is not enough. A woman must provide for her self-reliance, not suppose it, and must also provide for the associations on which she will willy-nilly depend. There is a utilitarian rationalism about Machiavelli's teaching, a planning for security through calculated subordination, that is alien to the antibourgeois and anticontrol bent of contemporary feminism. It is Sofronia's politic scheming that establishes her control. She anticipates her necessities in the long haul and is inventive in providing means. Sofronia is not overcome by fear, she scoffs at Nicomaco's transparent efforts to win her with love, and she keeps her wits when Cleandro loses his. Thus she can provide for the family respectability and wealth that is useful. She schemes to ridicule her husband for her purposes, but when he has been cowed she protects him and avoids offending him, also for her purposes. Machiavellian liberation is an enlightened liberation. In *Clizia* old Sofronia is the most Machiavellian of the prominent characters. Like Ligurio in *Mandragola,* she is the brains of the job. Also like Ligurio, she is most like the author of the play.

Clizia *and* Mandragola

What is the relation of *Clizia* to the more famous *Mandragola?* While some commentators speak of disparate literary qualities of the plays, judging *Clizia* inferior, they rarely consider the substantive relation.[48] Do the plot and teaching of *Clizia* complement, contradict, or duplicate those of *Mandragola?* That's the interesting question, and it is provoked by the *Clizia* itself. Two characters from *Mandragola,* Sostrata and Siro, reappear in *Clizia.* Two songs, as to the power of love and of trickery, reappear as well. More to the point, in *Clizia* Nicomaco expressly reminds Sofronia of Frate Timoteo's miracle working in *Mandragola* (to produce Lucrezia's pregnancy) before slyly suggesting that she allow this pliable friar to pick the servant that gets to marry Clizia (2.3).

But Sofronia rejects out of hand Nicomaco's scheme for priestly intervention. Her reaction is a clue to the differences in the plays. In *Mandragola* the pious Lucrezia had been bedded adulterously only after a friar had salved her conscience with theological casuistry. But in *Clizia* the female lead scoffs at any such resort and lewdly so: "As if one needed a miracle to explain a priest getting a woman pregnant" (2.3). The general relation appears to be this: in confronting the traditions from ancient Greece and Christian Rome, *Clizia* addresses chiefly but not solely Greek moral wisdom, *Mandragola,* Latin theological learning.

Edmund Burke once traced the European tradition of chivalry to a blend of the Greek tradition of the gentleman with the Christian tradition of piety. Both of Machiavelli's comedies take aim at this Great Tradition. Both fight on the same battleground, that of love and the sexes. Also, both treat of private things in a grave public context and the same context: contemporary Italian politico-military failings. Clizia had been won as spoil of war by a French captain during the invasion of Italy by Charles VIII in 1494. In *Mandragola* Callimaco returns from Paris, where he had fled because of the same French invasion. That is, both plays take their broad bearings from the Italian weakness familiar from Machiavelli's political diagnoses, a weakness there symbolized by this and other French incursions.[49] The problem is specifically modern, Machiavelli seemed to think. It is caused by the pretensions to power of pacific Christian gentlemen and of an unarmed Roman Church, a church that needs armed allies, including foreign kings. But the pious weakness is partly the result of a philosophic weakness — especially of a Socratic and Aristotelian tradition that rather disdains political virtue in favor of moral and contemplative virtue.

In addressing such paradoxes at the level of romantic comedy both plays use the character Sostrata to remind of the naturalness of passion, of sexual passion in particular. Sostrata is a feminine form of *sostrato,* which can mean substratum or hidden depths or, in more philosophic discourse, matter or substance. In *Clizia* and *Mandragola* alike Sostrata laughs at scruple, counsels indulgence in pleasure, prepares the bride or wife for lovemaking, and is happily in on the conspiracy. But she is never a planner, and she utters such pieties as "In the name of God." Human passion is without much foresight and defers to conventional formulations (*Clizia,* 4.2, 10, 12).[50]

Although the two plays make a joint assault upon religion and "onesta," one can see a concentration of labor even if no strict division. Greek things and opinions are more prominent in *Clizia:* Athens, Greek names, a philosophic theory of comedy, and a wise friend. This play satirizes chiefly aristocratic morality, the gentleman and his household, deference to superiors, and the naturalness of governance by fathers and by males in general. Yet it is also true that *Clizia* satirizes claims to divine authority and power, perhaps claims that Machiavelli finds somehow connected to the attitudes mentioned. "I am brought back to life," Nicomaco exclaims when his fear of losing Clizia is replaced by hope of getting her (3.7).

It must be granted that blaspheming seems to go quite deep in *Clizia.* One has to wonder about an unholy divine trio of Nicomaco, Cleandro, and Sofronia. Apart from seeming to have risen from the dead, Nicomaco is frequently identified with God or at least "the name of God," and he orders his servant to "stand with Christ" (3.6, 7). His son identifies himself with a man of "infinite sorrows" (3.2).[51] In light of such things, it may not be mere convention that Machiavelli occasionally calls Sofronia Madonna. Perhaps *Clizia* shows how to scoff at a blindly willful lord who would take vengeance on those who stand in the way of all good things for himself. He would take vengeance, as Catherine Zuckert suggests, even on his chosen people and would sacrifice even his only begotten son.[52] "I intend to be lord in this household," Nicomaco says after threatening to evict his wife, burn down their house, and imprison his son (3.1). He is "the foundation and cause of my harm," says Cleandro (3.2).

Still, religious scoffing is more prominent in *Mandragola*. It is thematic and not secondary. Also, the scoffing in *Mandragola* focuses less on the Lord and more on an otherworldly Christ, his worldly otherworldly church, and Latin learning, and the Roman learned such as Boethius. Hence the prominence of spirituality, the church, Christian theology and chastity, and Christian husbands and priests. Which is not to say that the play spares the claims of the Bible as such and of morals as such.

These differences pervade the particulars. The title character in *Clizia* is a woman never seen, who is called at one point a "fantasia." Perhaps the play spoofs as nonexistent the beauty or perfection that men, not least Aristotelians, imagine to accompany natural desire. The title of *Mandragola* refers to a supposed medical cure (the mandrake root) that is shown to be a funny fraud. This play spoofs as nonexistent a miracle that was supposed to change nature and produce "a soul for our Lord."[53] Clizia is a spoil of war left by a military gentleman; she proves to be the daughter of a worldly gentleman. But Lucrezia in *Mandragola* is distinguished by devotion to God — she seems almost a daughter of God — and is married to a gullible Christian gentleman. In *Clizia* Sofronia uses Nicomaco's strange confidence in friends and in established hierarchies to overcome the chance result of his strange confidence in the drawing of lots. In *Mandragola* Ligurio uses Nicia's faith in miraculous cures to overcome Lucrezia's faith in providence.

The plays differ above all in the different beddings. Both plays describe openly if indirectly acts that decency would shroud. Indeed, such descriptions might be expected to undermine sexual awe and especially feminine modesty. Both episodes lead to a revolution in the household. But *Mandragola*'s recounting of Callimaco's night with Lucrezia describes virtually a religious conversion — an antireligious conversion that follows an earlier black mass with Dr. Callimaco as high priest. Pious wife is "reborn" as enlightened woman.[54] Lucrezia departs from faith in God, holy fathers, and husband. She turns to worldly pleasure, spirited independence from husbandly authority, and acceptance of her strong young lover as "lord and master" behind the facade of a traditional household.[55] The sexual spectacle in *Clizia,* on the other hand, challenges the presumptive naturalness of heterosexuality and of the superiority of gentleman to servant. The final bedding of Nicomaco, if one can call it that, involves display of male intercourse, if one can call it that, and the power of a strong young servant over an old and foolish master. It symbolizes subversion of the aristocratic and paternal moral order — and of the Aristotelianism that upheld such an order as being in accord, more or less, with the best in human nature.

There is some reason to think of *Clizia* as a completion of Machiavelli's comic project for managed liberation, not just a complement to other parts. The servant who triumphs is Siro. Siro is the only character besides Sostrata who appears in both plays. In *Mandragola* a servant Siro appears as a perfect servant. He is so perfect as to seem unnatural, a parody, perhaps, of a servant of the Lord who takes on himself the sins of the world.[56] In *Clizia* Siro's clothes, discarded pretriumph, are used to hide Clizia on her way to a convent. In *Mandragola* Siro is not raised toward independence, despite the subversion of the Christian household and despite the fact that Siro is often astute and is finally the object of Ligurio's solicitude: "Is there no man who remembers Siro?"[57] In *Clizia* Machiavelli remembers the servant Siro. Siro triumphs, in memorably offensive gesture and deed, and his leading role in the ridiculing of the old master is expressly noted (5.1). It may be that *Clizia* subverts what Machiavelli thought to be the remaining pillars of the traditional household, an allegedly natural superiority in fathers and masters and an unconditional dutifulness before a lordly father who demands all worship for himself.[58] But there is little reason to follow further the blasphemies in which Machiavelli entangles his audience.

Finally, what is one to make of the fact that *Clizia*, like the *Discourses on Livy*, is a variation on a classical text, while *Mandragola*, like *The Prince*, is not?[59] Is there more to this parallel than coincidence? *Clizia* does seem in some ways more attentive to the conventionally moral and family-oriented than is *Mandragola*, just as the *Discourses* is more attentive to the legal and republican than is *The Prince*. Whereas *Clizia*'s prologue shows some effort to protect an appearance of morality, *Mandragola*'s justifies speaking ill. *Clizia* is about efforts of the old and feeble to keep a household; *Mandragola*, about efforts of the young and vigorous to introduce a love match under the veils of a household. In that respect too *Clizia* may be a completion of Machiavelli's comic project. While *Mandragola* in its focus on sex laughs at the household's focus on marriage and babies, *Clizia* rethinks the household's utility. It shows the use of babies and how in general to replace patriarchy with an enlightened alliance for security, wealth, and reputation. Accordingly, *Mandragola* seems the more intellectually radical of the two plays. There is nothing in *Clizia* to compare with Friar Timoteo's remarkable dialogue with Lucrezia about the difficulties of morality, nor are there prominent characters of the theoretical subtlety of the friar or even of Ligurio. Might it be that *Mandragola* is a comic put-down of love extending even to love of Christ—the unarmed prophet who conquered the world and whom Machiavelli means to replace with a new faith ("fede") of arms?[60] Ligurio, unlike Sofronia, might rise beyond household management. *Clizia* is a comic put-down of love that extends to the political philosophers' pretension to love of wisdom. Palamede, attuned to business, indicates Machiavelli's alternative — but he finds no business worth his time in *Clizia*. *Mandragola* is more oriented to individuals' pursuing their own business and hence also to Machiavelli's own business. *Clizia* is about a restricted application of the prince's art: liberating and reforming the little republic of the household.

Comedy of Enlightenment

In general, Machiavellian comedies promote for private life the reconstruction that *The Prince* and the *Discourses* promote for public life. They subvert and they construct. They subvert the traditional hierarchies of the household. They construct artificial associations for private satisfactions, whether it be an adulterous grouping within the household or a more equal and mutually useful household.

This private reform by comedy complements Machiavelli's grave treatises on public reform. Many have praised his special attention to public life, some for its encouragement of a participatory civic republicanism, others for its undistracted realpolitik. But this priority for public life rests upon a critique of the dignity of private life. Machiavellian comedies ridicule most the supposedly higher inclinations to piety, decency, nobility, and philosophy. They laugh at the allegedly natural and divine hierarchies of the household and of private life generally. Reformed private life is, then, a realm chiefly of play — so the boy-lovers Cleandro and Callimaco and the would-be boy-lover Nicomaco — and of domestic security — so the wiser heads Ligurio and Sofronia and the longing of the sentimental-timid Nicia for a "little cutie" who will be a "staff to sustain our old age."[61] Entertainment and everyday security are what private life is about, according to Machiavelli. Criticizing the allegedly higher inclinations, he allows public life to stand out as alone grave. For the pleasures of bodily play and small trickery ignore the dangers of death and war as well as our subjection to the big tricksters. A secure household is but small security. Consider Nicia's fear of "the Eight" and his dependence upon what he thinks is done by "kings and princes and lords."[62] Only peoples with power can secure themselves and their families, and only princes with their own states can obtain by glory an immortality of their own.

It is not surprising that the comedies' reform of the private sphere is accompanied by an insinuation of public reform. To that extent at least Machiavellian comedy is politicized comedy — a rhetoric of political reform. It is not solely political because of the pleasure in play and the necessity for association in households. The private sphere has its claims. But comedic rhetoric has in good part a public purpose, partly by subverting in small and partly by accustoming in small.

Without reform we stint ourselves, in the words of the first song. We are repressed, in today's lingo. The plays liberate us from deferential beliefs and instruct us in the key liberated belief: that we are put upon in the name of the old fogies and dominating creeds of the world. The young, strong, clever, and female have been especially put upon. Machiavellian comedy aims especially to liberate and instruct them.

Women are the primary beneficiaries, with playboys probably in second place, and the young and the clever of both classes are favored accordingly. Both Sofronia and Lucrezia are pretty much in control of their households by play's end. "Whoever offends a woman" must face a force that surpasses "all mortal force," according to the song after act 3 of *Clizia*. Machiavelli takes his own warning to heart. This first of modern political philosophers caters to women in the prologue to *Clizia* and caters to their desire for vengeance in the action. A young girl is protected from an old father, and the result is the punishment of an old lecher as well as an exhibition of a man's frustration without a woman. Both comedies could seem chiefly for the liberation and instruction of women — but that would be to forget the satisfactions supplied to the young men with whom they sympathize (at least when the women know what is really important) and who set the plots in motion by seeking them.

The conventionally prominent men of the plays are by and large forgettable. They are boys preoccupied with girls or old men preoccupied with domestic security or with girls. One sees little in Callimaco or Nicomaco of ambition and gravity. The male servants are generally no better; they are alternately cheeky, servile, and cheeky again. It is true that Ligurio is the brains of *Mandragola* and that other clever men, like Father Timoteo in *Mandragola* and to a lesser extent Palamede in *Clizia,* are memorable. But these men have instrumental roles or are irrelevant to the plot. Some are conspirators, indeed, but chiefly for someone else's benefit. They get only partial satisfaction in managing another person's domestic satisfactions, although Ligurio gets a leg up in his rising (but not in his loving). It may be that first-rate men wish for the power and glory of public life, a life inevitably grave and ruthless. The pleasures and security of love and of the household are primarily for second-rate men and for almost all women. Lucrezia, "fit to govern a kingdom," may be an exception, although even in her enlightenment she submits herself to Callimaco as "lord, master, and guide" as well as "my father" and "my defender."[63]

In the prologue to *Mandragola* the author says that he engages in such light literary pursuits only because he is "cut off from showing with other enterprises other *virtù.*" Machiavelli too gets only a secondary satisfaction from the domestic scene and from satisfying audiences with such stuff. A student must look to *The Prince* and the *Discourses* to understand the scope of Machiavelli's singular outlook, not least as to first-rate men.

Still, the two comedies are themselves a profound political innovation. Comedy had not enjoyed a particularly good press among the political philosophers who preceded Machiavelli. They saw a short road between laughing at rulers and the respectable — and losing reverence for law and morals. The road between satire and lawlessness or licentiousness is especially short for the young, whose character, whose stance toward life and the passions, is comparatively unformed. Some ancient philosophers had worried about a slippery slope. In his *Politics* Aristotle would have well-governed countries keep lampoons and comedies from young people, at least until their upbringing is completed.[64] The *Poetics* exhibits similar apprehensions, touching on the origins of comedy in preludes to phallic songs and in personal parodies and crude invectives. It connects the rise of comedy with the rise of democracy and common tastes and with wandering comedians dishonored in their towns. Still, such doubts do not exhaust Aristotle's relevant reflections. He credits the great Homer with the origin of comedy in his *Margites,* as well as of tragedy, for Homer rose above merely personal satire to the laughable as such. He takes care to record the first comic writer in Athens to give up the lampooning form ("idea") and generalize speeches and plot ("logoi" and "muthos").[65] Aristotle, like Horace, points toward an urbane and philosophic comedy. It is urbane about the troubles and joys of life because wise as to the range of human beings and as to the absurdities and sadnesses to be expected. The *Nicomachean Ethics* includes wittiness among the moral virtues of the gentleman.[66]

Shakespeare in his *Tempest* figures forth, I believe, such a philosophic poet. Prospero is a lover of studies and the liberal arts, but he also has magical powers with the aid of his darling "chick," Ariel. Ariel can be taken for the poet's imagination, his power of imaging forth characters and events. Still, precisely such a nature as Prospero's may incline him to neglect the evil possibilities from a twisted brother, say, or from the twisted nature of a Caliban. Even on his island, even after the lesson of his political disaster back in Milan, only Ariel's warnings and powers save Prospero from the various plots of Antonio, Caliban, and Stephano and Trinculo. We are shown the endangered position of the poetic and wise, confronted by the dominating, the viciously passionate, and the flighty but greedy crowd. The *Tempest* instructs such a nature about the storms of life, without forgetting or denying life's magical delights. Prospero finds it easier to care for the charms of the wonderful Miranda and the nobility of the ardent young prince Ferdinand. But this care too is partly in the light of his darling art and in the shadow of his impending death. Prospero takes care to provide for what he delights in, lovingly and not only because it is perpetually endangered by the low and vicious. Philosophic comedy of this kind ridicules rather tolerantly the low, while indicating its ubiquity and warning of its danger, but also illuminates the beautiful and noble, while reminding of both its preciousness and its fragility. In portraying all of this, a *Tempest* shows both the gifts of the poet and the capacious superiority of the wise. There is high comedy as well as low comedy. High comedy prepares the mind to discriminate among delightful possibilities as well as dangerous ones. It adds to the pleasures of imitation the pleasure of philosophic thoughtfulness. It is what Dante accomplished in his *Commedia*.

Machiavelli's is different comedy, although it too means to instruct. It instructs in policy and being politic. It does not ridicule the low, except as shortsighted, but it especially ridicules those who pretend to be high, that is, to be virtuous, spiritual, or devoted to wisdom. It is less high comedy than low comedy because it disdains the distinction between noble and base. But it is neither, for it exposes above all the foolishness of high and low that keeps each from the effectual ways of real satisfaction, which it also shows. It does elevate the wise, but chiefly in the cool form of the shrewd knowers of the world. So Ligurio and Sofronia. Machiavellian virtù is cool because it is all business and not warmed by love of the good, the beautiful, or the true.

Hence the peculiarly cynical, conspiratorial, and calculating flavor of Machiavellian comedy. Its humor is in exposing the pretension in others' airs of superiority and in enjoying one's own superiority in tricks and plots. Such twofold wit, malicious and proud, is characteristically Machiavellian. It is in the political writings as well as in the comedies. *The Prince* and the *Discourses* may be grim by the standards of ordinary morals and politics. But they are enlivened with the pleasure of seeing and surpassing the foolishness of well-meaning men and even of the princes who pride themselves on vice. Machiavelli's comedy is, then, farther from low comedy than is, say, Shakespeare's. There is an easy warmth about Stephano and Trinculo in the *Tempest* and Bottom in *Midsummer Night's Dream,* whatever the more ominous possibilities. And then there is Falstaff. Machiavelli's comedy is cold if raucous in its use of the ridiculous, for it is calculatingly in the service of politic reform.[67]

Clizia is a comic classic of enlightened rhetoric, a classic insinuation of the critique and the planning that underlie modern free society as well as modern effective government. But the play also expresses the versatile wit of one of the most powerful of thinkers. Machiavelli had his reasons. Whether they are adequate is a question considered, but not settled, in this essay.

3

Comedy, Machiavelli's Letters, and His Imaginary Republics

ARLENE W. SAXONHOUSE

I write about Machiavelli's comedy. But what is comedy? This is a question to which I shall keep returning throughout this essay; to begin with, though, I do not mean only the comedies as categorized by the literary critics who divide literature into comedy, tragedy, romance, and all such assorted genres. Neither is comedy only the plays written to be produced and enacted on stage, such as Machiavelli's *Mandragola* and *Clizia,* and categorized by scholars of the Renaissance as *commedia erudita,* which had its roots in the "antique inspiration" of Plautus, Terence, and Greek New Comedy.[1] After all, Dante entitled his great poem *The Divine Comedy,* taking comedy away from the earthy world of the comic stage.[2] While analyses of Machiavelli's comedies have provided insights into a variety of Machiavellian themes,[3] for my purposes I am thinking of comedy in broader terms, terms that recognize the much wider source of comedy in Italian literature of the Renaissance and especially in the *novella* tradition deriving from Boccaccio's *Decameron.*[4]

Beyond the literary forms whether derivative from ancient or more contemporary and local works, however, *comedy* as I use it throughout this discussion is the breaking of boundaries—the blasphemy that reduces the gods to our

Pamela Ramseyer was a model research assistant for this essay. I would like to acknowledge and to thank her for the help she has provided.

level and human beings to biological creatures with sexual drives and alimentary needs. One of the classic boundaries that we in political theory explore, debate, and criticize is that between public and private. Comic productions from Aristophanes onward had been the mechanism for transcending that boundary. In comedy the stage becomes an arena in which the distinctive and the peculiar are opened up to be shared by all, in which the traditionally private is revealed to the gaze of the many.[5] The private life of families and especially the sexual interactions of families become a spectacle laid bare to public viewing, and comedy builds on how this opening up reveals the tentativeness of the public's affirmed boundaries between male and female, between the upper and lower classes, between human beings and animals. These are the boundaries that at the end of comic literary works are, for the most part, reestablished through a restructuring of the comic world and the creation of a new regime, a new order. Comedy through its revelations, its taking away of veils of respectability and deceit, exposes private desires to public viewing and shows us human nature at its crassest; but it also translates those desires into a public and private order while the author of comedies becomes the founder of these new regimes through his art. Tragedy, in contrast, while teaching about the complexity of the world and about our own impotence in the face of that complexity, often leaves the audience barren of resolution — the plaything of the gods, or worse.[6] Machiavelli's letters, laden with self-mockery, are far more comic than tragic; they often evoke smiles if not outright laughter and open up to his readers his own and others' private desires for viewing, amusement — and education.

Machiavelli is explicit about his staged comedies being didactic. Arguing for the use of local dialects in literary composition in *Discourse or Dialogue Concerning Our Language,* for example, he writes,

> I say that many things are written which cannot be well written unless native words and expressions are used. In this category are comedies, for though the aim of comedy is to hold up a mirror to domestic life, the way it does this, all the same, is with a certain urbanity and with expressions which excite laughter, so that the men who come eagerly to enjoy themselves, taste afterwards the useful lesson that lay underneath. This is why it is difficult to use serious characters; for there can be no gravity in a cheating servant, a ridiculous old man, a love-crazed youth, in a wheedling harlot, in a greedy parasite, yet their actions can convey lessons, useful to our daily life. But to treat the subject in a comic fashion, it is necessary to use words and expressions which have such an effect, and they do not and cannot do unless they are local, popular, and understood by everybody.[7]

Similarly, at the beginning of *Clizia,* Machiavelli writes,

Comedies were invented to be of use and of delight to their audiences. It is indeed quite useful for any man, and particularly for young ones, to learn about the avarice of an old man, the frenzy of a lover, the deceit of a servant, the greed of a parasite, the indigence of the poor, the ambition of the rich, the wiles of a whore, and the bad faith of men. Comedies are filled with such examples, and they all can be represented with the greatest decency, but if the audience is to be delighted, it must be moved to laughter, and that cannot be done while keeping our speeches grave and austere; for speeches which evoke laughter are either foolish, or insulting, or amorous. It is therefore necessary to present characters who are foolish, slanderous, or love-struck.[8]

But what lesson are we to learn through this laughter? It is to behave like — or indeed to be — a prince. Comedies which detail our lives as private creatures provide the understanding of human nature and human potential whereby we can learn to control or adjust to the world in which we live. As Harvey Mansfield states it, "But a private man must behave like a prince because a private man if he is prudent, must become a prince. . . . Machiavelli's own suggestion, in his punning use of the word *privato,* is that a private man would regard himself as deprived of office."[9] Machiavelli's letters, however, illustrate how Machiavelli, as the author of comic tales and as one who imagines new republics while living the life of a private man, nevertheless is indeed a prince, a molder and founder of principalities through the imaginative exercise of his comic art. Through his letters he himself becomes a founding prince of imaginary republics and the educator of those who with the wisdom he teaches may be the founders of actual regimes.

According to scholars, Florentine comedies of the sixteenth century may often have had a "cautious moralistic tone," yet there was also an "alternative streak whereby intrigue, trickery [beffa] and even adultery can be celebrated for their own sake."[10] The exalting of trickery draws on the "comic structures in Italian literature before 1500," which revolved around a "competitive type of story, where some characters get the better of others in order to achieve satisfaction — and more often than not the satisfaction is one of which normal society disapproves." Boccaccio and the novelle lie at the heart of this comic structure, which usually narrates a "contest in which there are winners and losers. The losers qualify as such by stupidity, inadequacy, or sometimes (but not often) immorality: the winners triumph through their intelligence, energy, singleness of purpose and intensity of desire."[11]

These models, these contests, these personalities identified in the *Discourse* and in the preface to *Clizia* and inhabiting Machiavelli's comedies the *Mandragola* and *Clizia* and his one novella, *Belfagor,* all appear as well in many of Machiavelli's letters.[12] The letters, often straddling the line between literary narrative and informal reflection on events both public and private, bring out the fundamentally comic aspects of politics. The letters give us a deep sense of the daemons in Machiavelli's life, but also of his delights, his everyday engagement in "the affairs of the heart" (if I may express myself euphemistically without the full force of Machiavelli's cruder, but more vivid language here),[13] and his everyday engagement in political affairs.[14]

Most important about the comedy that emerges from the letters, though, is not so much what it tells us about Machiavelli's and his friends' lives, but how it helps us understand the foundations of his politics, how comedy in fact infiltrates the highest political activities and understandings. The letters illustrate how Machiavelli's legacy to the modern world is one of comic ambiguity and hopefulness rather than a sense of tragic impotence. The modern world as Machiavelli conceived it was one of comedy, of ambiguity, of transcendence, of human passions and human foibles that bring smiles to our faces — of successes that go to the trickster, the intriguer, to the one with "intelligence, energy, singleness of purpose and intensity of desire" rather than to the moralizer. The prince who does not recognize the comedy inhering in the ambiguity of natural boundaries cannot engage in the imaginative leaps at the base of political foundations and thus must fail. The letters help us recognize the necessity of comedy for the exercise of Machiavelli's politics — a politics that treats nature as fluid waiting to be channeled by the energies of a prince. In this essay, I focus on how the comic fluidity of nature surfaces in Machiavelli's letters and how the letters, by giving his readers an understanding of that fluidity and of the need to structure it, become a source of education to all who read them.

In a letter from 1515 to Francesco Vettori, Machiavelli notes the mobility of his attention from "weighty matters" to the "chimerical." While some might criticize this fluctuation, Machiavelli delights in it:

> Anyone who might see our letters, honorable *compare,* would be greatly astonished, because at first it would seem that we were serious men completely directed toward weighty matters and that no thought could cascade through our heads that did not have within it probity and magnitude. But later, upon turning the page it would seem to the reader that we — still the very same selves — were petty, fickle, lascivious, and were directed toward chimerical matters. If to some this behavior seems contemptible, to me it seems laudable because we are imitating nature, which is changeable: whoever imitates nature cannot be censured. [Letter 247 (January 31, 1515)]

Nature offers no permanent guide or form to which we find ourselves bound. Rather, nature is boundless and formless, challenging us to constant adaptation. To imitate a changeable nature: that is the comedy and the world Machiavelli presents us with. Nature itself makes men both comic and serious. Unlike the Nature of the ancients and medieval philosophers, Machiavelli's Nature demands that we not affirm a fixed form to ourselves lest we be broken by the rigidity of our characters, that we not mire ourselves in the moralistic pieties of those who lose in the comic stories of Italian literature. In chapter 24 of *The Prince* this rigidity is phrased in terms of cautiousness and impetuosity. The prince who finds himself cast firmly with one character trait or another and lacks the ability to adjust with Nature loses his state. The private (deprived) individual who does not understand and act on this need for fluidity never becomes a prince.

In his letters, Machiavelli demands that he and his readers move gracefully between the weighty and chimerical — or rather, be both when the times demand. Thus, the letter in which the above passage appears begins with a sonnet by Machiavelli acknowledging the power of Cupid, but it is only after Cupid learns that he must change his arrows that he conquers the resistant Machiavelli. Even the god adapts before he gains power over the object of his pursuit. Machiavelli's sonnet acknowledging his submission to Cupid's power is in response to Vettori's letter in which not Cupid's arrows, but idleness brought on Vettori's own subjection to love and to Vettori's conclusion that "I know of nothing that gives more delight to think about and to do than fucking. Everyman," Vettori had continued, "may philosophize all he wants, but this is the utter truth, which many people understand this way but few will say" [Letter 247 (January 15, 1515)]. While Machiavelli begins his letter with his reflections on Cupid the ruler and with stories of lust and love, he turns in this same letter directly to a discussion of "new states, taken over by a new ruler," how "they present countless problems," and what Machiavelli would do "were I a new prince." The move from sexual conquests and the language of the passions to discussions of political power is Machiavelli's lesson to his correspondents and readers — then and now. The seriousness of the political enterprise does not exclude the comic, and the comic is prelude to the serious. The construction of states builds upon the knowledge of lust and of Cupid and the necessity even for gods to transcend the rigidity of past forms. The prince must understand the comedy of nature.

In a letter from the previous year Machiavelli had written to Vettori about human hypocrisy and "how blind human beings are in matters that involve their sins and what implacable persecutors they are of the vices that they do not possess." After numerous jabs at particular friends and associates, he writes,

Magnificent Ambassador, there are nothing but crazies here; only a few are familiar with this world and are aware that whoever seeks to act according to others will accomplish nothing because no two men who think alike can be found. These people are unaware that whoever is considered wise by day will not be considered crazy by night and that whoever is deemed a decent, able man will occasion honor, not blame, whatever he does to refresh his spirit and live happily; instead of being called a sodomite or lecher, people will say he is well-rounded, easy-going and a boon companion. [Letter 227 (January 5, 1514)]

Machiavelli concludes his letter by urging Vettori to "stick with your natural dispositions" and turns those who criticize him into birds: their associate Brancacci (who reappears often in the letters) is "like one of those little wrens that is the first to squawk and to scold, and once the owl arrives, is the first to be caught." Meanwhile, Filippo (again, a frequent inhabitant of the letters) is "like a vulture who, when there is no carrion in a rural district, soars a hundred miles to find some" and "when his gullet is full . . . mocks eagles, hawks, falcons, and their ilk." Thus, Machiavelli tells Vettori, "Let the one squawk and the other fill its crop." This letter captures much of Machiavelli's perspective on political and social life: the interplay of day and night, the hypocrisy that distinguishes virtue from vice, and the imaginative similes that transform the human into Aesopian creatures no more elevated than the vulture or wren. The letter denies natural boundaries and natural forms, natural categories — or categories of any kind — and emphasizes instead the fluidity of our lives and the dangers of trying to rely on a bounded nature with prescribed forms.

In an early chapter of *The Prince* Machiavelli reflects on a prince's acquisition of polities that have lived by their own laws and in freedom. About holding them after they have been conquered, he offers this advice: "For in truth there is no secure mode to possess them other than to ruin them. And whoever becomes patron of a city used to living free and does not destroy it, should expect to be destroyed by it."[15] Comedy, whether on stage, in stories, or in letters, is the analogous process of destruction and reestablishment. The plots of Machiavelli's comedies (for example, *Mandragola*) show how an old order is destroyed and how the new institutions provide for a new and happier life for all. But the new order (or regime, if we prefer the political term) cannot be founded without the destruction of the old. In chapter 6 of *The Prince,* Machiavelli praises those who by their own *virtù* and arms founded new principalities. *Fortuna* does not help beyond offering the opportunity; the opportunity, though, is the disorder from which the new prince creates order. To create, the heroes of chapter 6 must start with a world in chaos — in which either old orders have failed or have never been established. At a minimum, the old must be destroyed before the creation of the new. Comedy, as it appears in Machiavelli's plays and in his letters, destroys the old as prelude to the creation of the new. As I shall suggest, the letters of Machiavelli in their comic expression, building on the lively literary tradition from Boccaccio onward, illustrate this destruction of the old with its traditional boundaries and the refounding and restructuring of a flexible nature.

The Letters

In these days of abbreviated e-mail exchanges in which style and personality are encoded in the relative placement of a colon, semicolon, and parentheses, we must return to a period when communication via frequent letters was the norm. Letters (then and now) often report events, make requests, deny requests, offer opinions, reveal anxieties or disappointments.[16] Machiavelli's do much more. His letters (and some of those of some of his correspondents) become an explicit arena for the exercise of his imagination, for the creation of stories and drama — for the leap from what is to what might be, from what we observe to what we suspect based on observation.

In an often cited passage from one of his letters to Guicciardini, Machiavelli, feeling isolated on a mission to the Minorite Friars of Carpi, writes, "For some time now I have never said what I believe or never believed what I said; and if I do sometimes tell the truth, I hide it behind so many lies that it is hard to find" [Letter 270 (May 17, 1521)].[17] Truth fades into lies, lies into truth, and we know not what to believe. While reading Machiavelli's letters, we must always keep this in mind. Ambiguity dominates his letters for we are always caught in the net of his imagination and we must tread between reading his letters as reports or as imaginary explorations by which he analyzes the absurdities of the world in which he finds himself. Certainly, not every letter hides truths, but many are filled with a teasing that warns us not to take his statements as more than dreams [see, for example, Letters 176 and 206] and explorations into the comic stories of human interaction.

In Letter 208 from April 9, 1513, Machiavelli writes to Vettori, "Because Fortune has seen to it that since I do not know how to talk about either the silk or wool trade, or profits or losses, I have to talk about politics. I need either to take a vow of silence or discuss this." To what would be the dismay of today's political economists, Machiavelli herewith separates trade from politics, but in saying that he can speak only of politics he assures us that his letters — letters filled with his and his friends' amorous and blasphemous adventures — are a part of the political world as he understands it. The private remains prelude to the political.

In the specific letters that I discuss in detail below, imagination dominates mostly with regard to the sexual exploits of Machiavelli and his friends, but Machiavelli also suggests how imagination must inform all readings or interpretations of the world around him. In perhaps the most famous passage of *The Prince,* from chapter 15, Machiavelli says that he himself pursues the "effectual truth" rather than relying on his imagination, and he urges his readers to abandon "imaginary republics and principalities which have never been seen or known to exist in truth." And yet in his letters Machiavelli makes clear to his readers that the imagination is necessary to analyze the politics of his times and to understand human motivations. The letters are filled with imaginary tales and a reframing of events so that we come to understand how the imagination is in fact the basis for learning "the effectual truth."[18] In his letters Machiavelli imagines both the thoughts and the actions of others. In July 1513, just at the time Machiavelli is writing *The Prince,* Vettori writes to him about an imaginary republic: "I wish I could be with you and see whether we could organize this world, and if not the world, at least this part here, which seems to me very hard to organize in fancy, so if it came to having to do it in fact I should think it was impossible" [Letter 216 (July 12, 1513)]. In his own speculation about the activities of political actors, Vettori writes to Machiavelli, "We must consider that each of these princes of ours has an aim and because it is impossible for us to know their inner thoughts, we have to judge it from their words, from their actions, and some part of it we imagine."

Vettori points to the necessity of exercising the imagination in any effort at reform or analysis. Machiavelli's effectual truth, while working against the imaginary republics of Plato and St. Augustine, is not as independent of the imagination as chapter 15 might make us believe. In his own letters, he frequently resorts to the sort of imagining Vettori encourages as he analyzes the political actions of his contemporaries. As if he were an actor in a play or comedy, he himself becomes the persona he is trying to analyze and advise. In a letter from June 1513 he writes to Vettori about the French campaign in Italy; to understand the situation and what ought to be done, he writes, "I have put myself in the pope's place and scrutinized in detail what I might now have to fear." The letter is replete with the phrase "were I the pope" or some such locution as the private person Machiavelli becomes in his imagination a public prince. The process of political analysis is one of imagining oneself as another, of playing the part of an actor, perhaps to be other than who we are by nature.[19] The successful reader of political life is one who has this capacity of imagination — and it is a capacity that allows the theorist to move fluidly from political analyses to the construction of comedies, whether on stage or in the stories one tells in one's letters. While the process of imagining oneself as another is the process of acting on the comic stage, of making oneself a Calli-maco or a Nicomaco when one is not, it is, as well, what is required of the prince, who must be what he is not, who must transcend himself to take on a variety of personas: to be stingy when one is liberal, to be bad when one is good. The actor, the Machiavellian letter writer who never says what he be-lieves, and the prince all practice (and must practice) this art of transcendence.

In his letters Machiavelli imagines both motivations and events; he turns political actors into men who have motives we can only guess at, and he turns friends into actors whom he directs in their comic interludes. Below I discuss some of the more famous letters to suggest how Machiavelli's comic imagina-tion leads to and reveals his political insights and how the lessons of comedy can move us from privation to princehood. Machiavelli himself as the com-poser of the letters moves out of the privations of his daily life in exile to the prince who, with the necessary knowledge of our fluid natures, structures a world of imaginary republics over which he rules and from which we learn. This is not to deny an underlying theme of these letters that leaves us thinking that as powerful a prince as Machiavelli may be over the imaginary republics he creates, he would have preferred to exercise power in an actual regime. Had Machiavelli been the ruler of an actual regime, though, we might not be the subjects of his reconstructed world.

In discussing these letters, I do not follow the chronological order in which they were written, but rather use them — as Machiavelli used Livy's history — to offer *exempli* in order to point to some more general themes.[20]

LETTER 178: DECEMBER 8, 1509

In one of the most unpleasant and coarsest letters in a collection of frequently coarse letters, Machiavelli describes an encounter he had with a prostitute during his stay in Verona in 1509. Writing to Luigi Guicciardini, he expresses his envy of Luigi's "fucking" and then goes on to describe how he was seduced into "fucking" a vile old hag by an old woman who washed his shirts. "The house she lives in is more than half under ground," he writes, " — the only light you see enters through the door." When Machiavelli chances on her one evening, she invites him in to offer for sale some "shirts," where-upon he "made out in the gloom a woman . . . affecting modesty." The "old slut" asked him to try on the "shirt" and pay for it later. Once alone in the dark with the cowering woman, Machiavelli "fucked her." Afterwards, "feeling like taking a look at the merchandise," he lit a lamp and discovered how physically grotesque she was. Machiavelli lingers in detailing the ugliness of the woman and concludes by telling Luigi that he vomited all over her, thus repaying her in kind and vowing never to get "horny" in Lombardy again. The letter is revolting, and Machiavelli spares no effort in making it so — but did it happen? Is it a tale that comes from Machiavelli's imagination and, if so, what does he accomplish with this story?

For the most part, scholars have chosen to read this letter as a parable rather than as a report of Machiavelli's experiences. Sebastian de Grazia, for instance, writes, "Luigi had encouraged his friend to give rein to whimsy in writing, and Niccolò had replied earlier that he was thinking of doing just that. . . . Whether true or false, all or in part, the tale is a popping concoction — one part merchandise, one part sexual appetite, and other parts thrown in from ancient and regional jars."[21] Hannah Pitkin reads the letter as a story of masculine insecurities: "With his guard lowered by sensuality, it seems a man is in danger,"[22] Giulio Ferroni argues that the letter, drawing from the tales of Boccaccio, follows a traditional story line that incorporates a repellant old woman (and the inherent misogyny with it).[23] Linda Carroll and Juliana Schiesari have the most extensive analyses. Carroll reads the letter as a metaphor of Machiavelli's experiences in Verona, with woman as a metaphor for the body politic. In her reading, the letter "employs the prostitute to convey his low opinion of Venice and its rulership of the mainland." Through "coded language," Carroll argues, Machiavelli could disguise his "dangerous opinion which portrayed the Venetians as cowardly and feminine."[24] Schiesari offers what she calls a feminist reading based on psychoanalytic categories. The letter, written in jealous response to Vettori's sexual success and in which the woman's physical attributes suggest "a degraded phantasm of phallic femininity," portrays for her Machiavelli's "unconscious struggle with economy and sexuality" and his anxiety about powerful women, which is really anxiety about "a changing economic order" governed by Lady Luck.[25]

Readers have had a hard time assuming that the tale is the report of an actual event, although his letters leave no doubt about Machiavelli's sexual drives, which he satisfied often. For one who later is to write that he cannot talk of "either the silk or wool trade, or profits and losses," this story, as de Grazia notes, frames the sexual engagement in the language of commerce and exchange. But more important in my reading of it is the attention to darkness and deception and to seeing and feeling as well as the self-mocking reduction of Machiavelli to a blind character who is tricked by others and left an unsatisfied fool, but who ultimately learns a lesson about himself and others. The letter presents almost a Platonic tale of descent into a cave, where vision is limited and where Machiavelli must function on the basis of what he is able to see in the shadows of the house "under ground"; he escapes, repulsed and sick, only when he brings light into the cave with "a piece of burning wood from the hearth."

In part, the letter shows Machiavelli engaging in a self-mockery that reveals his position as a subject rather than a prince, controlled by others rather than controlling, and brought to this condition by sexual famine. The self-mockery as a sexual creature present in this relatively early letter resounds throughout his letters and surfaces again in the *Clizia* of 1525 when he gives the foolish, love-crazed father/husband/guardian of that comedy the name Nicomaco. Both the young Machiavelli and the old Nicomaco, driven by sexual passions, become subject to the trickery of others. For Niccolò and Nicomaco alike, sexual longing means submission to women and a sense of shame at the weakness males show when faced with a woman's trickery; thus, they serve as a warning, respectively, to the friends who read the letter and to the young who see the comedy about the dangers of sexual longing to those who wish to rule. And yet, at the same time, Machiavelli in his letters and comedies delights in his and in others' sexual escapades; he and his friends may become fools as a result of their sexual adventures, but the comedy of the life he portrays means also the enjoyment of the foolery and the successes. The lesson is certainly not to deny one's sexual drives — from which Machiavelli and his friends so often get so much pleasure — but rather to approach them with a wisdom about the power that sex has to transform men into subjects rather than princes. In this letter from his youth he makes clear how he had been duped because of his longing, and he vows never to put himself in such a situation again — at least not in Lombardy. In the later comedy, his alter ego Nicomaco demonstrates how hard it is to learn and follow the lessons he himself tried to teach.

The prostitute letter reads in part like a mockery of such epic tales as the *Aeneid* and *The Divine Comedy*, in which the resolution and reaffirmation of order depend on the confrontation with death and darkness. This letter is built on the theme of a descent into darkness where Machiavelli can barely make out the form of the woman in the corner. In *The Prince* Machiavelli writes in chapter 18, "Men in general judge more by their eyes than by their hands, because seeing is given to everyone, touching to a few. Everyone sees how you appear, few touch what you are." In the darkness of the washerwoman's cave, though, Machiavelli can only feel: "her thighs flabby and her cunt damp — and her breath stank a bit." In this case touch was inadequate and brought no enlightenment to the young Machiavelli. He learned only when he brought light and sight down into the darkness. Then the confrontation with the ugly (death) can be acknowledged and becomes the basis for growth and an education about the relative power of the senses. The light brought to the cave reveals the ugly woman but also shows Machiavelli his own susceptibility to trickery. That potential to be tricked faces us all, driven by desires into places where we feel but do not see, whether we are the young Machiavelli of 1509, the old Nicomaco, or the young for whom Machiavelli writes his comedies.

In the epic framing of the letter, the dark descent educates Machiavelli and leads him to a resolution—namely, that he won't get horny again in Lombardy. This hardly has the epic stature of the founding of Rome or the divine purification of the soul captured in *The Divine Comedy*, but Machiavelli's epic mocks the old form of illumination from descent into an underworld confrontation with death and Hell and prepares his readers for their own confrontations with sexual famines and female trickery. Most seriously, the "epic" letter points to a world in which all is not what it seems, in which washerwomen are not just washerwomen but pimps, and in which a shirt is a vile old hag. In the dark of the cave Machiavelli is subject to trickery; only with the light he himself brings to the cave when he lights the log from the hearth can he learn to give what he claims is due and not let himself be ruled by others.

LETTER 229: FEBRUARY 4, 1514

By the time Machiavelli writes Letter 229 in 1514, he has endured imprisonment and torture at the hands of the Medici and is never again to engage as a citizen in the political life of Florence as fully as he had when it was a republic. About his experience in prison he writes succinctly to Vettori, "I shall not repeat the long story of my disgrace to you but shall merely say that Fate has done everything to cause me this abuse. Anyhow, thanks be to God, it is over. I hope not to come up against it any more" [Letter 204 (March 13, 1513)]. And in a letter a few days later again to Vettori he comments, "I should like you to get this pleasure from these troubles of mine, that I have borne them so straightforwardly that I am proud of myself and consider myself more of a man than I believed I was" [Letter 206 (March 18, 1513)]. The letters that he now exchanges with Vettori have a lightness as he overcomes the black moods that may darken his daily life.

In Letter 229, Machiavelli responds to a letter from Vettori describing an evening entertaining a neighbor widow, her daughter, son, brother, and two of Machiavelli's and Vettori's friends. As preface to the core of the letter, Machiavelli writes, "And when I think from beginning to end [dal principio al fine] of this, your and their story [istoria] . . . it appears to me as worthy a thing to be recited to a prince [ad un principe] as anything I have heard this year." First, Vettori's "story" as recorded in his letter did not have a beginning or an end. It wandered from a concern about offending a relative by entertaining female visitors to criticisms for his asocial behavior to the visit of the neighbor widow and her family, ending with the departure of the woman after an evening of flirtation and pleasantries and Vettori's admission that he has fallen in love with the daughter against plan and expectation.

More important, however, is the suggestion that his and his friends' story is worthy of being recited to a prince. Machiavelli has very likely finished *The*

Prince by this time and sent it off for Vettori's reaction.[26] In his letter of December 10, 1513 [Letter 224], Machiavelli had told him about his work on principalities and had written that Casavecchia (one of the dinner party guests) had seen it: "He will be able to give you some account of both the work itself and the discussions I have had with him about it, although I am continually fattening and currying it." On December 24, 1513, Vettori writes to Machiavelli, "Filippo [Casavecchia] also has told me, that you have written a certain work about states. I shall be grateful if you send it to me; and although I am not an authority, I judge it proper that I should judge your thing. . . . When I have seen it, I shall tell you my opinion about presenting it or not to the Magnificent Giuliano, as it may seem to me" [Letter 226]. Subsequently, in Letter 228 from January 18, 1514, Vettori remarks, "I have seen the chapters of your work, and I like them immeasurably. But since I do not have the entire work, I do not want to make a definitive judgment yet." He never does.

John Najemy proposes that the reference in Letter 229 may suggest Machiavelli's annoyance that Vettori has not offered his praise for this little work on principalities.[27] But the deeper question is, What is the relation between the story Machiavelli presents in his letter and what he would recite (or has recited) to a prince? why — even mockingly — would Machiavelli transform the casual events noted in Vettori's letter into a tale fit for princes? After describing the evening, Vettori had written, "I cannot help complaining to you that out of a desire to make my friends happy I have become almost a prisoner of this Costanza" [Letter 228]. Because of sexual longing, he has gone from ruler to subject. In Machiavelli's restructuring of the evening's events, in transforming it into a staged comedy deriving from a Boccaccian novella, Vettori appears (like Machiavelli in the prostitute letter) as one tricked, a failed prince conquered by Cupid, as one who had the opportunity to create a new regime but instead became subject himself. The problem is not so much that he allowed himself to feel the passions of men, but that he tried to control rather than adapt to the passions that were affecting. At the beginning of his letter Vettori had noted, "I believe in others more than myself, and I always want to please anyone else before myself," but this desire to please others made Vettori vulnerable — and his story can thus serve as a warning to others who would be princes in their own worlds. By transforming the story of Vettori into a tale about control and submission, about passions and resistance, Machiavelli has turned Vettori's descriptive prose into a comic parable that may not quite rival *The Prince* but alludes to the challenges and resources that that work illuminates.

Machiavelli's letter began with a curious suggestion. Thanking Vettori for his letter, he wrote, "I took great pleasure in it, as I realized with solicitude Fortune has dealt with you and has arranged matters so well that thanks to you Filippo and Brancacci have become one soul in two bodies, or rather to be correct, two souls in one body." What does becoming one soul in two bodies or two souls in one body mean? It may be a suggestion about the nature of the soul, but it could also refer to the creation of a unity out of a multiplicity. Vettori, like a prince, has united others and created something new; his success, though, has left him a prisoner, in agony rather than delighting in and gaining satisfaction from his accomplishment.

From this point on, Machiavelli transforms Vettori's letter into a play with himself as director, creating scenes and giving stage directions. As an imaginary director working only from the basic outline of Vettori's letter, he sets his characters into a series of motions, actions, glances, and speeches that attempt to cover up their passions and yet also reveal their internal feelings. Machiavelli seems to "see"[28] Brancacci "gazing, fidgeting, drooling . . . consumed by . . . Costanza's words." Casavecchia he sees gesticulating, nodding, playing the role of father, tutor, lover, while the boy whom he is eager to seduce is torn in different directions. He sees Vettori himself attending to the widow and her brother while watching the flirtations of his friends with each eye. He sees him "answering in generalities, and like Echo to their most recent words"; Vettori had written only that he had asked them "about a certain suit they have pending, so that, with them occupied in this conversation, they would give some time to the others." Then, creating a scene not in Vettori's letter, Machiavelli sends Vettori to the fireplace with "rapid, inch-long steps, stooping a bit" and gives him an innocuous sentence to speak.[29]

The elaborate dramatic presentation of the evening continues for much of the letter. Machiavelli moves all the characters to a table loaded with bread and glasses, but for the climax and to capture how the tables have turned with Vettori as host succumbing to Cupid's arrows, Machiavelli offers a line spoken by a character in Terence's *Brothers*. According to James Atkinson and David Sices, the sentence expresses "the older father's realization that he is a victim of a comic deception, enabling his younger son to go against his strict wishes in an affair of the heart." Given that Machiavelli writes these lines, are we to think that it is he who has been deceived by his friend, reading in the letter of how Vettori arranged the dinner party to help his friends only to discover that it is Vettori's own passion that has been aroused and that rather than acting the role of the facilitator or pimp (or prince) Vettori himself was smitten with love? Through literary allusions, Machiavelli in his turn transforms Vettori first into a bull and then into a swan, "so you could lay an egg in her lap . . . now into one animal, and now another [a female swan, no less] — as long as you are not separated from her."[30] The only way for Vettori to satisfy his longing is to imitate the gods, who in turn know how to imitate or, rather, become animals. The comic model of transcendence prevails. To succeed in love Vettori must become male bull and female swan. To succeed in politics, according to Machiavelli's work on principalities, the prince must become both lion and fox and learn from the human animal, Chiron the centaur.

The tale so engagingly told and directed in Machiavelli's letter is one of transcendence of boundaries, but Vettori does not control the transcendence. The capacity to transcend emerges not of his own will, but as the result of Machiavelli's control as literary artist. Vettori is subject, not ruler — subject to love and to Machiavelli's construction of him. The prince who allows himself to be put into a script rather than writing his own tale has not read with adequate care chapters 22 and 23 of *The Prince*. It is Machiavelli (whose little work Vettori has not acknowledged) who can, through this letter, transform Vettori — make him a comic rather than heroic character. The lesson a prince might learn from this recitation is precisely the power of a Machiavellian appropriation and reframing of the tales one considered one's own.

Machiavelli concludes his letter with a paragraph on his own willing submission to love, phrasing it all in the language of enslavement which has led to "more charms than if I had tormented him." Submission to love makes Machiavelli less of a fool than Vettori, who had provided a dignified dinner party to please his friends. But Machiavelli again — introducing complexity into everything he writes — reports how when he is in Florence he spends time with his friend Donato and with his lover La Riccia and how "both value me as an adviser." He worries, though, that "this good will not last long since I have given both of them some tidbits of advice that have never panned out." And he has heard La Riccia say to her maid, "Wise men, oh these wise men, I don't know what they have upstairs." Thus, should Vettori listen to or not listen to the "advice" that Machiavelli gives? Is Machiavelli only a "savio" with nothing "upstairs," ready to be bested and tricked by the wise women in his life? The "farewell" of Machiavelli's letter leaves the reader in a world of ambiguity in which success is the same as failure, control is submission, and wisdom is foolishness.

LETTER 231: FEBRUARY 25, 1514

Letter 231, also to Vettori, is explicitly described as a novella by Machiavelli and records a complex story about Machiavelli's friend Brancacci: "I have put off answering you until now because' I wanted better to learn the truth about a novella[31] that I am about to tell you." (Are novelle "true"? In what sense?) Machiavelli follows with an allusion to Ovid by commenting that the gentle business ("cosa gentile") is some "laughable metamorphosis" — one worthy of being noted in the "chronicles of old."[32] Lest he give offense, says one who seems seldom to worry about giving offense, he will recount the tale at first in the guise of a parable. Thus, he launches into the parable of Brancacci — or, rather, as he says, "someone, let's say Giuliano Brancacci." As Atkinson and Sices point out, "Machiavelli leaves it open whether this Brancacci is a fictive name or the real Giuliano Brancacci, who is actually in Rome, not Florence [where the story Machiavelli tells takes place]."[33]

Machiavelli's parable begins with Brancacci going into the "woods" to hunt birds. After wandering the alleys of Florence, Brancacci finally succeeds in engaging a "young thrush." The language describing the encounter is a faintly veiled description of a homosexual encounter.[34] Machiavelli, finding the parable and metamorphosis no longer serving him, goes back to actual names, or at least the characters become human and the young thrush metamorphoses into a young man with a name and a pedigree ("let's say, 'Michele,' the nephew of Consiglio Costi"). But the metamorphosis is not only of a young boy into a bird, but of individuals as well — a metamorphosis achieved through the exchange of names. Brancacci promises to pay the young man the next day for services rendered but tells him he is Filippo Casavecchia. When Michele arrives asking for payment, Casavecchia at first is confused and then senses blackmail. Casavecchia figures out who may be behind the "dirty work" (questa villania), arranges for Michele to be brought to where Brancacci is holding forth (like Machiavelli) telling stories ("novelle"). When Michele recognizes Brancacci's voice and thus the man who enjoyed his services the previous evening, Brancacci runs away and Casavecchia is exonerated.[35]

The letter is a tale told for amusement, perhaps even a "just so story," for we now know, Machiavelli explains, the origin of the phrase floating around Florence during carnival season: "Are you Brancacci or are you Casa?" Though he had written that he waited to respond to Vettori until he could confirm the accuracy of story, the story tellingly points to the unreality of the novella; he makes no pretense that the story in the end is a representation of the facts. Indeed, he reminds the reader throughout that the tale is a fiction as he interjects into the narrative three times the phrase "verbigrazia" (let's say) about the names of the characters, recalling that he as the author of this novella has discretion about who his characters will be, what tricks will be played on them, perhaps even where they will be, and how the tale will end. As narrator, he is the prince controlling the fates of the characters in his tales.

The story told in this letter is like many others, a tale of fluidity or, as Machiavelli explicitly says, of metamorphosis, of the way human beings become birds and then are transformed back again by a change simply in narrative structure, and of men transforming themselves into others through the appropriation of a name that is not theirs. This story follows the pattern of traditional novelle and of Machiavelli's comedies: there is a sexual desire, there is an effort at trickery in the attempt to satisfy that desire that backfires, and the initial trickster becomes the object of a ruse engineered by another. In *Clizia,* for example, Nicomaco devises a plan to gain access to Clizia by marrying her to his servant; the plan is foiled when his wife, Sofronia, turns that trick against him, and he lands in bed with another servant rather than with the girl after whom he lusts. In Letter 231, Machiavelli has his Brancacci — "who liked doing things on the sly"[36] — try to trick both Michele and Casavecchia, whom he had tricked before. But the trick is foiled when a relative of Michele brings him to the story-telling Brancacci. Brancacci, caught in his own trap, "completely flummoxed, got out of there immediately."

In the comedy of this letter, the resolution is the reestablishment of an order through the reaffirmation of identities, of " 'let's say' Brancacci" as Brancacci, of Michele as a boy and not a thrush, and of Casavecchia as Casavecchia and not Brancacci. The tale has charm and interest as a result of Machiavelli's making the character of Brancacci appear foolish in his attempts to upset identities, but in the end the identities reaffirm themselves and no one becomes other than who he is. Yet behind the tale, again, stands the author Machiavelli, who as narrator orders the novella of Brancacci's attempt to trick Michele and Casavecchia. Machiavelli first gives individuals their identities and then reaffirms the identities after the characters' efforts to introduce ambiguities. Narrating his novella, Machiavelli remains the prince within his narrative world.

Letter 231 is a response to a letter in which Vettori explained that he chose not to comment on Machiavelli's letter rewriting Vettori's dinner party. Instead, Vettori wrote of his continuing infatuation (and success) with Costanza, adding, "Do not think, however, that I have not had some reproofs about this, or let us say affectionate admonitions from Filippo and Giuliano" [Letter 230 (February 9, 1514)] — the same two characters who next appear in the parable of Machiavelli's letter. Machiavelli's construction of the story may in part be a response to the moralistic tone of Brancacci vis-à-vis Vettori. Machiavelli ends his letter by rejecting the admonitions of Filippo and Giuliano, saying to Vettori, "Give your love full rein and . . . whatever pleasure you seize today may not be there for you tomorrow. . . . I believe now, I have always believed, and shall continue to believe that what Boccaccio says is true: it is better to act and to regret it than not to act and regret it." These words and the reference to the great author of the novelle conclude Machiavelli's letter and his own novella. The story that mocks Brancacci (and perhaps himself) is prelude to an exhortation to pursue one's desires without restraint, without the moralistic chastising of one's friends and allies. Uncertainties, whether of identities or about the future, require action rather than passivity, and fortune favors those willing to engage in tricks. Brancacci may become the object of laughter, but he enjoyed the services of Michele.

LETTER 224: DECEMBER 10, 1513

In the most famous and most frequently anthologized letter of the Machiavellian correspondence, Machiavelli describes a day in his life on the farm outside of Florence where he lives in exile. The letter of December 10, 1513, is famous in part because it mentions a short study to which he refers as *De Principatibus,* in which "I delve as deeply as I can into the ideas concerning this topic, discussing the definition of a princedom, the categories of princedoms, how they are acquired, how they are retained, and why they are lost." The letter is famous as well for its vivid description of how Machiavelli retreats "when evening comes" into his study to converse with the ancients. Like the letter in which Machiavelli transforms an evening described by Vettori into a comedy, this letter is a direct response to one he had received from Vettori. Vettori had written, "So in this letter I have decided to describe to you what my life in Rome is like," and he proceeds to detail his housing, his daily activities, and his wish that Machiavelli would join him [Letter 223 (November 23, 1513)]. Machiavelli details his own daily activities, offering specifics about his business ventures (not successful), his reading of the love poets (which makes him happy "for a while"), his companions at the inn and in assorted games (not interesting). Numerous scholars have offered provocative readings of these passages;[37] I focus only on the paragraph detailing his discourse with the ancients.

Machiavelli returns home from the local inn, where the barroom games have provoked a "thousand squabbles and endless abuses and vituperations," takes off his workday clothes, and crosses a threshold; in his imagination he moves from present sorrows and the "malice of my fate" into an imaginary world in which he can discourse with men long dead. He creates this imaginary republic of letters in which he is received solicitously by the inhabitants of that court. Leaving behind a life "cooped up among these lice," he creates in his mind a world in which discourse is the only nourishment he needs, the food "for which I was born."[38] Engaging with the ancients is again an activity of transformation and metamorphosis. Atkinson and Sices render "tucto mi trasferisco in loro" both as "I absorb myself into them completely" and as "I transfer myself into them completely."[39] No longer himself, he slips into this world of the imagination and an imaginary self, transcending boundaries between past and present, self and other, body and intellect, even life and death. In the court of the ancients, "I am not terrified by death." Machiavelli becomes both ancient and modern, "two souls in one body."

In the other letters, Machiavelli turns friends into animals and sets them into traps of their own making, into characters who are not themselves, into actors in his plays. Here he turns himself into other than what he is, a man caught by contemporary circumstances, confined to selling wood, eating with his household "what food this poor farm and my miserable patrimony yield," and drinking and playing games at the local inn. After he crosses the threshold of the imagination, he inhabits the courts of the ancients, dressed in "clothes of court and palace." It is a world accessible only to the imagination, and it exists only as the result of the transformation of self. Only in this world of imagination can he write *The Prince*. His princes, like himself, must be able to transform themselves creatively, to imagine what is not, to transform themselves into others ("trasferisco in loro"), and expand beyond the apparent limits of the natural world. Throughout this letter Machiavelli plays a multiplicity of roles by which he destabilizes the world in which he lives.

The political process remains for Machiavelli the destructive and constructive endeavor captured by comedy and the imagination, but we also need to see the parallels to the analytical process. To understand the political world, as he writes to Vettori, he must imagine himself as pope, as Charles, as Lorenzo, he must transfer himself totally into them; likewise, to learn from the ancients with whom he discourses in his study, he must transform himself into them. To the degree that he remains himself, constrained by a fixed nature, he does not learn from the ancients or the moderns and cannot be an adviser to princes. Crossing the threshold into his study is crossing far more than physical space; it is crossing into a world in which he can enjoy the fluidity that lies for him at the basis of political action and political analysis. The comedy of trickery that characterizes the other letters is not present here; rather, the comedy of this letter lies in the willingness to ignore the boundaries that nature has set and to rely, instead, on the imagination to overcome that nature.

The destabilizing and restructuring of Machiavelli's politics depend on the exercise of the imagination, of transforming a man into a vulture or a wren or a thrush, of a willingness to go beyond the given set of experiences and the traditional boundaries of sight and form, to cross the threshold at evening and to become other than what we are. Early in his correspondence (1506), Machiavelli wrote to Soderini,

> But the reason why different actions are sometimes equally useful and sometimes equally detrimental I do not know. . . . I shall be presumptuous enough

to give you [my view]. . . . just as nature has created men with different faces, so she has created them with different intellects and imaginations. As a result, each man behaves according to his own pattern of intellect and imagination. . . . The man who matches his way of doing things with the conditions of the times is successful . . . because times and affairs often change — both in general and in particular — and because men change neither their imaginations nor their ways of doing things accordingly, it turns out that a man has good fortune at one time and bad fortune at another. And truly, anyone wise enough to adapt to and understand the times and pattern of events would always have good fortune or would always keep himself from bad fortune; and it would come to be that the wise man could control the stars and fates. But such wise men do not exist: in the first place men are shortsighted; in the second place, they are unable to master their own natures; thus it follows that Fortune is fickle, controlling men and keeping them under her yoke. [Letter 121 (September 13–21, 1506)]

Years before he writes his letter of December 10, 1513, and his chapters 24 and 25 of *The Prince*, Machiavelli recognizes the need for a fluid human nature. It is the comic art that captures this fluidity and that he incorporates in his letters and in his stage plays. Throughout Machiavelli's letters there is frequent reference to and enjoyment of Ovid's *Metamorphoses*, tales of human beings transformed into assorted natural forms, whether botanical or animal. *The Prince* is likewise filled with exhortations to the prince to go beyond the confines of traditional forms, to see the self as a part of, rather than in opposition to, this fluidity on which depends the recreation of our world.

While the *study* of politics entails this transcendence and fluidity, the political act, however, must be one of imposition. The letters and comic productions allow Machiavelli through literary composition to enact the princely role of the leadership inherent in a narrative control over characters and in the ability to transform them and set them into arrangements unheard of before. These become his imaginary republics.[40] As a storyteller, as the constructor of scenes and events, Machiavelli can play the prince, the orderer, the transformer. He does not need political power to accomplish what the princes of Italy may hope to do in their cities. To rule and to be the true prince, he needs only his imagination and the comic sense of the absurdities brought about by a world of flux.

In his letter of December 10, 1513, Machiavelli writes that he had learned from Dante "that no one understands anything unless he retains what he has understood," and so "I have jotted down what I have profited from in their conversation and composed a short study." Writing can transform the imagination into knowledge; it gives form to the wisdom gleaned from conversation. Machiavelli, like Dante, goes on his own journey guided by the mythical heroes of the past, from whose speech he learns of the present and the future. Like Dante, he puts that imaginary expedition into writing. *The Prince* becomes Machiavelli's divine comedy, the replacement for Dante's conversation with the ancients.

True to his inclination to undermine all he says and recalling his presentation of himself as mocked by his mistress as a "savio" with "nothing upstairs," Machiavelli ends this long letter of December 10, 1513, with the following: "Whoever has been honest and faithful for forty-three years, as I have, is unable to change his nature; my poverty is a witness to my loyalty and honesty."[41] Is this Machiavelli's tragedy, that he urges on others what he himself cannot accomplish? or is this his ultimate comic stance as the man who never said what he believed or believed what he said? I prefer the latter reading and find myself — along with Machiavelli's other readers — always caught in a world of ambiguity and uncertainty, a world in which I must impose order rather than relying on others to do so for me. But it is an order that will be accessible only if I engage in the processes of the comic imagination that Machiavelli teaches.

4

Machiavelli's Discourse on Language

SUSAN MELD SHELL

Machiavelli's *Discourse or Dialogue Concerning Our Language,* long a favorite among philologists, has generally been ignored by students of his thought.[1] Few besides Hans Baron have discussed its political implications,[2] and most, especially since Cecil Grayson raised again the question of its authenticity, have dismissed the work as either uncharacteristic or not Machiavelli's at all.[3] There is no denying the strangeness of the work, in which a dialogue with Dante is the occasion for a discourse on the nature of language generally, its cycles, modes, and orders, and its relation to the grave and comic forms assumed by Machiavelli's own writing. The interest of any treatment of language by so accomplished and self-conscious a user of language should be evident. It is almost universally believed that Machiavelli regarded his writing as a substitute for the political activity that fortune denied him, and for this reason alone we might expect his *Discourse* to be self-revealing.

The *Discourse* is a complex and difficult work, one that treats a number of subjects — literary, political, military, and erotic — his other writings tend to keep formally apart. The very features of the work which seem at first uncharacteristic make it of special interest to the student who would understand the place of language in Machiavelli's politics and with it, the integral character of the author's thought. One cannot, to be sure, expect too much of the *Discourse,* which, so far as is known, Machiavelli did not intend to publish and which may, like other works that bridge the boundary he usually drew between the comic and grave, be incomplete. Many of the sketchier arguments of the *Discourse* are elaborated in published writings to which this discussion will have recourse. There is, however, as we shall see, enough in the *Discourse* to refute the charge that it is un-Machiavellian (and most of the challenges to its authenticity amount to this)[4] and to shed light on important arguments that Machiavelli elsewhere left obscure.

I first take up the challenge to the authenticity of the *Discourse* that is posed, in the minds of some, by its aggressive treatment of Dante. Then I lay out in greater detail the general argument of the *Discourse* and follow with a consideration of some related themes developed in the *Florentine Histories* and the *Discourses on Livy*. Finally, I address the implications of Machiavelli's treatment of Dante for his understanding of the relation of language and politics more generally.

To state Machiavelli's overall argument briefly: In spite of Dante's brilliant literary efforts to combat the political power of the pope and to unify Italy under the aegis of the emperor, he remained, because of his continuing attachment to classical models of poetry and learning, the unwitting prisoner of modes and orders hostile to the political health of Europe. Nevertheless, Dante's use of poetry for political purposes and in the service of Italian greatness enhanced the literary power of the Florentine language and thus helped prepare for Machiavelli's own unarmed triumph.

Those who have challenged the authenticity of the *Discourse* do so, for the most part, on the basis of its harsh treatment of Dante, to whom Machiavelli in his other works seems to show respect. Resurrected from the dead, the great poet is subjected to a barrage of accusations as Machiavelli, with inquisitional zeal, makes him confess to the crimes of political ingratitude and indecency. Machiavelli, who claimed to love his *patria* more than his soul, poses as a kind of "anti-inquisitor," accusing the divine poet on behalf not of God but of his native city. Critics who have been most discomfited by this attack have taken it as if it were a true auto-da-fé rather than a piece of playful invective. Ignoring its parodic elements, they overstate even its apparent inconsistency with Machiavelli's usually decorous treatment of the poet. But most important, they fail to look beneath this general decorum to the differences which divide the two great writers and provide serious ground for Machiavelli's playful attack. The *Discourse* is a vehicle for criticizing not only Dante the poet, but also, and more significantly, the classical and Christian doctrines that he espoused in his *Commedia, Convivio, De monarchia,* and *De vulgari eloquentia.*

The last of these works, Dante's own celebrated treatise on language, had been lost for two hundred years when, in the early 1500s, it was recovered by Gian Giorgio Trissino, who in 1514 brought a copy to the Oricellari Gardens. Here it evidently came into Machiavelli's hands.[5] *De vulgari eloquentia* stirred controversy throughout Italy about the nature of the vernacular, and it is undoubtedly to such a controversy that Machiavelli refers in the opening passages of his own work.[6]

The early sixteenth century was a time of uncertain fortune for Dante's reputation as a writer. The Venetian cardinal Bembo, whose own influential treatise on language idolized Florentine, preferred Plutarch and Boccaccio, while other Neoplatonists and humanists eyed with discomfort Dante's eclectic Aristotelian sympathies.[7] In works other than the *Discourse* Machiavelli professed respect for Dante, though more for his achievements as a poet and partisan than as a thinker. Quotations from Dante are scattered throughout Machiavelli's works, usually in flagrant disregard of their original context and meaning. In 1.1 of *Discourses on Livy*,[8] for example, he attributes to Dante words which Dante places in the mouth of Sordello; and at 1.53 Machiavelli takes from Dante's *Convivio* an expression of his antipopular sentiment in matters of language and, wrongly attributing it to *De monarchia,* applies it to politics.[9] In Machiavelli's published works, passages from Dante are always misattributed or slightly modified in ways which better suit Machiavelli's argument, a fact which strongly suggests, if it cannot conclusively prove, willful misrepresentation. In a famous letter to Vettori (December 10, 1513), moreover, Machiavelli links Dante with the "lesser poets," whom he enjoys reading for their "amorous passions," rather than with the "ancient men" to whom he "give[s] himself over entirely" in rational discourse.[10]

Machiavelli's literary and erotic works also abound in imitations (frequently parodic) of Dante's style. His Tercets and Decennials follow the difficult terza rima of the *Divine Comedy,* as does *The Ass* (which also takes its bearing from the scurrilous *Golden Ass* of Apuleius). In this tonally ambiguous and morally troubling poem, Machiavelli assumes the persona of a donkey, which, bitten by ambition and desire, is led by an erotically obliging guide from a dark wood through the Valley of Circe, whose inhabitants include a pig who speaks like Epicurus but rises (in his case, from the mud) like Dante's Ugolino. Machiavelli naturalizes and bestializes the *Commedia,* translating its spiritual ascent into the worldly meanderings of an ass. In Machiavelli's Circean barnyard the sublime figures of the *Commedia* become ludicrous.

Machiavelli's critical stance toward Dante in the *Discourse,* then, is not as inconsistent in his general treatment of Dante as some critics have maintained. In the *Discourse* it is not so much Dante's poetic art which comes under attack—Machiavelli never denies him his place among the "buoni scrittori" (good writers) of Florence — or his "ingegno" (ingenuity) as his "dottrina" (doctrine) and "giudizio" (judgment), attributes of Dante that Machiavelli nowhere else chooses to praise. The *Discourse*'s accusation of the poet does not seem in itself to furnish ground for doubting the work's authenticity. Unless other, compelling evidence should come to light, it would seem reasonable to trust the good Bernardo, who claimed the *Discourse* as his father's own,[11] and treat its complex argument as the work of Machiavellian intelligence.

The structure of the *Discourse* is roughly as follows: the essay opens with an expression of high (or exaggerated) patriotic sentiment followed by a statement of the controversy to be decided, that is, whether the great writers of Florence wrote in the language of their native city or in a language common to Italy as a whole. After examining the statements of the writers themselves — from which Dante alone emerges as favoring a common language — Machiavelli briefly considers Dante's motives and then turns to a lengthy interrogation of the famous poet, punctuated by digressions on language and comedy and culminating in a "confession" on Dante's part that elicits Machiavelli's "complete contentment."

Written from the farm to which Machiavelli retreated following the fall of the Florentine republic, the *Discourse* begins with a vindication of the author's treatment of his native city. Whenever he has been able to honor his city, it asserts, he has done so willingly, even if it involved care and danger, for "a man is under no greater obligation than toward that on which depended, first, his existence, and later, all goods which fortune and nature have bestowed on him." Nor can any of a city's subsequent deeds weaken this obligation: "He who turns against his city, even if it has expelled him, deserves the name of patricide." "For if," says Machiavelli, "it is wicked to beat one's father [padre] and mother, for whatever reason, it follows that it is most wicked to attack one's *patria*" (2:805; 175). Machiavelli's pose as loyal native son is sullied only by the potential irony of his hypothetical constructions and by the swordless enemy against which he turns his courage.[12] For Machiavelli proposes not to fight his country's wars, but only to defend her language. The dispute which quickens his patriotism is only literary.[13]

His remarks are occasioned, he says, by a recent controversy concerning the language of the poets and orators of Italy.[14] Some, "the ones who are most dishonest" (inonestissimi), claim that the language is Italian, others, the "dishonest" (inonesti), call it Tuscan; still others, those with whom Machiavelli here means to throw his weight, call it Florentine (2:803; 175).

Machiavelli proposes to settle the dispute by comparing the various dialects ("parlare") with the modern vernacular ("questa moderna lingua") as employed by its most celebrated writers. Since among these celebrated writers, Dante, Boccaccio, and Petrarch "hold, beyond any controversy, first place," Machiavelli narrows his task by balancing them against the rest of Italy, to whose provinces ("provincia") all other places must, for "love surrounding the language of these three, concede." So compelling is the language of these three Italians that countries of far greater political power cannot compete with it. In literary matters, Italy is supreme. The languages of powerful Spain, France, and Germany can "presume even less" in this regard than that of weaker Lombardy[15] (2:806; 176). In modern times, one might conclude, political and literary strength do not necessarily coincide.

Having narrowed the field to Italy proper and wishing to avoid the Babel-like confusion ("fuggire questa confusiona") that would result from a division of dialects by town and village, Machiavelli settles for a division by province — boundaries that, with the exception of Lombardy (whose language, as we have just learned, is *not* Italian), recall the old political divisions of the Roman Empire.[16] Whereas Dante, in *De vulgari eloquentia*, had recognized the existence in Italy of thousands of ways of speaking, some varying even within a single city (and all ultimately following from the fall of Babel), Machiavelli "flees confusion" by looking to demarcations left behind by the extinguished Roman Empire. His subsequent division of Italy into Lombardy, Tuscany, Romagna, the territories ("terra") of Rome, and the Kingdom of Naples signals the ambiguous status of both Lombardy, whose inclusion in Italy is both denied and affirmed within a single page, and Rome, to whose "earthly" side Machiavelli draws verbal attention. Modern Italy includes, among its parts, one not clearly its own and one whose earthly estates point to another; it also harbors one ruled monarchically without embracing all together. The confusion of language is not (as it seemed to be for Dante) a divinely imposed sanction for human presumption,[17] but the more recent and altogether mundane result of Italy's political disunion.

To be sure, the "great differences" to be observed among the dialects of Italy are accompanied by a mutual intelligibility that lends false credence to the view that Dante used a language common to Italy. To explain these differences, it is necessary, Machiavelli says, to understand the reason for that mutual intelligibility — a line of inquiry his *Florentine Histories* pursues at length. According to the argument of the *Florentine Histories* (to be considered below in greater detail), whatever unity the languages of Italy enjoy derives from the political power of ancient Rome and the subsequent power of the Christian Church, which, adapting the political and linguistic institutions of Rome to its own use, transferred them to the barbarians. The peculiar unity and diversity of Italy's languages are a function of its special political and religious history.

In the *Discourse,* Machiavelli turns instead to those who, following the authority of Dante, identify the boundaries of a language with its affirmative particle, citing as they do Dante's reference to Italy as the place "dove il sì suona" (where the "sì" rings), along with examples of Germany's *iò*, England's *ies,* and France's *oc* and *ui*. (On this account, the languages of Europe distinguish themselves from one another by what they cannot, grammatically speaking, have inherited from Latin, which lacks a single word for *yes*.) In *De vulgari eloquentia,* Dante, citing the Spanish *oc* and French *uil,* presses a similar line of argument. According to Dante, each of these particles, along with other abstract and common terms (such as "heaven," "love," and "God"), are remnants of a language that predates the biblical confusion. As Dante sees it, Italy owes its linguistic unity not to the political dominion of ancient Rome, whose language could not be understood without the artifices of grammar, but to a pre-Roman (and divinely guided) community that emerged intact after the fall of Babel.[18]

Machiavelli indicates his disagreement with (the real) Dante by citing the examples of modern Spain and Sicily, where, beyond Italy's borders, the *sì* also sounds. Over time, Spain has lost its *oc* to France and acquired Italy's *sì*. Misled, it seems, by historical coincidence, Dante paid insufficient attention to the real political forces that help shape linguistic boundaries. And in any case, it is verbs rather than particles and nouns that regulate ("regolare") language; whenever verbs are similar, languages are mutually intelligible whatever the status of their other terms because verbs, the "sinews and nerves" (la catena e il nervo) of language, indicate the meaning of the unknown words they come between. It is thus necessary to be "ruled" (regolarsi) by grammar, not, as with Dante, as a means of contact with ancient authority, but in order to rank the power ("potente") of the terms to rule by pointing out meaning otherwise unknown (2:807; 177). Words that convey action in time, rather than those that express affirmation or denote static substances and properties, are the most powerful conduits of shared intelligence.

A final source of Italy's linguistic unity lies in the ability of accent and pronunciation to distinguish one idiom from another without making them mutually unintelligible, as with Lombardy's and Romagna's dropping of the final vowel (2:807; 177), a usage denounced by Dante in *De vulgari eloquentia* for its extreme harshness and barbarity.[19] Here, as with other barbaric accents (2:812; 182), Italy's peculiar linguistic landscape maps the history of its politics, in which (as Machiavelli notes in the *Florentine Histories*) neither Roman nor barbarian usage has been able to assert unqualified predominance.

Machiavelli's discussion here avoids the question of quality or aptness that preoccupied Dante, who concluded, after a lengthy review, that *no* local dialect was suitable for poetry and prose capable of expressing the highest (that is, "gravest" or most "tragic") matters. That such poetry (thanks to Dante and other exalted writers) in fact exists was, on Dante's account, itself the best argument for a vernacular common to Italy as a whole, both distinct from and superior to the local speech of any single region. For Dante (but not, as we shall see, for Machiavelli), apt language and language spoken popularly by a local community are mutually exclusive.

Dante's self-proclaimed task in *De vulgari eloquentia* is to discover and defend (in Latin and hence to an audience that extends beyond Italy) a noble or "illustrious" vernacular that combines the poetic possibilities of natural language with the power to carry the most elevated, or rational, concepts. As such, Dante's vernacular sets itself against the Latin of the Church, reaching especially to Italy's educated laity, who, divided among a variety of political jurisdictions, might nevertheless constitute a community of elevated discourse to rival the pretended temporal universality of the Church. In calling this vernacular "curiale," the language of the "court," Dante called attention to what Italy, owing to the harmful political pretensions of the papacy, was missing but which Dante wished it to enjoy — a single, politically authoritative court under the power of the emperor. Dante's defense of an illustrious vernacular was thus in keeping with his attachment, as a citizen of Florence, to the party sympathetic to the emperor against that sympathetic to the pope, a factor that led directly to his bitterly lamented exile. (Machiavelli's account of this sad chapter in Florentine history will be considered in due course.)

Resuming, Machiavelli compares the language of each region with that of the most celebrated writers, all of whom — as is "most noted" (notissima) — come from Florence and none of whom, with the exception of Dante, denies Florentine as his "lingua patria." The non-Florentine writers, whom Dante praised, are dismissed by Machiavelli for their piddling output (2:808; 178). Evidently, impressing one's literary peers, as Cino of Pistoia impressed Dante, does not guarantee literary success; to be deemed a writer of the first rank one must be generally and continuously celebrated. The judgment of as great a writer as Dante may diverge from future literary fashion; the good opinion of great men does not assure preeminence.

The task of the remainder of the essay is to extract a confession ("confessar") from Dante that he too used the language of his native city. In so doing, Dante will be made to affirm what Machiavelli himself believes ("credo"), namely, that the local and natural (rather than artful) idiom which conforms most closely to the language of the "primi scrittori" (first or early writers) should be called the language in which they wrote and deserves as such to be honored most highly (2:807; 178). Machiavelli's own confession of faith, which takes natural usage for its "scripture" (scrittura), ignores the possibility on which Dante had staked his claim — that of a vernacular that might be closer to one local dialect in this or that respect but whose superior beauty lay, above all, in measured avoidance (in characteristic Aristotelian fashion) of the extremes to which local idioms are prone.

That which Dante most praised in Cino was his capacity to transcend the parochial dialect of his native city. Like Dante himself, Cino aspired to a literary language common to Italy, against which native dialects might be judged. Such curial language drew its quasi-judicial authority from "the most excellent court of Italy," whose members, lacking a common prince, "are united by the gracious light of reason."[20] Such votaries of reason could be counted on to lay aside municipal prejudice (as did Dante in embracing Cino of hated Pistoia) in anticipation of the Imperial Court of Justice to which Dante looked forward expectantly. For the "sweetness of so glorious a language," Dante claimed, he "cast even [his] own exile behind [his] back" (though by saying so he showed that he had not forgotten it). In Dante's anticipatory court of the intellect, no local interests should predominate, though some might have a greater share, just as some men have a greater share in virtue. Dante's illustrious vernacular, part discovery, part creation of his own artistry, claimed "commonality" in the high sense of being suitable for conveyance of the highest thoughts. "Curial" (or "courtly") language was thus not only the medium of a most elevated poetry (which Dante associates in *De vulgari eloquentia* with tragedy as distinguished from elegy and comedy); it also was the vehicle for a kind of philosophic or spiritual world citizenship. "The world," he declared (echoing Cicero), "is now my native country," just as the sea is to the fish.[21]

In attacking Dante as a linguist, Machiavelli also attacks him as a citizen. In accusing Dante on behalf of Florence, he is also accusing Dante's alleged transcendence of his actual political and linguistic patrimony. Dante's refusal to recognize the native character of his language is symptomatic of his general failure to acknowledge what is properly his own. Dante has too much esteem for the universal, too little for the particular. What is more, his preoccupation with his exile, a subject none of his works fails to mention, suggest that he is less a fish than he pretends. As Machiavelli puts it,

> In his ingenuity, doctrine and judgment ["per ingegno, per dottrina e per giudizio"] Dante showed himself to be excellent in every part, except when he had to reason about his own city, which he persecuted beyond all humanity ["humanità"] and philosophic principle/institution ["filosofico instituto"] with every species of injury. And not being able to do other than defame her, he accused her of every vice, damned her people, blamed her site, spoke badly of her customs and her laws. And he did so not only in one part of his "cantica" but in all, diversely and in diverse ways, so offended was he by the injury of exile! . . . so that he did all that he could [2:808; 178–79].

If any of the miseries which Dante predicted had come to pass, Florence might rightly regret having nourished him. But fortune has given him the lie and made Florence "continually prosperous and celebrated . . . , leading her to such a state of happiness and tranquillity, that should Dante return to life and see her again he would either accuse himself or choose to die again, tortured by the blows of his innate hatred." A native son despite himself, it is no "miracle" (maraviglia) that Dante disowned his native language, wishing as he did to destroy the acclaim that his own reputation had created (2:808–09; 179).

Machiavelli's scabrous portrait of Dante does violence, of course, to his doctrines, but perhaps no more violence than Dante did to those whom he described in his *Commedia*. Forced to choose between self-accusation and damnation ("choosing to die again"), Dante could almost be mistaken for one of his own infernal characters.[22]

The excessive invective of which he accuses Dante matched by his own, Machiavelli turns to Dante's calumny against his native tongue, as if the poet had rejected Florentine and not localism ("lingua particular") as such. Ignoring Dante's defense of what is universal, Machiavelli reduces his rejection of Florentine to an expression of personal bitterness (or "vendetta"), no more to be believed ("credere") than that Dante "found Brutus in the widest mouth of Lucifer, five Florentine citizens among the thieves, and Cacciaguida in Paradise." The fact that Cacciaguida was his own ancestor does not make Dante's judgment any more credible (2:809; 179).[23]

Machiavelli calls the poet of the beatific vision "blind" to Florence. (Dante called the people "blind" to his vernacular.)[24] Where his native city was concerned, Machiavelli alleges, Dante lost all "gravità, dottrina et giudizio" (gravity, doctrine, and judgment) and became a different man, "so that if he had judged everything in the same way, he would either have been kept in Florence forever or expelled (as mad)" (2:809; 179). Nasty, blind, and foolish, Machiavelli's Dante has all the makings of a comic figure, stupefied by vengefulness like the populace that he himself condemned.

Having by exaggeration and sly parody laid the foundation of his attack, Machiavelli proceeds to the merits of the case, which he says he will consider with "ragioni vive et vere" (reasons alive and true) rather than general words and conjectures, "which are easily refuted." Having identified the conjectural and general with the easily refuted and the particular with the living and true, he proceeds to a definition of common language—a term that has an altogether different sense for Machiavelli than it did for Dante (2:809; 179–80). For Dante in *De vulgari eloquentia*, the common is the perfection of the particular, from whose accidental properties it abstracts and whose essential qualities it purifies.[25] His beloved vernacular is common by virtue of its excellence rather than of its popularity,[26] his emphasis on "eloquentia" rather than "vulgari." Common language for Dante is not that spoken by everyone or by most, but that to which the best, recognizing the inadequacy of local speech, presume.

For Machiavelli, who ignores these elevated subtleties, "common language" means the language most in use, not that to which the best aspire (2:809; 179–80). The universal neither perfects the particular, nor represents a higher order of being. "Local" speech means that which is understood locally, "common" that which is shared. Indeed, no language is pure; every language has a proportion of both native and common elements. A common Italian language ("parlare commune d'Italia") would have more of what is common than of what belongs to a particular idiom ("parlare proprio"); a particular idiom has more of the native than the common. For Dante, mixed languages were a degeneration; for Machiavelli they are as normal as human interchange itself. All languages borrow from one another: "for when men of different provinces converse with one another they exchange one another's words." And "when new doctrines or arts [arti] appear in a city, they are necessarily accompanied by words born [nati] in the language from which those doctrines and trades have their origin." Religion and the arts, so important to the late history of the Italian cities, are the forces that Machiavelli here singles out as primary causes of linguistic change. The bloodier and more drastic causes, whose absence from modern Italy he notes elsewhere,[27] go unmentioned here. Although most significant in the history of other languages, military conquest is apparently irrelevant to an understanding of "questa moderna lingua" (this modern language). In the modern Italian cities, new words are introduced by gentler means. New words take on slowly "through speech," rather than quickly through fear, the accents, cases, moods, and other differences of the language in which they find themselves. In this way, they at last "become its own," for "otherwise languages would be like patchwork, and not turn smoothly [tornerebbono bene]" (2:809–10; 180).

Dante's history of language, like his account of politics, takes its bearing from the original and final unity of men. Machiavelli, on the contrary, begins with human diversity and difference. Languages, like politics, are mixed bodies which, lacking innate wholeness, tend by themselves to disintegration, which only human effort can forestall. Linguistic unity is not a divine gift, in either a biblical or a poetic sense, but the effect of human interest, common or otherwise, and the exchanges it prompts. Like political interchange, linguistic interchange need not debilitate. So long as a language retains the power to dominate foreign elements and appropriate them as its own, it enriches itself, becoming "more beautiful as [it] become[s] more copious" (2:810; 180).

Eventually, however, a language takes in so many new words that it is "bastardized" (imbastardicono) and becomes "an entirely new thing" — a change that may occur so slowly that the language falls imperceptibly into ruinous barbarism. Gradually and by degree the native loses its ability to make what is foreign its own. A language's enrichment is only part of a repeating cycle in which vigor precedes corruption and decline. Such decline, Machiavelli observes, takes hundreds of years, unless accelerated by what he understatedly calls the "introduction of new population." Languages can (like Sparta) survive for a time in isolation. But forced, as they eventually are, to interact, they can continue to survive only by enriching themselves with the materials of others, a process that can (as in Rome) forestall but not prevent eventual destruction. In either case, lost language can, if one "so wills, be reemployed" (riassunto), by recourse to good writers, "as is presently done for Latin and Greek" (2:810; 180).

Leaving aside such considerations and the questions they raise about the future of the Florentine language as irrelevant to the present, since Florentine is not yet in decline, Machiavelli at last calls forward his great predecessor, demanding to know what Dante has taken from Latin, what from Lombard, and what he has himself invented. Dante gives examples of all three but insists that the mixture, combined with Tuscan, produces an entirely different language. He admits that in the *Paradiso* he relies heavily on Latin as most suitable to the expression of his "dottrina" but insists that he has adapted his Latin borrowings to the curial language of the *Commedia* as a whole (2:811; 181).

That the "confessional"[28] examples drawn from the *Commedia* are all self-referring arouses the hunch that Dante's problems, from Machiavelli's standpoint, are as much political (and spiritual) as linguistic. Dante's "lombardisms" — one alluding to his exile,[29] the other to his Tuscan birth[30] — raise the specter of his political failure. His invented words refer to intercourse with angels. And his "latinism" refers to his own reliance on example "because one cannot signify in words the surpassing of things human."[31]

The definition of curial language (or "cortigiana") Machiavelli's Dante advances is similarly suspicious — it is not, as a reader of *De vulgari eloquentia* would expect, the language of a court materially dispersed though intellectually united,[32] but instead the language of the actual papal and ducal courts, where literary men speak better than the locals ("nelle terre particulari d'Italia") (2:811; 182).[33] Curial language is presented as the language of the literary elite, which draws its strength not from reason and grace, but from the actual potentates of Italy. Machiavelli, in short, foists on Dante a loyalty to the court of Rome that Dante's own work explicitly rejects.[34] Dante, who in *De vulgari eloquentia* calls the language of Rome "most hideous," disavowed support for Rome in matters temporal, insisting on the independence of emperors from popes (many of whom find a place in the lower reaches of the *Inferno*).

Reinterpreting Dante's presumed "transcendence of things human," Machiavelli does not permit him the indulgence of his spiritualized politics. With examples that refer to the political transgressions of the papacy, he argues that Dante's loyalty to the court of Rome is false. In so accusing Dante it is, of course, Machiavelli, not Dante, who "tells lies" (2:811; 182). In doing so, however, he shows the effectual truth of Dante's effort to overcome through poetry the divided loyalties of European Christendom.

Machiavelli also confronts Dante with confessions drawn from the *Commedia* itself. Dante admits his use of Florentine or Tuscan, both in the circle of hypocrisy[35] and before Farinata, who was condemned for — so to speak — loving his patria more than his soul.[36] Farinata, who has the political astuteness to warn Dante of his coming exile, belongs among the followers of Epicurus, "who make the soul die with the body," and it may not be stretching things too far to see in the infernal shade something of Machiavelli's own reflection.

Machiavelli's accusation continues beyond the (seemingly) grave crime of political disloyalty to the genuinely comic ones of clumsiness ("goffo"), crudity ("porco"), and obscenity ("osceno"). If anyone should blush, says Machiavelli, it isn't Dante but Florence (2:814; 185).[37] Machiavelli's apparent priggishness here, inconsistent as it seems with his own comedic practice elsewhere, has given critics as much trouble as his overweening patriotism earlier in the *Discourse*.[38] Much of the difficulty dissolves, however, if one is open to the possibility of playful intention. Any of Machiavelli's accusations could be turned against the author, who, after all, is even here not too priggish to repeat Dante's indecencies verbatim. The instance of alleged clumsiness by Dante is in fact the product of a clumsy transposition by Machiavelli,[39] whose own comedies in any case abound with indelicacies. Indecency, like localism, is, as he elsewhere puts it, entirely natural. Dante could avoid neither indelicacy nor his native language because "l'arte non può mai in tutto repugnare alla natura" (2.813; 185).[40] Dante "dishonors" his work not because his usage is indecent but because his art holds nature repugnant.

Turning now to the opposing arguments, Machiavelli observes that since languages are not simple bodies but necessarily mixed with others, some use of foreign words on Dante's part should be expected. A language belongs to a country ("si chiama d'una patria") when it "converts" (convertisci) borrowed words "to its own use/usage" (uso) and is sufficiently powerful ("potente") that it disorders ("disordine") them rather than being disordered by them, drawing them to itself as if they were its own ("lo tira a sè in modo che par suo"). It matters little, then, that Dante used foreign words, since Florentine did the ordering (which amounts, for Machiavelli, to a *destruction* of the rule preceding it). Rule is not a relation between natural rulers and those naturally ruled (as Aristotle claimed), but the (violent) imposition of one's *own* discipline on that previously imposed by another. Machiavelli calls writers like Dante "amorevoli" (lovers) of their language, bound to do as he did but not as he said, there being nothing wrong in borrowing foreign words but only in claiming thereby to be speaking another language. Dante ought to have imitated the ancient Romans, who knew how to enrich their "lingua patria" without betraying her (2:814; 185–86).[41]

The Romans are exemplary in other ways. In military affairs, they were able to group their citizen soldiers with many more from other nations; and because "the Roman citizens and their captains were the nerve [nervi] of the army [esercito], since all fought under Roman order and discipline, these exercises assumed the name, authority, and dignity of Rome [il nome, l'autorità, e dignità romana]." It is thus foolish for Dante, who enlisted so many native legions of words as well as Florentine cases, tenses, moods, and endings, to believe that with foreign words he has transformed his language. The fact that Florentine and "cortigiana" share the same verbs is, moreover, offset by Dante's use of Florentine cases and endings (thus putting a native stamp on that which makes the languages of Italy mutually intelligible) (2:814; 186).

If Rome were able to rule an empire by "freely admitting strangers into her army, privileges and honors,"[42] she could manage them only so long as she had a well-regulated citizen force. Octavian, hailed by Dante as the "perfect monarch," one whose peaceful reign coincided with the life of Christ, is blamed by Machiavelli for disbanding the citizen army, an act to which he traces the fall of the empire.[43] Dante is too much the partisan of gentlemanly honor: in *De monarchia*, he attributed Rome's world conquest to her providential success in single combat.[44] With regard to single combat Machiavelli says that the Romans "could not have done a worse-considered thing."[45]

Nevertheless, Machiavelli presents Dante as a kind of founder who, by his example, leads others out of the barbarity of their local idiom, teaching them to reject what is their own and serve another. Before Dante, Petrarch, and Boccaccio, the Florentine language lacked the power to dominate the languages of other provinces. As Machiavelli insists, many words that seem to belong to Italy as a whole were in fact peculiar to Florence until Dante's influence brought them into common use, contributing to the mistaken belief that his language was initially so (2:815; 187).

As for Dante's claim to speak a courtly language, Machiavelli replies that the courts of Milan and Naples speak local idioms, while the court of Rome (Dante's attachment to which Machiavelli marvels at/deems miraculous ["maraviglia"]) uses "so many languages of so many nations" that "it can supply no mode of rule [regola] whatever." Unlike the ancient city, modern Rome cannot bring order to its polyglot constituency — no "miracle," since (as Dante in *De vulgari eloquentia* would himself agree) perverse speech and customs go together (2:815; 187).

Finally, Dante's celebrity leads others to try to imitate him, adding to the impression that he spoke a language common to Italy as a whole. Such efforts, Machiavelli adds, rarely succeed, not only because "art can't surpass nature" but also because many works, including comedies, suffer if they do not use local terms and endings — an opening that Machiavelli seizes on to give Dante a lesson in the art of comedy (2:815–16; 187–88).

Comedy, according to Machiavelli, aims to mirror private life, yet with "a certain urbanity" and "words that provoke laughter" and are "comprehensible to everyone," so that those who run to such "delectation" taste/enjoy ("gustino") afterward the "useful lesson beneath."[46] Comedy is thus not altogether opposed to gravity (as Dante in *De vulgari eloquentia* implies) inasmuch as it conveys lessons grave and useful to our lives ("effetti gravi e utili alla vita nostra") (2:816; 188).[47]

Machiavelli's use of "nostra," like his insistence on "termine proprii patrii," insinuates him with the general, popular audience he would instruct in spite of itself. To make men laugh, one must use language that is foolish, sarcastic, or amorous (as we learn from *Clizia*) but above all familiar, comedy's dependence on local speech contrasting nicely here with the *lack* of native speech in an effeminately lascivious Rome (2:815; 187). In the *Clizia* Machiavelli claims to have succeeded in presenting indelicate matters with the greatest decency (or honesty, that is, "onestà grandissima").[48] Because of the grave and useful lessons (Machiavelli does not quite say "moral") that comedy conveys — and owing, the *Discourse* suggests, to the peculiar immediacy of native speech — laughable themes involving love, slander, and buffoonery can be presented without impropriety. Whereas the comedies make use of love,[49] the *Discourse* employs buffoonery and slander: grave Dante "loses all dignity"; Ariosto finds it hard to maintain decorum; Trissino, Bembo, and Sannazaro cannot avoid pratfalls in attempting to write in a language not properly their own.

Machiavelli's comedies are also familiar in the way of repetition. Two borrow the form and one the plot of Roman comedies. A third, the *Andria*, which translates Plautus's work into the local dialect of Florence, makes other familiarizing adaptations, such as replacing Davus and Oedipus with David and Florence's "prophetic" Frate. In his prologue to the *Clizia*, Machiavelli playfully defends his adaptation of a Roman story to a local setting on the grounds that his audience does not speak the language of antiquity and that in any case events repeat themselves. (Indeed, the joke extends even further: Plautus borrowed *his* plot from an earlier Greek dramatist.)

Comedy, then, would seem to be a mere pastime — a "delectation" in which time is literally "consumed" and "passed"[50] — except that it is also able to instruct everyone, especially the young, as to humanity's deceitfulness, thus disabusing them of their credulity.[51] This disabusing of everyone, both male and female, goes together with "ridiculing" things of love and hence with the salty native terms that bring love down from the Latinized heights of an idealizing and aristocratic discourse (2:816; 188). Eros, for Machiavelli, may be sweet, indeed, the sweetest delight and consolation most human beings are able to enjoy; it never rises above the pleasures of the body.[52] In so reducing (or demystifying) love, Machiavellian comedy is more than the retelling of classical plots it sometimes pretends to be.[53] Machiavelli's comedy disdains the ornate style of an Ariosto for the "salt"[54] of terms that are "ordinary, complete [or 'recognized by all'], and obvious [or 'noted'] [soli, interi, e noti]" (2:816; 188). With "urbanity" (urbanità) replacing "courtliness" as the chief standard of literary merit, intellect distinguishes itself not by being elevated above the common but by a certain knowingness allowing one to penetrate further jokes all enjoy and through which all are benefited (or corrupted).

Speech, *pace* Dante, is the subject of accident and occasion, not the vehicle of redemption. It cannot escape its timely fate by conforming to transcendent standards. Eschewing Dante's pretensions to an "elevated, curial, and illustrious" vulgate, Machiavelli identifies the best language with the language "piu in prezzo" (more valued) (2:817; 189); if he does not know and use it, no writer, however talented, can succeed. Authors who would be "most celebrated" and "most noted" evidently can't be snobbish.

In his concluding discussion of language, Machiavelli may have especially in mind Lorenzo de Medici, who in his *Comento alcuni dé suoi sonetti,* disparaged language that is merely "in prezzo" rather than rising to a standard of excellence which *transcends* "il successo delle cose del mondo" (the success of worldly things).[55] Language ought to gain its stature, according to Lorenzo, not from worldly success, but through its aptness in expressing the soul's harmony and the mind's intelligence. But according to Machiavelli, language excels not through its aptness for expressing the worthiest things,[56] but through its aptness for domination through the imposition of a (borrowed) discipline currently in favor. Florentine, the language now "piu in prezzo," acquired its stature through its timely ability to accommodate both prose and poetry in a period when poetry was gaining in popularity. "Everyone [ciascuno] knows" that poetic usage started in Provence, then moved to Sicily, Italy, Tuscany, and at last to Florence, "for no other reason than that Florence was the most apt [atta]" (2:817; 189). Machiavelli's brief history illustrates the dependence of linguistic fortune on popular taste. In the absence of the popularly recognized occasion of a literary fashion which originated in Provence, the peculiar aptitude of Florentine "to accommodate both prose and verse" might have gone unrecognized, unused, and unesteemed. If Florentine "now merits being first, and procreating these writers" it is "not through commodiousness of site, through ingenuity [ingegno], nor through any particular occasion other than through her language accommodating [commoda] such a discipline [as poetry]" (2:817; 189). The literary fertility of Florence is due precisely to the "things of this world" that Lorenzo claimed to despise. Florence's poets owe their glory not to transcendent qualities of their language, but to good fortune, a fortune beyond Italy's borders and beyond her powers.

Viewed in this light, Machiavelli's extravagant praise of Florence earlier in the work takes on a different aspect. In literary matters Italy is dominated by the Florentine language, from which all idioms with universal pretensions prove to derive. Whatever the claims of Dante and others, Italy lacks a language that is truly common. But Florence is not the maker of her literary fortune. What is more, her literary success is politically ambiguous at best. The flowering of letters comes after that of arms,[57] and a literary culture is a sure sign of political corruption. The flowering of Roman letters followed Rome's imposition of Latin (albeit one enriched by Greek and other sources) on those it conquered. It is difficult, however, to see what military conquest preceded Florence's literary success. The fact that Italy has languages that both derive from Florentine and seem common testifies to the political weakness of Florence, which is unable to impose its language definitively on the rest of Italy, and to the political weakness of Italy as a whole, which lacks the political unity necessary to produce a language that is truly common. Italy's literary successes are a mirror image of its political failings.

In book 1 of his *Florentine Histories* Machiavelli considers in greater detail the relation between language and political conquest. Italy's peculiar linguistic development reflects its unique political and religious history, in the course of which Roman and barbarian elements have mixed but, owing to the presence of the Church, have never been properly ordered. Barbarians that might otherwise have conquered her decisively have repeatedly been checked, as Machiavelli shows, by "holy reputation."[58] Because of the same influence, the old empire held out for many years as a force too weak to rule but strong enough to prevent others from doing so by conquering the old empire decisively, until it finally succumbed to church authority in a way that brought further strife to Italy no less destructive for being internally rather than externally generated.

In relating this sad history, Machiavelli pays particular attention to the power of names, both as signs of rule and, more recently and perversely, as its implement. As he described Roman strength in terms of its ability to extend "il nome romana" (the Roman name), so he discusses that of the barbarians in terms of their ability to impose their own names on the territory they conquered. Regions like France, Burgundy, England, Brittany, Hungary, Slavonia, and Normandy, for example, have lost their old Roman names and taken on the new names of their conquerors, while Italy, never completely conquered in this way, retains a name of Latin derivation.

Titles of power, by way of contrast, have altered in Italy, along with the "forms" they accompany. Odoacer the Goth, the first barbarian to overrun and settle in Rome, "dropped the name of the Empire and had himself called King," so that with the change of power Rome might change its title.[59] Theodoric, who defeated Odoacer, assumed his title but established his capital in Ravenna, distributing his own commanders throughout the region. The memory of Theodoric, who restored order and stopped the barbarian influx, "would everywhere be worthy of every honor" except for certain "cruelties" caused by "suspicions" (sospetti) demonstrated by the deaths of Simmacus and Boethius.[60] It is not just corrupt Christianity but the effect of Christian holiness itself which Machiavelli blames (however slyly) for Italy's continuing political disorder; and, to emphasize the point, he juxtaposes the "cruelties" perpetrated against (or on account of) the two holy men with the far crueler disorders which these men through their holy influence indirectly perpetrated.[61] Under Theodoric, Italy had begun to live in an orderly fashion and recover from the "true misery" of her former instability. The effects of that instability were terrible. For, says Machiavelli,

> If one considers how much harm is caused to a republic or a kingdom by a change of prince or government, not through any external force but only through civil discord (where one sees how little changes ruin every republic and every kingdom, even the most powerful) it can easily be imagined how much Italy and the other Roman provinces suffered in those times; for not only did their governments and their princes change, but also their laws, customs, modes of life, religion, language, dress/habits and names [le leggi, i costumi, il modo del vivere, la religione, la lingua, l'abito, i nomi].[62]

The gradual linguistic changes of Machiavelli's and Dante's time, brought on by peaceful interchange and literary imitation, pale in importance before the drastic and terrible changes which, preceding them, made languages anew.

From these changes, sufficient to "terrify," by their mere thought, "every firm and constant spirit,"[63] ensued "new orders of speech" (ordini di parlare) as well as new names of places and men, the former, as his examples indicate, a mixture of Roman and barbarian, the latter based on the New Testament.[64] Even language, it seems, was affected by the Church, which allowed localities to assume local names but stamped men with its own nomenclature.

It is at this point in his narrative, as he describes how the Goths, after rebuilding Rome out of respect for the holy reputation of St. Benedict, were themselves driven from Italy, that Machiavelli notes explicitly the most grave tumults and discords ("tumulti e discordie gravissime") brought about by Christianity.[65] Longinus, the emperor's deputy, changed the provinces to dukedoms (whose rulers he "had called dukes"), took away the Roman consuls and Senate ("names until that day preserved there"), and gave Italy's ruler the (Greek) name of exarch. In so altering Italy's titles, says Machiavelli, Longinus gave it a "new form" that further weakened and divided it, invited the invasion of the Lombards, and so precipitated Italy's ruin.[66]

As Machiavelli observes in the next chapter, the Church both increased and benefited from this instability — a process that began with the (perverse) decision of the Roman emperors to combat disorder by adopting the religion that inspired it. Still, prior to the arrival of the Lombards, "the popes never acquired any greater authority than what reverence for their habits [costumi] and doctrine gave them."[67] Afterward, the popes, their political ambitions whetted by the vacuum left by the removal of the emperors to Constantinople, gained new respect as "nearly the heads" (quasi que cap[i]) of Rome, permitting alternating alliances with the Greeks and Lombards that further increased the papal "dignity." Deprived of their Greek allies by the inroads of the Slavs, the popes turned to others, opening the way for France's invasion of Italy — an event made possible by the Lombards' (foolish) reverence for the pope, and the pope's wish to convert rather than kill his enemy.[68] France gained the empire, however, only by giving new power to the papacy, so that "whereas the pope had habitually [soleva] been confirmed by emperors, it now commenced that the emperor in his election had need of the pope."[69] When the emperor Charles subsequently wished to "reorder" Italy, he gave the name of Lombardy to the province inhabited by the Lombards, now strangers only "in name," and he called the part near them (but subject to Exarchate of Ravenna) Romagna, so "that they might hold the Roman name in reverence." During the same period, the priests of Rome, prompted by their relative independence, began to call themselves cardinals," to honor their power with splendid title"; in doing so they arrogated to themselves so much "reputation" as to deprive the people of Rome of their power to choose the pope,[70] as they were deprived of their authority to help to choose the emperor,[71] so much did names newly matter. France's partial reforming and reordering of Italy at this time was possible only because the pope previously brought to Italy the "names of count and marquis," just "as Longinus, exarch of Ravenna, first established there the name of duke."[72] (Whereas Longinus did his own name changing, the reordering of Italy by Charles required an earlier name changing by others.) This litany of naming and renaming culminates (in recognition of the dependence of church power on the power of names) with the "Roman Pope Osporco" [or 'Piglips'] who, owing to the ugliness/filthiness of his name ("la bruttura del nome"), "made himself called 'Sergius,' " from which dates the practice of popes changing names on their election.[73]

The ascendency of names and naming as primary instruments of power goes hand in hand, for Machiavelli, with the new "importance of spiritual wounds," about which the French emperor soon learned: Henry IV, attempting to depose Pope Gregory V and appoint his own, found himself forced by his own subjects to kneel before the pope and beg for pardon. Such was the "seed" of the conflict between Guelphs and Ghibellines, in which Italy, no longer visited by barbarian floods, was lacerated by intestine wars.[74]

Thus did the authority of the Church rise as that of the empire fell. Lacking its own arms, the Church extended its temporal power by lending the authority of its names and discipline to the arms of others. The new religion was first adopted by the emperors because they thought it useful, then submitted to because they deemed it necessary. With the decline of the empire, the Church gained worldly power, but never enough to forsake the need of armed allies, who themselves proved divisive. Too weak to govern the empire by itself, the Church was too strong to permit another power to succeed where it had failed.[75] From Theodoric, who tried to settle Italy, to Niccolini, who tried to revive Rome's "ancient form," all attempts to reorder Italy have succumbed to the influence of the Church. The normal political cycle from order to confusion back to order has been disrupted by an extraordinary force. As Machiavelli observes at the beginning of book 5 of the *Histories*,

> Provinces, in the changes they are wont ["sogliono"] to make, most of the time come from order to disorder, and from disorder pass over to order — because, it not being conceded by nature to worldly things to stay ["fermarsi"], when they achieve their ultimate perfection, not having more to rise, they descend. Similarly, when they have descended, arriving through disorders to the lowest depth, of necessity, not being able to descend, they begin to rise: and thus from the good there always descends the bad and from the bad there arises good. Because virtue gives birth to peace, peace quiet, quiet leisure, leisure disorder, disorder ruin; and similarly, from ruin is born order,

from order virtue, and from this glory and good fortune. When it has been observed by the prudent how letters come after arms, and that in provinces and cities captains are born before philosophers. For good and ordered arms having given birth to victories, and victories to quiet, the strength ["fortezza"] of armed hearts ["animi"] cannot be corrupted with more honest/honorable ["onesto"] leisure than with that of letters, nor can leisure enter into well-instituted cities with greater and more dangerous deception ["inganno"] than this one. This Cato . . . recognized [when, the Roman youth began to admire Greek philosophers, he provided] that no philosopher should be received [henceforth] in Rome. By such means, then, provinces come to ruin, arriving at which, and men becoming wise through suffering ["battiture"], they return, as was said, to order, if they do not remain suffocated by an extraordinary force ["se già da una forza estraordinaria non rimangono suffocati"].[76]

In the case of Italy the ordinary cycle has been stopped by an extraordinary force—an unnatural stasis and stifling of vital impulse. Neither a united polity nor a common language has emerged from the ruins of the ancient empire. If Florence's literary influence extends beyond its borders, its authority does not. Its modest literary success is a sign of the political weakness of Italy generally.

Machiavelli's treatment, in the *Discourses on Livy,* of the effect of religion and language on human memory yields a further clue as to the reason for this stoppage of the ordinary course of nature:[77]

To those philosophers who would have it ["hanno voluto"] that the world is eternal, I believe ["credo"] that one could reply that if so much antiquity were true it would be reasonable that there be more than five thousand years of memory, if it were not seen how these memories of times extinguish them-selves by diverse causes: of these, part comes from men, part from heaven. Those that come from men are the variations of sects and of languages. Because when a new sect—that is, a new religion—arises, its first concern is to extinguish ["estinguere"] the old one to give itself reputation. One is ac-quainted ["si conosce"] with this thing from considering the modes taken by the Christian sect against the Gentile. The Christian sect annulled all the orders, all the ceremonies of the Gentiles, and extinguished ["spenta"] every memory of that ancient theology. It is true that they did not succeed in ex-tinguishing totally notice of the things done by the excellent men of it; this is born from [the sect's] having maintained the Latin language, which they did being forced ["forzatamente"], in that they had to write this new law with it. Because if they had been able to write with new language, considering the other persecutions they made, not one of the things of the past would have been recorded. And he who reads the modes taken by Saint Gregory and the other heads of the Christian religion will see with how much obstinacy they persecuted all the ancient memories, burning the works of poets and historians, ruining the images, and laying waste ["guastando"][78] to every other thing that gives any sign of antiquity. So that if to this persecution there had been added a new language, in short time everything would have been forgotten. And it is therefore given to be believed that that which the Christian sect wanted to do against the Gentile, the Gentile would have done against that which was prior to it/in its presence ["innanzi"].[79]

Machiavelli here overstates the extent to which Christianity, in its "obstinate" persecution of the old theology, is a model of conquest generally. Livy, for one, gives a very different picture of Rome's treatment of the language and religion of Tuscan/Etruscans, whom Rome defeated.[80] Indeed, as Machiavelli makes clear in the previous chapter, the obliteration of Etruscan memory is less the fault of Rome than of the lack of a "particular history [istoria] of [Etruscan] affairs" to maintain a record of their greatness.[81]

Still, Christianity has preserved a record of the past despite itself. Forced by its lack of arms to adopt Roman speech and institutions to its own use, the Church has kept alive the memory of ancient things. The circumstances that have maintained political disorder and stopped the cycle at its lowest ebb may also help a permanent reordering.

That Christianity has not wholly expunged the languages of former times is thus less a sign of its weakness with respect to earlier sects (who evidently did not always pursue this goal so obstinately) than of its failure to realize its own ambition — one that might otherwise be accomplished, Machiavelli elsewhere suggests, by a particularly wise and well-situated author.[82]

The best way to secure and enhance a name, as Machiavelli notes in the same work, is to begin ("principare") and found it on "fact and one's own work."[83] And yet the importance of name to Machiavelli himself is by no means obvious. Powerful rulers, as he insists, typically stamp their titles as well as those of their armies with their native tongue, as do powerful peoples in the provinces they occupy.[84] But, as the example of the Etruscans/Tuscans shows, the perpetuation of a name does not necessarily indicate the perpetuation of authority.[85] In the *Discourses,* Machiavelli attributes Rome's success, in no small measure, to the manipulation of titles: some rule in name alone, while others rule in all but name.[86] To what extent, one wonders, did Machiavelli intend his own authority (or authorship)[87] to remain anonymous?[88]

Language cycles between order and barbarism, governed, like other mixed bodies, by the vicissitudes of time. But language is also a human assertion against time. Like political laws, linguistic rules give human affairs a temporary order and stability. Even a language in decline can for a time be restored by recourse to its "buoni scrittori," who themselves brought it out of disorder. And yet, in the last analysis, fortune seems to set distinct limits to the ordering

powers of "buoni scrittori." The language of Florence's great writers conquered Italy not because they were more skillful than those of other cities, but
because they were lucky enough to be born into a language more apt than
others for the expression of literary genres that happened to be "in prezzo."
Their success must also be attributed to the weakness of the cities of Italy
generally, a circumstance favorable to the flourishing of a literary culture and
inimical to the political conquest of any city, a conquest which would probably have entailed linguistic supremacy as a matter of course. Languages prevail
not only through the skill of their poets but also and primarily through the political and religious conquests of their speakers. This takes nothing away from
the fact that Machiavelli's own literary—as distinguished from political—
fortune happens to be optimal. Though fortune has bestowed on him no
occasion for political conquest, it has given him a native fluency in the first
language of Italy, a language particularly suitable to the writing of both poetry
and prose, and a fluency particularly suited to the writing of comedy. If his
efforts are ultimately superior to those of Dante, it is the result not of superior
fortune—the fortunes of the two Florentine exiles seem about equal—but of
superior humanity, philosophic institution, and virtue. Although Machiavelli
elsewhere speaks of Dante's prudence[89] and acknowledges his understanding,[90] Machiavelli never mentions Dante's virtue.

In the *Discourse,* Machiavelli speaks with the living dead of this world, rather
than of another (as with Dante in the *Commedia*). Called forth (we know not
whence), Dante "confesses" that what Machiavelli says is "true" and then
"departs" (si partì) (we know not where). Unlike the Christian persecutions
that Machiavelli's treatment of the poet parodies, Machiavelli's literary inter-
rogations result in nothing crueler than an admission by Dante that Machiavelli is right, followed by "complete contentment" on Machiavelli's part on
having "undeceived him" (d'averlo sgannato) (2:818; 190).

To be sure, Machiavelli is not certain that he "will undeceive" those who "so
little recognize the benefits they have received from *nostra patria* that they
wish to assimilate [accomunare] its language with that of Milan, Venice, Romagna, and all the blasphemies [bestimmie] of Lombardy" (a parting speech,
on Machiavelli's part, blasphemous indeed!). Machiavelli does not know if he
will be able to overcome the ingratitude of his contemporaries—an effort that
will perhaps turn on his own future efforts as an author and which in any case
reminds us of the little stock he elsewhere puts in gratitude.[91]

It is easy to see a number of parallels between Machiavelli and Dante, two
great sons of Florence, each loyal in his own way to his native city, yet bitten by
high if not the highest philosophically political ambitions. Each was a master of

both poetry and prose, and each a theorist, in his own way, of the eloquence he practiced. This said, the differences that divide the two great authors count more than what unites them: whereas Dante turned to poetry and ancient philosophy to remedy the ills of a politically and spiritually divided Christendom, Machiavelli famously sought to found "new modes and orders." Perhaps nowhere is this difference more evident than in their respective approaches to comedy—a special theme of Machiavelli's essay on language. Like Platonic philosophy, Dante's masterpiece — a "comedy" that treats the highest themes — transcends the distinction (that he himself elsewhere acknowledged) between the tragic, the elegiac, and the comic. Machiavelli, on the other hand, does not so much transcend the distinction between gravity and levity as alternate between them on the plane of worldly pleasure and success.[92] Comedy is Machiavelli's special way of speaking directly (in "nostra lingua") to the people, whom Dante, as Machiavelli sees it, scorned to his detriment.

It may be best to end, however, on a note of (tempered) praise, taken from the famous letter in which Machiavelli speaks of his own "transformation" in(to) curial conversation:

> When evening has come, I enter my study and remove my workaday clothing, full of mud and mire, and I put on regal and courtly robes ["panni reali et curiali"], and appropriately reattired, enter the ancient courts of the ancient men, where, received lovingly by them, I feed on that food which *alone* ["solum"] is mine, and which I was born for; where I am not ashamed to speak with them and to demand of them the reasons for their actions, and where they, owing to their humanity, answer me. . . . And because Dante says that to have intended/understood ["intesi"] without retaining ["lo retenere"] does not make knowledge, I have noted what capital ["capitale"] I have made from their conversation and have composed ["composto"] a little work "On Principalities."[93]

The ancients into whom Machiavelli thus (in a parody of Christian communion?) "transforms [himself] completely" (tucto mi transferisco in loro)" evidently did not include the self-proclaimed poet and promoter of a special curial language. (One is, indeed, struck by the tonal contrast between Machiavelli's gracious inquiries into the "reasons" for the ancients' actions and his caustic interrogation of the poet, whose "reasons" are, it seems, all too obvious.) And yet Machiavelli does credit the authority of Dante as to the importance — if one would indeed "make knowledge" — of "retaining what one has understood." This phrase, which refers, in the *Commedia,* to the importance of opening one's mind to the "austere food" of heaven, is interpreted by Machiavelli as a gloss on the poem as a whole, in which Dante is also nourished by conversations in purgatory and hell. And the "retention" that for Dante signified a consumption perfect in being free of all material residue becomes, on the basis of Machiavelli's reading (*or* "gusto purgato"), what his communion with the ancients leaves behind as capital/compost. In this way too, Machiavelli exploits the truth of Dante's work (which he extracts from Dante in the *Discourse* and which furnishes, Machiavelli claims, his [proximate] reason for composing *The Prince*) against Dante's own intention.

5

Tragic Machiavelli

RONALD L. MARTINEZ

Machiavelli's letter of October 21, 1525, to Francesco Guicciardini, to which he signs himself "historico, comico et tragico," has, since Roberto Ridolfi's biography, been taken as a fitting summary of the career of the Florentine secretary. As Machiavelli wrote no known tragedy (and there is no tantalizing lost possibility analogous to the supposedly Aristophanic comedy *Le maschere*), the last term in the self-descriptive triad is sweepingly interpreted by Ridolfi as Machiavelli's formulation of the experience of Italy during the catastrophic epoch that had begun with the French invasion of 1494.[1] Ridolfi's interpretation is beyond cavil, but Machiavelli's lapidary self-description may warrant further scrutiny, especially in the context of theater history and dramatic theory in the early cinquecento. Giorgio Barberi-Squarotti, who has argued for a "tragic structure" in Machiavelli's work, especially *The Prince*, based on a conception of political existence as a heroic agon, has gone so far as to say that Machiavelli's tragic vision made Italian tragedy in the theatrical sense at once superfluous and impossible.[2] What I hope to show in this essay is, rather, that Machiavelli had reason to consider the word *tragico* not merely a description of his witness to (as he put it) "the ruin of Italy" or of the paradoxical *Prince,* but something close to a technical term. From such a perspective Machiavelli's work does not supplant and eclipse all possible tragedy but furnishes one voice, if indubitably a major one, in a tragic chorus: a metaphor I hope to justify in the course of my argument.

The triad of occupations suggested by Machiavelli's signature seems to vary the canonical parsing of theatrical types into comedy, tragedy, and satyr-play crystallized for Renaissance scenography by Sebastiano Serlio, who illustrated them in his influential *Libro dell'architettura,* published in 1547.[3] Machiavelli's probable allusion to the triad thus considerably anticipates the time when the three types had become proverbial, just as his ostentatious use of the dramatic unities in *Mandragola* (c. 1518) anticipates the wide diffusion of Aristotelian rules consequent on the Latin translation of the *Poetics* by Alessandro Pazzi de' Medici in 1524.[4] Both of these precocious uses by Machiavelli will emerge as significant later in my discussion; what I wish to emphasize here is that if indeed theatrical in provenance Machiavelli's signature fits snugly with his preoccupations during the waning days of 1525, a few months after he had presented his *Florentine Histories* to the Medici Pope Clement VII in Rome. In addition to worrying about the political situation, inevitable in exchanges with Guicciardini (the French loss of Milan to troops of Charles V, the first of the disasters that led to the Sack of Rome, was fresh in mind), Machiavelli was discussing with the historian a possible future production of his comedy *Mandragola* (the first performance of *Clizia* was itself recent, in March of 1525) and to this end explaining the Tuscan proverbs that lard the text of the comedy. One of these, the frog's riposte to the harrow ("la botta all'erpice") that flayed its back: "Don't bother to come back" — lends Aesopic clothing to a sardonic perspective on the passage of French troops over Italian soil during the previous three decades.[5] Thus at the end of 1525 Machiavelli was discussing with Guicciardini the *historical* resonances within a great *comedy* of the *tragic* situation of Italy.[6] Let me add here that Machiavelli was beginning to conceive of this national tragedy as a kind of historical fate or necessity: consider the citation to Guicciardini, in the same letter, of Dante *Purgatorio* 20.86–87, in which the suffering of the papacy at the hands of the Capetian monarchs of France is prophesied by Hugh Capet, the ancestor of the French dynasty, in language evoking the passion of Christ. This perception of history as inexorable nemesis as well as the genre of historical lament (*lamento storico*) exemplified by Dante's text also has tragic potential. I will return to these topics at the end of my essay.

Some ten years before his letter to Guicciardini, Machiavelli had participated in the meetings in Bernardo Rucellai's gardens in his Florentine villa, the Orti Oricellari. There Machiavelli came into contact with a wide spectrum of political and artistic opinion, joining in urgent debates over the question of the constitution of Florence.[7] A sporadic, restless Medicean, Bernardo and his son Giovanni were not above tolerating anti-Medicean views in the garden, and in 1522 the conversations ceased after members were implicated in the conspiracy against Cardinal Giulio de' Medici (although Machiavelli not among them). For my purposes, it is interesting that many of the Oricellarians, present and past, were playwrights, some of them tragedians: Luigi Alamanni, a principal conspirator, would during his exile translate Sophocles' *Antigone;* Iacopo Nardi wrote several comedies, and Giovanni Rucellai, Bernardo's son and sometime host in the Orti, was, with Giangiorgio Trissino—another sometime Oricellarian—among the earliest to attempt regular classical forms with his tragedy about the Gepid princess *Rosmunda* (1515), based on a barbaric episode that Machiavelli was to include in his *Florentine Histories* (1.8).[8] Bernardo was for his own part a historian, and his account of the French invasions set the fashion of dating Italian misfortunes from the cardinal year of 1494, as in the opening chapters of Guicciardini's *History of Italy.*[9] As we will see, Machiavelli himself adopts such dating in his two original plays. Without oversimplifying the variety of political ideas among the several generations of Oricellarians, how close was Machiavelli to one or another of the Oricellarians in his dramatic ideas?

Like Machiavelli, who spent the years of his attendance at the Orti gatherings writing his *Discourses on Livy,* two of the Oricellari tragedians, Trissino and Ludovico Martelli, chose texts from Livy for tragedies: Trissino the tale of Sophonisba, a classic by virtue of Petrarch's two treatments of it, and Martelli the account of the murder of Servius Tullius by the Tarquins for his *Tullia.*[10] Not merely the imitation of a classical text is in question, but the gesture of meditating on Roman origins in order to stimulate political reflection on post-1494 Italy.[11] From this vantage point, the suicide of Sophonisba that concludes Trissino's tragedy has been taken by several readers as a gesture of resistance to enslavement by superior force and referred to the circumstances of Italy; if on the mark, such a characterization of the queen seriously revises Livy, whose seductive Sophonisba is an inveterate enemy of Rome.[12] Martelli's *Tullia* also transforms Livy by imposing the plot of Sophocles' *Electra* on the historian's account and making the result a parable of Italy expecting her deliverer, rather than the preamble to the expulsion of the Tarquins, as it functions in the historian's text: Sophocles' Orestes becomes in Martelli's play the exiled, much-awaited husband Lucio Tarquinio.[13] For the neofeudal Medicean Martelli, the deliverer of Italy should have been Giovanni delle Bande Nere, the mercenary captain from a cadet branch of the Medici; as events fell out, Martelli, who died before 1530, seems to herald with his tragedy the epoch of Duke Cosimo de' Medici and the solution by despotic force, imposed in part by a deus ex machina, Romulus *pater patriae* in the play, Emperor Charles V on the historical stage.[14]

But it is not these Livy-inspired tragedies that are closest to Machiavelli's manner, although the topic of the much-expected external deliverer will return to concern us later. Riccardo Bruscagli has argued that Rucellai's *Rosmunda* pioneers the adaptation of Machiavellian ideas to the Italian stage. Expressed by ruthless tyrants and devious counselors, these ideas had become by midcentury the stock-in-trade of conventional anti-Machiavellianism, as in G. B. Giraldi Cinthio's *Orbecche*.[15] The pronouncements by Rucellai's tyrannical Alboino, in praise of cruelty in maintaining power, indeed resonate with Machiavelli's realpolitik in *The Prince*. But Bruscagli underestimates the influence on both Rucellai and Machiavelli of already theatricalized Senecan treatments of tyranny: the language of Rucellai's play could have more easily come from the pseudo-Senecan *Octavia* (itself a *fabula praetexta* drawn, like Rucellai's tragedy, from history rather than myth) than from chronologically unlikely conversations with the Florentine secretary.[16] Nevertheless, that Rucellai and Machiavelli were entertaining similar conceptions is very probable, and on at least one occasion a direct borrowing by Machiavelli from *Rosmunda* is arguable. Late in Rucellai's tragedy, Rosmunda's suitor, Almachilde, summarizes the array of forces pushing Rosmunda to marry her father's killer, Alboino: "Her servitude, fear for her honor, / the threats of the King; her ardent love / for me; and good Falisco was the go-between" (4.49–51). This is adapted, with a characteristically sardonic twist, by Machiavelli in *Mandragola,* when Lucrezia enumerates the corrupting forces that have bent her will to Callimaco's bidding: "Now that your guile, the stupidity of my husband, the naivete of my mother, and the wickedness of my confessor have led me . . . " (5.4).[17] If Machiavelli has adapted a passage from a contemporary vernacular tragedy to his comedy, it may not be out of place to make a more detailed examination of *Mandragola* and *Clizia* in relation to early cinquecento tragedy.

That Machiavelli pays scrupulous attention to the so-called dramatic unities in his original comedies has long been remarked. Most significantly, both works are compassed within a span of twenty-four hours or slightly more, as Aristotle had prescribed — but for tragedies, not comedies.[18] Also suggestive of tragic conventions is Machiavelli's concealment, in both plays, of the denouement behind closed doors, so that it must be related in detail by a messenger. Because in both cases the sexually "obscene" events related allude to tragic gestures (see below), a comic invocation of the Horatian proscription of onstage violence seems clear.[19] And both plays, as if exploiting Horace's concession that comic diction may sporadically rise to tragic eloquence,[20] contain clear parodies of tragic episodes. As several readers have seen, *Mandragola* parodies in its plot Livy's account of the suicide of Lucretia, whose aftermath, ably managed by Lucius Junius Brutus, led to the expulsion of the Tarquins and the establishment of the Roman republic,[21] concluding the series of outrages — including those of Tullia — that made Livy compare the Tarquins to the families of Greek tragedy.[22] *Clizia* in turn, as if recalling Lucretia's knife wielding in Livy, feigns a shift into tragedy when Clizia, the never-seen "virgo," is falsely reported to have seized a knife and threatened both Pirro and Nicomaco with death.[23] This moment is recalled in the climactic attempt of Nicomaco to substitute himself in Clizia's bed on her bridal night: when the servingman Siro, who has replaced Clizia, pokes his erect member into Nicomaco's flanks, he evokes memories of the nuptial-night murder of bridegrooms like those of the Danaids in Greek myth or of the Roman matrons in Livy's history.[24] Siro's feigned sodomitic assault also recalls the tragic parody of *Mandragola*: Nicomaco is "stabbed" in bed by Siro, as Sextus threatens to stab Lucretia unless she yields to his will.[25]

In *Clizia*, of course, Machiavelli's mock-tragic passages echo the source, Plautus's *Casina*, whose editors have suggested verbal parallels for Casina's madness in a lost *Andromache* by Ennius.[26] But the importance of the mock-tragic episode to the final trick makes it unlikely that Machiavelli was passively following his source here. Like one of the Boccaccian *novelle* that it draws from, the tale of Nicomaco and Pirro (*Decameron* 7.9), *Clizia* concludes with the humiliation and scapegoating of the old man, leaving him socially exposed and unredeemed.[27]

Mandragola too, in addition to its central parody of the tragic tale of Lucretia, includes fictive tragic episodes that are nevertheless part of the play's verbal and imaginary world: the supposed death of the "garzonaccio" who is to absorb the virulence of the poisonous mandrake and the "throwing away" of an "unborn piece of flesh" in the abortion scheme proposed to Timoteo to test his pliancy before criminal suggestions are specters of an easy ruthlessness lurking behind the jollity.[28] In this respect the name *Mandragola* itself has a cardinal role to play and suggests how Machiavelli's play is conceived as the evasion or, better, the privation of tragedy. As the author of *The Ass*, a work contemporary with the play, Machiavelli knew that in Apuleius's novel a benign physician substitutes mandrake for the poison requested by a murderous stepmother in order to frustrate her intent and subsequently accuse her before the authorities.[29] Thus, for Apuleius, the mandrake causes a false image of death that tricks the plot out of a tragic outcome; in Machiavelli's play, by contrast, the fiction of a lethal "mandragola" masks the play's real virulence, what Ezio Raimondi called "the poison of *Mandragola*": its withering reflection on Florentine corruption and fecklessness.[30] In fact, Machiavelli's disap-

pointment before the failure of republican ideals — signified in the comedy by
the *absence* of a heroic Lucretian sacrifice that might restore Florentine courage — is reiterated years later in another letter to Guicciardini (December 19,
1525), a letter in which no hope is seen for heroic resistance to the depredation
of Italy: "In short my conclusion is that this gang here will never ever do
anything honorable and bold worth living or dying for. I observe so much fear
in the citizens of Florence and such disinclination to offer any opposition to
whoever is preparing to devour us — and I see no exception to my conclusion."[31] It could be said Machiavelli's disappointment is precisely that his
Mandragola cannot be a tragedy. Whereas for Livy the Tarquins provided for
Rome a tragic royal house comparable to the Cadmeids and Atreides of Greek
tragedy and thus paradoxically brought about the "cure" of Rome through the
revolution led by Brutus, Machiavelli's implication is that the corruption of
the house of Calfucci, as of the citizenry in general, renders unthinkable the
tragic catharsis of the Florentine civic body. Thus, Machiavelli withholds from
his unworthy audience any but a parodic view of a tragic icon like Lucretia.[32]
In this sense the traditional purgative properties of mandrake make of the
play's title a bitter joke indeed, a metatheatrical reflection on the impossibility
of both tragic action and political renewal.[33]

But that such a purgative power was thought to potentially inhere in the
episode from Livy is beyond doubt. Lucretia's suicide was one of the repertory
of visual topics of revolution and tyrannicide that Florentines had drawn on as
a stimulus to resistance first of the Visconti and subsequently (between 1494
and 1512 and again in 1527–30) of the Medici themselves; in the terms of
Machiavelli's *Discourses* 3.26, the aftermath of Lucretia's rape typifies how
violence against women precipitates revolution in the state.[34] The finest sur-
viving image of the story of Lucretia is Botticelli's *spalliera* painting (usually
placed in the late 1490s) representing Brutus displaying the body of Lucretia
to the weeping citizens of Collatia, thus immediately before he uses her example to shame them into revolutionary bravery. Illustrated on the triumphal
arch behind the ostentation of Lucretia's body as well as on the friezes of
flanking buildings are other exempla of Roman republican heroism — Hora-
tius at the bridge, Mucius Scaevola before Lars Porsenna — as well as the
biblical patrons of Florentine liberty, David on a pillar, surmounting Goliath,
and Judith with the head of Holophernes on the left building frieze, of whom
more in a moment.[35] It is thus relevant that art historians have long associated
the Lucretia panel with the Vitruvian tragic scene divulged and canonized by
Serlio's volume. For early cinquecento Florentines, the death of Lucretia was
an established tragic icon, inviting to revolution and tyrannicide, complete
with a stage set rendered in the purest classicism available.[36]

The fashioning of a tragic icon had indeed already been exploited as a theatrical device by Machiavelli's fellow Oricellarians Trissino and Rucellai. Giulio Ferroni has emphasized how Trissino, in the preface to his *Sophonisba,* justifies the use of vernacular so that the tragic plot, the *mythos* or *fabula,* may be made more accessible to the audience. Trissino's vernacular rhetoric thus becomes the vehicle not only of what Aristotle called *dianoia,* which Trissino rendered as "discourse," and held to be essential for a tragedy of pathos like his *Sophonisba,* but of the spectacular aspect of drama, what Aristotle called *opsis.*[37] Cut off from a concept of tragic gesture—a failing that Marco Ariani has suggested profoundly hampered the histrionic range of Italian cinquecento tragedy—tragic *dianoia,* which Aristotle thought of as including political as well as rhetorical speech, is theorized by Trissino as descriptive rhetoric, again accenting visual imagery.[38] Such was, in any case, already the rhetorical tradition that Trissino inherited regarding Sophonisba, of whom Petrarch had given a famously elaborate verbal description in the *Africa.*[39] Trissino's accentuation of the visual is not entirely un-Aristotelian, however: in the *Poetics* Aristotle illustrates the most important part of tragedy, the plot, with analogies drawn from painting. And indeed the most important part of the plot, the recognition, is dominantly, though not exclusively, visual in character.[40]

Thus Trissino's tragic spectacle could count on, as Machiavelli's was to do, the preexistence of a well-engraved memory-image, at once rhetorical and iconographic, of tragic action. But Trissino's account of Sophonisba's dramatic gesture—unhesitatingly drinking off the poisoned cup Massinissa sends that she might evade display in a Roman triumph—was based not only on memories of Petrarch and Livy but on the contemporary cult of Sophonisba by Isabella d'Este, who had a grisaille of Sophonisba's suicide painted by Andrea Mantegna for her rooms in Mantua.[41] Thus when Ferroni berates Trissino for botching the gesture by delaying the queen's use of the cup, he overlooks how Trissino interrupts the suicide much as a cadenza delays the final chord in tonal music; the several hundred lines adapted from Euripides' *Alcestis* have an encomiastic purpose, showing a Sophonisba not only courageous and realistic, but affectionate, responsible, pious, and humane as well. For Trissino is doing more than refreshing an established image in a humanist key:[42] like the subsequent *blason*-portrait in his *Ritratti* of 1524 (also the publication date of the tragedy), Trissino's Sophonisba is a homage to Isabella herself, a rhetorical pendant to Mantegna's grisaille, offered perhaps as exemplary of the suitably heroic riposte to conquest by a foreign power.[43]

Rucellai's emphasis on tragic iconicity in *Rosmunda* is more concise and no less forceful and consistent with Rucellai's use of description, indeed formal ekphrasis, in his other tragedy, *Oreste.*[44] *Rosmunda* is arranged around two narrated scenes of tragic action, one of psychological, one of real violence (the second, of course, only narrated). The first scene includes Alboino's insistence that Rosmunda drink of the cup shaped from her father's skull and her compliance: "le labra al teschio pose" (she placed her lips on the skull, 4.140). The verse evokes *Inferno* 33.128–32, in which Ugolino places his mouth on the head of his adversary, Ruggiero, to gnaw at his skull: "li denti e l'altro pose / ... al teschio e l'altre cose" (he put his teeth to the other / ... to the skull and the other things); the pilgrim's sight of Ugolino, which he labels a "bestial segno" (bestial sign, 33.133), is itself recalled in the Counselor's horrified response: "tu narri una cosa da fere" (you tell of something bestial, 4.134).[45] The spectacular dimension of Rosmunda's ordeal is thus underscored by summoning to memory the most brutal scene in Dante's poem, one traditionally thought fully tragic even in medieval terms.[46]

Rosmunda's drink, the bitter cup ("amara tazza") of the tyrant's oppression of his wife, is then promptly avenged by the death of Alboino at the hands of Almachilde, who, dressed as a woman, decapitates the tyrant and retrieves his head — precisely as the biblical Judith, under the guise of amorous sport, compasses the seduction and decapitation of Holophernes.[47] The biblical reference justifies the tyrannicide and inserts the event in the Florentine repertory of civic icons, among which Judith held a place of honor, as we saw. Rucellai, a Medicean, would have conceived his tragedy as a call to repel the barbarians, an ambition that although not strictly current in the explicitly pacifist tenure of Leo X had been the principal rallying cry of Italian revanchism during the previous pontificate of Julius II and regained relevance after the battle of Marignano (1515), in which the French expelled the Swiss from Italy and exposed the inability of the pope to defend Milan from attack. From a Medicean perspective the barbarians would of course be the Swiss and Germans, not the French that had infuriated Julius.[48]

Which brings us to Machiavelli the historian. We saw that, like Rucellai, Machiavelli drew on the fierce tale of Rosmunda and Alboino as he began writing his *Florentine Histories* in the 1520s.[49] The placement of the episode seems both ominous and pivotal, for it immediately follows the expulsion of the Goths by Belisarius and Justinian that was to become the ideal pattern for driving invaders from Italy,[50] and immediately precedes Machiavelli's analysis (1.9) that it was the rise of the papacy, favored by the fragmentation of Italy upon the Lombard invasions, that led to the contemporary ruin of Italy. In a radical turnaround of the tale of Lucretia, whose outraged chastity galvanized Romans to depose a tyrant, Machiavelli emphasizes, as Rucellai had not, Queen Rosmunda's ruthless sexual blackmail: having substituted herself for the girl Elmelchilde expected to find in his bed, she gives him the choice of murdering Alboino and assuming the throne or facing death for having out-raged the queen. So fierce and so desperate are the expedients necessary to repel invaders—and they fail in the end.[51]

Whereas Guicciardini chose to begin his history of Italy by leading up to the disastrous year 1494 and continue until the pacification of Italy after the Peace of Cambrai (1529) and the death of Clement VII (1534), Machiavelli made the dissolution of the Laurentian balance of power (1492) the final act of his Florentine history. He concludes, "Immediately Lorenzo was dead, those bad seeds began to grow which, not long after, there being no one alive who knew how to quell them, ruined and still ruin Italy" (8.36). Machiavelli has Calli-maco and Nicomaco echo these formulas in his plays (*Mandragola* 1.1, *Clizia* 1.1), for in the comedies it is the unpredictable fortunes of war that set com-plex plots in motion: Callimaco continues his Parisian sojourn to avoid the invasion of Charles VIII, "which ruined that province," while Clizia, found among the spoils of Charles's sack of Naples in the following year, is lost again as the French king's return across the Alps was harassed at the crossing of the Taro. Such allusions provide a kind of textual perspective in which comic foregrounds spring from and are juxtaposed to the tragic background of the historical record.

Because for Renaissance thinkers history was seen as largely dominated by Fortune, it had a traditional tragic structure that Machiavelli was to develop in his historical and political writing: indeed the techniques, scenes, and imagery of tragedy—tyrants, reversals of fortune, stunning acts of cruelty, prophetic dreams and visions, bitter laments—were conspicuous in historical writing during the period of the Italian crises, often with explicit invocation of tragic form.[52] In Machiavelli's *Florentine Histories,* the Florence of Dante and the early chroniclers,[53] plunged into civic strife on the murder of Buondelmonti, is finally pacified and unified under the authority of the Medici—this much is clear in Machiavelli's dedicatory epistle to Clement VII, who commissioned the work. In the text, Machiavelli takes pains to juxtapose two extreme types of government that characteristically failed in Florence and in Italy: revolu-tionary republicanism (the type that reflects Machiavelli's deepest idealism) and tyranny. For Machiavelli, both of these types begin and end with sudden reversals of Fortune. Thus the ill-organized class revolt of the Ciompi and the self-deluded republican insurgencies of Niccolò Cola di Rienzo and Stefano Porcari in Rome; and on the other hand, the despotisms of Charles of Calabria and the duke of Athens.

In the *Histories* as in the earlier *Prince,* however, Machiavelli is fascinated above all by the external despot, or condottiere, who challenges the autonomy of Florence and exposes the weakness of its constitution. He reserves his closest attention for such figures as Castruccio Castracani and Cesare Borgia, the duke Valentino, whose ambitions regarding Florence remained darkly ambiguous but whose lightning success at forming a state in central Italy in 1500–03 was considered by Machiavelli both a model and a warning to the Florentines and Valentino himself potentially the type both of the redeemer and the tyrant. For Machiavelli such figures both embodied and were themselves subject to the mystified principles of Fortune and necessity. As such, they were preselected to be actors on a tragic stage, where Fortune raised and ruined the mighty at her whim.[54]

Of course the whims of Fortuna had been the fundamental, almost the exclusive, characteristic of the medieval conception of tragedy and would continue to figure as a prominent subject in Renaissance theories of tragedy. Chaucer's sixteen narrative "tragedyes" in the *Monk's Tale* ("I wol biwaille, in manere of tragedie") include the tale of Dante's Ugolino, which, we saw, itself exhibits canonical tragic subject matter by medieval standards: cannibalism and the sacrifice of young children (with echoes of Seneca to boot): but in every case the principal tragic feature is the revolution of Fortune's wheel, bringing low the great and mighty ("thanne wayteth she her man to overthrowe").[55] Raimondi demonstrates in his reading of Albertino Mussato's *Ecerinis* how the principle of Fortuna's rule, which had such a fertile Renaissance progeny, organizes that Latin prototragedy; the concept of *Fortuna* itself, of course, left its mark on the theorists of tragedy later in the cinquecento.[56] Both the humanist Latin tradition and the series of classically correct vernacular tragedies initiated with the plays of Trissino and Rucellai drew their concept of Fortuna in part from Seneca (especially the pseudo-Senecan *Octavia*) and in part from the humanist tradition of moralizing biography made popular by Boccaccio (*De casibus virorum illustrium, De claris mulieribus*) and Petrarch (*De remediis utriusque fortunae*).[57] To mention an instance that will be significant later, near the conclusion of Boccaccio's *De casibus,* the narrator sees, in nearly last place among Fortune's victims, Dante: the proud exile has no time for his own misfortunes and points instead to the disastrous effects on Florence of the mercenary French despot the duke of Athens. Machiavelli's reflections on the struggle of Fortuna and *virtù* emerge, though of course only in part, from these traditions; indeed his narratives of success followed by abject defeat draw on the same defensive psychology as the medieval narratives, even if they reconceptualize the terms of the struggle to those of a timeless heroic agon against fortune and Nature, as Barberi-Squarotti argues. If they leave out the explicit moralizing, they retain the potential for visual representation in drama.[58]

Thus Machiavelli's sample for the commission of the *Histories* was the tale of Castruccio Castracani, the condottiere who became the tyrant of Lucca and, militarily, ran the Florentines ragged for a decade. Addressing the story to the former Oricellarians Zanobi Buondelmonti and Luigi Alamanni, Machiavelli takes well-known liberties with the historical record to fashion the biography as an exemplum of Fortuna's whimsical work, as Castruccio is first raised from obscurity to fame and success and then undone by a chill caught as he gazes over the field of his most complete (and fictional) victory over the Florentines.[59] For Machiavelli, the account of Castracani stages the play of forces that every such agent must consider and hope to avoid if full success is to be achieved. But, with almost medieval inevitability, the fragility of the body or a small oversight is enough to undo the achievements of virtù in the heroic struggle against a malicious Fortuna.

Although Franco Gaeta suggests that Castruccio most resembles the Prospero Colonna of *The Art of War,* the story of the Lucchese condottiere also evokes the figure that more than any other held Machiavelli's fascination over the decades: Duke Valentino, Cesare Borgia, who appears in *The Prince* as an explicit example of the heroic agonism of virtue against fortune.[60] Machiavelli made numerous recensions of Borgia's biography, drawing for his account in *The Prince* from his copious *Legations* to the Florentine *Dieci di libertà* (also known as the *Dieci di Balìa* [Ten of war]), written during his tenure as Florentine legate to Valentino's mobile court.[61] In its brief brilliance Borgia's rush for mastery of the world's game was even more the stuff of tragic Fortune than that of Castracani, especially given the set of circumstances that brought about his fall: the fact that he and his father, Rodrigo Borgia, Pope Alexander VI, fell ill at the same time. Since the pope was bankrolling his son, with Alexander's death Cesare's power rapidly withered; and as he himself was incapacitated there was little he could do to break his own fall.[62] Guicciardini would later relate that the Borgias fell victim to their own misdirected poisons, giving to their ruin the pattern of nemesis.[63] Although this aspect is not explicit in *The Prince,* Machiavelli, who does emphasize Cesare's regret at not foreseeing the circumstances that defeated him, was undoubtedly aware of it.[64]

But it is not merely in his rapid rise and fall that we can identify tragic aspects to Borgia's career: Machiavelli documents with evident admiration Borgia's scapegoating of his effective, but overly harsh lieutenant-general for the Marches, Remirro dell'Orca.[65] Choosing the moment just before the populace was goaded to revolt, Borgia had Remirro imprisoned, killed, and discovered neatly sawn in half in the main square of Cesena on the morning of the day after Christmas. The spectacle of the butcher butchered astonished the citizens of Cesena, who were both gratified and terrified by the specter of violence that could check, indeed overmatch, that of Remirro himself. But they remained pacified by the execution of their tormentor, as if he had indeed been the "orca" (ogre) of fable: "The ferocity of which spectacle rendered that population at once satisfied and astonished." Though painfully real, Remirro's death is also a sign pointing to a fiercer and more powerful agent behind him, one who had held his life in the balance.[66] But this was also the very irony that would defeat Cesare: the background forces of Fortune and Nature that he could not hope to fully control. Thus the episode, whose conscious theatricality has been often remarked,[67] functions in ways later theoreticians would describe as the psychological mechanism of tragic catharsis: a spectacular event that by virtue of being a staged representation leads to the discharge of awe and terror that is yet pleasurable and instructive.[68]

This same implicit logic informs another of Valentino's tricks, one that also ironically adumbrates his own fall. The episode was excerpted by Machiavelli for special treatment as the *Description of the Way Duke Valentino Killed Vitellozzo Vitelli, Oliverotto da Fermo, Signor Pagolo, and the Duke of Gravina Orsini.* A narrative some eight pages long in a modern edition,[69] it is masterful in its focus, not only tragic in structure but articulated with tragic topics and imbued at appropriate moments with a tragic mood. Given how closely he had followed events as they unfolded, Machiavelli was likely aware of the dramatization made of these and related events in a historical play, produced at Urbino on February 19, 1504, barely a year after Valentino's coup.[70] The spectacle may have influenced Machiavelli's decision to shape his account — which editors place as early as 1504 — in ways that put the reader in mind of tragic form.

Although there is no question of detecting tragic unities in the *Description* (the sequence of events occupies several months), Machiavelli's rearrangement of some historical data makes it clear that he was firming up the logic of the "plot": thus the fall of Rocca San Leo to Guidobaldo da Montefeltro occurs immediately after, rather than before, the diet of Mangona, where the Vitelli and Orsini, hitherto allied with Borgia, gather to worry about his power and decide to check it; the vicissitudes of the pinnacle-fortress, soon recaptured by Borgia, foreshadow the decisive role of the fortress of Sinigaglia, where the final events will take place. The action can be summarized in a sentence: Borgia lays a trap for his faithless allies and, after luring them into a position of vulnerability with shows of reconciliation, springs the trap and kills them. Thus the whole episode revolves around the question of the "faith of princes" and its reliability,[71] a topic that, as Bruscagli argues, is also central to the plot of Giraldi Cinthio's influential *Orbecche* (1541), where it is discussed in strikingly Machiavellian terms.[72]

Especially brilliant is Borgia's exploitation of the Vitelli and Orsini offer to join forces "either for the venture of Tuscany, since they were for that; and if not, they would proceed to the reduction of Sinigaglia." Choosing Sinigaglia, the duke appears merely to respond to an overture, a demonstration of passivity that deceives his enemies into thinking they hold the initiative. Equally deceptive is Borgia's parading of the rhetoric of fidelity and friendship, which persuades his prey to walk into his trap despite their misgivings. Here Vitellozzo breaks a cardinal rule laid down by Machiavelli in the text (and echoing his advice elsewhere): Never trust a prince or a people to whom one has previously done injury.[73] Between Borgia's ruse and Vitellozzo's error, the outcome is foreordained.

At this point in the text, Machiavelli begins to draw the net closed, both with regard to Borgia's plot and in terms of his own narrative: thus there is a textual mimesis here of the onset of tragic necessity. For the first time, Machiavelli dates the events (December 30), narrowing the temporal scope to the two days before the final act in Sinigaglia. In the next paragraph, he describes the physical approach to the city as a narrowing funnel, with the road hemmed in on the one side by the sea, on the other by mountains, while the entrance to the citadel itself is enclosed by a piazza surrounded on one side by buildings, by the river on the other.[74] Between these gestures of temporal and spatial constriction Machiavelli inserts a backdrop of historical perspective: he imagines Borgia and his troops on the very last day of 1502, December 31, on the banks of the Metauro, five miles from Fano. Why mention this river, notorious in the annals of Roman history as the site where Roman legions destroyed Hamilcar Barca and the Carthaginian army during the Second Punic War? One editor suggests the allusion underscores Borgia as an *imperator* in the making. I would argue that Machiavelli here evokes a moment of fateful decision and crisis, thus, as so often, juxtaposing current events to the heroic annals of notably successful Republican Rome. But though in one sense the allusion places Borgia in a heroic frame, it is left to the reader whether to place the Catalan Borgia with the victorious Romans or with the ultimately doomed Carthaginians.[75] Borgia's role remains ambiguous, which provides some ironic distancing from his exploit—although telegraphing the eventual defeat of Borgia himself is not the purpose of this text.

What follows, too, is tragic in action and in the commonplace of tragic premonition: Vitellozzo arrives at the place of his betrayal and death disarmed, "with a cloak lined in green, afflicted as if he was aware of his future death. . . . and it is said that when he left his people to come to Sinigaglia and go to the Duke, he made a kind of final departure from them." To be sure, as editors point out, Vitellozzo's farewells recall those of characters in Plutarch's *Lives* who foretell disaster; but analogous premonitions, sometimes in the form of nightmarish prophetic dreams, are topics of Senecan tragedy routinely adopted in the vernacular tragedies of the cinquecento: both of the "new" vernacular tragedies, *Sophonisba* and *Rosmunda,* begin with such dreams.[76] Pathetic farewells, too, constellate the tragic stage. Trissino's tragedy concludes with the queen's tender leave-takings of her retinue, a scene emulated in Lodovico Dolce's *Marianna* (1565), among other examples.

In the last paragraph of his text, Machiavelli, like the messenger of classical tragedy, relates the final moments of Vitellozzo and Liverotto, who are taken to a secret room (offstage, as it were) and strangled. Machiavelli then adds that after an interval of eighteen days, subsequent to arrests made in Rome, the other principals, Pagolo Vitelli and the duke of Gravina, were also strangled. Once again a date serves to nail down the event, and our sense of how the conspirators have been checked is hammered home by the final word in the text: "strangolati." To Guicciardini, describing later the events of December 31, it fell only to apply the suitable generic label: "The next day, which was the last day of December, so that the year of fifteen hundred and five should end with this tragedy, [Cesare] had Vitellozzo and Liverotto strangled in a chamber."[77]

More important than the use of such tragic apparatus as the anticipation of death and the leave-takings is Machiavelli's apparent wish to study how a set of circumstances is guided and shaped by the virtù of Borgia so that the options of his adversaries are reduced to zero; in other words, how events are seized by a kind of historical necessity working through its (temporary) agent, Borgia. This daemonic aspect of Borgia's career fascinated Machiavelli, and, just as important, it is this aspect that corresponds to the effect of the tragic "marvelous" — later to be advocated by Aristotelian theorists as a necessary ingredient of the reversal and recognition scenes.[78] For Machiavelli, that the pity and fear of his audience will be engaged is guaranteed largely by his emphasis on the relevance of Borgia to Florentine politics, as both example and threat. The Florentine reader can never forget that Borgia might at any moment level his ambitious gaze on Florence: it is thus no accident that Machiavelli recalls the alternative to Sinigaglia offered to Borgia, the "impresa di Toscana." Indeed, from the first textual detail — Borgia's trip to Lombardy to clear himself of Florentine accusations — to the last — one of the men seized at Rome by Alexander is the archbishop of Florence — Machiavelli keeps the Florentine context in mind, just as he had necessarily addressed his reports on Cesare to the *Dieci di libertà.* In one sense Machiavelli makes it easy for sympathies to run with Cesare, given the reminder of Paolo Vitelli's execution in 1499 by the Florentines for his betrayal during the war with Pisa. Yet, with the baseless claim that the Florentines promised Cesare support against the Vitelli and Orsini, Machiavelli distorts a record he himself had helped to write, adding even that this imaginary comfort was brought to Cesare by Niccolò Machiavelli himself. It seems our author can be as perfidious as his subjects.

But this documentary perfidy has an artistic purpose, in that the Florentine reader, alerted by the testimony of Machiavelli himself, is brought to closely consider the consequences of dealing with Cesare Borgia. Let the Florentines, like the Cesenati, take note.

Arguably, Machiavelli's role as the eyewitness of Borgia's rise and fall helped warrant his assumption of the role of tragic choragus when he came to consider the situation of Italy at the end of *The Prince:* indeed, as we will see, Machiavelli resumed a traditional rhetorical posture, going back to the time of Dante, of chief mourner of Italian political subjugation. But Machiavelli did not wait until *The Prince* to reflect, however subtly, on the ironies of Borgia's own fall. As I have anticipated, Borgia too is trapped in the net of Fortune, whose design it was that he and his father should have become sick on the same day. In the *Decennials,* contemporary with the *Description* (1504), unflattering language, very different from that of *The Prince,* is used of the deceiver of Sinigaglia.[79] Using terza rima, Machiavelli's language veers into the Dantesque and snatches language from the *Inferno* — the belimed devils ("Malebranche") in the Malebolge, for example, evoked by words like "ghermire" and "unghioni" (grapple, claws) (see *Inferno* 22.69, 138) — to describe the plotting of Valentino and his former allies against each other. The seductive Catalan is compared to a basilisk, whistling Vitelli and Orsini victims into his net (again in terms — "fischio," "vischio" [whistle, birdlime] — that evoke *Inferno* 22.104 and 144, where Dante uses "suffolare" and "inviscare" [whisper, belime], respectively). In this vision, Borgia and his victims are reduced to the same level of bestiality, indeed to the Aesopic terms of the mouse, the frog, and the kite that Dante invokes for his tricked-trickster devils. In that fable, the struggling of the mouse when the frog perfidiously attempts to drown it attracts the kite's attention, fatal for both smaller animals. Borgia thus degraded, it becomes clear that the focus of tragic interest in the first *Decennial* is less on the human actors than on the subject mentioned near its beginning, personified Italy ravaged by barbarian invasion:

> quando in sè discordante Italia aperse
> la via a' Galli, e quando esser calpesta
> da le genti barbariche sofferse. (16–18)

> [when in conflict with herself Italy opened
> the way to the Gauls, and when she suffered
> herself to be trampled by the barbarian peoples]

With lines like these, Machiavelli was picking up a traditional refrain of lament for the suffering of Italy, a refrain that will lead me back to the letter to Guicciardini of October 21, 1525.

First, however, let me note that Machiavelli's persisting interest in Borgia's depredation of Urbino was itself ominous, given the role that the dedicatee of *The Prince,* Lorenzo de' Medici, was to play as the usurping duke of Urbino upon the accession of Giovanni de' Medici as Pope Leo X in 1516. Urbino, recurringly the pawn of papal imperialism in the early cinquecento, functions in Machiavelli's political writing like the small hinge on which turns the destiny of greater Italy. It is thus fitting that Urbino should furnish the link for reconnecting my argument with that refrain of political lament I noted above of Boccaccio's Dante in the train of Fortune. Speaking, in the same first *Decennial,* of Cesare as a hydra (v. 404), Machiavelli anticipates Nicola Grasso's use of the same description in *Eutichia,* one of the plays offered during the Urbino carnival of 1513.[80] A companion piece to the brilliant *Calandria* by Bernardo Dovizi da Bibbiena, Grasso's comedy (the Greek name suggests "good fortune") is furnished with a plot springing from Borgia's depredation of Urbino in 1502; the play was also punctuated with *intermezzi* that portrayed the trials of Urbino besieged by Cesare but ultimately redeemed by the house of Montefeltro.[81] Even the *Calandria* itself was staged with *intermezzi* that Baldassare Castiglione, who produced the theatrical festivities at the Urbino carnival, interpreted as alluding to the tragedy of Italy; and Castiglione himself appended to the *intermezzi* of Grasso's play seven octaves on the misfortunes of Italy that might have functioned as a chorus for a contemporary tragedy.[82]

But tragedy, as Walter Benjamin observed, "is a preliminary stage of prophecy." If in 1504 Machiavelli could look back across the decade to the first invasions of 1494 and draw the sorry implications of Italian disunity, in his letter to Guicciardini of October 21, 1525, it was toward a new, future crisis that he bent his powers of political prognostication. Musing on the recent fall of Milan to imperial forces, Machiavelli cites the words of Dante's Hugh Capet on the crimes of the Capetian house; but whereas Hugh's vaticination is *ex eventu,* Machiavelli offers an authentic prophecy of the fall of Rome and the capture of Clement VII, Christ's vicar, by the army of Charles under the constable de Bourbon, which would occur after Machiavelli's death in late June of 1527: "I see the fleur-de-lys return from Alagna / And in his vicar, etc." ["Christ is captured"].[83] Machiavelli prefaces his prophecy with reference, in Latin, to divine providence ("sic datum desuper" [thus given from above]), suggesting the irrevocability of events; his omission of the final words of the quotation underlines the oracular effect.[84]

In prophesying the fall of Rome and capture of the pope, Machiavelli was part of a trend, not only that of Grasso and Castiglione but one that finds echoes among contemporary Italian tragedies and the tragedians themselves. The plays of Trissino and Rucellai, though written about 1515, were published in

1524 and 1525, respectively, just as the greater crisis began to loom, in late April of 1524, with the loss of Milan to Bourbon's army. Among the Oricellarian tragedians, it was reported that in March of 1525 Rucellai, the castellan of Sant'Angelo, the pope's refuge during the future sack, pronounced from his deathbed the doom of the tightfisted Medici pope;[85] Martelli, despairing at the death of Giovanni delle Bande Nere, the city's — and Italy's — strongest hope of defense, fled both Florence and Rome for Naples, leaving poems in which he lamented the invasion of Italy by "Scythians and cannibals."[86] The year 1527 itself opened with a salvo of prophetic announcements, including one by Aretino as well as an illustration, conceived by Baldassare Peruzzi, of the papacy perched on the summit of Fortune's wheel, the direction of the wheel's movement being disputed between an angel and a devil.[87] Indeed, it is largely because of Machiavelli's analysis in the *Histories,* ironically dedicated to Clement VII himself, that the popes were to find themselves on the hot seat, so to speak, taxed as villains in the drama of Italy's suffering:[88] an analysis that dominated historical reflection until Alessandro Manzoni, with his tragedy *Adelchi* (1822), gave a neo-Guelph and pro-Catholic slant to the papal role in the history of Italy.

In quoting Dante's lines on the invasion of Italy and humiliation of the papacy, Machiavelli was aligning himself with a chorus of voices in drama, lyric, and journalism that were lamenting misfortunes past, passing, and to come. This literature of tragic anticipation is striking precisely for its sense of history as veering, with the approach of the constable's army, into tragic inexorability. Ten years earlier Machiavelli, in the "sublime rhetoric" of the last chapter of *The Prince,* had attempted to arouse the Medici to expel the barbarians; in other words, he had attempted to inspire the sense of fatedness, of an opportunity, or *kairós,* for the cause of defending Italy.[89] Where by 1525 the choruses of lament in lyric and tragedy sang the burden of what contemporaries would call "the end of Italy," Machiavelli in 1516–17 had used similar literary traditions to encourage active resistance. But the Petrarchan optimism was not, even then, without a vein of tragic pessimism: although Machiavelli explicitly cites Petrarch's rousing canzone "Italia mia" to conclude the final chapter of *The Prince,* his invitation, earlier in the chapter, to gaze on Italy calling for help ("be it seen how she begs God to send her someone who will redeem her from this barbaric cruelty and insult") alludes rather to Dante's display ("Come and see") of personified Rome calling on the emperor to rescue her ("My Caesar, why do you not keep me company").[90] As Dante's prayers in the *Purgatorio* went unanswered, by 1525 Machiavelli's voice had adopted fully the melancholy tone of Dante's abandoned Rome. Although it has been overlooked by readers of *The Prince,* Dante's personification of a widowed Italy tearfully calling for her redeemer, partially through its mediation by Machiavelli, was to become for the next four centuries the principal rhetorical device for expressing the anguish and vehemence of Italian irredentism.[91] Signing himself historian, comedian, and tragedian, Machiavelli foresaw all too well how the history of Italy was shaping itself into a tragic plot.

6

Lost in the Wilderness:
Love and Longing in L'Asino

MICHAEL HARVEY

One of the chief themes in Machiavelli's work is that the political actor must not be restrained by any sentimental tenderness, whether self-pity or compassion for others. The political actor must be able to act freely, without being checked by such qualms. The best political actor, Machiavelli insists, never takes off his armor. His startling condemnation of Cesare Borgia in *The Prince,* after almost a whole chapter of unstinting praise, can be understood from this perspective: in the end Machiavelli says Borgia fell because at one critical moment, after a lifetime of treachery, he was too soft, allowing sentiment and vanity to obscure his understanding of who his enemies were and how he had to treat them.[1]

The need for emotional imperviousness is the major reason that Machiavelli says great founders must be their own makers, with no family, no fathers, no ties to others that might make them vulnerable. And even if a political actor has such ties, he must learn to set them aside. One thinks of Junius Brutus, founder of the Roman republic, whose "severity" Machiavelli emphasizes in presiding over the trial and execution of his own sons.[2] This is, I think, the major psychological theme of Machiavelli's teaching — to harden men enough

I am grateful to Vickie Sullivan for generous and penetrating comments.

that they can, in effect, always wear their armor, or even let the armor become their very skin.[3]

Many critics have deplored this theme: "Have not all readers of Machiavelli," asked one, "felt how his heroes have no inside?"[4] It seems to many readers that Machiavelli, so intent on teaching his hard lessons, is oblivious to the psychological and moral costs to those who seek to live such lives and to those who are their victims. But this hollowness — or as Sheldon Wolin called it this "exteriorization of virtue" — is for all but the most inhuman of men achieved at great cost.[5] Machiavelli, I believe, understood this. There is a tremendous psychological toll exacted in living as a Machiavellian. Wolin remains one of the most eloquent critics of the suffering implicit in the Machiavellian actor: "Machiavelli has given us something more than a single-dimensional portrait of a power-hungry figure. What we have is a portrait of modern political man drawn with dramatic intensity: if there was heroism, there was also anguish; if there was creativity, there was also loneliness and uncertainty."[6]

Repeatedly, alongside his endless admonitions to act, one finds Machiavelli brooding over the falseness and inadequacy of appearance, over the stifling or loss of one's true self. Often one senses anguish beneath the surface of Machiavelli's writing, anguish over the very political life that he so persistently analyzed and advocated: "Let everyone flee from courts and governments," he says in "On Ingratitude," "for there is no road that sooner leads a man / to weep for what he wished, once he has it."[7] It is almost more than humans can bear, he hints, to live as he says they must live. In his thought such a pessimistic perspective never really triumphs, but it insinuates itself into all of his writing, undermining the directness and simplicity of his prescriptions and adding a note of postmodern doubt to his bold modernist voice.

The way that Machiavelli's troubled vision tends to struggle with itself is very much on display in *L'Asino,* his most complex, ambivalent, and moving work. Written with equal dollops of lyricism and didacticism, *L'Asino* is a poem with tightly interwoven themes: a sweet love story, a teasingly explicit sexual romp, a Dantesque pilgrimage of the weary soul, an epitome of Machiavellian political analysis and education, even a withering assault on the Machiavellian perspective itself. Comically echoing Dante, *L'Asino* works in part as a sly story of the redemption of manhood, albeit a redemption that has nothing to do with heaven and everything to do with the fall and rise of human things. The poem binds its disparate elements in part through its careful attention to one key Machiavellian term, *virtù. L'Asino* is largely built around this term, which occurs eleven times in a bundle of erotic, political, and moral senses.[8] The poem in a sense serves as a critical interrogation of Machiavellian virtù, juxtaposing stark and hopeful understandings of the term — and of Machiavelli's thought as a whole. Tracing the ups and downs of virtù, *L'Asino* can be read as a kind of Viagra for the soul.

The poem begins with braying laughter and ends with pathos and slapstick — a stinking, excrement-covered pig delivering a dour lecture on the superiority of life as an animal over that of a man. Machiavelli himself seems to peep out from the poem's verses, particularly in the identity of the poem's narrator, who is thrust into the poem's harsh landscape. Conclusions about *L'Asino* are tentative because of the poem's apparently unfinished state — it ends abruptly, before the events alluded to in the opening chapter ever take place. Its inconclusiveness has led most critics to emphasize an artistic disjunction between the lyrical first five chapters and the more didactic final three chapters. The argument has been made even that Machiavelli wrote the two portions of *L'Asino* at widely different times or that he wrote only a portion of the work, his son Guido, perhaps, writing the final three chapters.[9] But such conjectures lack any textual or historical basis and serve only (as they are meant to) to dismiss or diminish *L'Asino* as a significant text in Machiavelli's oeuvre.

I take a different tack. The poem's complexities and seeming indeterminacy seem to me to help constitute its meaning, part of what is in fact an artistic and thematic whole. The poem's main movement is the rehabilitation and education of its downcast narrator by a beautiful and mysterious woman. The woman articulates Machiavelli's own oft-expressed perspective on the necessity of action and violence. But *L'Asino* as it stands ends with what on its face seems to be a passionate renunciation of the woman's perspective. The poem, that is, gives us a defiant and rhetorically powerful last word which — because we know it is not the end of the story related in the poem and because it is put in the mouth of a very weak character — is really part of the text's essential irresoluteness, its inability to answer the question of virtù, of human worth. The lament of *L'Asino*, that human beings are "born naked of every defense" and that human life is filled with "pained and straining" weeping (8.121, 125), is a fundamental theme in Machiavelli's writings, just as surely as the poem's contention that brutality and struggle are burdens that human beings — or, more to Machiavelli's point, men — must bear.

L'Asino opens with a characteristic Machiavellian yoking of mordant humor and morose self-pity (Machiavelli never could live up to his advice against the indulgence of self-pity). The first lines promise a story of grief: "The varied chances, the pain and the grief / that under an Ass's form I suffered, / I shall sing, if fortune allows" (1.1–3). But right afterward the narrator also promises to spread the sound of braying and mocking laughter everywhere. Gratitude is deaf, he says, and so he expects nothing better than bites and blows. The rest of the first chapter is given over to a comic tale about a Florentine youth whose peculiar compulsion it is to run through the streets. Countless efforts to cure him through prayers and medicine fail, until one doctor promises to cure him. But that doctor too, a charlatan, fails as well: the boy, finding himself on the street one day, cannot restrain himself from yielding to his old compulsion, and he spends the rest of his life running headlong. The narrator — here Machiavelli peeps irresistibly out from the text — applies the moral to himself, saying that for a time he tried to cure himself of his mocking nature, but that now he will return to spilling venom and exposing the follies and failures of the world: "And whoever wants to take offense should loosen his belt" (1.121).

After this opening chapter the tone changes abruptly. The narrator describes a dark, rough wilderness into which he has fallen, and his despair at his situation. The allusion to the "dark wood" (selva oscura) in which Dante finds himself at the beginning of the *Inferno* is deliberate. Like Dante's journey, this will be a spiritual descent and a reckoning of human affairs and human lives.[10] But unlike Dante, Machiavelli presents a pagan vision of the underworld, and there will be no redeeming ascent afterward. The work draws most overtly from the *Metamorphoses* or *Golden Ass* of Apuleius.[11]

Initially, the narrator finds himself in a powerless, dependent position, stranded "there where I lost all my liberty" (2.24). It is a world of war between men and women, a war in which women have all the power. The threatening woods in which the action is set are vaguely imagined as a sexual landscape, the wild and threatening terrain of the body. The opening description can be read as a myth of infancy. The narrator is like a newborn — he knows nothing about where he is, cannot say how he came there, is terrified by deafening sound and bright light, and cannot move or even stand on his own. The darkness and then loud noise and blinding flashes of light leave him terrified and unmanned. He is unable to stand erect, his virtù "cast down and conquered" (2.36). He supports himself against a tree stump — a mutilated phallic icon, one might see it, in this wild landscape. Before he can pull himself away from the trunk, a beautiful, commanding woman appears. She is carrying a horn and a lantern and is followed by many beasts. She tells him that this wild forest is Circe's domain and that she is one of those who tend Circe's animals.

Circe, the sorceress of mythology who changed Odysseus's companions into swine, lives as queen of this wilderness attended only by women. "To men an enemy" (2.110), she keeps as animals all the men who lose their way in her woods. Describing Circe's magic, the woman says, "This special virtù is given her by heaven, / that to different shapes she can change a man, / as soon as she gazes fixedly at his face" (2.139–41). This is the fate, she warns, that threatens the man if he does not follow and obey her. Here Machiavelli grants women — or at least Circe — a virtù of their own, though it contrasts with manly virtù, which is at once an aspect of the male body and a harsh code of conduct. As so often in Machiavelli's treatment of male-female relations, he depicts a woman's power as overarching, uncontrollable (by men), and virtually inhuman — and thus largely irrelevant to political analysis — while he emphasizes the vulnerability, contingency, and fragility of the man's power.[12]

Is there a salacious meaning in the description of the power of Circe's gaze to change a man's shape? The woman's words suggest the very human and earthy virtù that she herself will exercise on the man, the power to change his shape by giving him an erection. The chief theme of *L'Asino* is the ups and downs, in various senses, of human — and for Machiavelli, read "manly" — virtù. Here Machiavelli perhaps ties women's virtù to his main thematic treatment of manly virtù, meaning for the reader to catch the bawdy play in the woman's words. And again, perhaps, Machiavelli has drawn the reader further into his world.

These first instances of virtù in *L'Asino* — the man's virtù "cast down and conquered," Circe's special virtù — raise the question of how to make sense of this term. *Virtù* is the single most notorious and important term in Machiavelli's thought. Long-running scholarly debates over the term tend to boil down to asking to what extent *The Prince*'s brutal lessons about virtù are supported by Machiavelli's other writings. Those who see *The Prince* as for any reason atypical can move to dismiss its teachings and try to identify a more appealing "authentic" Machiavelli, the genius of modern republicanism, and a more pleasing virtù. John Plamenatz, for instance, notes some distinctions between the ugly and solitary "heroic" virtù of *The Prince* and the "virtù of the citizen" he locates in the *Discourses*.[13] But Plamenatz, sensibly, does not see a vastly different Machiavelli in the latter work. Indeed, in the *Discourses* and in Machiavelli's other works the vision of virtù that predominates is one of solitary, manly achievement.

For Jakob Burckhardt, Machiavellian virtù was "a union of force and ability."[14] Hanna Pitkin says that in Machiavelli's writing virtù "tends mostly to connote energy, effectiveness, virtuosity." Noting the word's Latin root, *vir* (man), she observes, "*Virtù* is . . . manliness, those qualities found in a 'real man.'"[15] J. G. A. Pocock asserts that for an actor in the unstable, threatening world which Machiavelli perceived, "action is *virtù*."[16] *Virtù* is the term Machiavelli uses for the excellence of the greatest founders of states — Moses, Cyrus, Romulus, and Theseus. It refers to their ability to found great and enduring states as well as to their originality, their boldness, and their capacity to impose their will on the world. It is, as Hannah Arendt put it, "the specifically political human quality."[17]

Machiavelli thumbs his nose at any consistent effort to impose a moral sense on this "specifically political human quality." Sometimes it seems he accepts a conventional moral sense of *virtù*, as in his well-known discussion of the tyrant Agathocles in chapter 8 of *The Prince*. But by the end of that discussion, Machiavelli elevates Agathocles above moral scrutiny for having achieved lasting success. To drive home the point, Machiavelli sets his praise of Agathocles against his condemnation of a modern would-be tyrant who differs only in that he did not succeed. In such passages Machiavelli systematically strips virtù of its moral content. Mercy and cruelty are equally good, if they work. There is no enduring measure of human worth beyond political success; there is no value beyond the seizure and continuance of rule. Efficacy drives even morality. Agathocles' political success, for instance, allows him in the end to remedy his position even with God.[18] Machiavelli's conception of virtù thus directly attacks a moral and a Christian understanding of virtue, putting in its place a notion of value based on restless aggression, the primacy of politics, and the willingness to use whatever violence, cruelty, or treachery it takes to achieve one's ends.

Machiavellian virtù thus begins with the skills of the warrior. And since for Machiavelli war pervades life, Machiavellian virtù applies the warrior's art and standpoint to every facet of life — it represents, in Bernard Crick's phrase, "man militant in civic life as well as in the field."[19] *Virtù* can connote even man militant in sexual life. Translations like "potency," "vigor," and "manhood" connote in English the sexual implications of virtù as Machiavelli conceives it. Most readers of Machiavelli must have perceived the connection he makes between virtù and manliness, and some of the most perceptive have described virtù in images that betray — or even blare — a sexual understanding, as in Arendt's description of the "interplay" between *fortuna* and virtù: "*Virtù* is the response, summoned up by the man, to the world, or rather to the constellation of *fortuna* in which the world opens up, presents and offers itself to him, to his *virtù*."[20] Sometimes Machiavelli himself, as in the famous chapter 25 of *The Prince*, plainly sexualizes his political doctrine.

But in *L'Asino,* Machiavelli is at his most blatant: he uses *virtù* to mean, quite literally, a man's erect phallus. On one level, the work unfolds as a series of phallic references: from virtù "lost," "cast down and conquered," fallen, "not of iron," despaired of, and "little," to virtù restored by a woman's solicitude and enjoyed in a night of passion between the narrator and the woman. Upon this erotic frame of potency lost and regained hangs another level of meaning and another sense of the term, the tale's meditations on human virtù and the mutability of human things. The narrator, at the beginning of the story, has lost not only his physical potency but his strength of spirit; the woman ministers not only to his body but to his spirit as well, through her kindness but also through her teachings on the necessity of force and conquest in the world. The poem's structure thus blatantly sexualizes Machiavelli's political thought and presents an understanding of virtù in which sex, violence, and politics come together in a single male principle.

Oddly enough, Pitkin, whose pioneering study of sex and gender in Machiavelli remains the best work on the topic, failed to see the centrality of virtù in the text. While calling *L'Asino,* among Machiavelli's works, "the richest but also the most confusing single source on women in relation to politics," she never helps sort out the confusion by discerning the key role of virtù in the poem.[21] Thus she never comes to terms with *L'Asino.*

The mysterious, beautiful woman whom the narrator meets in the woods knows the whole course of his life and takes pity on him, bidding him to come with her and her animals. She appears to have the force and wisdom of a mother. She knows his name and tells him that she has been watching him for many months. She is his protector, telling him he must follow her "if in these woods you do not wish to die" (2.144). She tells him to crawl on all fours so that Circe will not see his face. He creeps after her among the animals, and when they come to the ditch that lies before the palace he splashes through the water with her animals while she walks across the narrow beam that serves as a bridge.

In the castle, she treats him at first like her child, leading him by the hand to her chamber, drying him, and cooking a meal for him. But she is more than a mother figure. Bidding him to eat, she alludes not too obliquely to his fallen virtù and to what is to come shortly: "for I know you need it — not a little perhaps, / if your condition is not of iron. . ." (4.23–24).[22] After they eat, she invites him into her bed, but at first the narrator wraps the bedsheets around himself, shrinking from her "like one who in his virtù does not hope" (4.102). "Shrinking and shy," he compares himself to "the new bride" lying petrified next to her husband (4.97–99). The woman smiles at his bashfulness and tells him teasingly that many men have longed and fought for the place she gives him willingly and that surely he would do whatever he could to be with her — "Then why do you have so little virtù that these / clothes that are between us make war on you, / and keep you so far from me?" (4.112–14). Her words finally stir him to action. He moves near her, touching her body, and is almost overwhelmed by the sensation. His hand roving over her body, he says, "My lost virtù quickly returned" (4.129). At last, timid no longer, he embraces her, and they enjoy a night of sweet passion — so sweet that he swoons on her breast.[23]

The next day, she treats him as a jealous husband would his domiciled and docile wife. She commands the narrator to wait for her while she does her day's work: "You will remain alone in this room. . . . Do not go outside; . . . do not answer if one calls" (5.10–14). The easy switching of traditional gender roles here is one of the charms and interests of *L'Asino.*

Throughout *L'Asino,* the woman is in addition the man's teacher. She tells him some of what he has suffered and what he must undergo. She unfolds a vision of the world's mutability. Later, it is this theme upon which he meditates when she leaves him alone, echoing and developing her vision. She takes him to see the animals Circe keeps in order to learn their nature, and as she leads him, she offers him her hand and he takes it "so as not to be separated from her at all" (7.131). At every turn, he obeys and follows her. The triad of dependencies in which the narrator is placed — child, student, passive lover — echoes the snares of seduction that Machiavelli conceived in a letter to Vettori, in which he imagined their calculating friend Filippo da Casavecchia talking to a youth "now as a father, now as a tutor, now as a lover."[24]

But if this is a seduction, it is a very complicated one. The relationship between man and woman in this poem is unlike any other in Machiavelli's writing — indeed it is, I think, the sweetest interlude in all of Machiavelli's writings. Theirs is a relationship of friendship and mutuality as well as eros; their tender friendship adds a layer of complexity and richness to this fable. When she first encounters him, she greets him by name — "as if," the narrator says, "a thousand times she had seen me." He says, "I was completely reassured by that action" (2.75–76). Later, he describes their dinner together as not so much a seduction but a mingling of spirits: "Leaving all the troubles and the griefs, / happily we ate together, and talked / of a thousand little songs and a thousand loves" (4.46–48). In bed, it is not sarcasm or derision but her good humor and "kind speaking" (4.121–22) that kindle his virtù. The day after, when she returns from her labors, he is tongue-tied and ashamed of "the sweetness that subdued me" (6.21), but her gentle embrace overcomes his silence: "After a time, she and I / spoke of many things together, / as one friend with another talks" (6.22–24).

In this unfinished poem, the nature and identity of the young woman are not clear, but that she serves as friend as well as lover and teacher is surely important to her role in reawakening the narrator's virtù. It is also significant that in their interactions, most notably in bed, the woman plays the man and the man plays the woman. For once in Machiavelli's writing, a man is not forced to erect his virtù by his own efforts: and to drive home the lesson with comic exaggeration, Machiavelli makes the attainment of virtù quite literally an erection achieved and enjoyed by two lovers, with the conventional sexual roles reversed. There is freedom here, and real happiness. One thinks of Arendt's patently erotic description of the "harmony between man and world" that is the "interplay" between Machiavellian virtù and fortuna — "playing with each other and succeeding together."[25] Arendt's words suggest that this happy play is the usual state of affairs in Machiavelli's world, but I disagree. In its happiness, *L'Asino* undermines or dissents from Machiavelli's usual understanding of virtù. Usually, he portrays the attainment of virtù as part of a great solitary struggle for autonomy and mastery by a man, a struggle in which the world or fortuna or a state is sometimes an acquiescent partner but too often a thing to be seized, held down, beaten, and even raped.

At times, Machiavelli celebrates such violence; at others, he details with joyless but dogged persistence the swath that violence cuts through human affairs. At all times, he claims that in order to live as more than a victim, one must embrace the very harshest violence. Men have no other choice if they wish to live in the world. Machiavelli himself, the singer of this dark vision, often seems to stagger under its weight. Sometimes one feels that he would gladly cease playing a man if he could, as the narrator of *L'Asino* is briefly allowed to do and as the protesting pig at the end of the fable has done.

The narrator of this fable, whom we are meant to identify to some extent with Machiavelli, possesses an extreme measure of the anxiety, self-pity, and brooding sense of injustice that Machiavelli himself carried. It is one of the narrator's satisfactions to be told that his suffering is on a heroic scale:

> "Among modern peoples and among ancient,"
> she began, "never has any endured
> more ingratitude, nor greater hardship.
>
> This, indeed, by your fault did not happen to you,
> as happens to some, but because Luck
> to your good action came contrary." (3.76–81)

One is reminded of the lachrymose self-pity in *The Prince*'s dedicatory letter to Lorenzo de' Medici: "If your Magnificence will at some time turn your eyes from the summit of your height to these low places, you will learn how undeservedly I endure a great and continuous malignity of fortune."[26] The narrator of *L'Asino* is offered the kind of consolation that would have appealed to Machiavelli and that in a sense he achieved through his writings: "Perhaps you will yet win glory, / recounting to these peoples and to those / your long history of hardships" (3.112–14).

It must please the man to be told that his sense of suffering is justified and to have another person so intuitively understand his cares. One of the recurring motifs of *L'Asino* is the man's silence and inability to speak — but another is the woman's mysterious understanding of him, which renders speech superfluous. When she first encounters him, she asks him how he came there:

> My cheeks, which were wan and pale,
> changed color and became like fire:
> and, silent, I shrugged my shoulders.
>
> I would have liked to say, "My little sense,
> vain hope and vain opinion
> have brought me down into this place,"
>
> but I could not form this speech
> in any mode — so much shame
> for myself seized me, and such compassion.
>
> And she, laughing: "You need not
> fear to speak among these stumps;
> just speak, and tell what yearning fills your heart." (2.82–93)

This is, in a sense, a fantasy of intimacy without vulnerability — the woman's magical understanding of the narrator releases him from the need to express himself, while her wisdom and power release him from the usual need to depict himself as a true man in Circe's kingdom. It is as if her understanding has pierced his heavy armor and begun to heal the suffering spirit within. The narrator's burdens of being a man in a harsh world have unmanned him and crushed his virtù: "I had come to the end of my life, / in a place dark, shadowed, and sightless, / when I was overtaken by the night" (3.55–57). The woman rescues him and restores his virtù. The poignancy of *L'Asino* is that it provides a tantalizing glimpse of a kinder world than the one Machiavelli inhabits, a world of mutuality and friendship between men and women, where men can gain virtù through friendship rather than solitary conquest and through equality of relations rather than seduction and violent assault.

But this is only one aspect of the world of *L'Asino*. The wild place the woman inhabits, "this place so fierce and strong" (3.84), is no refuge. If Circe finds the man, he will be killed: behind the love and friendship of the man and the woman is a backdrop of sexual warfare. She who rescues him can treat him kindly, but she cannot give him a kinder and more loving vision of human life. She can help him only by recognizing his pain as the pain of being human, of being a man in Machiavelli's world:

> You see the stars and the heavens, you see the moon,
> you see the other planets go wandering,
> now high, now low, without any rest.

Sometimes you see the heaven cloudy, sometimes
lucid and bright — so nothing on earth
remains in its same state.

From this come peace and war,
from this ensue the hatreds among those
whom one wall and one moat lock up together.

From this came your first torment;
from this sprang all the cause
of your labors without relief.

Nor has Heaven changed opinion
yet, nor will it change while the fates
keep toward you their bitter purpose.

And those humors which were to you
so very adverse, and so very hostile,
not yet, not yet are purged. (3.88–105)

The vision is Machiavelli's own, on display in all of his life's writings. The woman imparts it to the narrator and affirms his own manly code: "Because weeping has always been unseemly to a man, / he ought, to his fortune's blows, / turn a face unstained with tears" (3.85–87). She gives him the strength to carry this dark vision; significantly, she does not give him a kinder one: "Do not become disheartened; but freely take this weight / upon your shoulders firm and strong; / for yet it will avail you to have taken it" (3.130–33).

Later, when she leaves him alone, he takes up her theme: "I wanted to examine the cause of variations in earthly things" (5.35–36). His meditations on human ambition, discontent, and violence are a powerful epitome of Machiavelli's thought:

That which tumbles kingdoms from the highest hills,
most of all, is this: that the mighty
with their might are never sated.

From this it comes that they are discontented
who have lost, and their passion is aroused
to bring down those who stand triumphant.

Whence it comes that one rises and another dies;
and the one who has risen is ever consumed
by new ambition, or by fear.

This appetite destroys our states. (5.37–46)

Solicitude and kindness have restored the narrator, but they have not wrought any deeper change in him. He does not reject his part in the hard world he envisages, as he observes about people generally: "But it's even more astonishing that everyone / recognizes this error, but no one flees from it" (5.47–48). Nor have the woman's ministrations changed his understanding of how survival and success in this world depend on an aggressive conception of virtù: "That kingdom which is pushed by virtù to act, or by necessity, will be seen ever to turn upwards," he says, with a little echo, perhaps, of the poem's phallicism (5.79–81). That city which has "bad customs," by which he means whatever weakness or softness keeps it from preparing for war, "must consume herself" (5.85–88). His own virtù has been restored, but only to make him a warrior again, ready to bear arms in this hard world: "Virtù," he concludes, "makes countries tranquil" (5.94)—but only by means of the sword, and tranquillity itself is inevitably a sign of corruption and decline. The poem's lovemaking had hinted at a kinder world, one with room for love, but the narrative quickly leads back to a hardened understanding of human things.[27]

But having seemingly resolved the question of virtù, Machiavelli at once proceeds to call it into question at the end of *L'Asino*. The poem ends with an abrupt change of tone, an eloquent assault on the Machiavellian perspective. But that assault is put into the mouth of a pig, hardly the most heroic or praiseworthy of creatures—especially this pig, covered in excrement and content to wallow in muck. The point we're left with is by no means clear, unless it is to add a final muddling interrogative to what would otherwise be a clarion call for Machiavellian manhood.

The woman takes the man to see Circe's animals in order that he may learn the nature and circumstances of their lives. After seeing many animals and learning what types of men they had been, the narrator encounters a pig. This is the only animal he talks to, and the only one who talks with him. Offered the chance to be human again, it rejects the offer. In the *Inferno*, Dante had asked the gluttonous spirit wallowing in mud why Florence was so torn by discord;[28] in Machiavelli's fable, the muddy pig addresses the same question. He blames human virtù, attacking the narrator's high estimation of it: "I see well that you are in that error, / that for a long time held me too. / So greatly does your self-love deceive you / that you don't believe there's any good / apart from human existence and its worth" (8.29–33). He promises to correct the narrator's error of founding his conception of the good on human things.

It is better, the pig says, to found one's notion of the good on nature. Men learn to be prudent—an "excellent virtù" (8.38)—but animals are naturally so, making them better able to apply prudence. Animals follow nature's wishes, and their virtues are in harmony with their needs. But men follow their insatiable appetites and are given only hands, speech, ambition, and avarice, so that they endlessly move about, unable to remain in a peaceful, frugal civil life. The pig describes a human world of strife, grief, and isolation: "Yours are ambition, licentiousness, lamentation and avarice." Only men do violence to each other, he says. The pig concludes the fable with a final renunciation of manhood:

> Think now how you want me to become once more a man,
> being spared from all the miseries
> that I endured while I was a man.
>
> And if any among men seems to you divine,
> happy and joyful, don't too easily believe him,
> for in this mud more happily I live,
>
> where, without thought, I soak and wallow. (8.145–51)

What are we to make of these words? The poem ends with them, and thus they have immense rhetorical power. But at the same time we know the pig will not win the narrator over; from the poem's opening lines we know that the narrator will eventually return to human form after suffering his own transformation. The narrator's focus remains the human condition and a human conception of virtù. In this, his perspective is obviously Machiavelli's. When the pig tells the narrator, "You don't believe there's any good / apart from human existence and its worth" (8.32–33), he is claiming the natural good for himself and challenging the narrator (and readers) to follow him in this. But is the pig to be believed? He speaks as if it is natural to be docile and unnatural and human to be aggressive. The pig neglects the fact that each creature in Circe's realm has assumed his particular form as a reflection of his human character — the violent became bears, the ambitious and discontented became wolves, and so on. In human form, the pig lacked any spark of energy or ambition: is such a one to be our teacher? No; the appeal to nature proves unreliable; there are many different natures, and it is the clash between them that must shape any understanding of how we ought to live. In the end, thus, the pig's perspective is a powerful lament, nothing more and nothing less; the pig's eloquence holds no resolution to the problem of virtù. But, if they offer no alternative, the pig's and the poem's final words do undermine any effort to read the story as a simple narrative of recovery, of the healing of a man's body and spirit.

Machiavelli turns away not only from nature as a guide, but also from God. Machiavelli hints at this by modeling *L'Asino* closely on Dante's descent into the underworld but neglecting to follow the rest of his journey. In this poem as throughout his works he rejects any effort to set up a conception of value above human things. Men inhabit the middle world, and it is in this world that their hopes and salvation lie. The narrator of *L'Asino*, meditating on the human condition, concludes his thoughts by saying that religion and prayer are necessary for political reasons — "altogether mad is he who forbids people their ceremonies and their devotions; because in fact it seems that from them may be reaped union and good order" — but he says also that men and states are responsible for their own fates and that their own action is essential:

> To believe that without you, God vies for you,
> while you're idle and on your knees,
> has ruined many kingdoms and many states.
>
> Indeed are prayers necessary:
> and wholly mad is he who to the people forbids
> their ceremonies and their devotions:
>
> because from those, truly, it seems are reaped
> union and good order; and from that
> then follows good and happy fortune.
>
> But there shouldn't be anyone of so little brain
> that he believes, if his house is falling,
> that God will save it without other support;
>
> because he will die beneath that ruin. (5.115–27)

It is, in a sense, a hopeful vision that locates human salvation in human action. But, as we have seen, in countless ways Machiavelli sows doubts about men's ability and freedom to act and about how much men's action can accomplish. The sublunary world, the only world for Machiavelli, is filled with the anxieties and fears of men, their knowledge of the world's mutability, and their own weakness. There is little refuge from these, only brief interludes when men may forget themselves. We may consider the moment in *L'Asino* when, after a sweet night of lovemaking, the woman leaves the narrator. No sooner is he alone than his sense of suffering returns: "As soon as I was parted from her, / the arrow of reflection once more filled / that wound which through her I had healed" (5.22–24).

The narrator's fear and anxiety unmanned him, and even after he is restored, his memory — "the arrow of reflection" — returns to wound him. One of the themes of *L'Asino* is how painful it is to remember, and how sweet can be the luxury of forgetting. Yet forgetting *is* only a luxury, and soon one must always return to the remembrance of one's condition. Men in Machiavelli's world have very little respite from their solitary, hard existence. If they impose great violence upon the world, they also are tyrannized by their own roles. The relentless pursuit of manhood in action means endless anxiety because one is always judged by one's most recent performance. A man can continually be unmanned by his own fragile self.

The situation of the Machiavellian actor is precarious, and the precarious situation is worsened by the paradox that the Machiavellian man must found his greatness on his own virtù and his own strong appetites — but then he must learn to control those appetites. The true Machiavellian is no sensual, pandering adulterer or drunkard but a tightly controlled man, like Cyrus or Castruccio Castracani or the Prince himself, who controls his sexual appetites for his political good.[29] The Machiavellian must master his mind and body. Then he must hope that Fortune lets him master her. Harvey Mansfield, considering the central Machiavellian image of political action, puts the case quite suggestively: "He makes the politics of the new prince appear in the image of rape. . . . Whether he says what he appears to say about the status of women may be doubted, however. The young men who master Lady Fortune come with audacity and leave exhausted, but she remains ageless, waiting for the next ones. One might go so far as to wonder who is raping whom.[30]

The Machiavellian aggressor, Mansfield says, is really the victim. One must not embrace this view without reserve — there are real, suffering human victims of human violence in the Machiavellian world, victims whom we should not lose sight of by classing them with their oppressors — but there is an undeniable sense in Machiavelli's thought of injury even, and in a sense especially, to the wielders of violence, the usually young Machiavellian men who must hold themselves to such superhuman, or inhuman, standards. This awareness of the agony of manhood is one of the chief features of *L'Asino* and is in fact its last word.

Why should we read *L'Asino* — a poem, a fable, a kind of love story — if we want to understand Machiavelli's political ideas? Because we should read Machiavelli, I suggest, as we would read an artist — in Antonio Gramsci's phrase, "an artist of politics."[31] His political ideas emerge not merely in the surfaces, the overt statements, of his works — the rise and fall of states, the lives and acts of political figures — but in the dramatic forms he employed in his writings, in their ironies, hints, and silences, in the quips, confessions, and emotional appeals that occur in all his works. Machiavelli is one of the subtlest, slyest, and richest of political writers. His vision is one of extreme contrasts, sudden changes of tone or perspective that disorient many readers, leaving them with a kind of moral vertigo. A future reader of his letters, Machiavelli imagines, "would suppose now that we were grave men, wholly concerned with important matters, and that into our breasts no thought could fall that did not have in itself honor and greatness. But then, turning the page, he would judge that we, the very same persons, were light-minded, inconstant, lascivious, concerned with empty things."[32]

Machiavelli described himself not as a political scientist but as a storyteller. "Niccolò Machiavelli, historian, comic and tragic writer," he signs a letter late in life.³³ The mingling of comic and tragic strains, one might say, is Machiavelli's most characteristic response to human life as he saw it, with its violence and wickedness, its inconstancy and insecurity, its deceptions and self-deceptions. The comedy appears in his plays, in his dissection of the sexual follies and schemes of men, but also in his historical writings, in his dissection of the folly and weakness of modern Italian rulers, notably in the *Florentine Histories*. The tragic strain appears in his consciousness of the terrible suffering that rulers' weakness and folly caused throughout Italy. Both strains, comic and tragic, appear throughout his work in the bitter contrast between the past glory of Rome and the degradation of Italy in his day.

Here Machiavelli's political vision is rooted. The chief failing he saw in the rulers and people of his day and place was an inability and an unreadiness to fight in a terrain which could erupt in war at anytime. Thus the fundamental requirement of the Machiavellian actor is to be ready at all times to wage war. The loneliness of the Machiavellian actor begins with this insistence on the violence and insecurity of life and its corollary that any true notion of human worth depends on one's strength and power. Machiavelli erected a definition of virtue that resided in the external life of humans — not in right action but in *effective* action. Machiavellian virtù is nothing more than the skill and art of the warrior, in the armed camp that is the world of men.

The Machiavellian political actor, in Felix Gilbert's words, "must live for politics to the exclusion of all else."³⁴ The plainest contrast with this single-mindedness is Baldassare Castiglione's contemporaneous depiction of the courtier, whose various aspects are to be integrated into a complete life: scholar, soldier, political actor, royal counselor, lover. The last book of Castiglione's *Courtier* is on the relevance of love to the political life of the courtier and the political health of the court. When Machiavelli overturned the conceptions of virtù of Petrarch, Castiglione, and a whole tradition of moralizing political thinkers, narrowing their concerns to the elemental question of survival, he removed love from the political equation. There is virtually no place for love in Machiavelli's view of human affairs. He seems to delight in stories that violate our expectations about the power of love to soften human relations. Instead of the romantic or familial love that one might expect, one finds in so many of Machiavelli's stories baser, crueler emotions: lust, malice, ambition, pride, and terrible aloneness.

Machiavelli denies the relevance of religious things to human things and sees no way to achieve transcendence through human things. All human life, in Machiavelli's bleak view, consists ultimately of "cose vane" (empty things). Survival is the one fundamental objective in such a world, but survival for its own sake cannot create meaning — or creates a babble of meanings, contention without mastery. Machiavelli's actor, Wolin concludes, "performed in a universe hushed in moral stillness."[35] Moral ends in Machiavelli's world, Wolin observes, have been replaced by ironies. Answers have been replaced by questions. In this morally hushed world, Machiavelli's lessons are precarious and dangerous. When he overturns classical and Christian notions of the good, denying their use and their truth, Machiavelli leaves his political actor naked and alone, with nothing but his understanding and strength to defend him. But one's strength is insecure, and one's understanding complicates and undermines as well as protects.

The human condition, as it emerges in Machiavelli's thought, is an eternal oxymoron, violence and suffering yoked together. Both violence and suffering are inevitable, imposed on humans by restless, insatiable human nature and by the systemic logic of individuals living together. But both violence and suffering are the products of human will, for the Machiavellian project consists in choosing the right violence to commit, the right suffering to inflict and endure. In the play of these dialectics — violence and suffering, necessity and choice — emerges the tragic element in Machiavelli's thought.

At the end, *L'Asino* is incomplete. We have been told that the narrator must still undergo self-transformation, as the woman has prophesied: "It falls to you / to search the world, wearing a new skin: / for that providence which maintains / the human species intends that you endure / this privation for your greater good" (3.116–20). The fable had begun after this transformation, with the narrator returned once more to human form, promising to tell the whole of his story: "The varied chances, the pain and the grief / that under an Ass's form I suffered, / I shall sing, if fortune allows" (1.1–3). Life in the form of an ass, he says, inured him to pain: "Bites and blows I don't reckon as much / as I used to, having become / of the nature of he whom I sing" (1.16–18).

Machiavelli, one is tempted to say, saw himself less as a lion or a fox than an ass — small of valor, steadfast of blows, a beast of others' burdens. Near the end of his life, just a few weeks before he died, he wrote a letter to his son concerning, among other affairs, the treatment of one of the family mules: "The little mule, though he is crazy, needs to be treated quite differently from other crazy creatures, because the other crazy ones are tied up, and I want you to untie him. . . . [T]ake off his bridle and halter and let him go where he will to get his living and rid himself of his madness. The territory is large; the animal is small; he can't do any harm."[36]

Machiavelli writes as if he understands the mule. One is tempted to read this passage as a kind of final reckoning by Machiavelli of his own life, of his own wanderings, of his own madness. Machiavelli granted that in many ways his vision of human life was a mad one, as he acknowledged in a letter to Guicciardini: "I say one thing that will seem to you crazy; I shall bring forward a plan that will seem to you either foolhardy or ridiculous; nonetheless these times demand decisions that are bold, unusual and strange."[37] In his strange times, in his strange and suffering world, Machiavelli was driven to strange wanderings and wonderings. He devoted his life to writing about politics as war, to urging his readers and listeners to prepare for war, but to no discernible good. Perhaps he knew he was only playing at war, as in the neat military diagrams that he drew to accompany *The Art of War*. But no matter, he might conclude: "The territory is large; the animal is small; he can't do any harm."

Whether or not one identifies Machiavelli closely with the wanderer caught in the world of *L'Asino,* the poem is an essential text for coming to terms with Machiavellian virtù and with Machiavelli's thought in general. His vision enshrines an aggressive masculine identity as the political ideal. But what elevates Machiavelli above fascism — what will make him forever a fascinating and troubling thinker on the human condition — is that the inescapable duty of every political actor in Machiavelli's world, the quest to achieve manly identity, is dogged at every step by brooding anxiety about failure. The pig's lament at the end of *L'Asino,* that human virtù leads inevitably to sorrow, is one of the strands woven throughout Machiavelli's thought. But at the same time, *L'Asino* is a celebration of virtù as male sexuality, of the joy of potency and the sweetness of love. In its stark contrast between joy and despair, the work is a window on Machiavelli's troubled vision.

Wilderness, declared that grim preacher Cotton Mather, is a temporary condition through which we are passing to the promised land. That is how Christians of all sorts have always made sense of the world, how they have sought consolation even in the starkest of Machiavellian environments. But for Machiavelli, we must understand, wilderness has become a permanent condition. It is the world in which we live and in which all our dreams and longings are contained and must find expression. All of Machiavelli's pessimism is rooted in this conviction. His fitful, hopeful efforts to build something that lasts, something that matters, are always pulled back to earth, to wilderness, to the necessary anguish and impermanence of the human condition.[38] The real wilderness of *L'Asino* is not the desolate place the narrator finds himself in, but the human world he has come from — and to which he will return. In that human world, a man's virtù is his strength and his identity, his armor and his sword. In *L'Asino* Machiavelli uses the metaphor of the male body as explicitly as he ever does to connote the rise and fall of men's lives and human affairs. In *L'Asino,* we see virtù as erection — for a sweet, fleeting moment signifying love as something more than conquest, but also, and always, signifying loneliness, and suffering, and the necessary art of brutal violence.

7

The Politician as Writer

FRANCO FIDO

My purpose is to discuss some instances of the connection between Machiavelli's practical concerns as a diplomat and politician on the one hand and his extraordinary ability, on the other, to elevate those concerns to the sphere of theory and literary creation. As Machiavelli's career as a writer develops amid the chaos of Florentine and Italian politics and personal losses and disappointments, he relinquishes his early hopes for the possibility of a princely redeemer. Although his confidence in the possibility of human beings' mastering fortune diminishes, his own power as a literary artist capable of creating unforgettable characters and indelible images and of revealing the universal in the particular remains unchanged.

From Diplomacy to Literature

VALENTINO AND THE SLAUGHTER OF SINIGAGLIA

In 1501–02 Cesare Borgia, the duke Valentino, was trying to aggrandize his domains in various directions along a circle stretching dangerously around Florence: the Romagna, Arezzo with the Valdichiana, Piombino, and Urbino. It was precisely to Urbino that Machiavelli was sent along with the bishop of Volterra, Francesco Soderini, in June of 1502, to sound Valentino's intentions and, at the same time, to keep him at bay with the promise of an appointment as condottiere. He returned a few months later to Cesare Borgia in Romagna, not only as representative of the Republic, but also, this time, as the personal agent of Piero Soderini, who in the meantime had been elected gonfalonier for life.

This second mission to Valentino, between October 1502 and January 1503, in Imola, then in Cesena and Sinigaglia, always trying to stay at the duke's heels, permitted Machiavelli to observe closely the crisis with which Borgia was confronted when his generals assembled in Magione, near Perugia, and revolted against him. This left Florence wavering between two equally disliked adversaries and, as usual, wanting to buy time.

In Urbino Machiavelli had been impressed by the intelligence, energy, and secretiveness of the duke: "This lord is very splendid and magnificent, and so spirited at arms that there is no great thing that does not seem small to him; and [in striving] for glory and for acquiring [new] states [dominions] he never rests, nor recognizes fatigue or danger. He arrives at a place before one can find out from where he is taking his departure; he makes himself well-liked by his soldiers; he has got the best men in Italy: which things make him victorious and formidable, with a perpetual [good] fortune in addition."[1]

During Machiavelli's second mission his admiration, but also his uneasiness, grew as he tried in vain to probe the intentions of the duke. He became increasingly aware that Florence should make a choice and that its "swinging" from side to side could only harm it. Having no clear instructions and consequently no good cards to play, he sounds in his letters to the Ten more like an attentive and fascinated spectator than like a diplomatic agent or even simply a good informant such as the shrewd Giustinian, Venetian ambassador to the pope, also present on the scene. Rather, the historian and the storyteller were awakened in him by the spectacle before his eyes of a "virtuous" leader caught up in a situation fraught with risks but also, if rightly confronted, with potential for great gains.

A letter written to him on October 21 by Biagio Buonaccorsi, his colleague in the Chancery, reveals that Niccolò had asked for Plutarch's *Vitae* to be sent to him from Florence, as if out of the need to compare a modern hero to the great ones of the past.[2] At the same time, his letters to the Ten often tend to turn into the recording or recreation of direct discourses. These speeches — filled with reticences, calculated boastings, veiled threats, mysterious allusions — may be those delivered by Cesare himself, or they may be attributed (according to a technique he will develop further in the last books of the *Florentine Histories,* the ones closest to the recent and sensitive Medicean past) to a fictitious character who speaks in the first person and thus conveys

Machiavelli's own opinion without compromising him. The "friend" quoted in the letter of November 8 is an example: "Now if you asked me, what could be done? Let's get down to brass tacks: I would answer that on your part, you have two plagues that will kill you, if you don't cure them. One is Pisa, the other Vitellozzo."[3]

The fascinated attention of the witness tends to turn into artistic ambition and narrative undertaking. But such a process appears to be justified by the author's awareness of the enlightening function and heuristic power that literary elaboration may exert on the interpretation of historical events.

This is why Machiavelli left us two versions of the last act of the drama, from the moment Valentino, apparently scared and ready to compromise and forgive, asked the conspirators to meet him in Sinigaglia to that of their capture and execution. The first and more detailed version is contained in the dispatches (with a few blanks due to the loss of some letters) sent to the Ten between late December 1502 and January 9, 1503. The second is the rightly famous *Description of the Way Duke Valentino Killed Vitellozzo Vitelli, Oliverotto da Fermo, Signor Paolo, and the Duke of Gravina Orsini*, which was most likely written shortly after his return to Florence and was therefore the first piece of writing he did for a purely literary purpose, that is, entirely independent of any practical goals.[4]

The comparisons of the two versions often made by scholars show, quite predictably, the greater stylistic care and narrative ambition of the *Description*, evident for instance in the thorough, elegant depiction of Sinigaglia and the road leading there.[5] No less noticeable in the *Description* is Machiavelli's desire to emphasize the contrast between the supposed initial bewilderment of the duke — "who was in Imola full of fear, because all of a sudden and unexpectedly, having his soldiers turned into enemies, he found himself facing a war at home, and disarmed"[6] — and the tactical skill and cold-blooded cruelty with which he will set the trap for the conspirators.

As other interpreters have correctly observed, however, the similarities between the chronicle written on the spot and the literary reelaboration are stronger than their obvious differences.[7] For example, both texts have a powerful description of Orsini's and Vitelli's entrance into Sinigaglia, the observer's gaze falling upon the poor mount and the worn-out coat of Vitellozzo, who is pale and stupefied, "as if he were conscious of his impending death."[8]

In this sense the *Description* does nothing more than acknowledge and make explicit a speculative and creative impulse already present in the dispatches from the mission: both works are evidence of the same propensity (though put to different uses) to represent events by rapid touches and striking, meaningful details. At the same time, through his writing Machiavelli aims at seizing, beyond the brutal contingency of political actions (treasons, deceit, massacres), a play of forces and of laws which demands an absorbed and almost solemn contemplation in order to be fully appreciated.

THE *FIRST DECENNIAL*

In 1503, following Pope Alexander's death, a pope "of transition," Pius III Piccolomini, was installed — but he lived less than a month after his election. Then an old enemy of the Borgias, Giuliano Della Rovere, became pope with the name of Julius II. Astonishingly, his election took place with the acquiescence of Valentino. Almost immediately, the new pope began a series of military operations intended to bring several cities in central Italy back under the authority of the Church. As he did the slaughter at Sinigaglia, Machiavelli happened to witness most of these events, first as a Florentine representative to Rome during the second conclave of 1503, in which Julius II was elected pope, and later as an observer during the pope's campaign against Perugia (a city poorly defended by Giampaolo Baglioni, its ruler, as he will remember much later in 1.27 of the *Discourses on Livy*).[9] But none of these important occurrences inspired him to write anything comparable to the *Description*.

Machiavelli continued to follow his literary calling in different forms, even as he pursued his interest in contemporary history. Toward the end of 1504 he wrote the *First Decennial*, a chronicle in tercets of the events that occurred in Italy between Charles VIII's invasion in 1494 and the death of Valentino in 1504, which he dedicated to Alamanno Salviati, the future father-in-law of Francesco Guicciardini.

The metrics and the at times forced energy of the images betray the deliberate intention of imitating Dante, either directly or through other fourteenth-century models like the *Centiloquio,* in which Antonio Pucci had versified Giovanni Villani's *Cronica* in terza rima. At a time when Florence was clearly losing, as Carlo Dionisotti has observed,[10] its preeminence in the field of vernacular poetry — this is the period between the publication of Matteo Maria Boiardo's *Amorum libri* and *Orlando Innamorato* and Jacopo Sannazaro's *Arcadia* on the one hand and of *Orlando Furioso* and Pietro Bembo's rhymes on the other — such a return to Dante falls halfway between the manifestation of a conservative literary taste and a gesture of Florentine patriotism.

In the dark picture of the contemporary political situation drawn by the author, the Italian princes' factious divisions and dependence on mercenary troops and on venal and unscrupulous commanders appear to be the deep-rooted causes of a political disaster that overwhelms all the protagonists. The French, Spanish, Venetians, Florentines, Medici, Borgias, and Ludovico il Moro are all brought together in a harsh condemnation from which only a few well-intentioned but isolated individuals are excepted, like Alamanno Salviati among the "ottimati" (patricians) and Piero Soderini of the popular party. The chronicler's contempt for the present and his obvious admiration for Dante manifest themselves in a long series of animalizing metaphors, or "blasoni," which transform the poem into a bitter and grotesque bestiary: Capons (from the Capponi family) and Roosters ("Galli," that is, the French), the Wolf (Siena) and the Panther (Lucca), the Viper (from Visconti's coat of arms), the Bears (Orsini) and the Calves (Vitelli), and so on. On the crest of this zoomorphic wave is Cesare Borgia: a basilisk-like Valentino tackling his faithless, snakelike commanders:

> Turned against one another, these serpents full of poison began to use their
>   claws and with their talons to tear one another, and with their teeth,
> and since Valentino could not escape, he was forced to cover himself again
>   with the shield of France, that he might avoid the hazard;
> and to catch his enemies with birdlime, and to get them into his den, sweetly
>   this basilisk whistled.[11]

These are among the few of the *First Decennial*'s 550 lines that are still remembered, along with those evoking with dark irony the end of Savonarola:

> I speak of that great Savonarola who, inspired with heavenly vigor, kept you
>   closely bound with his words.
> But many feared to see their country ruined, little by little, under his
>   prophetic teaching;
> hence no ground for your reunion could be discovered, unless his light divine
>   continued to increase, or unless by a greater fire it was extinguished.[12]

At the end of his narrative the poet goes back to the present:

> Therefore my spirit is all aflame; now with hope, now with fear it is
>   overwhelmed, so much that it wastes to nothing bit by bit;
> because it seeks to know where your ship can sail, weighted with such heavy
>   weights, or into what harbor, with these winds.
> Yet we trust in the skillful steersman [obviously, Piero Soderini], in the oars,
>   in the sails, in the cordage; but the voyage would be easy and short if you
>   would reopen the temple of Mars.[13]

The shortage of "armi proprie" (weapons of one's own) denounced in the last lines was one of the causes of Italy's weakness when confronted with those European powers that, in the meantime, Niccolò had come to know firsthand, never as a full-fledged ambassador, but as the escort of the "en titre" (orator) or else as the Signoria's temporary envoy on a particular mission.

OF FRENCH AND GERMAN MATTERS

Machiavelli went to France four times between 1500 and 1511. The first time he went with Francesco Della Casa and stayed for several months, occupied with the difficult assignment of warding off Louis XII, who demanded repayment of the salaries he had advanced to the Swiss mercenaries who, without much zeal, were besieging Pisa on Florence's behalf. Along with his colleague, he was also faced with the task of persuading the king to put a stop to the ambitious undertakings of his protégé Cesare Borgia in central Italy. The successive missions were no easier, being always in pursuit of the Court, which was constantly on the move between Lyon and the cities of the Loire Valley, from Nevers to Nantes through Blois and Tours. Now Florence was faced with even more complex problems: to steer a middle course between a belligerent, dangerous neighbor like Julius II and a distant ally like Louis XII (July 1510); or to keep away from Pisa, finally reconquered, the assembly of a Council hostile to the pope (September 1513).

Between the second and the third legation in France, at the end of 1507, Machiavelli was dispatched with Francesco Vettori to the emperor Maximilian I, that is, to Bolzano and Innsbruck by way of Switzerland, to discuss the financial contribution of Florence to the emperor's anticipated "descent" to make himself crowned in Rome.

His strongest impression of France was probably the one he got from his first, longer stay, during which he had, among other interesting experiences, a famous meeting with the king's powerful minister Georges d'Amboise cardinal of Rouen. He proudly recounted the exchange in *The Prince:* "I spoke about this at Nantes with Cardinal Rouen when Valentino (for this was what Cesare Borgia, son of Pope Alexander, was commonly called) occupied Romagna; for when the Cardinal of Rouen told me that Italians understood little about war, I replied to him that the French understood little about politics; for if they did understand, they would not permit the Church to gain so much power."[14]

In fact, the importance of his European experience, precisely in terms of politics, that is, to use a modern expression, in the area of political science, is fully attested by the short historical-literary works that Machiavelli wrote sometime between 1508 and 1512, after he had returned from these legations.

In the short *De natura Gallorum* (On the character of the Gauls, undated) and *Discorso sopra le cose della Magna e sopra lo Imperatore* (Discourse on Germany and the emperor, 1509) the prevalent anthropological and prosopographic interests are brought to bear on the sphere of political judgment

(the harshness, greediness, and realism of the French; the pathological inde-
cisiveness of the chivalrous Maximilian), while in the longer *Description of
French Affairs* and *Report on German Affairs* (1508; revised in 1512 with a
new title, *Description of German Affairs*) the picture is enriched with geographical and economic details (for example, France's agricultural wealth resulting from its large size and from its numerous and easily accessible water-
ways, the scarce circulation of currency, and so on); remarks on national
character (for example, the frugality and individualism of the Germans) and
political considerations (for example, the loyalty of the French barons to the
Crown, either because of their being reassured in their right to property by the
law of majorat or because of the fact that, related as they are by marriages or
otherwise to the reigning dynasty, they could always hope for the succession).

At the same time, in the eyes of the Florentine citizen, the two great northern
countries appeared to embody opposite political examples: France of the successful transition from feudal fragmentation to the unity of a great, modern
monarchy, thanks to a wise political balance between barons, bishops, and
officers representing the central power and also to a fiscal balance between
local privileges and taxes paid to the king; Germany of the substantial failure
of imperial authority, incapable of reconciling the conflicting interests of the
feudal nobility and those of the free communities and of applying the land's
immense resources to a national policy.

Although not as precise and useful on the level of immediate information as
the Venetian ambassadors' reports written in those same years,[15] Machiavelli's
accounts of Germany and especially of France exhibit an acuteness and a
power of synthesis unprecedented in the history of essay writing in compara-
tive politics. They deserve to be associated with the masterpieces of the following years more closely than an often provincial criticism has allowed so far.

In the Ancients' Footsteps: Writing about War

It has often been pointed out that both the inspiration and the initial
form of Machiavelli's *Discourses on Livy* came out of the meetings in Cosimo
Rucellai's gardens or house. There the former republican statesman who was
disappointed with the Medici found attentive listeners among the young, dem-
ocratically inclined men who frequented the gardens, three of whom, Luigi
Alamanni, cousin of the poet by the same name, Zanobi Buondelmonti, and
Batista della Palla, would participate in 1522 in the conspiracy to kill Cardinal
Giulio de' Medici.

The *Art of War* is close to the *Discourses* both in the time in which it was
written (around 1517–20) and in the fictional framing device that Machiavelli

adopted for it. Published in Florence by Filippo Giunta's heirs in 1521, it is the only one of his major works to appear while he was still alive. It recounts a dialogue (modeled after such famous dialogues of that time as Leon Battista Alberti's *Libri della famiglia* and Bembo's *Asolani*) that takes place on the occasion of the appearance in the Rucellai gardens of Fabrizio Colonna, a Roman condottiere who was passing through Florence (most likely in 1516: *terminus a quo* for the writing of the work). For seven books Colonna talks to the master of the house and his friends, among them Buondelmonti, Palla, Alamanni, and a silent and attentive listener, Machiavelli himself. Like the work of the Riminese Roberto Valturio, *De re militari libri XII* (1483), the Machiavellian dialogue makes use of Latin military theorists and historians like Vegetius, Frontinus, and Livy but adds the author's age-old passion for a problem — that of a national army — personally experienced since the time of the Florentine *Ordinanza* of 1505–06[16] and tirelessly dealt with in all of his major writings. If this brings us back to the genesis of the *Discourses on Livy*, the *Art of War*'s dedication to Lorenzo Strozzi (the brother of that Filippo who had married Clarice, daughter of Piero de' Medici, and had been adviser to Lorenzo, duke of Urbino, his brother-in-law) reminds us to some extent of *The Prince*'s dedication to that same Lorenzo de' Medici.

Machiavelli's creative and speculative processes are always influenced by the issues of the present and do not seem to obey any too meticulous planning. But the clear relationship between *The Prince*, the *Discourses on Livy*, and the *Art of War* may tempt one to see them as panels of a triptych on the art of founding, governing, and defending the state, respectively. In fact, in this sense, the *Art of War* represents a conciliation of the first two, inasmuch as, like the *Discourses on Livy*, it extols the harmonious and lawful cooperation of all the components of the social organism and, at the same time, stresses the necessity of a unified military command that is reminiscent of the concentration of all power in one person expounded in *The Prince*: "The kingdoms that have good laws do not give absolute command to their king except in their armies; in this place alone sudden decision is necessary, so in it there must be one and only one authority."[17]

Once again, as in the *Discourses on Livy*, the strength of the argument springs from the contrast between the disastrous failure of the Italian ruling class splendidly described in the concluding chapter —

> The common belief of our Italian princes, before they felt the blows of Trans-
> alpine war, was that a prince needed only to think of a sharp reply in his study,
> or write a fine letter, to show quickness and cleverness in quotable sayings and
> replies, to know how to spin a fraud, to be adorned with gems and with gold,
> to eat and sleep with greater splendor than others, to be surrounded with

wanton pleasures, to deal with subjects avariciously and proudly, to decay in laziness, to give position in the army by favor, to despise anybody who showed them any praiseworthy course, and to expect their words to be taken as the responses of oracles. It did not enter the mind of these wretched that they were preparing themselves to be the prey of whoever attacked them. From that came in 1494 great terror, sudden flights, and astonishing losses; and thus three of the most powerful states in Italy have been many times spoiled and plundered[18]

—and the example, never as deeply admired as here, of the Roman republic:

To honor and reward excellence, not to despise poverty, to esteem the methods and regulations of military discipline, to oblige the citizen to love one another, to live without factions, to esteem private less than public good, and other like things that could easily fit with our time.[19]

Through his spokesman Fabrizio Colonna (a double who is made all the more authoritative by his military past), Machiavelli tackles, in the first book, the problems related to the formation and drafting of an army. After insisting on the strong connection between "good laws" and "good arms" (each needs the other since only civil power can assure a healthy military policy), Fabrizio plunges into a vehement denunciation of war as a business or trade and of volunteers and professional soldiers in general, claiming that they have chosen the occupation of killing as a result of failing at other, more productive activities. Fabrizio favors the figure of the civil soldier—who will fight effectively because he believes in values (patriotism, liberty, family) for which he is willing to die and will return home after the war and reinsert himself into the serene routine of civilian life—to the corrupt, inefficient mercenary troops, which remain Machiavelli's obsessive and polemic target.

Thus, no less important than the "reading of the ancient things" is the "experience of the modern ones," from the economic and administrative resources of a centralized system like the one observed in France and the plans for a national army that was already envisaged in that country, to the fitness of the German mountain dwellers for periodic military service, to the implicit defense of the Florentine militia stubbornly called for by Machiavelli between 1505 and 1512 (the year the secretary's infantrymen were crushed at Prato by the Spanish soldiers).

In the following books Fabrizio's discourse becomes more technical and detailed, but the basis of his reflections lies in the discovery of the importance of infantry in recent wars, after centuries of supremacy enjoyed by the feudal cavalry: a discovery that concurs with Machiavelli's sympathies for the popular party. But this domination of foot soldiers armed with pikes, as demonstrated, above all, by Swiss tactics and successes, appeared to him to be a return to the model of the Macedonian phalanx. And since the Roman legion had proved capable of disrupting the phalanx, likewise a modern infantry organized according to the Roman model could defeat even the Swiss.

Apart from the reduction of Roman military history to a single moment, the project of bringing antiquity back to life is only one of the shortcomings of Machiavelli's military utopia. His exaltation — paradoxically entrusted to a career soldier par excellence like Fabrizio Colonna — of a drafted army made up of citizens doesn't take into consideration the fact that the Roman army was actually composed of well-trained professionals; and his faith in the classical example makes him underestimate firearms in general and artillery in particular and consequently also field fortifications.

On the one hand, then, the *Art of War* dwells on a double prejudice: that patriotic and civic motivations are enough to assure an army of temporary soldiers a basic superiority over expert but corrupt mercenary troops; and that the military craft of the ancients can still provide all the answers to the strategic and tactical problems of the present. On the other hand, the book celebrates and articulates an important idea, or better, a discovery, that of the deep connection between the art of war and healthy political life. If Machiavelli's work on strategy is still read and admired today, it is mostly because of the force with which the figure, new for those times, of the citizen-soldier emerges from the discussion: a figure which personifies in terms of dedication and discipline the great thesis underpinning the *Discourses on Livy,* that of a necessary participation of all the people in the life of the city and in the defense of the state.

From Statecraft and Rhetoric to History

THE *DISCOURSE ON FLORENTINE AFFAIRS*

Between 1515–16 and the publication of the *Art of War* in 1521, Machiavelli's writings, which probably circulated in manuscript form among friends and admirers, were for the most part of a literary rather than political character: a couple of comedies, the *Discourse or Dialogue Concerning Our Language,* the unfinished *Second Decennial, The Ass,* and the "favola," or tale, of *Belfagor arcidiavolo.* In that same period, the gatherings at the Orti Oricellari, which the unemployed Niccolò would participate in, most likely made him assume the role of *maître à penser* for the young Florentine patricians of the Rucellai entourage.

All these circumstances were to promote an image of him that differed from the old one of a clever politician, secretary of the Second Chancery and of the

Ten, and the right-hand man of the fallen Piero Soderini: an appointment for him under the new masters of Florence became conceivable — if not, understandably, an assignment in the sphere of public affairs or a decisionmaking position, at least in some harmless role, say, a cultural endeavor or (to use a modern term for an old idea) political propaganda.

In April 1520 Cardinal Giulio de' Medici was authorized by Pope Leo X to award Machiavelli, as his friend Battista della Palla gladly wrote him from Rome, "una provvisione per scrivere o altro" (a grant for writing etc.).[20] Such permission made possible his appointment to the Studio, that is, the University of Pisa, in November 1520, with a salary of one hundred florins and the task of composing some "annals or chronicles of Florence."[21]

The composition of the *Florentine Histories* will occupy Machiavelli until 1525. But before dealing with this last of his major works, I want to consider two other texts, both from 1520, which in different ways are related to it in that they are almost its antecedents.

When Lorenzo, duke of Urbino, died in May 1519, the future of the Medici family seemed for the moment compromised by the lack of descendants. Giulio de' Medici solicited, on the pope's behalf, the opinion of several local experts on constitutional reforms that could possibly be enacted in Florence. Toward the end of 1520 Machiavelli replied with his *Discursus florentinarum rerum post mortem iunioris Laurentii Medices,* published two and a half centuries later as *Discourse on Florentine Affairs after the Death of Lorenzo* (Florence, 1760), but also extant, with the original Latin title, in an early sixteenth-century manuscript.

Machiavelli begins with the remark that, at least since the end of the fourteenth century, Florence had never been either a true republic or a true principality. The rule of the "ottimati" established by Maso degli Albizzi in 1393 was followed by the latent and tolerant dictatorship of Cosimo and Lorenzo; then, between 1494 and 1512, by a republic that was soon qualified by the institution of a permanent gonfalonier ("gonfaloniere perpetuo") in the person of Piero Soderini — who, however, "had nobody at hand who could defend him"[22] — and finally by the short-lived principate of Lorenzo, the grandson of Lorenzo the Magnificent. As a result of this situation, the patrician group of the "ottimati" had grown progressively weaker, to the point of practically disappearing as a political force.

To this point, Machiavelli's analysis coincided with the opinions expressed by the partisans of the new regime, for example, Goro Gheri or (before Lorenzo's death) Niccolò Guicciardini and Ludovico Alamanni.[23] But while all of them saw the downfall of the patricians as a good opportunity to turn Florentine citizens into good subjects once and for all and thus to strengthen the

Medici's power, Machiavelli notes on the contrary that such a great "equalità di cittadini" (equality among citizens) exists now in Florence that the republican political order is the only possible one left. In contrast, Machiavelli maintains that the opposite condition, the great "inequalità" among citizens, made the principality unavoidable in Milan, for instance, where the duke's power was based on the mediating role between subjects and ruler that the class of gentlemen played in Lombardy: a class so important there or, say, in France, but by now nonexistent in Florence.

Machiavelli is aware, to a certain extent, of the paradox involved in proposing a republican restoration to the Medici, the actual masters of Rome *and* Florence. Therefore he tries to convince Pope Leo X and Cardinal Giulio that their party would remain in power by adopting the complex political structure he has contrived, and that the control of the situation would safely be left in their hands. The functions of the government would be carried out by authorities appointed by the pope: a council of sixty-five notables, among whom a "gonfaloniere di giustizia" would be chosen every two or three years; a council of two hundred members, open to middle-class citizens; and the "Otto di balìa," the Eight, entrusted with foreign and military affairs. These three magistracies holding executive power would be backed by a Great Council ("Consiglio grande") consisting of six hundred to one thousand elected citizens; and by the sixteen gonfaloniers heading the Companies of the People: these last two bodies representing the popular participation in the government of the state. Machiavelli hints at a system of mutual controls among these various institutions, but how these controls would work is not clear, and the future of his republic after the death of the two powerful addressees of his project, Giulio de' Medici and Leo X, is even less clear.

We do not know exactly how the *Discourse* was received in the Medici circles, but one can easily surmise that they saw in it a good reason to stick to the decision already taken by the cardinal, namely, to employ Niccolò as historian, not political counselor.

THE *LIFE OF CASTRUCCIO*

In 1520, the task assigned to Machiavelli to go to Lucca on behalf of the Florentine creditors of the bankrupt Michele Guinigi was another modest sign of a thaw in Machiavelli's long political freeze. In July and August, during his moments of leisure in Lucca, he wrote a *Summary of Lucchese Affairs* and the far more ambitious *Life of Castruccio Castracani of Lucca* (published in 1532 by Blado in Rome and by Bernardo Giunti in Florence with *The Prince* but also preserved in several reliable manuscripts of the sixteenth century).

The idea of writing the life story of the famous Ghibelline condottiere

(1281–1328) was suggested to him by the *Vita Castrucci Antelminelli Lucensis Ducis* published in 1496 by the Lucchese humanist Niccolò Tegrimi. But as can be seen immediately in Machiavelli's dedication to Zanobi Buondelmonti and Luigi Alamanni (both frequenters of the Orti Oricellari and among the characters speaking in the *Art of War*), the chief aim of the booklet was to provide his faithful old friends as well as the new patrons who had appointed him to write about Florence with a sample of good historical prose. At the same time, he was probably tempted to tackle again, this time with changed mind and different interests, the absorbing theme of an individual who having done "very great things" deserved to be brought back to the memory of men as a "very great example" of the power of both human skill and Fortune.

The goals of the work, at the same time rhetorical and ideological, are reflected in the casualness, so many times disapproved of by later historians, with which Machiavelli manipulates the fabric of known events, omitting or altering facts recorded by Tegrimi and adding details either invented or taken from what he read of other great characters in various classical sources: Plutarch's *Lives,* Diodorus Siculus's *Life of Agathocles,* Sallust's *Bellum Jugurthinum,* Xenophon's *Cyropaedia,* and for Castruccio's *dicta* at the end of the short biography, Diogenes Laertius's *Vitae philosophorum.*

The Orti Oricellari friends and first addressees of the booklet were immediately aware that Machiavelli's patchwork composition did not claim in any way to be factually exact, but rather — as Zanobi remarked on his own and his colleagues' behalf — to be recognized "as something good and well written," and such that it made one wish that the author "set out with the utmost diligence to write his [*announced*] history" (letter of September 6, 1520).[24]

From the very beginning, legendary origins worthy of an ancient hero are attributed to Castruccio (found as an infant in a vineyard and adopted by the noble Lucchese canon Antonio Castracani); the character of Francesco Guinigi, a second and more distinguished foster father, is fictional; Montecatini's victory is attributed to the young Castruccio, while, in fact, Uguccione della Faggiuola was the only one in command of the Lucchese-Pisan army; fictitious feats of arms, like those of Serravalle and Fucecchio, are described through details taken from real and overlooked battles, like those of Altopascio and Carmignano.

Could it be that through this systematic idealization Machiavelli was trying to depict and project into the past the figure of the perfect prince, already hoped-for in the future, as if it had really existed in bygone days? To answer in the negative it is enough to consider the historical and psychological context that distinguishes the biographical exercise of 1520 (the same year in which a republican program was presented to the Medici family in the *Discourse*) from the treatise of 1513, *De principatibus*.

To be sure, certain acts of calculated but politically expedient brutality on the part of Castruccio, for example, the repression of the Pogginghi rebellion in 1320, resemble those of Cesare Borgia; and the trivial fever that kills the still-young Lucchese leader is a reminder of the illness that prevented Valentino from running for cover after his father's unexpected death. But it is precisely a comparison of Castracani to Borgia that gives us a measure of the distance between the two works. In 1513, looking ahead beyond Valentino, Machiavelli saw a young Medici, Giuliano or Lorenzo; instead of a future, Castruccio has only a mythical past, so that behind him stand Philip of Macedon and Scipio Africanus: and the defeat of the fourteenth-century ruler compared to the success of those great models can be explained first by the difference between strong Macedonia and Rome on the one hand and puny Lucca and Pisa on the other, and second by the dissimilar and by now overwhelming role played by fortune. This Castruccio himself bitterly admits on his deathbed, taking leave of the young Paolo Guinigi:

> If I had known, my son, that Fortune had wanted to cut me down in the middle of that journey's path leading to the glory which I, through my many successful deeds, had promised myself to attain, I would have toiled less and left you fewer enemies and less envy, though a smaller state. I would have been happy to rule Lucca and Pisa and I would not have taken the Pistoians and angered the Florentines with so many injuries; rather, making each of these two peoples my allies, I would have led a quieter, if not longer, life and would have left you, without a doubt, a more stable and secure state, although a smaller one. But Fortune, who wishes to be the arbiter of all human affairs, did not grant me sufficient judgment early enough to understand her, nor enough time to be able to overcome her.[25]

The struggle of the man of action against fortune, whose outcome was still undecided but promising in *The Prince* and practically settled in 2.29 of the *Discourses on Livy* ("I repeat, then, as an incontrovertible truth, proved by all history, that men may second Fortune, but cannot oppose her; they may develop her designs, but cannot defeat them")[26] now appears to be definitely lost, and in that sense Castruccio's is the idealized life of an impossible hero. This pessimism in the sphere of heroic competition is accompanied by a withdrawal toward a more moderate stand, toward a skepticism that implies not total discouragement, but rather a more resigned stance toward human weaknesses and a feeling of solidarity that arises from the shared experience of a difficult condition. From this point of view, the wisdom regained by Nicomaco in the subdued ending of *Clizia*, or the very idea of converting the Medici family to democracy, are announced by the words of dying Castruccio to his pupil Guinigi.

The "memorable sayings" and the first-person discourses like the one quoted above are the visible manifestations of a more conscious rhetorical commitment than in the great political treatises of 1513–19. They place the *Life of Castruccio*, even on a stylistic basis, between the elegant dialogues of *The Art of War* and the prose of the *Florentine Histories,* of which *Castruccio* was in fact meant to be a sample. Another obvious connection between the *Life* and the *Florentine Histories* lies in their focusing on great exemplary figures when reconstructing the past: in the former the Lucchese ruler, in the latter Theodoric, Giano Della Bella, Benedetto Alberti, Michele di Lando, Rinaldo degli Albizzi, Braccio da Montone, Niccolò and Tommaso Soderini, and so on, not to mention the compelling and towering Medicean protagonists: in this sense, the portrait of Cosimo the Elder at the end of the chapter on his life in the *Florentine Histories* (7.6), concluded by a collection of witty and thoughtful "sayings and replies," represents an appropriate, concise application of the method already tested on Castruccio.

THE *FLORENTINE HISTORIES*

Machiavelli probably set to work on the *Florentine Histories* at the beginning of 1521 and was, with a few interruptions (for example, his mission to the Franciscans in Carpi), occupied with it for about four years. In November of 1523 Giulio de' Medici became Pope Clement VII, and in May of 1525 Niccolò went to Rome to present him with the completed work in eight books. The first editions of the *Florentine Histories* were published practically at the same time by Blado in Rome and by Giunta in Florence in March of 1532. Modern editions also take into account various reliable manuscripts of the sixteenth century. The first book, or "universal treatise," acts as an introduction to the others and deals with the history of Italy from the death of Theodoric to 1414. The three subsequent books mainly cover the internal affairs of Florence: from the origins of the city to the plague of 1348 (book 2); from the middle of the fourteenth century to the death of Ladislao, king of Naples (book 3); and from 1414 to the return of Cosimo de' Medici to Florence in 1434 (book 4). In the following books the scope broadens to include the complex Italian affairs: the war between Filippo Maria Visconti and Florence, dominated by the figures of Niccolò Piccinino and Francesco Sforza (book 5); and a continuation of Italian events between 1440 and 1462 (book 6). Book 7 describes Cosimo's government and the first years in power of the young Lorenzo and closes with the conspiracy against Galeazzo Maria Sforza in Milan in 1476; book 8 treats events from the Conspiracy of the Pazzi to the death of Lorenzo the Magnificent in 1492. It's likely that the decision to stop at that year, after twice expressing in the course of the work (5.1 and 8.18) the intention of reaching Charles VIII's invasion of Italy, was taken when a new Medici pope succeeded Adriano VI, the foreigner, and when, therefore, dealing with the disastrous two-year period that culminated in Piero di Lorenzo and all the Medici being driven out of Florence became a much more sensitive matter.

If instead of simply continuing the *Historiae florentini populi* of Leonardo Bruni (translated into Italian by Donato Acciaiuoli) and Poggio Bracciolini (translated by Jacopo Bracciolini), Machiavelli prefers to start his account from the origins of the city (in fact, in the first book, from the fall of the Roman Empire), the reason given in the preface is that those illustrious predecessors had passed over the internecine divisions of Florence; consequently they overlooked an element that is essential for Niccolò from the *Discourses on Livy* on: the idea that in a final analysis a society's success (as in the case of the Roman republic) or its corruption (as in Florence) depends on the greater or lesser capacity which that society shows in "managing" the inevitable differences of classes. And an additional reason to keep his distance from the two humanist chancellors remembered and criticized in the preface could be the Guelph polemic against all the enemies of the Church that runs through their *Historiae,* especially Bruni's.

Besides Leonardo Aretino and Poggio, Machiavelli is familiar with and uses without quoting Biondo Flavio's *Historiarum ab inclinatione romani imperii decades,* published in 1452–53, and the *Chronicles* of the Villani brothers, of Marchionne di Coppo Stefani, and of Gino di Neri Capponi (and for the first book also Procopius's *History*) in the early part of the narration. In the part closest to the present and for book 4 in particular, he relies again on the fundamental Biondo and on Giovanni Cavalcanti's *History of Florence,* which wouldn't be published until the 1800s but was circulating in manuscripts by the second half of the fifteenth century.[27]

Usually Machiavelli freely uses one source at a time, following it for a while and then abandoning it for another. He doesn't worry about confronting differing versions of the same event or searching for documented confirmations of the events narrated. In this respect, his historiography appears to be radically different from that practiced a few years later by his fellow citizen and friend Francesco Guicciardini. But in his *Istorie* there is an already Guicciardinian bitterness.

Whereas *The Prince* and the first book of the *Discourses on Livy* had aimed at establishing some positive rules or examples with a view to encouraging an action that at that point still looked possible, now the disorder and gratuitous violence that characterized the unfolding of Florentine events make that action appear to be hopeless. This is the irretrievable result of having ignored for too long those basic political laws. From this point of view, the history of Florence and of Italy "resists," owing to its illogicality, a historical interpretation like the one Livy and Tacitus had gloriously offered of Roman history: as Machiavelli remarks when speaking of the conspiracy against the duke of Athens in 1343, the Florentines "cannot keep their liberty and yet cannot endure servitude" (2.36).[28]

The responsibility for "these horrors" and "these hatreds" falls on all the protagonists of the history of Italy. His judgment on the papacy vigorously confirms the one pronounced in 1.12 of the *Discourses on Livy:* "The pontiffs, now through love for religion, now through their personal ambition, did not cease to provoke new dissensions in Italy and to stir up new wars, and when they had made a prince powerful, they repented of it and sought his ruin; thus that country which through their own weakness they could not hold, they did not permit any other to hold" (1.23).[29]

But approaching the present, Machiavelli reserves his most serious denunciation for nepotism, a practice invented by Niccolò III: "As before this time no mention had ever been made of any pontiff's nephews or relatives, so in the future they will fill history; and at last we shall come to sons; and there is nothing left for the pontiffs to try except that, as up to our times they have planned to leave their sons as princes, in the future they may strive to leave them the popedom as hereditary" (1.23).[30]

And one feels the same harshness when Machiavelli points out the other two sore points in the history of Italy, inept political leaders and mercenary soldiers: "Of these slothful rulers and of these dastardly armies my story will be full" (1.39).[31]

Popes, princes, mercenary armies: they are the same targets hit since the *First Decennial,* at the beginning of his career as a historian. But a bitter detachment has now replaced the excited participation one felt in the terza rima chronicle. In the steady flow of the prose discourse all the characters are ironically reappraised: and the vacuum left by their irremediable mediocrity is, as it were, filled by the alert intelligence of the historian, especially in those privileged places ("nooks" Alessandro Manzoni would call them) that the author reserves for his own philosophical and metahistorical meditations. This happens especially in the preambles to the various books and, in a different way, in the great speeches attributed to certain characters.

In the opening remarks of each book one recognizes the intellectual atmosphere of the *Discourses on Livy:* The "mutations" in the republics are due to the nobles' tendency to enslave the people and the people's desire to remain free (book 4). These hostilities between common and noble men are natural because they are "caused by the formers' inclination to rule, and the latters' not to obey"; but in Rome such conflicts were dealt with through debate in accordance with the laws and became an incentive for civic virtues and military valor (book 3); and at the beginning of book 5 the Polybian theory of *anakyclosis* — the cyclical repetition of forms of government throughout history — is lucidly reformulated.

Nevertheless, with respect to the *Discourses on Livy,* one notices in the *Florentine Histories* a clear weakening of the old naturalism on the one hand and of popular or democratic sympathies on the other. Now, Machiavelli distinguishes between three components of Florentine society: the political and economic aristocracy, the people, and the class of artisans or (in Roman terms) plebeians. Starting with the second half of the fourteenth century the people did not want to share power with the nobles and by governing alone not only alienated the other social forces but prevented all healthy competition, paving the way for new, more serious divisions in its very bosom: "The enmities in Florence were always those of factions and therefore always dangerous. Not even a victorious faction ever remained united, except so long as the opposing faction was vigorous. But when a beaten faction was destroyed, since the party in power no longer felt any fear that could restrain it and had no law of its own to check it, the victor became divided" (7. 1).[32]

In the introduction to each book Machiavelli comes back to and corrects the perspectives of the great commentary in Livy with a more severe judgment on his own class or party, and open regret for the political and economic contribution that influential good men would have been able to make in the public sphere if they hadn't all been automatically excluded from power. But the most effective rhetorical moments — and most enjoyable from a literary perspective — are those in which some characters, often of lofty origins, less frequently of humble, anonymous ones, take the floor in order to analyze the situation or to reflect upon their actions.

It is impossible to quote all of these characters, but a few should be mentioned: the discourse of the Florentine citizens in their attempt to dissuade Gualtieri, duke of Athens, from becoming a tyrant is a commendation of freedom and a demonstration of the impossibility of eradicating its memory in a city like Florence — it obviously reasserts ideas already found in the *Discursus to Pope Leo X* and in the *Discourses on Livy* but (if one considers the pathos that shapes it and the result that it is seeking) sounds rather like a sort of "*Anti-prince*" (2.34); the leave of his consorts taken by Benedetto Alberti before going into exile (3.23); the discourse of the Serravezzani to the Ten after being betrayed by the Florentine commissioner Astorre Gianni during the unjust War of Lucca (1429); the response of Niccolò of Uzano to the enemies of Cosimo (4.21 and 27) the following year; the discourse made by the people of Milan to Francesco Sforza in the hope that their present unhappiness caused by the mercenary armies at least will serve as an example to their descendants, "even though that of Thebes and of Philip of Macedon has been of no use to us" (6.20);[33] Lorenzo the Magnificent's oration to the Signoria and the citizens following the Conspiracy of the Pazzi and the excommunication of Florence by Sixtus IV (8.10).

In the speech of the Milanese comparing themselves to the Thebans one recognizes the resurfacing of a small subgenre of classical historiography. But the instinct of the man of theater, deeper in Machiavelli than any humanistic reflex, allows him to put himself in the shoes of the people he is talking about, adopting for a moment their outlook and their interests, even though he does not share them. This is why the Lucchese officer who calls the people to resist the Florentines can effectively depict them as greedy and cruel (5.11), and (in one of the best passages of the work) the anonymous leader of the Ciompi, "one of the most fiery and of greatest experience" among them, can explain their rebellion in strictly political and economic terms, passionately and eloquently defending the oppressed in that which, already at that time, cannot be called anything other than a class struggle: "If you will observe the way in which men act, you will see that all those who attain great riches and great power have attained them by means of either fraud or force; those things then, that they have snatched with trickery or with violence, in order to conceal the ugliness of their acquisition, under the false title of profit they make honorable (3.13).[34]

The ancient historian brought to mind by such magnificent dramatization of political thinking is, paradoxically, the one whom Machiavelli seems to remember the least: that Thucydides who, in a famous dialogue, takes notice of and unmasks the brutal triumph and "ideological" justification of Athenian power over the innocence and weakness of the Melians.[35]

The closer Machiavelli's account of events comes to the present, the more delicate becomes the problem of what to write of the Medici. The Medici had been the protagonists of Florentine history since the second third of the fifteenth century, and one of them, Cardinal Giulio, the family member who always showed the most esteem and sympathy for Machiavelli, had asked him to write the *Florentine Histories*. On the one hand, the attention given to them in the last books accords with the importance attributed to exceptional individuals throughout the course of the work. On the other hand, it was precisely the predominance of the Medici that encouraged that tendency to exile and persecute the patricians, by which acts "Florence was deprived not only of able men but of riches and industry" (4.33).[36]

Cosimo the Elder seems to embody the clairvoyance recommended earlier to the prince in order to overcome chance: "Since [Cosimo] was very prudent, he recognized ills at a distance and therefore he was early enough either not to let them grow or to get ready in such a way that after they had grown, they did not harm him" (7.5);[37] but the author doesn't forget his special relationship with Cosimo's descendants and the potential accusations of sycophancy to which he knows himself to be exposed: so, he warns his reader, even if he praised Cosimo "nobody should be astonished; since he was a man rare in our city, I have been obliged with an unusual method to praise him" (7.6).[38]

On the whole Machiavelli maintains a remarkable impartiality, as could be expected, and although his *Florentine Histories* is not exactly, as an influential interpreter has written, a "determined and coherent demolition of the Medicean legend from Cosimo to Lorenzo the Magnificent,"[39] it is not by chance that the most intense criticism of their power comes in the words of the dying Piero di Cosimo to his supporters:

> I know now that I have greatly deceived myself, since I little realized the natural ambition of all men, and still less yours. It does not suffice you to be leaders in so large a city, and for you who are so few to have those offices, dignities, and advantages with which earlier many citizens were wont to be honored; it does not suffice you to divide among yourselves the goods of your enemies; it does not suffice you to distress all the others with taxes, while you, free from them, have all the public profit, and distress everybody with every sort of injury. (7.23)[40]

Neither is it less significant that in the last book the historian's admiration should go not to the Florentine regime under Lorenzo, but to that of Genoa under the Bank of San Giorgio, a perfect example of "privatization of power" on the part of a practically anonymous group of austere and competent bankers (8.29).

The misgivings Machiavelli had expressed in a letter to Francesco Guicciardini of August 30, 1524, were certainly justified, but no less reasonable were his expectations about the great work he was writing:

> I have been staying and now stay on my farm to write the *History,* and I would pay ten soldi — I do not intend to say more — to have you by my side so that I could show you where I am, because, having to come to certain particulars, I need to learn from you if I give too much offence either by raising or by lowering these things. But I shall keep on taking counsel with myself and shall try to act in such a way that, since I tell the truth, nobody will be able to complain.[41]

In conclusion, the assessment of recent Italian history that Machiavelli draws out at the end of his career sounds catastrophically pessimistic: but such a picture of vile tricks and deceptions will not be without value: "It is perhaps as useful to observe these things as to learn ancient history, because if the latter kindles free spirits to imitation, the former will kindle such spirits to avoid and get rid of present abuses" (5.1).[42]

From the bitterness of this negative lesson come swift and lapidary reflections, as in *The Prince* — "He who is the Pope's friend in wars and in dangers will in victory have a companion but in defeat will be alone, since by his spiritual power and reputation the Pontiff is supported and defended" [8.17])[43] — but also great descriptive moments in which the author seems to celebrate his revenge, as a writer and as a rhetorician, against the dullness of history, as in the truly Leonardesque representation of a storm that hit central Italy in 1456:

> The shattered clouds, now rising toward the sky, now descending toward the earth, crashed together; and now in circles with the greatest speed they moved on, and before them stirred up a wind furious beyond all measure; flames and the most brilliant flashes appeared thick among them as they fought. From these clouds so broken and confused, from these winds so wild and these thick flashes came a noise such as from no sort or size of earthquake or thunder was ever heard before. From this resulted such terror that everybody who experienced it judged that the end of the world had come, and that the earth, the water and the rest of the sky and the world, confusing themselves together, were going back again to the ancient chaos." (6.34)[44]

The *Florentine Histories* has been for a long time the least studied and least understood of Machiavelli's major works. Only recently have scholars come to realize the powerful originality of a text in which the events are grasped in their essentialness from above, as it were, by an intelligence that integrates them and interprets them. It is an impressive instance of philosophical historiography without which, in all probability, the more analytical and philologically reliable work of Guicciardini himself would have been different, if not impossible.[45]

8

Beyond Limits: Time, Space, Language in Machiavelli's Decennali

BARBARA J. GODORECCI

For my own part I think — though all writers may not agree with me — that the shortest way to good prose is by route of good verse.
— *Thomas Hardy, "A Plea for Pure English"*

Machiavelli was a greater poet when he wrote in prose than in verse.
— *Roberto Ridolfi, Life of Niccolò Machiavelli*

It was in the autumn of 1504, in the aftermath of Florence's failed attempt to capture Pisa by diverting the waters of the Arno, that Niccolò Machiavelli wrote the first *Decennale,* changing the course — albeit briefly — of the flow of his own writing. The impact of the event in Pisa would be gauged in many ways: militarily, by the loss of a city of great strategic importance; politically, by the loss of prestige and reputation in failing to capture a long-time adversary; economically, by the stunning loss of seven thousand *ducati.* In a letter to Machiavelli from Cardinal Francesco Soderini (brother to Piero Soderini, gonfaloniere of Florence) dated October 26, 1504, the magnitude of the Florentine defeat may also be measured by the level of disbelief expressed at the outcome of the unfortunate enterprise:

> Assai c'è doluto, che in quelle aque si sia preso tanta fallacia, che ci pare *impossibile* sia stata sanza colpa di quelli maestri che si sono ingannati sì in grosso, forse anche che piace così a Dio, a qualche miglior fine *incognito* a noi altri.

[Much did it pain us, that such fallacy was taken (in) in those waters, that it seems to us *impossible* to have happened without the fault of those masters ("maestri") who erred so grossly, perhaps it pleases God thus, to some greater end *unknown* to the rest of us.][1]

The degree of denial on the part of Cardinal Soderini, evoked by the repetition of a negating *in*-("inpossibile," "incognito") relative to the grave error ("fallacia") of the engineering "maestri" is further amplified by the three augmentatives "assai" (much), "tanta" (such), and "grosso" (grossly). The enormity of Florence's loss to Pisa, therefore, is here expressed vis-à-vis Soderini's reaction to it.

There is no record of Machiavelli's direct response to Soderini's letter regarding the Pisan disaster, but the impact of such a grand event resounds nevertheless in the Florentine secretary's move only a few weeks later to chronicle all of the major historical and political occurrences ("tante *gran* cose" [so many *great* things]) of the previous ten years in his *Decennali*. The first *Decennale* was in fact originally dedicated on November 8, 1504, and focuses on affairs in Italy beginning with the invasion of Charles VIII and ending with the death of Cesare Borgia. Equally notable is the nature of Machiavelli's move: he chooses the poetic medium, rather than prose, for this work. More specifically, the first *Decennale,* composed of 550 verses, is written in terza rima.[2] Much can be speculated regarding the author's choice of poetry over prose and of terza rima in particular.[3] One cannot help conjecturing, for example, about Dante and Petrarch and the extent to which the two figured in this choice. One calls to mind Machiavelli's celebrated letter to Francesco Vettori, written years later of course (December 10, 1513), in which the two masters of Italian poetry are named. In the context of the author's anecdotal recounting to Vettori of his early morning itinerary — of his erring from "bosco" (woods) to "fonte" (spring, source) — Machiavelli takes advantage of a metaphorical *occasione* in order to point to his own literary sources: "Partitomi del bosco, io me ne vo a una fonte, et di quivi in un mio uccellare. Ho un libro sotto, o Dante o Petrarca." (Having departed the woods, I go on to a spring, and from there to my aviary. I have a book in my pocket, Dante or Petrarch.)[4] Dante and Petrarch explicitly figure in as part of Machiavelli's underlying literary legacy ("Ho un libro *sotto* [under, underneath] . . ."), and in the case of the *Decennali,* both the *Divina Commedia* and the *Trionfi* might well have served as exemplary sources for the Florentine secretary's poem,[5] though the use of terza rima was not limited solely to the works of these two illustrious poets. Quite the contrary. The tradition of terza rima to which Machiavelli was heir was both varied and extensive. Over the centuries, the form had proven itself capable of adapting to virtually any tone or style and any sort of subject matter,[6] not least of which was chronicle writing (*cronaca*).[7] As Allan Gilbert writes, "Observation and brief characterization of current history were for [Machiavelli] a necessary occupation";[8] terza rima as a poetic form, with its combined capacity for concatenation and synthesis, was particularly suited to the task at hand and was also in keeping with a characteristically Machiavellian tendency to adopt well-established forms for his works.[9] There is a logic, therefore, in the choice of terza rima for the *Decennali* which is grounded historically, and, interestingly, the historical *terminus ad quem* for *cronaca* written in terza rima is identified as the *Decennali*.[10] Tradition ends with Machiavelli.

All speculation aside with regard to terza rima and Machiavelli's possible imitative sources, one problem related to the secretary's poetic choice emerges from the text itself, and that is his concern with time and space. The question of time and space as it relates to the passage from the realm of human experience to that of language is the focus of the *Decennali*. This concern, quintessentially poetic, is historical, political, and philosophical as well in its implications. Herein lie Machiavelli's most enduring interests, and herein lies, therefore, the relevance of the *Decennali* with respect to Machiavelli's other, later "major" writings. The *Decennali* chronicle historical events leading up to and occurring during the period of Machiavelli's political and diplomatic engagement (1494–1509 and 1498–1512, respectively). Numerous events presented in the *Decennali* will acquire pivotal importance in *The Prince,* the *Discourses,* and even in the comedies: the invasion of Italy by the French king Charles VIII, the political maneuvers of Popes Alexander VI and Julius II, the events at the courts of Caterina Sforza and Cesare Borgia, to name a few. But the *Decennali* represent more than just an archival repository of historical facts, more than just a documentary on political action. They are concerned with language's making of history and the politics of letters, a fundamental concern of all Machiavelli's writings. I have suggested elsewhere that the manner in which Machiavelli deals with the problematics of spatiotemporality by means of his passage through the poetic medium in the *Decennali* represents a turning point for his future writings (*The Prince* in particular): that "discovering the proper 'weight,' 'volume,' and 'speed,' the proper rhythm and timing" of a story is central to his composition of exemplary prose (perhaps the sort of "poetic prose" to which Roberto Ridolfi refers in his biography).[11] Machiavelli's understanding of this process of discovery could not have been one accomplished in the abstract, but rather it had to have taken place within the context of a rhetorically philosophical act, that is, *in writing.*

In the spirit of the observation by Thomas Hardy cited in the epigraph, which takes into account the *act* of passage as well as the *fact* of passing, in this essay I propose to examine the workings of language in Machiavelli's *Decennali,* diverting attention away from *The Prince* and the other familiar works in prose. By focusing on this text in poetry, we pay attention to the threshold of Machiavelli's poetic prose. We are obliged to hear the historical facts recounted in a different manner, wherein they yield to the limits and constraints of scansion, meter, and rhyme. What will follow years later in *The Prince,* the *Discourses,* and Machiavelli's other writings will be profoundly influenced by the rhetorical strategies of the poetic rendering of experience that make up the *Decennali.* Those limits, therefore, are themselves the means, the vehicle by which Machiavelli's language reaches beyond itself.

The terms of this essay are not to establish that the poetic prose which characterizes Machiavelli's most well known works can be traced back to his *Decennali* and that the *Decennali,* as a result, be revisited and revalued. This could be a project for a literary historian. Rather, the impetus for my close reading of Machiavelli is born of the text itself; from the exigencies presented therein. To move in any direction above, beside, or beyond what is written before investigating *what* is written would be to take the text for granted. One cannot take Machiavelli for granted. One can, however, take what Machiavelli grants, that is, an *occasione* to inquire into the question of time and space in (his) language and of (his) language's time and space.

Dedication(s)

The text opens with dedicatory remarks addressed to Alamanno Salviati, patriot and former leader of the Signoria, said to have been the "savior of the [Florentine] Republic at the time of the rebellion in Arezzo."[12] Machiavelli, in homage to "an excellent man," dons him with the epithet of "viro praestantissimo." Some years later, Salviati will reciprocate by labeling Machiavelli a "rogue" (ribaldo). Nevertheless, in the interim, Niccolò notes that he has undertaken to write the *Decennali* on Salviati's invitation ("quae tuo invitatu edimus").

There are two versions of the opening remarks. The first, written on November 8, 1504, appears in the vernacular, and the second, dated "V Idus Novembris MDIIII" (that is, November 9, 1504), in Latin. The two versions have been judged "generally equivalent" by Gilbert,[13] who, as a result, opted to translate only the vernacular passage and to dispense with the subsequent Latin version in his well-known three-volume edition of Machiavelli's chief works. In other complete works editions, privilege is not given over to primacy, and it is instead the authoritative voice of the Latin rendering that speaks first. Given these facts, it is nevertheless legitimate to observe that the two versions have much in common. Both passages address the problem of time and space; the semantic field of reference is one of restriction, limits, tightening, closure. Both make a point of emphasizing the magnitude of the reductive process: of rendering things "so great" and "so numerous" in so few words. In the economy of the process of synthesis and condensation, it stands as a wonderful irony that Machiavelli, quite anomalously, wrote two dedications. But if this is so, then the two merit closer scrutiny. A look at the opening sentence of both passages reveals an immediate and shared concern about the question of time and space:

> Leggete, Alamanno, poi che voi lo desiderate, le fatiche di Italia di dieci anni e *la mia di quindici dì.* (939; emphasis added)

> Lege, Alamanne, postquam id efflagitas, transacti decennii labores Italicos, *nostrum quindecim dierum opus.* (939)

> [Read, Alamanno, since you wish to, the vexations of Italy for ten years and mine for fifteen days. (1444)][14]

One's attention in each case is made to focus on the disparity between the chronology of historical time and that of literary time and specifically on the reductive process operating between the amount of time elapsed in the making and unfolding of events in Italy (ten years) and the amount of time elapsed in Machiavelli's textual remaking of those events (fifteen days). From the outset, we take note of a rhetorical parallel within the text: in both versions there occurs an actual syllabic reduction in the latter part of the sentence (happily conveyed even in the English translation) that corresponds to the poet's literary reduction of history as represented by the *Decennali*. Beyond this, there are also distinct mechanisms at work in the two introductory sentences. In the vernacular version, the passage from years to days occurs with the swiftness of a pen stroke that transforms a dot to an accent mark at the end of an alliterative chorus which plays on the phoneme "di": "le fatiche *di* Italia *di di*eci anni e la mia *di* quin*di*ci *dì*" (the vexations of Italy for ten years and mine for fifteen days). The final, accented "dì," product of a metamorphosis both grammatical (di → dì) and temporal (anni → dì), signals an abrupt end to the rapid succession of repetitions as well as the ultimate end to this historical-poetic journey. The Latin version, on the other hand, emphasizes the passage from the historical to the literary through the use of chiasmus, reversing the order of words in one of the two otherwise parallel phrases. The vexations of Italy and Machiavelli's own (that is, "labores Italicos, nostrum"), at opposite extremes in terms of time and space, are represented nonetheless as specular equivalents, owing to the symmetrical structure of this crossed rhetorical figure. The chiasmus, whose echoing symmetry eliminates a gradual, logical transition within the sentence, greatly accelerates and condenses time, so that the passage between the one and the other occurs in the briefest of periods.

The metaphor extends into the ensuing sentences, where the disparity between historical time and literary time easily becomes a drama of temporal restrictiveness.

> So che v'increscerà di lei e di me, veggendo da quali infortunii quella sia suta oppressa, e me aver voluto *tante gran cose infra sì brevi termini* restringere. So ancora escuserete l'uno e l'altro: lei colla necessità del fato, e me colla *brevità del tempo* che mi è in simili ozi concesso. (939; emphasis added)

> Fortasse nostri aeque ac Italiae vicem dolebis, dum quibus ipsa fuerit periculis obnoxia perspexeris, et nos *tanta infra tam breves terminos* perstrinxisse. Forsitan et ambos excusabis: illam necessitudine fati, cuius vis refringi non potest, et nos *angustia temporis,* quod in huiusmodi ocio nobis adsignatur. (939; emphasis added)

> [I know that you will sorrow for her and for me, seeing her borne down by such misfortunes and me trying to include *so many great things within such narrow limits*. I am sure also that you will excuse us both: her because of fate's necessity and me because of *the short time* allowed me for such advocation. (1444)]

Italy is at once twice oppressed by bad fortune: first, as object of the disastrous events ("infortunii" / "periculis") of her own history, and again as they are recounted in such limited space. This story of Italy, filled with a great number of things grand, is violated *of necessity*—wounded, pricked, and ultimately obfuscated (this is the sense of the Latin "perstrinxisse")—because of its brevity. The drama of Italy is then intensified by Machiavelli's drama; his own temporal poverty with regard to writing the *Decennali*. He laments his lack of time ("ozio") "for such advocation."

By tracking the language of the text on the level of the performative, we discover several corroborative cues to this drama. The first is the actual "squeezing" of the equivalent phrase "so many great things within such narrow limits" between verbal pillars denoting stricture—"aver voluto tante gran cose infra sì brevi termini restringere"—thereby creating, vis-à-vis the split infinitive, a figurative rendering of the process which is here problematized. The coincidence of conceptual and syntactical stricture, dually emphatic, is further accentuated by its placement against a backdrop of implicit augmentation. It co-responds to the "sorrow" of Alamanno, expressed in terms of the verb in-*crescere* (where *crescere*, the root verb, means "to grow"): "So che v'increscerà" (I know that you will sorrow).

The Latin text enters into play with the Italian text by maintaining its role as a contrapuntal voice. We note, for example, an almost verbatim echoing of "tante gran cose infra sì brevi termini" in the Latin "tanta infra tam breves terminos." The concept of the abbreviation of time is demonstrated here by means of the remarkably short leap from the vernacular to its Latin rendering. By manifesting linguistically the extreme likeness between the two languages, all difference (historical, grammatical) and therefore *distance* is compressed. As for Machiavelli's repeated use of the root word *breve* in the phrase "brevità del tempo," we note that the Latin version adopts "angustia temporis" instead. And while this may be accounted for as a simply formulaic rendering in Latin for "the brevity of time," it is nevertheless also true that "angustia" in Latin has principally to do with narrowness and stricture, therefore complementing the image of temporal / syntactical stricture evoked in the Italian version. "Angustia" is also etymologically linked to *anguish* and thus to the pain ("dolebis"), the painful reading of this text. (The anguish of the text.)

The dedicatory passages end with these words:

> E perché voi, col mantenere la libertà di un de' suoi primi membri, avete suvvenuto a lei, son certo suvverrete ancora a me delle sue fatiche recitatore; e sarete contento mettere di questi mia versi tanto spirito, che del loro gravissimo subietto e della audienzia vostra diventino degni. Valete. (939)

> Verum obsecro te ut nobis non desis, sicut illi ac labanti patriae tuae non defuisti, si cupis carmina haec nostra, quae tuo invitatu edimus, non contemnenda. Vale. (939)

> [And since you, by preserving the liberty of one of her chief members, have supported her, I am certain you will support me too as the narrator of her vexations, and will be willing to impart to these my verses so much spirit that they may be worthy of their serious subject and of your reading. Farewell. (1444–45)]

Machiavelli enlists Alamanno Salviati to come to the aid ("suvvenire") of Italy, the poet, and the poem itself. To the "cupis carmina" a "vir praestantissimo" must lend himself; a man who will "be willing to impart to these [. . .] verses so much spirit that they may be worthy of their serious subject and of your reading." Ultimately, it is implied, the reader accomplishes this succoring act through the use of memory ("suvvenire"), the human means to the end of reversing the reductive process, and experiencing the fullness of time. Much of the task of imparting "spirit" to Machiavelli's brief tercets will involve being aware of this reductive process in the text; of comprehending the workings of language on the level of the performative.

The two dedicatory passages to the *Decennali* represent the first of a series of rhetorical attempts in this work to illustrate how language deals with the question of spatiotemporality. In light of this, the two should not be viewed as copies, the one "generally equivalent" to the other — which would make of each merely a clone — but rather as two distinct texts that dovetail one with the other and that as a whole exemplify the explosive and implosive impeta that characterize the relationship between languages and between language and history.

The Poem

The opening verses of the first *Decennale* are indebted to the dedicatory passages. The initial tercets re-present the themes and vocabulary already presented in the dedication(s) and parallel the rhetorical devices found therein, endowing, in this manner, the beginning of the poem proper with some historical depth and an aura of familiarity. To start, we take note of the first three lines. The perception is one of a point of return, rather than a departure *ex novo*:

> Io *canterò* l'italiche fatiche,
> seguite *già* ne' duo *passati* lustri
> sotto le stelle al suo bene inimiche. (940, vv. 1–3; emphasis added)

> [*I shall sing* Italian hardships for those two lustres *now just over,* under
> planets hostile to her good. (1445)]

Machiavelli takes up again with the "fatiche" of Italy, the vexations suffered during the prior ten years ("duo passati lustri"): the lexical echoes and the reiterated temporal time frame make this beginning resemble a cinematographic retake of what immediately precedes it. And as in a retake, the return is altered with respect to what transpired in the first sentences of the dedicatory passages, in particular regarding the problem of time. Here the time is radically out of joint, as what is about to begin has already come to pass ("già ... passati"). The one who will sing ("canterò") appears — sequentially in the verses — prior to what is "now just over." The disparity between historical time and literary time described earlier is not here a focal point on the level of the performative, having been supplanted altogether as a concept by the verbal juxtaposition. The notion (already a conceit!) of historical chronology is subverted from the outset by the very vehicle which purports to represent it.

A second future tense is offered us in the subsequent tercet, in which the poet makes a promise of all that he will narrate. The magnitude, in number, of the "italiche fatiche," mirror reflection and chiasmatic companion of "le fatiche di Italia," is here signaled by the recurrent use of "quanti."

Quanti alpestri sentier, *quanti* palustri
narrerò io, di sangue e morti pieni,
pe 'l variar de' regni e stati illustri! (940, vv. 4–6; emphasis added)

> [Of *how many* mountain paths, of *how many* swamps I shall tell, filled with
> blood and dead men by the vicissitudes of splendid states and kingdoms!
> (1445)]

"Quanti" (how many) stands in the verse both as a marker for the reductive
process operating in the text and as an interrogatory response to the "tante
gran cose" (so many great things) of the dedication. The exchange between
poem and prose is both complementary and augmentative, contrapuntal and
emphatic. Within these "narrow limits" a subtle strategy of amplification,
consisting of an illusion of movement in a linear trajectory enveloped within
the repeated return to the same point, begins to reveal itself.

In order to make it through the poetic journey, the poet calls upon Apollo
and his "sisters" in the third tercet:

O Musa questa mia cetra sostieni,
e tu, Apollo, per darmi *soccorso,*
da le tue suore accompagnato vieni. (940, vv. 7–9; emphasis added)

> [O Muse, hold up this harp of mine, and you, Apollo, come to give me *aid,*
> companioned by your sisters. (1445)]

Machiavelli's call for help ("soccorso") from the god and the Muses recalls
his earlier plea for aid ("suvvenire") from the political muse, Alamanno Salviati. The network of lexical correspondences renders plausible the suggestion
that this is a path already trodden, a familiar point in the landscape. It is a
point at which the text remembers both tradition and itself and in this manner
resonates beyond its own structured / strictured confines in a move toward
expansion that belies "brevi termini."

This perception is countered in the verses immediately following, which
offer an exemplary gesture of irrefutable demarcation of limits:

Aveva 'l sol *veloce* sopra 'l dorso
del nostro mondo ben termini mille
e quattrocen novanta quattro corso. (940, vv. 10–12; emphasis added)

> [The swift sun over the surface of our world had run full a thousand, four
> hundred ninety-four courses (1445)]

One thousand four hundred and ninety-four years pass quickly as the words
run from "aveva" to "corso" (had . . . run). The two components of the
pluperfect tense, auxiliary and past participle, are the first and last words of

the terzina, which between them enclose all grammatical / temporal referents. "Termini" (v. 11) in the strictest sense, "aveva" opens as a *terminus a quo* and "corso" closes as a *terminus ad quem,* summing up, in a most decisively abbreviated form, that period of history prior to the start of the *Decennali.* Temporal velocity, the principal theme of this tercet, acquires figurative weight by the placement of "veloce" (swift) at the center of the first verse (v. 10), perfectly balanced in its symmetry and scansion. The middle verse cannot contain the number "one thousand four hundred ninety-four," which spills into the following verse. The number — "mille/e quattrocen novanta quattro" — cannot contain itself, as indicated by the truncated "quattrocen," whose final syllable is lopped off in the verse. This all stands, however, as a reminder of the anguished excess which is nevertheless reined in: "tanta infra tam breves terminos." This echoes Machiavelli's use of the split infinitive in the dedicatory passage, and the recurrence here of a similar rhetorical tactic reemphasizes the close ties between the initial verses of the poem and the dedication and Machiavelli's preoccupation with the workings of time and language.

The compression of time in language continues as a performative act throughout the *Decennali.* Functioning as a propulsive force, this concept manifests itself in the poem by means of a number of linguistic turns, all concerned with the brevity of time.

An example of this sort of linguistic turn occurs at the beginning of the poem. Having opened the narrative with a description of the French invasion of 1494, Machiavelli focuses his verses on the phenomenon of the French passing through Italy. The "Gallo" (Gaul, cock) becomes, in the following simile, like a falcon or some other "bird of swifter flight" as he swoops down precipitously on his victims:

> E com'e' fu passato nel sanese,
> non prezzando Alessandro la vergogna,
> si volse tutto contr'al Ragonese.
>   Ma 'l Gallo, che passar securo agogna,
> volle con seco del papa 'l figliuolo,
> non credendo a la fé di Catalonia.
>   Così col suo vittorioso stuolo
> passò nel Regno qual falcon che cale,
> o uccel ch'abbia più veloce volo. (940; vv. 40–48)

[And when he had moved into Sienese country, Alexander, making no
    account of shame, turned wholly against the Aragonese.
But the Gaul, who aspired to pass on securely, determined to have the Pope's
    son with him, not trusting Catalonia's promise.
So with his conquering army he moved upon the kingdom like a falcon that
    swoops or a bird of swifter flight. (1445–46)]

The metamorphosis of the one bird into the other, an overt image adopted to describe the swiftness of the turn of events, is accompanied throughout by the verb "passare," signal for this linguistic act of passing. We are prompted to note this turning by the appearance of "si volse" (he turned) and "contr'al" (against) in verse 42. The simile, a figurative rendering of the rapid transition, is the historical event which reveals itself as an event in language.

The poet's interest in lightness and speed is constantly countered by the ponderous vexation ("fatica") of reporting on paper the events in their entirety. The restraints of time and space as they weigh upon the dynamic of the historical account are expressed in verses 223–25 (geographical center of *Decennale I*), in which the poet registers his awareness of the daunting task — still before him — of recounting the lengthy chain of events:

> Lungo sarebbe narrar *tutti* e' torti,
> *tutti* l'inganni corsi in quello assedio,
> e *tutti* e' cittadin per febbre morti. (940, vv. 223–25; emphasis added)

> [Long would it take to tell *all* the injuries, *all* the deceits encountered in that siege, and *all* the citizens dead from fever. (1450)]

Despite the illusion of deceleration offered us on a semantic level, the poet does not really slow the flow in order to dwell within the problem. Indeed, this central moment is one of temporal acceleration and compression, such that what we are left with, by means of Machiavelli's skillful use of *abreviatio,* are only the traces of what has been eliminated. A fleeting reference to its lengthy (and time-consuming) character ("long would it take") and to a myriad of tacit details ("*all* the injuries . . . *all* the deceits . . . *all* the citizens") replace the unfolding of the "facts" of the story in order to press on.

The swiftness of the French returns as a theme in several of the subsequent tercets, giving Machiavelli the opportunity to muse anew on the metaphor of the "Gallo" as bird of prey. Present in the verses, once again, is the figure of the duke Valentino, though in the following sequence, contrary to vv. 40–48, the adversities of fortune are upon him as the Gaul turns the tables, leaving him, along with his father, "high and dry" (in secco):

> ma 'l Gallo, più veloce ch'io non dico,
> in men tempo che voi non diresti "ecco,"
> si face forte contr'al suo nimico.
> Volsono e' Galli di Romagna el becco
> verso Milan, per soccorrer e' suoi,
> lasciando il Papa e 'l Valentino in secco. (944, vv. 253–58)

> [But the Gaul, swifter than I can tell, in less time than you can say "Ecco" rose up against his enemy.

> From Romagna, the French gamecocks turned their beaks toward Milan to
> rescue their fellows, leaving the Pope and Valentino high and dry. (1450)]

Present too, as in verses 40–48, are the linguistic signals "volsono" (*volgere,*
to turn) and "contr'al" (against), turning phrases which mark the turn of
events, and the key term "veloce," positioned midway in verse 253. The reference to speed in that verse is accompanied immediately by an example of
speed in language: "swifter than I can tell, in less time than you can say
'Ecco,' " where, in point of fact, the word "ecco"[15] (here he is) is briefer than
the word "ve-lo-ce"; the appearance of the Gaul swifter than "speed" itself in
terms of scansion. The poet profits from the metric and semantic valences of
the word.

Three tercets further on, the opening phrase "Volsono e' Galli" (the Gauls
turned) reappears, giving added rhetorical forcefulness to this sequence which
focuses on the French passage through Italy. These events, however, are quickly
followed by the reprisal of Duke Valentino, left "high and dry" in verse 258,
but who now gains the upper hand politically by overturning "in short order"
the order of things:

> el duca Valentin le vele sua
> ridette a' venti e verso *'l mar di sopra*
> *de la sua nave* rivoltò la prua;
>   E con sua gente fe' mirabil opra
> espugnando Faenza in tempo curto
> e mandando Romagna sottosopra. (945, vv. 289–94; emphasis added)

> [Duke Valentino again spread his sails to the wind, and *toward the Upper*
>   *Sea turned his vessel's prow;*
> and with his soldiers did wonders storming Faenza in short order and
>   turning Romagna upside down. (1451)]

A Dantesque Ulysses points "his vessel's prow" to sea. An impossible sea
which lies above his ship — " 'l mar di sopra / de la sua nave" — and which
immediately sets in motion a syntactical inversion in the following line (v.
291). A form of *rivoltare* (to turn [over]) — "rivoltò" — is central to the verse,
which turns upon itself as it speaks of political turns and re-turns. The terzina,
too, repeats this motion of rapid overturning in its chiasmatic structure. These
events of the performative preempt "in short order" what is recounted as
historical fact in the next tercet, such that the "turning upside down," a miraculous feat ("mirabil opra"), poetically has already taken place.

The tension between the acts of the text and the facts of the text resurges a
number of tercets beyond, in a sequence involving Vitellozzo Vitelli, ally (and
later, foe) of Duke Valentino,[16] who in the following passage turns against the
city of Florence ("contra di voi"):

> Ma Vitellozzo e sua gente superba,
> sendo *contra di voi* di sdegno pieno,
> per la ferita del fratello acerba,
>   al Cavallo sfrenato ruppe 'l freno
> per tradimento, e Valdichiana tutta
> vi tolse, e l'altre terre, in un baleno. (946, vv. 331–36; emphasis added)

> [But Vitellozzo and his arrogant soldiers, bursting with anger *against you*
>   because of your bitter stroke at his brother,
> by treachery broke the unbridled Stallion's bridle, and took from you in a
>   flash all Valdichiana and the other cities. (1452)]

The motive given for the turn, "per la ferita del fratello acerba" (because of your bitter stroke at his brother), foreshadows the manner in which it will be carried out: "per tradimento" (by treachery). The preposition *per* quickly changes definition from "for," or "because," to "by (means of)." Between the two *per,* the motive and the *modus,* lies the act of betrayal, Vitellozzo's double-cross: his liberation of Arezzo from Florentine rule. The turn of events occurs in the turn of a phrase. In the verse, "al Cavallo sfrenato ruppe 'l freno" (broke the unbridled Stallion's bridle) this double-cross is expressed in Italian by the implicit restoration of a negating *s,* the rapid change of state from "freno" back to "sfrenato," consequence of an intervening act of rupture ("ruppe"). This all transpires within the space of one hendecasyllable, so quickly as to surpass the only reference to speed, which arrives, tardy, in order to conclude the sequence: "in a flash."

The reductive process in the text reaches a point whereupon time seems to overtake itself. Nowhere is this more evident than toward the end of the first *Decennale,* where we find ourselves confronted by the beginning: a remembrance of the opening so familiar in its wording and imagery as to seem a re-presentation of the same:

> Ha volto el sol duo volte l'anno quinto
> sopra questi accidenti crudi e fieri,
> e di sangue ha veduto il mondo tinto;
>   e or raddoppia l'orzo a' suo' corsieri,
> acciò che presto presto si risenta
> cosa, che queste vi paia leggieri. (949, vv. 517–22)

> [For the second time the Sun has finished the fifth year's time above these
>   happenings cruel and savage, and with blood has seen the world imbrued;
> and now he is giving his coursers double barley that speedily speedily such a
>   thing may be heard that these will seem to you slight. (1456)]

The reference to the ten years passed, cited once in the dedication and again in the opening tercet of the poem, returns here in the text as a "now" (or): the point to which all events in their (feigned) unfolding were leading, but contemporaneously a point from which we have never departed.

The totality of the poem is enclosed within the doubled reference (in verse 2 and verse 517) to a single event. To this end, the rhetorical tactic of the split infinitive employed in the vernacular dedicatory passage, and that of a split pluperfect in the fourth tercet, is repeated here by the poet in an analogous gesture — that of the reiterated reference to ten years passed — to squeeze "so many great things within such narrow limits." The individual tactics adopted in the dedication, beginning, and end when combined, suggest a systematic rhetorical strategy, one designed to ponder and challenge the vexing temporal problem of "then" and "now" as a function of language. This is a matter that relates directly to the tradition of terza rima, to Dante in particular, and perhaps it is at this point, "now," that one may further comprehend the relevance of Machiavelli's poetic choice.

All dissolves into a singular "now." The phoneme *or* multiplies ("raddoppia") implicitly in the words that resonate beside it ("*or*zo," "c*or*sieri"), insistent in the urgency ("presto presto" [speedily, speedily]) of its own centrality. It is a moment that contains within itself only itself and, as such, all other moments. "Now" denies "then":

> *Non* è ben la fortuna ancor contenta,
> *né* posto ha fine a l'italiche lite,
> *né* la cagion di tanti mali è spenta;
>   *non* son e' regni e le potenzie unite,
> *né* posson esser, perché 'l papa vuole
> guarir la Chiesa de le sue ferite. (949–50, vv. 523–28; emphasis added)

> [By *no* means is Fortune yet satisfied; she has *not* put an end to Italian wars,
>   *nor* is the cause of so many ills wiped out;
> and the kingdoms and the powers are *not* united and *cannot* be, because the
>   Pope is trying to cure the Church of its wounds; (1456)]

In the verses cited, this is accomplished by two separate means: first, by a pattern of negation ("non," "né," "né," "non," "né"), which refutes the past by forcefully denying the conclusion of "what was"; and second, vis-à-vis a transfer that takes place across the text, in which "l'italiche fatiche," ten years' vexations, reappear transformed in "l'italiche lite" (Italian wars), something other — now — than what they were.

This "now" manifests itself as a paradox of temporality, its capacity to *be* at odds with its own state of suspended finality. This is reflected in the subsequent description of events taking place in Italy in 1504 (vv. 529–37), colored by references to will and desire,[17] the most striking of which, in the context of the writing of the *Decennali*, is Machiavelli's reference to the consuming Florentine ambition to possess Pisa: "e voi di Pisa troppa voglia avete" (v. 537) (And you for Pisa have too strong desire);[18] and it is marked by a defining moment which at present hangs in the balance, as witnessed in the following example:

> Marco pien di paura e pien di sete,
> fra la pace e la guerra tutto pende; (950; vv. 535–36)

> [Mark, full of fear and full of thirst, between peace and war is wholly in suspense, (1457)]

In the enduring and insistent now lies the between ("fra") on which all hangs ("tutto pende"). "The world was altogether held in suspense" (Era sospeso il mondo tutto quando) are the words that reflect back upon the events of 1504 which follow shortly after in the second *Decennale* (v. 16), while at the end of *Decennale I* the poet turns from the world to the first person in his final figuration of this phenomenon:

> Onde l'animo mio tutto s'infiamma
> or di speranza, or di timor si carca,
> tanto che si consuma a dramma a dramma. (950; vv. 541–43)

> [Therefore my spirit is all aflame; now with hope, now with fear, it is overwhelmed, so much that it wastes to nothing bit by bit; (1457)]

"Or" occupies the between of the spirit as well as the verses of the terzina. It is a now that changes in nature, as a genitive *di* in "or di speranza, or di timor" (now [of] hope, now [of] fear) would suggest, rendering poetically possible two states of being depicted in the enveloping verses by the immediacy of the all-engulfing flame and the slow wasting away to nothing. These two states, far removed from each other on the most immediate level of the logical, nevertheless share a bond grammatically — both are identified by reflexive verbs) — and semantically — both are metaphors for an act of self-effacement; an ultimate end. The chiasmus which crosses the two, "*tutto* s'infiamma . . . si consuma *a dramma a dramma*" (all *is aflame . . . it wastes to nothing* bit by bit), offers a means to track textually this poetic possibility by setting up a symmetry between the two extremes, a bond of equivalence that is further reinforced by the circumstance of terza rima itself, which draws them together through rhyme.

The drawing close of the two extremes *is* the drawing to a close. Indeed, we find ourselves at the end of *Decennale I*. An end full of the "now" of suspended finality, propelled by the impetus of the desire to know:

> perché saper vorrebbe dove, carca
> di tanti incarchi, debbe, o in qual porto,
> con questi venti, andar la vostra barca. (950, vv. 544–46)

> [because it seeks to know where your ship can sail, weighted with such heavy
> weights, or into what harbor, with these winds (1457)]

An end that in this respect is not a *terminus* — for it does not conclude — but rather a "falling silent," a laying down of the poet's pen (*Decennale II*, 950, v. 3).

This, however, is a provocation. Machiavelli's work is filled with *termini* of all sorts (rhetorical, grammatical, temporal), as indicated throughout my analysis. The last in this series of linguistic signals is to be found implicitly in the use of terza rima itself. This pattern of rhyme, celebrated for its characteristic capacity of concatenation, is counterdistinguished by an anomalous beginning and end. Whereas each word in the "chain" rhymes with two other words, the first and final rhymes break the pattern of three, diminished by one. In fact, as the poem opens with only two *A* rhymes ("fatiche," "inimiche"), so does it close in symmetry with only two words rhyming ("sarte," "Marte"). The limits of the poem are here clearly marked metrically, two ends of a narrative chain of events; a gesture complementary to the one marking the two temporal *termini* in verses 2 and 517 (see above). Two ends, two beginnings, drawn together by a "now" that represents the briefest point of passage between the two.

The poem seems to dissolve in a sort of facile recommendation, a shortcut to hasten the conclusion of a decade of vexations:

> ma sarebbe il cammin facil e corto,
> se voi il tempio riaprissi a Marte. (950, vv. 549–50)

> [but the voyage would be easy and short if you would reopen the temple of
> Mars. (1457)]

Indeed, the critical explanation offered by the translator suggests that these verses are "best explained as meaning that if Florence would form her own citizen army, instead of relying on mercenaries, she would be more likely to prosper in her foreign policy."[19]

> Pur si confida nel nocchier accorto
> ne' remi, ne le vele e ne le sarte;
> ma sarebbe il cammin facil e corto,
> se voi il tempio riaprissi a Marte. (vv. 547–50)

> [Yet we trust in the skillful steersman, in the oars, in the sails, in the cordage;
> but the voyage would be easy and short if you would reopen the temple of
> Mars. (1457)]

But the final verses of the poem resound with a now ("or") that is knowing ("accorto") and quick ("corto") and that contains the elements of a new beginning ("riaprissi"). Trust ("si confida") in the steersman ("nocchier") is expression of a trust in the means ("remi," "vele," "sarte"): a language capable of going beyond limits.

9

The Classical Heritage in Machiavelli's Histories: Symbol and Poetry as Historical Literature

EDMUND E. JACOBITTI

As many have noted, the key metaphysical support of the past three centuries of Western culture has been the concept of progress, the conviction that history is neither aimless nor cyclical, but a constant overcoming of the inferior by the superior.[1] Without this reliable canon, we would have no assurance of the survival of the fittest peoples and institutions nor any guarantee that democracy and secularism are better than monarchy and religious awe. It is, therefore, difficult for us to imagine a time when history was not so reassuring, when it was conceived as merely the constantly recurring cycle of the birth and death of peoples and cultures, a succession of things in an eternal world whose exact record had no more meaning than a chronicle of the annual change of seasons.

Yet for ancient Greeks and Romans, history was conceived as just such an unending cycle, an inexorable round whose recurrence was more significant than the superficial events that occurred along the way. In such a mental framework, cataloging events exactly as they happened could only be seen as trivial, the equivalent of a factual record of the sequence of leaves dropped from a certain tree in autumn or the dates on which flowers appeared on a particular branch in spring. Indeed, rather than focusing on empirical facts or on change, overcoming, or the path-changing event, ancient historians found meaning in what occurred again and again. Precisely because history did not progress but merely repeated itself, the past was always prologue, filled with meaning for the present and the future. The task of the historian, therefore, was not to record data, but to interpret the past for the conduct of present life. The writing of history, consequently, was conceived as the creation of figurative or allegorical symbols from the natural cycle, a kind of epic poetry filled with imaginative characters, motifs, and ideals like Achilles or Helen who served as models of courage and beauty. The result was that literature and history were understood not as separate disciplines, but as allied forces engaged in providing models of citizenship and statecraft.

With the revival of classical learning in the Renaissance, this poetic and rhetorical conception of history and literature again came to provide a model for numerous writers like Cervantes, Shakespeare, Rabelais, Bruni, and, of course, Machiavelli. For Machiavelli, literature and history were forms of writing freighted with symbols meant to serve as examples or lessons in the conduct of political life. Thus not only were extraordinary humans like Moses, Romulus, and Savonarola made to serve as symbols, but half-humans like Chiron and *fortuna,* animals like the fox and the lion, and even ordinary humans like Cesare Borgia, Agathocles, Oliverotto da Fermo, and Remirro de Orca were crafted into timeless figures of political life.

In this essay, however, rather than exploring the way Machiavelli composed individual humans into symbols, I want to concentrate on the way Machiavelli transformed actual historical cities like Rome and Florence into timeless poetic models of political behavior. I begin by examining the way the ancients made history into poetic symbol, the way this concept of poetic history arrived in the Renaissance, and finally I turn to the way Machiavelli deployed cities as poetic symbols.

Poetic history is, of course, much different from our own scientific history, which focuses on "what really happened" (wie es eigentlich gewesen), as Leopold von Ranke, one of the deans of modern historiography, famously called it. But it could be that one of the unintended consequences of our postmodern "incredulity toward metanarratives" like progress is that modern scientific history too will be revealed as an imaginative whistle-in-the-dark, a symbol of an age that thought it had overcome not only poetry but decline. If so, we, too, may come to appreciate historical writing as creative rather than scientific. In any case, even if the premodern understanding of history has only antiquarian value and does not recur, it is always enjoyable to read alternative metanarratives.

Though Machiavelli lived in the world before it acquired its modern historical anchor, like any person, he accepted *res gestae.* Yet he seemed incorrigibly immune to the idea that an accurate and detailed record of such things meant anything. In any case, even if an accurate record *had* mattered, he said in *Discourses* 2.5, there was no point in trying to put it together; for the world had existed forever, and historical records had been destroyed by human beings and by heaven so many times that recovery of the past was out of the question.

It was not just the general chaos that resulted when a people was conquered or fell into disorder that stood in the way of recovering the record. Rather, it was that the survivors of such calamities were almost always "rustics from the mountains [uomini tutti montanari], who, since they knew nothing of antiquity themselves, could not leave any [such knowledge] to posterity." And worse, "if there be among the survivors any who do have knowledge [of the past], they hide or pervert it for their own use to gain a name and reputation for themselves in the present" (per farsi riputazione e nome, la nasconde, e la perverte a suo modo).[2]

Unlike Alasdair MacIntyre in *After Virtue,* however, Machiavelli was not disturbed by the fact that humanity retained only bits and pieces of earlier events and beliefs.[3] It was simply normal, to say nothing of prudent, that when one people replaced another in the seat of power, they would try to expunge from the historical record as much of the political, social, and cultural institutions of the vanquished as possible. Thus when the early Christians gained the upper hand they "burned the works of the [earlier pagan] poets and historians" so as to leave no "sign of antiquity" (segno della antichità).[4] In fact, the only reason that we have any record of pagan antiquity, said Machiavelli, was because the Christians had been unable to erase the Latin language, for they used it themselves.[5] In short, had the Romans succumbed to Asians with an alien language, the Greco-Roman foundation we find so solid might well have been transformed into the archaeological flotsam and jetsam of an ancient order subdued by oriental civilization.

How is it that Machiavelli could not have been disturbed by the ephemeral nature of human records and human things? The reason, I think, was that he believed that all people, everywhere and always, led similar histories. Like individual species, collective bodies naturally arose out of barbarism, ascended to a mature period of strength, and then declined to weakness and passed away.[6] This did not mean that knowledge of history was pointless. On the contrary, it was useful, but in a way many today will find strange if not erroneous: What was important about history was not, as the Israelites thought, the unique events of a particular people or, as moderns imagined, the record of human progress. Rather, it was the shared experience, in particular, the apparently ineluctable rise and fall of every human order. The world might be eternal; but everything in the world, "all worldly things have a limit to their lives."[7] Instead, therefore, of seeing past people's institutions and practices as remote, quaint, or long since overcome, Machiavelli, like earlier classical historians, saw all human history in phylogenetic terms, the succession of forms through which every city, including one's own, passed from birth to death.

The cyclical idea of history is remote from our understanding of history as progress; but it also has other implications moderns no longer accept. Like Christian theology, cyclical history implied that humans could not be perfected. Indeed, it characterized them as feral, reverting back to savagery after brief periods of unnatural order. Perhaps strangest of all, in cyclical history nothing new ever happened. This was not simply because the historian saw all human orders as running the same course throughout time, but also because in the interminable rise and fall of untold human orders, it was clear that, apart from chance events, everything that had happened once must have done so again and again. Indeed, knowing no industrial revolution or concept of "technological breakthrough," premodern people had good reason to think that the important things never changed. As J. G. A. Pocock has noted, "The Greek and Roman intellects saw little reason to expect anything very new to happen in the human future, and doctrines of cyclical recurrence or the supremacy of chance (*tyche* or *fortuna*) arose and interpenetrated . . . to express this lack of expectation, which sometimes occasioned world-weariness and *angst*."[8]

But "world-weariness and angst" need not be the only response to cyclical history. Indeed, one might well respond that if every order of things must some day end, then political life must be as prudent and moral as possible so that the end not come too quickly. Indeed, as has often been pointed out, the modern notion that history is inevitable progress can, even more easily than the cyclical view, lead to "world-weariness and angst," for if history is perpetual progress, human cooperation or opposition to history is irrelevant. If, on the other hand, history is, like the life of an individual, of limited but uncertain duration, then prudent action rather than passivity seems called for. It is this view that I ascribe to Machiavelli.

For Pocock, of course, as well as for Leo Strauss and many other commentators, Machiavelli was the great "innovator" who set in motion the idea that history could be whatever humanity wished it to be.[9] Humanity, in this modern view, was the only actor in the field, and history must therefore be the product of solely human action. History, therefore, was not something to be tamed but merely to be told; and when the recounting was complete, fortuna, providence, divine hierarchy, and custom would be revealed as mere human creations. History, in short, reveals humanity's own divinity and omnipotence.

It seems to me that Machiavelli would have been the first to criticize this modern arrogance. He understood, as he says in *Discourses* 2.29, that "men can assist fortune but not oppose it; they can weave with her threads [orditi suoi] but never break them." This did not mean, however, that political action was meaningless. Precisely because the life of a state was conceived as the life of an individual human writ large, it was obvious that prudent behavior, while it could not prevent the chance lightning bolt, still seemed to produce a longer and more fruitful life than dissolute and reckless behavior. To think otherwise would have meant that because an individual could not in the end defy death, the best thing to do would be to lie down and read Marcus Aurelius or Epictetus. Machiavelli understood that, notwithstanding repeated renewals and despite all human endeavor, death would someday come. But since no one knew when, it was pointless to be passive. "But one should never surrender to apathy [non si abbandonare mai]," said Machiavelli in *Discourses* 2.29, "for not knowing the ends of fortune, which are always pursued in hidden and devious ways, man should always be ever hopeful and never surrender." In short, though "all worldly things have a limit to their lives," the aim of any normal person was to live in a manner that would allow one to live out that limit.

Thus history was the constant rising and falling of human things. But because of this, it was also the appearance of certain kinds of situations and persons again and again; and it was the appearance of those same crises, characters, and events that attracted interest. The historian, therefore, engages in the use of the past to challenge the present. Significance in historical events derived from the historian's ability to cull from the record eternal symbols and compose them into models that would have heuristic value for the present. History, therefore, always depended on imaginative insight and focused on the present. As such, it was a form of rhetoric that suggested ways to act in an uncertain world.

This kind of rhetorical history seems odd in our time not only because of its rhetorical flourishes, but because with its emphasis on eternal poetic universals, it ignores the huge gaps of time between ancients and moderns that seem obvious to us. To Renaissance humanists, however, the idea of the "rebirth" did not mean, as it does to many of us, that the modern era had begun, but that a new *cycle* had begun. It was this revolution or turning of the wheel that not only allowed the historical symbols to retain their meaning but also brought the ancients into relevance. Indeed, because the humanists saw an identity between past and present, they found it perfectly natural to imitate the ancients, for Petrarch to write letters to Cicero, and in general to act as if a live encounter with Cicero or Livy would not have been awkward. This imitation of the classics in Renaissance history is evident not only in the tropes of the poetic universal, but in the openly political and rhetorical purpose of Renaissance histories.

To suggest that, far from progressing, history simply repeats itself, let alone that the historian resort to imagination in the search for symbols, indicates how far Renaissance historians like Machiavelli are from our own era.

Ancient History, Rhetoric, and Poetics: The Role of the Poetic Universal

Because Machiavelli's notion of history seems so remote from our own, so filled with imaginative symbols and events, it is worthwhile considering the classical historical tradition from which Machiavelli came. In classical times and, in fact, until quite recently history was always regarded as an art form rather than as a philosophy or science.[10] Indeed, in Plato's *Republic,* in which art is generally scorned,[11] there was no place in education for history.[12] Serious subjects belonged to philosophy and religion, which supervised lesser forms like poetry, literature, and rhetoric. Similarly, Aristotle argued that poetry was more serious than history, for the poet had sense enough not to simply "relate . . . things that have happened."[13] Instead, the poet dealt with

> things that may happen, that is, things that are possible in accordance with probability or necessity. For the historian and the poet do not differ according to whether they write in verse or without verse. . . . The difference is that [history] relates things that have happened, [poetry] things that may happen. For this reason, poetry is a more philosophical and more serious thing than history; poetry tends to speak of universals, history of particulars. A universal is the sort of thing that a certain kind of person may well say or do in accordance with probability or necessity — this is what poetry aims at. . . . A particular is [merely] what Alcibiades did or what he suffered.[14]

The only way history could become serious was to rise to the level of poetry and rhetoric. Then, as a branch of rhetoric, it could, with the help of philosophy, address the question of how to live rather than merely recording events. The earliest history, in fact, was associated with Homer's poetry. And this marriage of poetry and history remained a solid relationship throughout the classical period.[15] Thus Quintilian (c. 35–100), the older contemporary of Tacitus (55–120), noted that "history is very near to poetry, and may be considered in some sense as poetry in prose."[16]

It is this association with poetry rather than with science that appears to give ancient history so different a flavor from our own. We are, of course, suspicious of any kind of *ornatus* in history for we are used to thinking of history as a stream of data "received" from the past and recorded without embellishment. But poetic history derived from the Greek concept of *poiesis,* "to make" or "create." Giambattista Vico provided an illuminating example of the etymological heritage of this idea of the poet as creator when he observed that the earliest poets were the savage man-beasts, or *bestioni,* the first figures on the evolutionary ladder. These terrifying and terrified subhumans *created* the gods and the gruesome morality they thought would appease their invented deities.[17] Bloody, unconscious creators or poets thus were the original founders of civilization, the first to bring humanity to order by inventing or creating symbols, rituals, and sacrifices that would support an order of things. Vico, in fact, went so far as to suggest that it was from this originary poetic tree that philosophy itself eventually bloomed.[18] In any case, it is this form of poiesis that underlay the classical concept of history.[19]

Composition, invention, and creativity were, therefore, the tools of early history. There was little reason, therefore, for the historian to be scrupulous in recovering the actual events of history; for such chronology taught nothing. The task of the historian was to take situations, events, or characters from the past and make them fit current needs. If the actual record did not do so, if it was incomplete or silent, it simply needed to be embellished and recomposed in order to provide the examples. Thus when Cicero looked back to Greece, he had Antonius praise their histories not for their accuracy, but for their poetic skill: Thus Antonius praised Herodotus because it was he "who first *embellished* this kind of writing [that is, history]," and Thucydides was important because "in my opinion, [he] has certainly surpassed all historians *in the art of composition.*"[20]

When we realize that poetic history was meant to compose universal types from the flotsam and jetsam of events, we can understand why Cicero scorned early unembellished historical writing as mere chronicles without eloquence or meaning. Until the famous rhetor-historian of the Second Punic War, Coelius Antipater (180/70–after 170 B.C.), said Cicero, Roman "history was nothing else but a compilation of annals. . . . the occurrences of every year. . . . without any ornaments of style . . . simple chronicles of times, persons, places, and events." Then "Antipater, an excellent man, the friend of Crassus, raised himself a little, and gave history a higher tone; the others were no embellishers of facts, but mere narrators."[21]

Antipater's history, like most early histories, was not for private reading but created, like a drama, for a public presentation. As such, the history was filled with all the rhetorical and oratorical devices that would induce awe and wonder in the audience. Thus, according to Antipater, Scipio's army was a force so large that summoning it depopulated all Italy; its numbers and might were so strong that it was preceded by "horrendous earthquakes" and storms; and when its soldiers let out a collective shout, "the birds fell dead from the sky."[22]

The obvious absurdity of such hyperbole did not trouble Cicero, for he understood that history's purpose was to exhort and entreat the citizens to uphold tradition and morality. Since morality does not rest on reason, rhetorical history could not be measured by the standards of truth used in critical philosophy.[23] Those who always want to know whether something is "fiction or fact" or demand that the historian "stick to the truth" do not understand the nature of history. They "display ignorance by demanding in such a matter the kind of truthfulness expected of a witness in court rather than of a poet." Those who accept such a standard probably also "believe that Numa [Pompilius had really] talked with [the nymph] Egeria, and that the cap was placed on Tarquinius' head by the eagle."[24]

Cicero described himself as a true historian because he knew that history and oratory were related. Thus, when he composed *De Legibus*, he had Atticus beg him for a proper Roman history:

> There has long been a desire, or rather a demand, that you should write a history. For people think that, if you entered that field, we might rival Greece in this branch of literature also. And to give you my own opinion, it seems to me that you owe this duty not merely to the desires of those who take pleasure in literature, but also to your country, in order that the land which you saved [in the Catiline Conspiracy] you may also glorify. For our national literature is deficient in history, as I realize myself and as I frequently hear you say. But you can certainly fill this gap satisfactorily, since, as you at least have always believed, this branch of literature is closer than any other to oratory.[25]

In the classical era, therefore, history was supposed to be political, moral, pragmatic, and rhetorical. Its purpose was to influence what happened in the present by examining things that had in one form or another happened again and again in the recurring cycle.[26] The idea that a historian should surrender his place in the present in order to see through the eyes of the past, was unknown; for the point was *not* to lose one's place in the present.

Livy (59 B.C.–17 A.D.), Machiavelli's source for the poetic *Discourses,* provided an example of history composed to address such current political and social problems. Earlier historians like Cato the Censor (the Elder, 234–149 B.C.)[27] and Sallust (ca. 86–35/34 B.C.)[28] had warned that internal forces were destroying Rome; but in Livy's tumultuous time the problem had become more visible. By comparing the moral shortcomings of contemporary Rome with the political virtue of Old Rome, Livy's history of the founding (*Ab Urbe Condita*) was an effort to compose, that is, make or create, a history that would bring his contemporaries to their senses. Livy was not, therefore, interested in recovering the actual record of the past but in using early legends and myths to illustrate what contemporary Romans should strive to emulate. Livy writes,

Here are the questions to which I would have every reader give close attention — what life and morals *were* like; through what men and by what policies, in peace and in war, empire was established and enlarged ["quae vita,
qui mores fuerint, per quos viros quibusque artibus domi militiaeque partum
auctum imperium sit"]; then let him note how, with the gradual relaxation of
discipline, morals first gave way, as it were, then sank lower and lower, and finally began the downward plunge which has brought us to the present time
when we can endure neither our vices nor their cure ["labente deinde paula-
tim disciplina velut desidentis primo mores sequatur animo, deinde magis
magisque lapsi sint, tum ire coeperint praecipites, donec ad haec tempora
quibus nec vitia nostra nec remedia pati pussumus perventum est"]. What
chiefly makes the study of history wholesome and profitable ["salubre ac fru-
giferum"] is this, that you behold the lessons of every kind of experience set
forth as on a conspicuous monument [and] no state was ever greater, none
more righteous or richer in good examples, none ever was where avarice and
luxury came into the social order so late, or where humble means and thrift
were so highly esteemed and so long held in honor.[29]

In short, the study of history for Livy could be "wholesome and profitable"
provided that an imaginative historian composed the material so that it would
stimulate political virtue in the present. To be neutral or objective in historical
matters would have implied that one could be neutral about morality. So
obvious was it that history was about the present, in fact, that a historian had
to be cautious about his composition; for "Roman officials," noted Ernst
Breisach, "understood clearly that the historians, by describing the past, com-
mented on the present and, implicitly, defined their expectations for the future."[30] Modern historians, many of whom also aim to influence the present
and future, have the same problem, though government censors have today
been replaced with those of orthodoxy.

Like Livy, Tacitus, in his *Annals,*[31] endeavored to mobilize history onto the
political field of the postrepublican age by presenting a series of historical
types, poetic universals, so vivid that the audience could easily find them in
present life. "Opposition did not exist," he wrote of the beginning of the
Augustan period. "War or judicial murder had disposed of all men of spirit.
Upper-class survivors found that slavish obedience was the way to succeed,
both politically and financially. . . . The more distinguished men were, the
greater their urgency and insincerity. They must show neither satisfaction at
the death of one emperor, nor gloom at the accession of another; so their
features were carefully arranged in a blend of tears and smiles, mourning and
flattery."[32]

This symbol of the figure who advances himself "politically and financially" through pusillanimous insincerity is so effective because it resonates down to present time as a type we have all seen. In short, it is a composite of careerism, a poetic universal that makes such individuals difficult to miss. What Tacitus, Livy, and for that matter Thucydides and many other ancient historians shared was this ability to compose such symbols from history so they became heuristic models for all time.[33]

The Return of Poetic History in the Renaissance

The classical tradition of history passed out of favor in the medieval and early Renaissance eras, dominated as they were by the schoolmen and their interpretation of the *organon* of Aristotle. The era had little use for history, generally ignoring it in favor of philosophical truth which scorned composition in favor of logic and rational algorithm. History was, therefore, not included in the *trivium* (grammar, logic, and the [empty] rules of rhetoric) or the *quadrivium* (arithmetic, geometry, astronomy, music) and was considered simply a minor form of one of the three great styles of rhetorical literature — usually of epideitic or panegyric.

It was not until later on in the Renaissance that growing secularism and the revival of civic virtue and the *vita activa* made the classical tradition of history again relevant to political life.[34] As a result, the classical idea of concrete, moral, present-tense history slowly reemerged as Renaissance humanists began to use it as a foil to neo-Scholastic abstraction.

What above all distinguished Renaissance rhetoric from the earlier Roman form, however, was the fact that it was no longer confined to oral performance but had also infiltrated the written word.[35] "All the power and skill of the ancient orators," noted Brian Vickers, "was claimed by Renaissance writers, so that the ability to move the affections through language — now written — became a fundamental property of literature."[36] And it was because of this movement from oral presentation to the written page that the rhetorical ideals of persuasion, service, and duty in the vita activa returned to historical writing, where they had once been among the ancient orators. History again came to be regarded as a form of rhetoric valuable for its ability to move an audience by taking known or legendary events and giving them symbolic and moving import.

The standard form of such history was exemplified in the works of Florentine secretaries of the Chancery like Leonardo Bruni (1427–44),[37] Poggio Bracciolini (1435–58), and Bartolomeo della Scala (1465–97). The general formula of such histories relied on Roman models like Livy and Cicero[38] and employed invented speeches, general remarks on universal themes at the beginning of books (chapters), the use of history to create poetic and heuristic examples, and an eloquent style stressing dramatic and rhetorical effect.[39] The primary purpose of these rhetorical devices was, of course, to urge the citizens to follow examples of civic virtue that were drawn from history.

Machiavelli's Rhetorical History

Nowhere is this rhetorical style clearer than in Machiavelli's works. Because of this poetic purpose, it is important to judge Machiavelli's work not for its literal accuracy, but by the moral purpose of its symbols. Examples of elevating an event or a character into a symbol abound in all Machiavelli's works. The discovery of the baby Castruccio by Madonna Dianora, for example, is composed to evoke memories of the origins of Moses or Romulus.[40] Often he takes the stark messages of his diplomatic correspondence, the *Legazioni,* and reworks them until they are elevated into symbols or poetic universals. Thus, the grisly murder of Remirro de Orca (Ramiro de Lorqua), for example, is raised from the initial description in the *Legations to Duke Valentino* to a spectacular example of purification and political advancement in chapter 7 of *The Prince.*[41] Likewise, Borgia's murder of his opponents at Sinigaglia was refined from a mere chronology of savagery in the *Legations* into an account of exceptional ability in the *Description of the Way.* Thus in the original *Legation,* Borgia was described as arrogant, ruthless, and calculating, a master of treachery. In the *Description,* on the other hand, it is Borgia who is surrounded by treachery in a situation filled with danger. Reconfiguring the situation into something ominous and open-ended rather than completely predetermined by the duke heightened Borgia's *virtù,* his ability to seize the *occasione* and destroy his potential betrayers.[42]

Machiavelli's literary intent here was clear. The actual events were secondary to the symbolic interpretation to which the events could be put. In short, the more Machiavelli infused mere empirical reality with poetic interpretation, that is, the farther he moved from chronological description of reality, the more instructive the writing became for use in reality. Every rewriting took the initial description to a higher and more meaningful level than could a mere carbon copy of the things themselves. Borgia thus became a symbol of the effective and ruthless use of virtù, while Vitellozzo became a symbol of hesitancy and vacillation. As Peter Bondanella points out, where the *Legations* were stark, direct, and historical, the *Description* rose to the level of high drama. Indeed, like a standard Renaissance drama, it was composed in five parts.[43] In short, history was an art form.

The greatest of Machiavelli's symbols, however, was that of Rome, the city whose citizens had been the most successful at maintaining their virtue and the only city in the West that had survived a thousand years. Rome, in short, was a poetic universal of the ideal city, all the more significant to the Italian Renaissance because of geographical, cultural, and linguistic ties. The symbol of the city of Rome as the model of civic virtue was common among ancient thinkers like Cicero, who contrasted it with Athens, the symbol of philosophy.[44] Machiavelli's *Discourses*, which created the poem of Roman virtue, therefore, can be contrasted to Plato's *Republic*, which creates the symbol of Athens, famous for philosophy.

In Machiavelli's symbol of Rome as the ideal city, it appeared that political bodies, like human bodies, might have a natural life span, a metaphorical "thousand years." If a city survived the initial challenges and reached maturity, it should, barring chance, run the full course that Rome had run. The mystery, however, was that so few lived out this natural life span. Some never rose to maturity; others died long before their time. This did not, however, invalidate the rhetorical symbol of Rome any more than the death of a generation of young men in wartime would invalidate the model that humans generally live three score and ten. What the idea did do, however, was to allow Machiavelli to raise the question of *why* some cities died an early death.

To Machiavelli, it seemed natural to turn to Roman authors to see what they had suspected had brought states to ruin. Like the Greeks,[45] the Romans believed that it was moral corruption rather physical exhaustion that brought states to eventual ruin; but since moral corruption seemed to always follow on the heels of success, perpetual life seemed out of reach. Seasons of triumph, in short, were also the incubation periods of hubris and decline, so that if a city overcame adversity it became hedonistic and dissolute and then succumbed to cities of greater virtù. Cyclical history, in short, was a tragic drama played out again and again. No order of things could endure beyond its three score and ten; and only those that preserved their political virtù could run this full course: "All things of this world have an end to their lives ["termine della vita loro"], only those that do not allow their bodies to fall into disorder run the full course ordained for them by heaven ["quelle vanno tutto il corso che è loro ordinato dal cielo . . . non disordinano il corpo loro"].[46]

Rome vs. Florence: The Florentine Histories

The symbol of a Rome that had escaped premature death became a fixture of Machiavelli's mental architecture. History, as he began to conceive it, became an attempt to disclose the natural or ideal pattern of human existence and the crises that could derail a people from completing this natural course. In the *Florentine Histories,* Machiavelli created Florence as a symbol to contrast with Rome, enabling him to further explore the kind of moral behavior that could best maintain ability or virtù. This again was not a question of recording history as it really happened, but of creating models of instruction for statesmen in the present.[47]

Earlier histories of Florence, like Bruni's, had been aimed at establishing Florence as the birthplace of the ancient Roman republic in order to beef up Florence's republican heritage and patriotism for the confrontation with the tyranny in Milan.[48] Their aim was to generate patriotism by evoking historical images and symbols of the rise and fall of republics faced with the more efficient government of tyrannies. Machiavelli, on the other hand, composed a different and much less flattering history. If Rome was Machiavelli's symbol of the people who had most exemplified civic virtue and political success, then Florence was the symbol of a city without civic virtue and political success. Machiavelli's aim was no less political or rhetorical than Bruni's, but his advice was different. Whereas Bruni suggested that republics collapsed because they could not compete with more efficient tyrannies like Milan, Machiavelli blamed the collapse on the lack of political virtù necessary to contain the explosive internal divisions that characterized free republics. In short, he took the same city of Florence and gave it a quite different historical diagnosis, making it a symbol for all time of what political bodies should avoid.

The idea that Florence represented more than the city itself, that it was to be viewed as an emblem of political failure intended to have eternal significance was hinted at in the title, *Istorie fiorentine.* The use of the archaic *istoria,* rather than the by-then more common *storia* indicated that Machiavelli's history was infused with poetic or legendary meaning; for the verb *istoriare* meant to illustrate an argument with historical or legendary figures and events. This was "history" turned *into* rather than rescued *from* instructive legend. *Istoriare,* therefore, implied a poetic "making" (poiesis) or composition of historical events, a *rafigurazione* of events into meaningful ideals and symbols. Likewise, the use of the plural "*histories,*" which implied that Florence could have more than one history, foreshadowed his intention to rearrange known events and situations into a different history. In Machiavelli's history, it was not the efficiency of Milan's tyranny, but Florence's inability to handle its internal conflicts that was to blame for its misfortunes. The *Florentine Histories,* in fact, raised those divisions and their repercussions into a poetic symbol of the maladies faced by every republic.

Initially, as Machiavelli says in the preface to the *Florentine Histories,* he had intended to write only of events from 1434, when Cosimo returned from exile. But when he discovered that the earlier histories had skipped over the internal divisions of the city, he composed a longer history centered around the eternal problem of divisions in republics.[49] Thus whereas Bruni and earlier historians had written hymns to their *patria* to inspire it to live up to its history, Machiavelli composed a poem urging his fellow citizens to overcome their past.

Though he begins with the idea that reading about one's own patria is more moving than about some other,[50] his aim was to advance the theme of decline in Florence:

> If in describing the following things that happened in this wasted world ["in questo guasto mondo," that is, Florence] one does not tell of the strength of soldiers, or the virtue of the captain, or the love of the citizen for his fatherland, one will see [instead] with what deceits ["inganni"], with what guile and arts the princes, soldiers, and heads of republics governed themselves in order to maintain the reputation they have not deserved. It may, perhaps, be no less useful to know these things than to know the ancient ones, because, if the latter excite liberal spirits to follow them, the former will excite such spirits to avoid and eliminate them.[51]

It is impossible to discuss every one of the symbols Machiavelli raised with respect to the internal divisions in Florence, but at least two of them can be accommodated here. According to Machiavelli, one factor in the failure of Florence and the success of Rome lay, oddly, in the fact that Florence leveled out its divisions into an egalitarian homogeneity, while Rome preserved its noble and plebeian classes and the conflict between them. Machiavelli attributed this difference to the "diverse ends" (diversi fini) of the nobility and the peoples in the two cities.[52] Thus whereas the ancient nobles of Rome had been, in Machiavelli's model, reasonable and compromising, the nobles of Florence were pigheaded, selfish, and not "content to live with that modesty which is required by civil life [vita civile]. . . . Every day produced some example of their insolence and arrogance [insolenzia e superbia]."[53] And like the Roman nobles, the Roman people were reasonable and made modest and piecemeal demands for a share of political power, desiring "to enjoy the highest honors together with the nobles [insieme con i nobili]." On the other hand, "the desire of the Florentine people was injurious and unjust." They did not want to share power with the nobles but "wanted to be alone in the government [essere solo nel governo] *without* allowing the participation of the nobles."[54] The result was catastrophic; for instead of the Florentine people being elevated by participation in noble life, the nobles, in order to survive, were forced into the measure of the common people. Thus even if a virtuous person wanted to serve the patria, rather than retaining his virtue, he was forced "not only to be but to seem like the men of the people in their spirit and mode of living [con lo animo e con il modo di vivere simili ai popolani non solamente essere ma parere]."[55]

Therefore, Machiavelli suggests that Rome survived longer because it did not resolve the "very great inequality" (disaguaglianza grandissima) that existed between the ranks, while Florence failed because its "inequality" was resolved into a "miraculous equality" (mirabile ugalità). Thus, said Machiavelli, "the virtue in arms and the generosity of spirit [virtù delle armi e generosità di animo] faded out among the nobility, and in the people, where [these virtues] had not existed, they could not be rekindled; thus Florence became ever more humble and abject."[56] Finally, "the ruin of the nobles was so great and afflicted their party so much that they never again dared to take up arms against the people; indeed, they became continually more ordinary and abject [più umani e abietti]."[57]

Machiavelli's interest here was certainly not in historical accuracy. One could easily write a different history of Rome, citing examples of pigheaded Roman aristocrats and immodest demands by the Roman people. Likewise, his interest was not in taking sides between the Florentine nobles who would not share power and the people who wanted only power and nothing noble.

Machiavelli's aim, rather, was to point out the importance of maintaining the conflict between the two classes and the malevolent consequences for Florence (and all people) of the popular victory and the leveling out of virtue: "Thus was Florence stripped not only of its arms but of all its generosity."[58] In short, Machiavelli raised the internal conflict itself to the level of an instructive poetic universal and argued that far from resolving it, the effort should have been to preserve it.

It has often been said of Machiavelli that he takes exceptional circumstances and turns them into the norm. Such a statement, of course, depends on what is normal and what exceptional. For moderns, the norm is tranquility, resolution, and absence of tension. Anything that puts conflict at center stage, therefore, is, in modern terms, taking the exception and making it the rule.[59] The salutary benefits of continued conflict can be understood only within the framework of premodern cyclical history, which regards struggle as healthy political aerobics, good for the system as long as it does not become excessive. Conflict is, in short, the emblem or symbol of a healthy city.

The second poetic universal that Machiavelli raised in the *Florentine Histories* (and elsewhere) was the danger posed by learning and letters as opposed to "effective truth."[60] Whether wealth was a cause of corruption had, of course, been raised by earlier Roman historians,[61] but the idea that a city had anything to fear from increasing the learning of its citizens raised different matters. It was not simply that Machiavelli doubted that learning was a commodity that, because of some "difference principle," could be redistributed through education, but that learning might, in fact, cause the city to lose its virtù, its political and military skill. Certainly, learning and letters always coincided with the beginning of military descent. "Letters come after arms" and "captains come before philosophers."[62]

Cities reached the apex of their development because of a resolute virtù, their ability or skill to resist internal and external dangers. But having reached the highest stage on the cycle and "having no further to rise, they must descend"; for having defeated their opponents and seeing no reason to retain their virtù, they were easily seduced by the temptations of leisure. To Machiavelli, the most iniquitous of seductresses were letters, learning, and philosophy, nouns he usually coupled with such pejoratives as "sluggishness" (ozio) and "corruption" (corruzione) and "deceit" (inganno).[63]

In ancient Rome, said Machiavelli, the subversive nature of the *vita contemplativa* had been avoided by the timely actions of Cato, who intervened "when the philosophers Diogenes and Carneades were sent to Rome by Athens as spokesmen. When he saw how the Roman youth were beginning to follow them about with admiration, and since he recognized the evil that could result to his fatherland from this honest idleness [onesto ozio], he saw to it that no philosopher [niuno filosofo] could be accepted at Rome."[64]

The danger that lay in learning and letters was that it suggested that philosophical truth might be more effective than arms, more civilized. What bothered Machiavelli about learning, in other words, was that it seemed to imply that there were eternal answers to the human condition, whereas the constant rising and falling of human things excluded such a solution. Thought had to be directed at questions of the moment. In short, philosophy was otherworldly, having nothing to do with the rising and falling of the real world.

Of course, the philosophy that Machiavelli had in mind here was Christianity. There were many reasons for his rejection of Christianity,[65] but his primary reservation was that Christianity was imprudent because it ignored the problems of concrete life, its founder "not being of this world." It directed human attention to the preservation of the soul, to life after death, rather than to the *vita attiva*. And since, as we know, Machiavelli loved his patria more than his soul, it was not surprising that he rejected Christianity.[66] In this sense, Machiavelli was the case limit of the classical humanist tradition, determined to focus on practical matters rather than the eternal verities of the schoolmen. Many humanists were somehow able, as was the mainstream of Christianity itself, to marry otherworldliness and worldliness. It is, however, difficult to imagine that any philosophy would have satisfied Machiavelli; for he was too aware of the impossibility of making *res* and *verba* congruent. Moreover, the

Church seemed to Machiavelli to be, despite its avowed interest in the other world, too much of this world. The Church, in other words, taught its adherents to keep their eyes on heaven while it seized the earth.

In short, the advocates of learning were self-interested and no different from any other adversary. They were, however, more clever; and Machiavelli, in the end, believed they would always win people over. Thus, in the *Florentine Histories,* he portrayed the men of letters as engaged in a deadly game of mastery over *la vita attiva* or *vivere civile.* Because learning and the *vita contemplativa* appeared after the "Captains" and "arms," when citizens were exhausted and the price of victory obvious, men of letters were easily able to enter the "fortress of well-armed spirits" (la fortezza degli armati animi). Like a fifth column, they began to teach the benefits of reason over warfare and by this "great and most dangerous deceit" (maggiore e più pericoloso inganno) they bring the city to ruin. But so cleverly decked out in the "most honest idleness of corrupting learning" (il più onesto ozio . . . delle lettere corrompere)[67] were the philosophers that they always defeated prudence.

Against this assault of theory on vigilance and prudence, Machiavelli opposed an ideal of discord and struggle, of a ceaseless opposition to the idea of resolution represented by philosophy. In short, as he had suggested in the case of the struggle between noble and plebe, healthy life was conflictual. Without that conflict, a city would succumb to Nietzsche's last men.

In conclusion, then, one may say that Machiavelli's historical perspective forces us into a situation in which there are no answers. Choosing how to combine such antinomies as liberty and equality, individual interest and the common good, political religion and religious politics, wealth and virtue is always necessary and in a healthy republic always present. The idea that the disputes at the roots of human society cannot be, or should not be, eliminated by philosophy implies that these disputes are the equivalent of Aristotle's "starting points," the self-evident principles upon which a healthy state must be founded. It implies that these issues can be treated only hermeneutically, literarily, as in a conversation rather than as chronological history. A world without resolution, in which reason can never provide common ground, however, seems to turn all philosophy into a question. It is this that makes Machiavelli so incompatible with modernity.

Contributors

Robert Faulkner, Department of Political Science, Boston College

Franco Fido, Department of Romance Languages and Literatures, Harvard University

Barbara J. Godorecci, Department of Modern Languages and Classics, University of Alabama

Michael Harvey, Department of Business Management, Washington College

Edmund E. Jacobitti, Department of History, Southern Illinois University, Emeritus

Harvey C. Mansfield, Department of Government, Harvard University

Ronald L. Martinez, Department of French and Italian, University of Minnesota

Arlene W. Saxonhouse, Department of Political Science, University of Michigan

Susan Meld Shell, Department of Political Science, Boston College

Vickie B. Sullivan, Department of Political Science, Tufts University

Notes

Introduction

1. Niccolò Machiavelli, *The Prince,* trans. Harvey C. Mansfield (Chicago: University of Chicago Press, 1998), 33.

2. The letter is dated January 31, 1515, and is quoted from *Machiavelli and His Friends: Their Personal Correspondence,* trans. and ed. James B. Atkinson and David Sices (DeKalb: Northern Illinois University Press, 1996), 312.

3. The letter is dated October 21, 1525, and is quoted from *Machiavelli: Tutte le opere,* ed. Mario Martelli (Florence: Sansoni, 1971), 1224.

4. Atkinson and Sices, *Machiavelli and His Friends,* 371.

5. Roberto Ridolfi, *The Life of Niccolò Machiavelli,* trans. Cecil Grayson (Chicago: University of Chicago Press), 219.

6. Machiavelli, *Prince,* 4.

7. Niccolò Machiavelli, *Mandragola,* trans. Mera J. Flaumenhaft (Prospect Heights, Ill.: Waveland Press, 1981), 10.

8. Hanna Fenichel Pitkin, *Fortune Is a Woman: Gender and Politics in the Thought of Niccolò Machiavelli* (Berkeley: University of California Press, 1984), 169. Anthony Parel identifies a different controlling force in Machiavelli's thought, but one that has the same effect. He maintains that Machiavelli's writings reveal him to be indebted to a premodern cosmology that understands human action to be determined by the movement of heavenly bodies: "It follows that we cannot explain human destiny solely in terms of human autonomy" (Anthony J. Parel, *The Machiavellian Cosmos* [New Haven: Yale University Press, 1992], 63).

9. Wayne A. Rebhorn, *Foxes and Lions: Machiavelli's Confidence Men* (Ithaca: Cornell University Press, 1988), 38–39, 170–83, 187. Ultimately, however, he concludes that Machiavelli's view is not tragic (247–48).

10. Giorgio Barberi-Squarotti, *La forma tragica del "Principe" e altri saggi sul Machiavelli* (Florence: Olschki, 1966).

11. See, for example, Roberto Ridolfi, *Studi sulle commedie del Machiavelli* (Pisa: Nistri-Lischi, 1968), 65–66, and Luigi Russo, *Machiavelli* (Bari: Editori Laterza, 1957), 94. Ronald Martinez has more recently offered a dark interpretation of Machiavelli's comedy when he compares *Mandragola* to its source, the story of the rape of the virtuous Roman matron Lucrezia contained in Livy's history. In so doing, Martinez finds "Lucrezia is transformed from the single remaining spark of ancient virtue to the absolute mistress of the corrupt world of the play"; and "cured of her resemblance to Roman Lucretia, Lucrezia comes to stand for an ambiguous female power that thwarts the ideal political agendas of the male *virtù* that, in Machiavelli's typology, strives to conquer history and fortune" (Ronald Martinez, "The Pharmacy of Machiavelli: Roman Lucretia in *Mandragola,*" *Renaissance Drama* 14 [1983]: 39–40).

12. Martinez's interpretation of *Mandragola,* discussed above in note 11, exemplifies this particular view.

13. Leo Strauss, *Thoughts on Machiavelli* (Glencoe, Ill.: Free Press), 292.

14. Mera J. Flaumenhaft in her interpretation of *Mandragola* expresses this view ("The Comic Remedy: Machiavelli's *Mandragola,*" *Interpretation* 7 [1978]: 59). Although Carnes Lord's allegorical reading of *Mandragola* finds much that is "uncomic" in this comedy, he maintains that while "Machiavelli's political vision is not simply comic, . . . it has an affinity with comedy if one understands by comedy the archetypical celebration of the triumph of youth and desire over age, authority, and duty" (Carnes Lord, "Allegory in Machiavelli's *Mandragola,*" in *Political Philosophy and the Human Soul,* ed. Michael Palmer and Thomas Pangle [Lanham, Md.: Rowman and Littlefield, 1995], 150–51).

15. Strauss, *Thoughts on Machiavelli,* 171–73, 253. The phrase "new modes and orders" appears in the preface to book 1 of Niccolò Machiavelli, *Discourses on Livy,* trans. Harvey C. Mansfield and Nathan Tarcov (Chicago: University of Chicago Press), 5.

16. Harvey C. Mansfield, *Machiavelli's Virtue* (Chicago: University of Chicago Press, 1996), 3–4, 43–44, 109–10, 262–63. For an additional discussion of the character of Machiavelli's rule, see also Vickie Sullivan, *Machiavelli's Three Romes: Religion, Human Liberty, and Politics Reformed* (DeKalb: Northern Illinois University Press, 1996), 10, 121, 172–73, 176–80.

17. Machiavelli uses these terms in *Discourses* 1.9 when he explains that the writings of Agis, revealed posthumously to his successor Cleomenes, inspired the latter to attempt to carry out the former's plans for the reformation of Sparta.

18. Strauss, *Thoughts on Machiavelli,* 40.

19. Machiavelli, *Discourses,* 138–39.

20. Ibid., 139–40.

21. Plato, *The Laws,* trans. Thomas L. Pangle (New York: Basic Books, 1980), 676b–677b.

22. Machiavelli, *Discourses,* 139–40.

23. For a discussion of what this knower of antiquity who survives the flood shares with Machiavelli, see Sullivan, *Machiavelli's Three Romes,* 132–39.

24. Machiavelli, *Discourses,* 257.
25. Ibid., 266.
26. Ibid.

1. *The Cuckold in Machiavelli's* Mandragola

1. See Leo Strauss, *Thoughts on Machiavelli* (Glencoe, Ill.: Free Press, 1958), 40.

2. See Roberto Ridolfi, *Studi sulle commedie del Machiavelli* (Pisa: Nistri-Lischi, 1968), 11–35; Sergio Bertelli, "When Did Machiavelli Write *Mandragola?*" *Renaissance Quarterly* 24 (1980): 317–26; Gennaro Sasso, "Considerazioni sulla '*Mandragola,*' " in Niccolò Machiavelli, *La Mandragola,* ed G. Sasso (Milan: Rizzoli, 1980), 5–18.

3. See Strauss, *Thoughts on Machiavelli,* 284–85.

4. I am using the excellent translation by Mera J Flaumenhaft, *Niccolò Machiavelli, Mandragola* (Prospect Heights, Ill.: Waveland Press, 1981).

5. See Marvin T. Herrick, *Italian Comedy in the Renaissance* (Urbana: University of Illinois Press, 1960), 165; cf. Mark Hulliung, *Citizen Machiavelli* (Princeton: Princeton University Press, 1983), 101.

6. For remarks on the parallel, see Benedetto Croce, *Poesia populare e poesia d'arte* (Bari: Laterza, 1933), 246; Luigi Russo, *Machiavelli* (Bari: Laterza, 1988), 109; Ezio Raimondi, *Politica e commedia; dal Beroaldo al Machiavelli* (Bologna: il Mulino, 1972), 202; Hanna F. Pitkin, *Fortune Is a Woman* (Berkeley: University of California Press, 1984), 47; Ronald L. Martinez, "The Pharmacy of Machiavelli: Roman Lucretia in *Mandragola,*" *Renaissance Drama* 14 (1983): 1–43; Michael Palmer and James F. Pontuso, "The Master Fool: The Conspiracy of Machiavelli's *Mandragola,*" *Perspectives on Political Science* 25 (1996): 130; Mera J. Flaumenhaft, *The Civic Spectacle* (Lanham, Md.: Rowman and Littlefield, 1994), 89–90; Carnes Lord, "Allegory in Machiavelli's *Mandragola,*" in *Political Philosophy and the Human Soul,* ed. Michael Palmer and Thomas L. Pangle (Lanham, Md.: Rowman and Littlefield, 1995), 154.

7. Livy 1.57–60; St. Augustine, *City of God,* 1.19.

8. Niccolò Machiavelli, *Discourses on Livy,* trans. Harvey C. Mansfield and Nathan Tarcov (Chicago: University of Chicago Press, 1996), 1.44.1.

9. Machiavelli, *Discourses on Livy* 3.5.1, 3.26.2.

10. Ibid., 1.16.4, 3.5.1.

11. Harvey C. Mansfield, Jr., *Machiavelli's New Modes and Orders* (Ithaca: Cornell University Press, 1979), 316.

12. Cf. Croce, *Poesia populare,* 248.

13. Niccolò Machiavelli, *The Prince,* trans. Harvey C. Mansfield (Chicago: University of Chicago Press, 1998), chap. 17.

14. Machiavelli, *Discourses on Livy* 2.13.1.

15. Francesco DeSanctis, *Storia della letteratura italiana,* 2 vols (Turin: Gallo, 1958), 2:597; Richard Blank, *Sprache und Dramaturgie* (Munich: Wilhelm Fink Verlag, 1969), 146–56.

16. Machiavelli, *Discorso o dialogo intorno alla nostra lingua,* 777a26, 40, in Niccolò Machiavelli, *Discorso o dialogo intorno alla nostra lingua,* ed. Bortolo Tommaso Sozzi (Turin: Einaudi, 1976), 23.

17. On levity and gravity, see Machiavelli's Letter of January 31, 1515.

18. Machiavelli, *Discourses on Livy* 3.2.

19. Machiavelli, *Clizia* 1.3.

20. Franco Fido, "Politica e teatro nel badalucco di Messer Nicia," in Fido, *Le metamorfosi del centauro: Studi e letture da Boccaccio a Pirandello* (Rome: Bulzoni, 1977), 103.

21. See Harvey C. Mansfield, *Machiavelli's Virtue* (Chicago: University of Chicago Press, 1996), 8–9.

22. Cf. Russo, *Machiavelli,* 97.

23. On Nicias, see Machiavelli, *Discourses on Livy* 1.53.4, 3.16.1.

24. In his foolishness Messer Nicia fears the infinite ocean will threaten his home.

25. The song in praise of Dinah contains a warning: "Dinah! Is there anyone finah? In the state of Carolina? If there is and you know her, show her to me."

26. Machiavelli, *Discourses on Livy* 3.6.11.

27. See Herrick, *Italian Comedy,* 81: In the *Mandragola* "no move, no word is wasted"; also, Raimondi, *Politica e commedia,* 213; Giorgio Cavallini, *Interpretazione della Mandragola* (Milan: Marzorati, 1973), 16; Mireille Celse, "La Beffa chez Machiavel, Dramaturge et Conteur," in *Formes et significations de la "Beffa" dans la littérature italienne de la renaissance* (Paris: Université de la Sorbonne Nouvelle, 1972), 101.

28. Plato, *Republic* 346d.

29. Machiavelli, *Discourses on Livy* 3.6.7. Cf. Niccolò Machiavelli, *Florentine Histories,* trans. Laura Banfield and Harvey C. Mansfield (Princeton: Princeton University Press, 1988), 3.13.

30. Cf. Sasso, "Considerazioni sulla *Mandragola,*" 73: "This tragedy dissembled in the forms of comedy." But the forms are important.

31. See Raimondi, *Politica e commedia,* 256–58.

32. Machiavelli, *Discourses on Livy* 3.1.4.

33. See Russo, *Machiavelli,* 113–14. There are eleven speeches in this scene (3.3).

34. See Blank, *Sprache und Dramaturgie,* 162.

35. Ligurio mentions seven good things that will be achieved by this abortion, including the return of the girl to her father, i.e., the maintenance of respectability which Messer Nicia preserves by allowing himself to be cuckolded (3.4).

36. See Strauss, *Thoughts on Machiavelli,* 285.

37. Ligurio will speak to Brother Timothy "between you and me," as if God were not in the church (3.6).

38. Machiavelli, *Florentine Histories* 7.34, 8.6.

39. The monologues are: Siro, 2.4; Messer Nicia, 3.7, 4.8; Brother Timothy, 3.9, 4.6, 4.10, 5.1, 5.3; Callimaco, 4.1, 4.4. See Russo, *Machiavelli,* 115.

40. Machiavelli, *Prince,* chaps. 13, 24; *Discourses on Livy* 2.10, 2.20.

41. Desdemona to Emilia, speaking of adultery: "*Desdemona:* Wouldst thou do such a deed for all the world? *Emilia:* The world's a huge thing; it is a great price for a small vice" (William Shakespeare, *Othello,* 4.3.67–69, in *William Shakespeare: The Complete Works* [New York: Viking Press, 1979]).

42. One must pay attention to Brother Timothy's arguments, not merely to his venality; cf. Cavallini, *Interpretazione della Mandragola,* 16.

43. As Flaumenhaft points out, this argument "is almost a parody of the extended

discussion of Lucretia's chastity in the *City of God*" (*Civic Spectacle,* 103). See also Raimondi, *Politica e commedia,* 202.

44. Cf. Giulio Ferroni, *Mutazione e riscontro nel teatro di Machiavelli* (Rome: Bulzoni, 1972), 68, who says that Lucrezia's act comes from an "autonoma decisione." Any "autonomy" is really a gift from Machiavelli insofar as he makes apparent how Lucrezia's will is taken away from her, thus suggesting how it might be restored. One could also say that the liberation from Christianity presupposes the experience of Christianity.

45. See Raimondi, *Politica e commedia,* 203; Ferroni, *Mutazione e riscontro,* 84–85.

46. In 2.6, Callimaco says that he would not want to be married if his wife wasn't "a mio modo." Machiavelli shows him how he would.

47. Allegedly similar, of course! See Gen. 19.

48. See Machiavelli, *Discourses on Livy* 3.30.1.

49. See Pitkin, *Fortune Is a Woman,* 111–12; Russo, *Machiavelli,* 109–10; Paulo Baldan, "Sulla la vera natura della *Mandragola* e dei suoi personaggi," *Il Ponte* 34 (1978): 393; Jack D'Amico, "The *Virtù* of Women: Machiavelli's *Mandragola* and *Clizia,*" *Interpretation* 12 (1984): 266; Susan Behuniak-Long, "The Significance of Lucrezia in Machiavelli's *La Mandragola,*" *Review of Politics* 51 (1989): 264–83.

50. The angel Raphael brought relief to Sarah by giving her eighth husband, Tobias, a remedy for an evil demon who had killed the previous seven on their wedding nights; Tob. 2–9. See Flaumenhaft, *Civic Spectacle,* 102; Raimondi, *Politica e commedia,* 203–05.

51. See Matt. 26:23; Martinez, "Pharmacy of Machiavelli," 30.

52. He says "I" (Io) twelve times, teasingly, in one paragraph.

53. Callimaco reports Lucrezia's remarks, but they are not funny (5.4).

54. See Boccaccio, *Decameron* 8.6.

55. Brother Timothy says that "if I were he and you were she, we wouldn't sleep." So, Brother Timothy wants to play Callimaco to all the spectators! The prologue says, "And I would wish that you [the audience] might be tricked as she [Lucrezia] was." "Tricked," as Flaumenhaft points out, is *ingannate,* in the feminine plural (*Mandragola,* 10).

56. See Flaumenhaft, *Mandragola,* 49.

57. Machiavelli, *Prince,* chap. 18.

58. See Raimondi, *Politica e commedia,* 263; Cavallini, *Interpretazione della Mandragola,* 49

59. The "donne" are still "in casa" (56); see Ferroni, *Mutazione e riscontro,* 99–100.

60. See Pitkin, *Fortune Is a Woman,* 30; Cavallini, *Interpretazione della Mandragola,* 61; Raimondi, *Politica e commedia,* 211; Fido, *Metamorfosi del centauro,* 105; Baldan, "Sulla vera natura," 390, 396; Lord, "Allegory in Machiavelli's *Mandragola,*" 158; Ruth Grant, *Hypocrisy and Integrity* (Chicago: University of Chicago Press, 1997), 46. Opposed are Joseph A. Barber, "La strategia linguistica di Ligurio nella *Mandragola* di Machiavelli," *Italianistica: Rivista di letteratura italiana* 13 (1984): 395; Felix Fernandez Murga, "Una possibile fonta classica della *Mandragola* del Machiavelli," in Vittore Branca et al., eds., *Il Rinascimento: Aspetti e problemi attuali* (Florence: Olschki, 1982), 379; Celse, "Machiavel dramaturge et conteur," 100–01, 104; Palmer and Pontuso, "Master Fool," 126.

61. At the most, he says, "I want to be the captain" (4.9). To understand this claim, one must reflect on Machiavelli's use of "captain" in the third book of the *Discourses.*

62. Not merely to Lucrezia, as D'Amico, "*Virtù* of Women," 270–71, maintains.

63. If Lady Fortune can allow herself to be raped (*Prince,* chap. 25), Messer Nicia can allow himself to be cuckolded. Consider again Emilia in Shakespeare's *Othello,* 4.3.74–76: "Who would not make her husband a cuckold to make him a monarch? I should venture purgatory for't."

64. Anyone who wants to get to the bottom of the *Mandragola* needs to reflect on the "king of France," here and elsewhere in Machiavelli's writings.

65. Machiavelli, *Discourses on Livy* 32. Palmer and Pontuso, "Master Fool," 130. Ferroni, who discusses *pazzia* at length, *Mutazione e riscontro,* 56–61, does not mention the possibility, or this instance, of feigning it.

66. Cavallini, *Interpretazione della Mandragola,* 51n; Pitkin, *Fortune Is a Woman,* 31.

67. Machiavelli, *Discourses on Livy* 3.17, 3.22.3.

68. Ibid., 1.pr.2.

69. Ibid., 2.26.

70. Machiavelli, *Prince,* letter dedicatory.

2. Clizia *and the Enlightenment of Private Life*

1. The account expands upon my introduction to Daniel T. Gallagher's translation of *Clizia* (Prospect Heights, Ill.: Waveland Press, 1996). I am grateful to Waveland Press for permission. Quotations from the play are from Gallagher's translation; references are by act and scene. For suggestions as to the original essay, I thank especially Mera J. Flaumenhaft and also Kent Cochrane, Daniel Gallagher, and Sharon Johnson.

2. *Discourse or Dialogue Concerning Our Language,* which is entitled *A Dialogue on Language* in *The Literary Works of Machiavelli,* ed. and trans. J. R. Hale (Westport, Conn.: Greenwood Press, 1979), 188.

3. Hale, *Literary Works,* xxvi. Daniel C. Boughner, *The Devil's Disciple: Ben Jonson's Debt to Machiavelli* (New York: Philosophical Library, 1968).

4. *Henry VI,* Part 1 (5.4.74), in *Shakespeare, The Complete Works,* ed. G. B. Harrison (New York: Harcourt Brace, 1952); *Merry Wives of Windsor* (3.1.101), in *Shakespeare, The Complete Works;* consider the vicious but thoroughly calculating Antonio in the *Tempest* and the grand but also thoroughly calculating Augustus—the "universal landlord"—in *Antony and Cleopatra.* See David Lowenthal, *Shakespeare and the Good Life* (Lanham, Md.: Rowman and Littlefield, 1997), 35–36; as to Caesar Augustus, see Robert Faulkner, *Francis Bacon and the Project of Progress* (Lanham, Md.: Rowman and Littlefield, 1993), 131–33.

5. See Richard Andrews, *Scripts and Scenarios* (Cambridge: Cambridge University Press, 1993), 205, 52, 253n33.

6. Roberto Ridolfi, *The Life of Niccolò Machiavelli,* trans. Cecil Grayson (Chicago: University of Chicago Press, 1965), 210. Ridolfi explains Machiavelli's motive for writing the play as simply to ready an entertainment for a feast—thus to please his host or his lady friend (208).

7. Boughner, *The Devil's Disciple,* 12.

8. Titus Maccius Plautus (c. 254–184 B.C.). Twenty-one of Plautus's comedies survive.

9. *Clizia,* in Niccolò Machiavelli, *Il teatro e gli scritti letterari,* ed. Franco Gaeta (Milan: Feltrinelli Editore, 1965), 116–18.

10. Does the rhetorical attention to women help explain the plot of the play? The plot results in protection of women young and old against an errant husband and repulsive lecher — one old enough to be the girl's grandfather and related enough to be in effect her father.

11. Latin versions of the *Poetics* appeared in 1498 and 1536; Greek texts were printed in 1508 and 1536. See E. Lobel, *The Greek Manuscripts of Aristotle's Poetics* (Oxford: Oxford University Press, 1933), 11. Compare Douglas Radcliffe-Umstead, *The Birth of Modern Comedy in Renaissance Italy* (Chicago: University of Chicago Press, 1969), 3; *Aristotle's Poetics,* trans. George Whalley, ed. John Baxter and Patrick Atherton (Montreal: McGill-Queen's University Press, 1987), 6.

12. Horace, *Art of Poetry* in *Satires, Epistles, and Ars Poetica,* trans. H. Rushton Fairclough (Cambridge: Harvard University Press, 1991), ll. 391–407.

13. Horace, *Art of Poetry,* ll. 193–201.

14. Aristotle, *Poetics,* ed. and trans. W. Hamilton Fyfe (Cambridge: Harvard University Press, 1965), 1460b37–1461a12.

15. Ibid., 1448b30–35.

16. Ibid., 1461a 5–12.

17. Ibid., 1448b14–17.

18. I use the translation by Mera J. Flaumenhaft (Prospect Heights, Ill.: Waveland Press, 1981).

19. Leo Strauss, *Thoughts on Machiavelli* (Glencoe, Ill: Free Press, 1958), 292.

20. *Mandragola,* in Niccolò Machiavelli, *Il teatro e gli scritti letterari,* ed. Franco Gaeta (Milan: Feltrinelli Editore, 1965).

21. Andrews, *Scripts and Scenarios,* 52.

22. Hale, *Literary Works,* 188.

23. Ibid., 187, 189–90.

24. Ibid., 190.

25. *Il Principe,* in Niccolò Machiavelli, *Il Principe e Discorsi sopra la prima deca di Tito Livo,* ed. Sergio Bertelli (Milan: Feltrinelli Editore, 1960), chap. 17.

26. *The Prince,* trans. Harvey C. Mansfield (Chicago: University of Chicago Press, 1985), chap. 15.

27. *Prince,* chaps. 12, 17. *Discourses on Livy* 1.27.

28. Hale, *Literary Works,* xii.

29. Ibid., 188.

30. *Clerumenae,* or "the lot drawers," a lost work by Diphilus.

31. Andrews, *Scripts and Scenarios,* 111–12.

32. Horace, *Art of Poetry,* ll. 270–74.

33. Horace, *Epistles,* in *Satires, Epistles, and Ars Poetica* 21.168–76.

34. Horace, *Art of Poetry,* ll. 268–69, 309–11.

35. Ronald L. Martinez, "Benefit of Absence: Machiavellian Valediction in *Clizia,*" in *Machiavelli and the Discourse of Literature,* ed. Albert Russell Ascoli and Victoria Kahn (Ithaca: Cornell University Press, 1993).

36. Marvin T. Herrick, *Italian Comedy in the Renaissance* (Urbana: University of Illinois Press, 1960), 45.

37. See Harvey C. Mansfield, *Machiavelli's Virtue* (Chicago: University of Chicago Press, 1966), 297, 13–16, 74–77, 179–80; see also *Discourses on Livy,* trans. Harvey C. Mansfield and Nathan Tarcov (Chicago: University of Chicago Press, 1996), Introduction, xxxvi, xxxviii.

38. If one ventures to play around with names, "Nicomaco" could remind of the *Nicomachean Ethics.* The *Ethics,* which takes the gentleman as moral model and is *the* philosophic defense of moral virtue, was supposedly addressed to Aristotle's son, Nicomachus. Nicomaco's strange mixture of hypocritical moralism and uncontrolled passion might be Machiavelli's little comment on the practicability of Aristotelian moral virtue as a disposition to select the "mean." Might *Clizia* also hint maliciously that Aristotle's moralism denies to young sons the pleasures that fathers secretly desire and would appropriate for themselves?

39. William Shakespeare, *A New Variorum Edition of Shakespeare,* ed. Horace Howard Furness (New York: Dover Publications, 1964), 1.2 and 4.1.

40. See Mansfield's note 4 to chap. 2 of *The Prince.*

41. Hanna Fenichel Pitkin, *Fortune Is a Woman: Gender and Politics in the Thought of Niccolò Machiavelli* (Berkeley: University of California Press, 1984), 119.

42. *Prince,* chap. 25.

43. *Discourses on Livy* 1.4.5; see especially Martin Fleischer, "Trust and Deceit in Machiavelli's Comedies," *Journal of the History of Ideas* 27 (1966): 374; also Martinez, "Machiavellian Valediction in *Clizia,*" 120, and Timothy Lukes, "Fortune Comes of Age (in Machiavelli's Literary Works)," *Sixteenth Century Journal* 9 (1980): 44–45.

44. *Discourses on Livy* 3.1.

45. *Prince,* chap. 23.

46. *Prince,* chap. 7.

47. Martinez, "Machiavellian Valediction in *Clizia,*" 131.

48. Consider Ridolfi, *Life of Machiavelli,* who dismisses without serious argument the "theory" that the two plays make up a "diptych designed for particular moral ends" (209). He refers to a work, which I have not considered, by G. Tambara, *Intorno alla Clizia di Niccolò Machiavelli* (Rovigo, 1895).

49. *Prince,* chaps. 3, 7, 8, 12.

50. See also *Mandragola* 2.6; 3.1, 9, 10, 11; 5.5, 6.

51. Cf. Isa. 53:3.

52. Catherine Zuckert, "Fortune Is a Woman—But So Is Prudence: Machiavelli's *Clizia,*" in *Finding a New Feminism: Rethinking the Woman Question for Liberal Democracy,* ed. Pamela Jensen (Lanham, Md.: Rowman and Littlefield, 1996), 34, 37n5.

53. *Mandragola* 3.1.

54. Ibid., 5.5.

55. Ibid., 5.4.

56. Cf. Isa. 52:3–9, 13, 14.

57. *Mandragola* 5.6.

58. Cf. Isa. 66:4–12, 57:11–14, 59:17–19, 62:11–12, etc.; Ezek. 44:10–14.

59. Zuckert, "Fortune Is a Woman—But So Is Prudence," 25.

60. Cf. *La Vita di Castruccio Castracani da Lucca,* in *Istorie Fiorentine,* Niccolò Machiavelli, *Opere,* ed. Franco Gaeta (Milan: Feltrinelli, 1962), 13.

61. *Mandragola* 5.2, 5.

62. Ibid., 2.6.

63. Ibid., 1.3, 5.4.

64. Aristotle, *Politics,* trans. H. Rackham (Cambridge: Harvard University Press, 1972), 1336b20–35.

65. Ibid., 1448a32,36–39, 1449a12–13, 1448b35–1449a2, 1449b 5–9.

66. Aristotle, *Nicomachean Ethics,* trans. H. Rackham (Cambridge: Harvard University Press, 1975), 1127b33–1128b9. See Susan D. Collins, "The Ends of Action: The Moral Virtues in Aristotle's *Nicomachean Ethics,*" Ph.D. diss., Boston College, 1994, 159–72.

67. Lukes suggests that "the triviality and humor of the dramatic medium may have best suited Machiavelli's intentions — to relate truly revolutionary and immoral ideas without being labeled a gross revolutionary and atheist himself" ("Fortune Comes of Age," 37n4). This is compatible with a clever man's perceptions of "how dangerous" such a play was "for a young man." Consider the first encounter with *Mandragola* of the playwright Carlo Goldoni, who "devoured" it and immediately reread it "at least ten times" (*Memoirs of Carlo Goldoni,* trans. John Black [Boston: James Osgood, 1877], 72).

3. Comedy, Machiavelli's Letters, and His Imaginary Republics

1. Douglas Radcliff-Umstead, *The Birth of Modern Comedy in the Renaissance* (Chicago: University of Chicago Press, 1969), 2. The recently recovered and printed texts of Plautus and Terence in the late quattrocento were not alone in their influence on comedy in the cinquecento; it drew most especially on the *Decameron* of Boccaccio (ibid., 59–61). Cf. note 4 below. Some authors suggest that it drew as well on *commedia dell'arte,* but the timing appears to be off, at least as far as Machiavelli is concerned because *commedia dell'arte* develops during the middle of the cinquecento, after Machiavelli's comedies were produced. Cf. Richard Andrews, *Scripts and Scenarios: The Performance of Comedy in Renaissance Italy* (Cambridge: Cambridge University Press, 1993); Jackson I. Cope, *Secret Sharers in Italian Comedy: From Machiavelli to Goldoni* (Durham: Duke University Press, 1996), 3–4.

2. I have been unable to find in the scholarly literature on Dante a satisfactory explanation of why Dante used the word "comedy" in the title for his work. Alessandra Fussi has pointed me to Dante's letter to Cangrande in which Dante himself (assuming the authenticity of the letter) explains that he used the term *commedia* in the title of his work because comedies end happily, and while at the beginning of the poem the content is "horribilis et fetida, quia Infernus," he assures that at the end it is "prosera, desiderabilis et grata, quia Paradisus" (Dante Alighieri, *Epistola a Cangrande* [Florence: Giunti Gruppos Editoriale, 1995], 12). Teodolinda Barolini, *The Undivine Comedy: Detheologizing Dante* (Princeton: Princeton University Press, 1992), 67, 292n8, points to the place in the *Divine Comedy* where Dante uses "commedia" and identifies comedy with that which makes truth out of lies ("ver c'ha faccia di mensoga," *Inf.* 16.124). Dorothy Sayers's chapter "The Comedy of the *Comedy,*" in which she notes places in the poem that evoke a

smile or suggest self-mockery on Dante's part, has the following priceless passage: "I have sometimes played with the idea of writing a story, and dropping into it, casually and without comment, the following sentence: 'George was curled up comfortably in the big arm-chair, chuckling over *The Divine Comedy*'" (*Introductory Papers on Dante* [Chicago: University of Chicago Press, 1954], 151).

3. For example, see Catherine Zuckert, "Fortune Is a Woman — But so Is Prudence: Machiavelli's *Clizia*," in *Finding a New Feminism: Rethinking the Woman Questions for Liberal Democracy*, ed. Pamela Jensen (Lanham, Md.: Rowman and Littlefield, 1996); Mera Flaumenhaft, "The Comic Remedy: Machiavelli's *Mandragola*," *Interpretation* 7 (1978): 33–74; and Hanna Fenichel Pitkin, *Fortune Is a Woman: Gender and Politics in the Thought of Niccolò Machiavelli* (Berkeley: University of California Press, 1984), 29–32, 110–15.

4. E.g., Andrews, *Scripts and Scenarios*, 18, argues that the *novelle* tradition and especially Boccaccio's *Decameron* was "no less important" a source for Italian Renaissance comedy than Plautus and Terence. Radcliff-Umstead, *The Birth of Modern Comedy*, 241, suggests that Boccaccio, perhaps even more than Plautus and Terence, inspired the growth of comedy and that Italian dramatists, with the example of the *novelle*, explored domestic relations more deeply than the Roman playwrights had ever dared to attempt; Marvin T. Herrick, *Italian Comedy in the Renaissance* (Urbana: University of Illinois Press, 1960), 58, makes similar claims.

5. Old comedy of Aristophanes certainly had a public focus with attention to the political life of Athens, but the mechanism for evoking comedy was to draw attention to the private foibles of the public characters and often to reduce the city to the realm of the family, cf., e.g., *Lysistrata* and *Ecclesiazusae*. New Comedy, stretching from Menander to Terence to the *commedia erudita* of the Italian Renaissance, focused directly on domestic life.

6. Flaumenhaft, "The Comic Remedy," 59, appropriately notes, "It has been said that there is no place for tragedy in the works of Machiavelli [the reference is to Leo Strauss, *Thoughts on Machiavelli* (Glencoe, Ill.: Free Press, 1958), 292]. His view of human *virtù* and Fortune preclude a world where pity, fear, and the recognition of divine justice constitute the proper human attitude. One effective way to undermine the sacred doctrines of older teachings is to refuse to recognize their seriousness."

7. Quoted from *A Dialogue on Language* in *The Literary Works of Machiavelli*, trans. J. R. Hale (London: Oxford University Press, 1961), 188.

8. Prologue to the *Clizia*, *The Comedies of Machiavelli*, trans. David Sices and James B. Atkinson (Hanover: Published for Dartmouth University Press by University Press of New England, 1985).

9. Harvey Mansfield, Jr., *Machiavelli's Virtue* (Chicago: University of Chicago Press, 1996), 262–63.

10. Andrews, *Scripts and Scenarios*, 115.

11. Ibid., 18.

12. In what follows I refer to the letters in the volume edited and translated by James B Atkinson and David Sices, *Machiavelli and His Friends: Their Personal Correspondence* (DeKalb: Northern Illinois University Press, 1996), by number and date. About the humor, comedy, and paradoxes which fill the letters, see especially Giulio Ferroni,

"'Transformation' and 'Adaptation' in Machiavelli's *Mandragola*," in *Machiavelli and the Discourse of Literature* (Ithaca: Cornell University Press, 1993), 81–116.

13. Many of the letters describe in vivid language Machiavelli's own love affairs and reflections on love's power. The analogy is often made between love and political rule. Love "binds me with his fetters," such that Machiavelli is "in absolute despair of my liberty" (Letter 247, March 1, 1515).

14. We also come to recognize through Machiavelli's frequent allusions to the literature of the Italy of his own time his deep knowledge of the artistic and comic literary works of his compatriots. Here I rely heavily on John Najemy, *Between Friends: Discourses of Power and Desire in the Machiavelli-Vettori Letters of 1513–1515* (Princeton: Princeton University Press, 1993), who traces the relationship between Machiavelli and Vettori through a study of their correspondence. Najemy identifies the literary allusions and provides detailed analyses of how Machiavelli's own incorporation of the literary allusions play out in his own presentations — and justify our working through to below-the-surface readings of Machiavelli's own writings. Though some of Najemy's psychoanalytic speculations on occasion wear on this reader, I found the book a goldmine of subtle readings and explorations of Machiavelli's complex relationship with Vettori and more importantly of his nuanced usage of literary references.

15. *Prince,* chap. 5. All translations are from Harvey Mansfield, Jr., *The Prince* (Chicago: University of Chicago Press, 1985).

16. Najemy, *Between Friends,* has an extremely helpful chapter (chapter 1, pp. 18–57) on the art of letter writing in the Renaissance. He summarizes the generally accepted humanist tradition of letter writing: "a written substitute for speech among friends, whose purpose is to preserve friendship in the face of separation" (47) and, after quoting Kristeller, who wrote that "perhaps the most extensive branch of humanist literature is that of epistolography," he notes, "I would add that it was also the Proteus among Renaissance literary genres. It slipped into the *novella,* the treatise, and the essay, into poetry and the theater; it was public and private, political and personal" (57).

17. This letter begins, "*Magnificent One, my most respected superior,* I was sitting on the toilet when your messenger arrived, and just at that moment I was mulling over the absurdities of this world" and includes a description of how he is trying to trick the Friars into believing that he is carrying on a correspondence with Guicciardini of the utmost political significance. The playfulness of the letter continues throughout — on through the phrases about telling the truth and not telling it — so we do not know whether to believe or not believe. We are left in a sense in an infinite regress of lies and truth.

18. Mansfield, *Machiavelli's Virtue,* 268–69, suggestively raises the place of images and imagination in the education of the prince: "It takes a rare brain to see an invisible similitude in a visible one," Mansfield notes and shortly thereafter concludes, "More attention might be given to the use of imagination in Machiavelli's behavioral political science." I contend that the letters may help us focus this attention on Machiavelli's "imagination."

19. Najemy, *Between Friends,* 137–38, has a very different reading of this passage. He sees Machiavelli's putting himself in the place of the pope as an attempt not to offend Vettori; i.e., by expressing his views as if they might be the pope's, Machiavelli avoids the possibility of appearing to disagree with Vettori. This reading reduces the letters to

personal interactions "between friends," as is the general thrust of Najemy's book. I see a more theoretical import to Machiavelli's comments here.

20. Machiavelli's letters provide a magnificent trove of information and insight into Machiavelli's life and into his imaginative, creative, and speculative talents. Any full analysis would require a far more elaborate study than the present one. In this essay I begin with only a few of the letters which point to some of the comic themes that are relevant to Machiavelli's politics.

21. Sebastian de Grazia, *Machiavelli in Hell* (Princeton: Princeton University Press, 1989), 126.

22. Pitkin, *Fortune Is a Woman,* 116.

23. Giulio Ferroni, "Le 'cose vane' nelle *Lettere* di Machiavelli," *La Rassegna della letteratura italiana* 76 (May–December 1972): 215–63.

24. Linda Carroll, "Machiavelli's Veronese Prostitute: *Venetia Figurata,*" in *Gender Rhetorics: Postures of Dominance and Submission in History,* ed. Richard C. Trexler (Binghamton, N.Y.: Medieval and Renaissance Texts and Studies, 1994), 99.

25. Juliana Schiesari, "Machiavelli and Fortune's Rape," in *Desire in the Renaissance: Psychoanalysis and Literature,* ed. Valeria Finucci and Regina Schwartz (Princeton: Princeton University Press, 1994), 177, 173, 181.

26. Quentin Skinner, *Machiavelli* (Oxford: Oxford University Press, 1981), 48, is correct to note that Vettori "responded with an ominous silence" to Machiavelli's manuscript and requests for responses, and that Vettori "instead began to fill up his letters with distracting chatter about his latest love affairs." That Machiavelli responded to this "chatter," however, does not reduce his own letters to chatter. As I hope to suggest, the letters transform chatter into explorations of political possibilities and limits.

27. Najemy, *Between Friends,* 265.

28. Atkinson, in Atkinson and Sices, *Machiavelli and His Friends,* translates this as "imagines," but that is not an accurate reflection of the Italian. See Franco Gaeta, *Opere di Niccolò Machiavelli,* vol. 3, *Lettere* (Turin: Unione Tipografico-Editrice Torinese, 1984), 442.

29. Vickie Sullivan wonders whether this movement toward the hearth parallels Machiavelli's use of a burning log to bring light in the prostitute letter. It very well may and thus show Vettori's failure to take the opportunity to know with the depth of insight that Machiavelli gains when he brings light into the subterranean dwelling of the washerwoman.

30. Atkinson and Sices, *Machiavelli and His Friends,* 518nn5,6, indicate that these references are allusions to myths about Jupiter, but we need to note that they are also myths that emphasize the transformation of a god into an animal, i.e., the transcendence of the boundaries between god, human, and animal.

31. The dinner party of Letter 229 had been referred to as an *istoria.*

32. About the dinner party he had written, "Had I not lost my notes I would truly have included [the story] among the Annals of Modern Times" (Letter 229).

33. Atkinson and Sices, *Machiavelli and His Friends,* 519n2; Najemy, *Between Friends,* 272–73, suggests that Brancacci in this tale may be a cover for Machiavelli himself.

34. In Letter 210 (April 4, 1513), Machiavelli makes reference to his friend Donato opening a new shop that sells doves. According to Najemy, *Between Friends,* 111–12, this is a reference to selling young boys for sex.

35. As Najemy, *Between Friends,* 274–75, points out, Machiavelli ends this recitation with a quote from Ovid's *Metamorphoses* (4167–89) that refers to the story of the net of Vulcan which captured Mars and Venus in the act of love. The gods made to look ridiculous are no different than the Florentines looking ridiculous in his own time.

36. Here Atkinson and Sices, *Machiavelli and His Friends,* 282, miss the opportunity to capture Machiavelli's punning — Machiavelli describes Brancacci as a "macchiaiuolo," which Gaeta, *Opere di Niccolò Machiavelli,* notes is "un tipe che faceva le cose di soppiatto" (a guy who has done things he wants to hide).

37. Again Najemy, *Between Friends,* 221–40, has the most extensive and creative reading — sometimes perhaps too creative, but he alerts us to the many literary allusions in this letter. See also John Najemy, "Machiavelli and Geta: Men of Letters," in *Machiavelli and the Discourse of Literature.*

38. If we knew that Machiavelli had read Plato's *Republic,* it would be worth speculating on the relation of this phrasing to the taunt that Thrasymachus casts at Socrates at the end of book 1 of *The Republic;* the same would be true of the relation between this imaginary conversation with the ancient sages and Socrates' vision of an afterlife of conversation that he offers in *The Apology.* Unfortunately, it is unlikely that Machiavelli read Plato that carefully.

39. Atkinson and Sices, *Machiavelli and His Friends,* 264, 514n13.

40. I think Najemy, *Between Friends,* 150, goes too far with suggestions such as the following about the letters from the summer of 1513: "But could Vettori have been hinting at the notion that these characters — Louis, Leo, Ferdinand and the rest — were, as far as it would ever be possible to tell, no more than what Vettori and Machiavelli or any other interpreter, made of them? . . . Vettori was implying that the only political world they could know was the one each of them created from signs whose perceived meanings had as much to do with the reader's own presuppositions and *fantasia* as with the largely unknowable reality that Vettori presumed lay behind the signs."

41. Again, shades of Socrates' *Apology* provocatively appear.

4. Machiavelli's Discourse on Language

1. *Discorso o dialogo intorno alla nostra lingua.* References are to *Tutte le opere di Niccolò Machiavelli* (Verona: Mondadori, 1968), followed by a semicolon and citation of the English translation in Machiavelli, *Literary Works,* ed. J. R. Hale (London: Oxford University Press, 1961). Translations of Machiavelli's work provided below are my own.

2. See Hans Baron, *"Machiavelli on the Eve of the Discourses: The Date and Place of His Dialogo intorno alla nostra lingua,"* in *Bibliothèque d'humanisme et renaissance* 23 (1961): 449–73; and Cecil Grayson, "Lorenzo, Machiavelli and the Italian Language," in *Italian Renaissance Studies,* ed. E. F. Jacob (New York: Barnes and Noble, 1960), 410–32. See also Daria Perocco, "Rassegna di Studi sulle Opere Letterarie di Machiavelli (1969–1986)," *Lettere Italiane* 39 (1987): 544–79.

3. Cecil Grayson, "Machiavelli and Dante," in *Renaissance Studies in Honor of Hans Baron,* ed. Anthony Molho and John A. Tedeschi (DeKalb: Northern Illinois University Press, 1971), 363–84; see also Mario Martelli, *Una giarda fiorentina: il "Dialogo della lingua" attribuito a Niccolò Machiavelli* (Rome: Salerno, 1978), and, from an earlier period, O. Tommasini, *La vita e gli scritti di N. Machiavelli,* 1 (Turin: E. Loescher, 1883).

For a defense of the work's authenticity on historical and philological grounds, see the introduction to Machiavelli, *Discorso intorno alla nostra lingua,* ed. Paolo Trovato (Padua: Antenore Università di Padova, 1982).

4. See, for example, the remarks of Dante della Terza in *Machiavelli nel v° centenario della nascita,* ed. R. Aron et al. (Bologna: M. Boni, 1974), 88–89; and Fredi Chiappelli, *Machiavelli e la "Lingua Fiorentina"* (Bologna: M. Boni, 1974). On Dante and Machiavelli generally, see the helpful bibliography in Larry Peterman, "Dante and the Setting for Machiavellianism," *American Political Science Review* 76 (1982): 630–44. For somewhat different treatments of the relationship of Machiavelli to Dante, see John Freccero, "Medusa and the Madonna of Forlì: Political Sexuality in Machiavelli," in *Machiavelli and the Discourse of Literature,* ed. Albert Russell Ascoli and Victoria Kahn (Ithaca: Cornell University Press, 1993), 161–78; and Albert Russell Ascoli, "Machiavelli's Gift of Counsel," in *Machiavelli and the Discourse of Literature,* 219–57. Freccero and Ascoli draw useful attention to Machiavelli's implicit reference, in his famous recommendation that princes be both "lion and fox," to Dante's opposing view of the matter (see *Inferno* 25).

5. On disagreement concerning the dating of the *Discourse,* see Trovato, Introduction to Machiavelli, xxvi–xxxix.

6. Compare Machiavelli's reference to "our" language and Dante's reference to "the" vulgar language/eloquence, which he defines as aptness in one's original or natural language for communicating the highest things (*De vulgari eloquentia* 1.1) — an aptness that is "common" insofar as all human beings are moved to attain it to the (varying) degrees that they are able. Though common in this special sense, the vulgar eloquence is more noble than the artificial language ("grammatica") that is the fruit of study, and this not because all men are equally able to use the vulgar eloquence, but because men's original or natural language provides the most adequate sensible medium for communicating the highest things. Dante's (biblically doubtful) account of the Adamic origins of this natural language (as a fuller treatment of his argument would show) blurs the distinction between what is first chronologically and what is first in order of being.

7. On Dante's relation to Aristotle especially, see Marianne Shapiro, *De Vulgari Eloquentia: Dante's Book of Exile* (Lincoln: University of Nebraska Press, 1990), 7–9. On Dante's affinities with averroism, see Ernest L. Fortin, *Dissidence et philosophie au moyen age: Dante et ses antecedents* (Paris: J. Vrin, and Montreal: Bellarmin, 1981). For a more conventional view, see, for example, Charles T. Davis, "Dante's Vision of History," *Dante Studies* 93 (1975): 143–60.

8. Machiavelli, *Discourses on Livy,* trans. Harvey C. Mansfield and Nathan Tarcov (Chicago: University of Chicago Press, 1996), 36n.

9. Ibid., 106n.

10. Niccolò Machiavelli, *Lettere* (Milan: Feltrinelli, 1961), 301–06.

11. See Trovato, Introduction to *Discorso,* lviii.

12. Readers of Machiavelli's *Clizia* will recall at least one favorable case in which a father receives a cudgeling with his son's approval if not connivance.

13. Machiavelli's remarks here seem to parody Dante's in the *Convivio* (1.13), where he asserts his supreme obligation to the vernacular as responsible for both his "existence" and his "greatest benefactions" (*The Convivio of Dante Alighieri,* trans. P. H. Wicksteed [London: Dent, 1903]).

14. For a useful discussion of the historical context, see Carlo Dionisotti, "Man of Letters," in *Machiavelli and the Discourse of Literature,* 46ff.

15. The special significance of Lombardy, whose "blasphemies" are cited at the conclusion of the *Discourse,* will appear below.

16. The Latin *provincia* originally denoted a subject territory of the Roman Empire.

17. See, for example, *De vulgari eloquentia* 1.2 and 1.17. Dante associates the confusion of language with humankind's "shameful" and "dishonorable" presumption to "outdo not only nature but the source of our own nature," and thus "not equal but excel God." The illustrious vernacular, whose users are more to be "honored" than "any king, count, marquis or warlord," seems to go some way toward removing the shame of that presumption. Indeed, Dante goes so far as to suggest that users of his vernacular, insofar as they communicate rationally, are like unto God. For these and other reasons, it is difficult to reconcile his defense of the illustrious vernacular with conventional biblical piety.

18. Still, Dante insists, since the confusion "no human language can be lasting and continuous, but must vary like . . . our manners and our habits [mores et habitus]," being rendered stable "neither by nature nor by intercourse" (*De vulgari eloquentia* 1.9). Grammar is an artifice constructed to offset the mutability of languages, the better to communicate with others living at a distance and to remain in contact with "the deeds and authoritative writings of the ancients."

19. Ibid., 1.15.

20. Ibid., 1.18.

21. Ibid., 1.16.

22. Dante's projected fate also calls to mind that of Savonarola, when his own prophecies for Florence failed to come true.

23. Cacciaguida, about whom we know nothing from Dante except that he was Dante's ancestor, rejoices over Dante in Paradise: "O fronda mia . . . io fui la tua radice (O my branch, . . . I was thy root)" (*Commedia* 3.15.89 in *The Divine Comedy of Dante Alighieri,* Italian text and trans. John D. Sinclair [New York: Oxford University Press, 1961]). In the *Discourses on Livy* (1.11) Machiavelli quotes Dante, agreeing with him that "human probity rarely descends by the branches" (cf. *Commedia* 2.7.121–23 [Dante's own text says "rises by the branches"]). Dante claimed to put service to his city before service to his family and service to "virtue" before either. But Dante's own actions, as Machiavelli recounts them, do not seem always to have reflected this theoretical ranking. As Machiavelli notes in the *Florentine Histories,* Dante's own political fortunes were caught up in the struggle between the Neri and Dante's own (antipapal) Bianchi, familial factions whose vengeful spirit almost ruined Florence. Whereas Machiavelli's expulsion resulted from attachment to Soderini's regime, Dante's resulted from family attachment. To be sure, Machiavelli was only too eager to switch his visible loyalties to the Medicis, and Dante tried to reconcile Florence's familial factions; this effort, however, did not prevent Dante's expulsion along with the rest of the Bianchi.

24. Cf. *Convivio* 1.11: blinded, the people "cry life to their death and death to their life." In the *Discourses* (1.53) Machiavelli gives the phrase a more political reading and misattributes it to *De monarchia.*

25. *De vulgari eloquentia* 1.15.

26. Ibid., 1.16.

27. See below pp. 94–95.

28. Compare (2:809; 179): "Because things that impugn with general words or conjectures are easily parried [riprese], I wish to show with live and true reasons how [Dante's] speech was wholly Florentine, and even more so than that which Boccaccio by himself admits [confessa per se stesso] to be Florentine." Seen in this light, Dante's ultimate "confession" (at 2:818; 190) is something of a forced extraction.

29. See *Purgatorio* 3.128.

30. See *Paradiso* 22.115.

31. See ibid., 1.70.

32. See *De vulgari eloquentia* 1.18.

33. Given the likely date of the *Discourse*'s composition and the interests of its author, the explanation for this "error" on Machiavelli's part put forward by some scholars — that Machiavelli was unfamiliar with Dante's actual texts — is difficult to credit.

34. *De vulgari eloquentia* 1.11.

35. *Inferno* 26.76.

36. Ibid., 10.25–27.

37. Cf. *De vulgari eloquentia* 1.7, where Dante "blushes" over the false human pride leading to the fall of Babel. Dante's own professed intention to restore human glory by overcoming that fall is not lacking in presumption.

38. See, for example, Grayson, "Machiavelli and Dante," 365.

39. Machiavelli runs together *Inferno* 26.13 and *Inferno* 20.30. The offending term ("introcque") is derided in *De vulgari eloquentia* (1.13) as a Florentine localism.

40. "Art can never entirely contest nature."

41. Machiavelli quotes Horace's *Ars poetica* 55–57: "quum lingua Catonis et Ennuii Sermonen patrium ditaverit [when the tongue of Cato and Ennius has enriched our native speech]" (Loeb Classical Edition, 1926). Horace defends the (sparing) use of new words, especially when drawn from a Greek source; new terms are like the leaves that seasonally replace the old. This praise of Greece does not prevent him from asserting that "[as] all mortal things shall perish, much less shall the honor and grace of speech live" (68–69). Ennius (Ennius Quintus 239–170 B.C.) is traditionally credited with introducing to Rome an elevated literary language especially apt for tragedy and enriched by Greek modes of expression. Ennius, who learned Latin only as a young man, grew up knowing Greek, the main language of the upper classes of lower Italy. Cato the Elder, famous for his opposition to Greek influence, especially that of poets and philosophers, brought Ennius to Rome as a result of his outstanding service in the Second Punic War. (Cf. Machiavelli, *Florentine Histories* 5.1; the success of Ennius seems to be a special case of Machiavelli's general rule that letters flourish after arms.) The Cato to whom Horace here refers would seem to be Cato Publius Vaerius (100 B.C.–?), a Latin poet known for his adaptation of Greek meters and themes.

42. *De monarchia* 1.16, in Dante Alighieri, *Monarchia*, trans. Prue Shaw (Cambridge: Cambridge University Press, 1995).

43. Machiavelli, *Art of War* 1:459; *Machiavelli: The Chief Works and Others,* trans. Alan Gilbert (Durham: Duke University Press, 1958), 2:578.

44. *De monarchia* 1.16.

45. *Discourses* 1.23, 22, 24.

46. Cf. Horace, *Ars poetica* 333.

47. According to the Prologue to Machiavelli's *Clizia,* comedies teach the untrust-worthiness of human beings — a lesson especially useful for the young.

48. Compare Machiavelli's insistence in the Prologue to *Clizia* that ladies can enjoy his comedy without embarrassment.

49. See the Prologue to *Clizia.*

50. *Mandragola,* first *canzone.*

51. See the Prologue to *Clizia.*

52. See especially *The Ass,* whose alternating cantos take as their theme sexual love as a (temporary) salve for frustrated political ambition. On Machiavelli's own alternations between love and politics, see the *canzoni* to *Mandragola* and the letter to Vettori (January 31, 1515).

53. Cf. the Prologue to *Clizia* with that of *Mandragola,* which presents to those willing "to stop making rumors/noises" a "new thing born in this earth [un nuovo caso in questa terra nato]."

54. "Sale" (salt) also means judgment or wit. Cf. Horace's criticism of Plautus: "Handle Greek examples night and day. You say your forefathers praised both the measures and the wit [salus] of Plautus. Too tolerant, not to say foolish, was their praise, if you and I know how to distinguish the coarseness/inurbanity [inurbanum] from smartness [lepido], catching the lawful/correct speech [dicto legitimmunque] with finger and ear" (*Ars poetica* 268–74). Machiavelli's wit takes the coarseness from wit and leaves the salt (and thus succeeds where, in Horace's terms, Plautus failed), without recourse to the law or reliance on the "wisdom of Socrates" that Horace regarded as essential to good writing (*Ars poetica* 309–10). (I am indebted to Robert K. Faulkner for calling my attention to Horace's "socratism.")

55. Lorenzo de' Medici, *The Autobiography of Lorenzo de' Medici the Magnificent: A Commentary on My Sonnets,* trans. James Wyatt Cook, together with the text of *Il Comento* (Binghamton, N.Y.: SUNY Binghamton, 1996), 46–49.

56. Cf. *De vulgari eloquentia* 2.1.

57. *Florentine Histories* 5.1.

58. Consider, for example, Attila's removal from Italy (*Florentine Histories* 1.3), the defeat of the Longobards (1.10), and the humiliation of Henry (1.11). The (relatively) successful Theodoric, by way of contrast, is distinguished by his lack of respect for the holy reputations of Simmacus and Boethius (1.4).

59. *Florentine Histories* 1.2, 3; 2.13.

60. Ibid., 1.4; 2.14, 15.

61. Cf. ibid., 1.6, where Theodoric is praised for raising Italy to such greatness that "the old afflictions [le antiche battiture] were no longer known there"; and 1.9, where he is blamed for abandoning the Romans to their own devices, thus inadvertently giving the pope a larger role in Italy's affairs. A more ultimate source of Italy's disorder seems to be the earlier abandonment of Rome by Christianized emperors, who preferred retirement in Constantinople to defending their empire from the place it could be managed most effectively (1.1).

62. *Florentine Histories* 1.5.

63. Ibid. Among these changes, as Machiavelli notes, that in religion was not of "least moment." Living thus, "among so many persecutions [by the Church]," men "bore the terror of their spirit written in their eyes," enduring as they did "infinite evils" without the "help or hope" that most men find in religious certitude. Machiavelli's claim that a united Church would have prevented these calamities is undercut by his persistent showing of why such a unity is politically impossible.

64. This unnerving effect of a "mere thought" contrasts sharply with the encouraging effect, in the case of earlier peoples, of actual defeat. Whereas earlier peoples were inspired by conquest of their land to attempt to conquer that of others (1.2, 6), modern peoples (like those who figured in the history of Venice) are inspired, at best, to make habitable (through the building of dams and dikes) previously unoccupied territory. Compare, too, the rise of Pisa as a refuge for the conquered (1.12). Although Machiavelli explicitly blames the disunity of Christianity for people's loss of hope and consequent misery (1.5), Christianity as such is responsible — as Machiavelli elsewhere makes clear — for modern men's inability to pluck courage from the jaws of necessity.

65. *Florentine Histories* 1.5, 6.

66. Ibid., 1.7–8.

67. Ibid., 1.9.

68. Ibid., 1.10.

69. Ibid., 1.11.

70. Ibid., 1.11, 14.

71. Ibid., 1.13.

72. Ibid., 1.11.

73. Ibid. "Osporco" suggests a term meaning "pig snout."

74. Ibid., 1.15.

75. See also *Discourses* 1.12; as Machiavelli there makes clear, the Church's baleful influence arises not only from the corruption of its prelates, but also from the politically destructive effect of Christianity itself.

76. *Florentine Histories* 5.1.

77. See the title to *Discourses* 2.5: "That the Variation of Sects and Languages, Together with the Accident of Floods or Plague, Extinguishes [spegne] the Memories of Things."

78. Compare Machiavelli's use in the *Florentine Histories* (5.1) of the phrase "this wasted world" (questo guasto mondo), in reference, apparently and conventionally, to a humanity unredeemed by Christ, but also, and, in light of his discussion in the *Discourses,* more truthfully, to the world after the advent of the Christian sect.

79. *Discourses* 2.5.

80. As Mansfield and Tarcov note in their translation (139n.), citing Livy 1.35, 55; 5.21–22; 7.3; 9.36. See also Livy 1.2: "The power of Etruria . . . had filled with the glory of her name not only the lands but the sea as well, along the whole extent of Italy from the Alps to the Sicilian Strait" (Livy, *Ab urbe condita,* Loeb Classical Library, 1976).

81. See *Discourses* 2.4: "Although of [ancient Tuscan] things there is no particular history, nevertheless there is some small memory and some sign of their greatness" — enough, indeed, for Machiavelli to urge modern Tuscans to imitate their ancient forebears, who, if they could not make an empire like the Romans, "could acquire the power

in Italy that their mode of proceeding conceded to them." This, Machiavelli adds, "was secure for a great time with the highest glory of empire and of arms, and a maximum praise for their customs and religion. This power and glory was first diminished by the French, then extinguished by the Romans, and so much so that . . . there is at present nothing but some [little] memory of it." Cf. John Hall, ed., *Etruscan Italy* (Provo: Brigham Young University, 1996); despite the power and literary flowering of the Etruscans, the absence of a record of its doings (i.e., no history in Machiavelli's sense) means that we are forced to study the Etruscan people "as if they were a prehistoric culture" (Hall, *Etruscan Italy*, 3). Evidently names, without a particular history to support them, are insufficient as witnesses to greatness. Machiavelli's own "histories" (and in particular his *Istorie fiorentine*) are perhaps intended, in part, to make good Tuscany's ancient defect. (See also, in this regard, *Discourses* 3.43).

82. See Machiavelli's discussion in *Discourses* 2.5 of the writer in whom knowledge of antiquity has been "saved" and who, wishing "to make a reputation and name for himself . . . , conceals and perverts [that knowledge] in his mode," so that "what he wishes to write alone, and nothing else, remains for his successors" (see also Vickie B. Sullivan, *Machiavelli's Three Romes: Religion, Human Liberty, and Politics Reformed* [DeKalb: Northern Illinois University Press, 1996], 132–41; and Mansfield and Tarcov, *Discourses on Livy* xxxix). Such a writer (whose flood-defying powers call to mind Machiavelli's likening of himself, in chapter 25 of *The Prince*, to a builder of "dams and dikes") would break the cycle that has heretofore set natural limits to the duration of names and other monuments to human greatness. In so doing, he would not only overcome the devastation of "this world" but also make available to human memory a perpetuity that previous philosophers, asserting the eternity of the world, have merely "wished for" (hanno voluto). As Machiavelli also observes, "the hands and tongue [lingua] of men," two "most notable instruments of human ennoblement," reach their highest level of perfection (or "obstinacy") only by being driven by necessity (*Discourses* 3.12).

83. *Discourses* 3.34.

84. In *Discourses* 2.8, Machiavelli distinguishes wars motivated by princely or republican imperial ambition, which typically allow the vanquished to retain their laws and customs, and the exterminating wars conducted by a whole people driven by necessity to occupy the territory of another, i.e., wars over the "salvation of everyone." Christian domination of Europe would seem to represent an amalgam of the two—one arguably motivated by imperial ambition rather than necessity, yet over the salvation of everyone.

85. Machiavelli's advice to a new prince, namely, "to make everything new," including "new governments with new names, new authorities, new men," contrasts with the successful conquests of republican Rome, which let old names remain and which, indeed, appropriated the language of Latium (on the latter point, see *Discourses* 2.13). See also 2.16: although alike in language, order, and arms, Rome defeated the Latins (owing, as Machiavelli says, to Rome's "extraordinary" obstinacy). So little do words, in this sense, matter that he can associate the *Latin* "name" with the foundation of the Roman state (2.30). On the contrast between ancient Rome and Christianity on this point, see Harvey C. Mansfield, Jr., *Machiavelli's New Modes and Orders: A Study of the Discourses on Livy* (Ithaca: Cornell University Press, 1979), 203.

86. See, for example, 1.34, 39, 55; 2.13.

87. See *Discourses* 1.25.

88. Cf. Machiavelli's deprecation of nouns (or names) in the *Discourse*. On Machiavelli's willingness to sacrifice his own (good) name, see Catherine Zuckert, "Fortune Is a Woman—But so Is Prudence," in *Finding a New Feminism: Rethinking the Woman Question for Liberal Democracy,* ed. Pamela Jensen (Lanham, Md.: Rowman and Littlefield, 1996), 35. See also *Discourses* 3.34; and Leo Strauss, *Thoughts on Machiavelli* (Glencoe, Ill.: Free Press, 1958), 290–93.

89. *Discourses* 1.11.

90. *Florentine Histories* 2.2.

91. Should one conclude that Florentine is more threatened by "assimilation" than Machiavelli had earlier admitted? Or does he mean to imply that Florentine will continue to dominate de facto, whether or not its preeminence is generally recognized? In any case, the (false) confusion of Florentine with other Italian dialects would not be altogether disadvantageous to Machiavelli as a writer of "serious" political treatises directed to Italy as a whole (and beyond).

92. Cf. the letter to Guicciardini, October 21, 1525, in which (following a discussion of how to extract a dowry from the pope, the fate of the duchy of Milan, and his own progress on the *Histories*) he (playfully) signs himself "historico, comico et tragico." See also Strauss, *Thoughts on Machiavelli,* 292.

93. Letter to Vettori (December 10, 1513). Cf. *Paradiso* 5.40–41, where Beatrice says to Dante, "Open thy mind to what I lay before thee and hold it fast there, for to have heard without retaining does not make knowledge." The context is the thorny question of whether vows may ever be broken, Beatrice allowing (in a spirit perhaps more Platonic than Christian) that it is sometimes better to admit one's error than to allow worse to happen (as in the sacrifice by Jeptha and Agamemnon of their daughters). The practice of buying indulgences to make up for broken vows, on the other hand, is called "charity from plunder," a phrase that nicely anticipates, albeit from a negative direction, Machiavelli's own definition of liberality in *The Prince*. See Clifford Orwin, "Machiavelli's Unchristian Charity," *American Political Science Review* 72 (1978): 1217–28.

5. Tragic Machiavelli

1. For the letter of (after) October 21, see *Machiavelli and His Friends: Their Personal Correspondence,* ed. James Atkinson and David Sices (DeKalb: Northern Illinois University Press, 1996), 369–71; Niccolò Machiavelli, *Lettere,* ed. Franco Gaeta (Milan: Feltrinelli, 1961), 440–44; and see Roberto Ridolfi, *The Life of Machiavelli,* trans. Cecil Grayson (London: Routledge and Kegan Paul, 1963), 207–19, 319–20.

2. See Giorgio Barberi-Squarotti, *La forma tragica del 'Principe' e altri saggi sul Machiavelli* (Florence: Olschki, 1966), esp. 103–280. Barberi-Squarotti's passionately argued thesis concerns the "abstract form" of the tragic in Machiavelli's work rather than Machiavelli's practice as a writer in relation to written tragedies in the cinquecento. See also Riccardo Bacchelli, "'Istorico, comico, et tragico,' ovvero Machiavelli artista," *Nuova antologia* 95 (1960): 3–20.

3. The types go back to Vitruvius. For Vitruvius in the quattrocento, see Richard Krautheimer, "Vitruvius and Alberti," *Acts of the Twentieth International Congress of the History of Art* (Princeton: Princeton University Press, 1963), 2:42–52; Pier Nicola

Pagliara, "Vitruvio da testo a canone," in *Memoria dell'antico nell'arte italiana,* ed. Salvatore Settis (Turin: Einaudi, 1986), 3:7–85. For Vitruvius and the theater, see Robert Klein, "Vitruve e le théâtre de la Rénaissance," in *Le lieu théâtral à la Rénaissance* (Paris: Editions CNRF, 1968), 49–61.

4. Machiavelli would have known Horace's *Ars poetica* and Seneca's tragedies, important for Latin tragedy in the trecento and quattrocento; see Federico Doglio, "Il teatro in latino nel Cinquecento," in *Il teatro classico del '500* (Florence: Accademia nazionale dei Lincei, 1971), 163–96; and note 16 below.

5. See the letter to Guicciardini of 16–20 October, Atkinson and Sices, *Machiavelli and His Friends,* 367–68; Gaeta, *Lettere,* 438–40.

6. See Bacchelli, "Istorico," 4–5. Indeed, the three genres are reiterated in a few consecutive lines just before Machiavelli's signature: cf. Atkinson and Sices, *Machiavelli and His Friends,* 371: "Give my regards to Maliscotta and let me know how far along the *comedy* is, and when you intend to put it on. I received that raise to a hundred ducats for the *History.* I am just now beginning to write again, and I vent my feelings by accusing the princes have all done everything they can to bring us to this *situation.* Farewell. Niccolò Machiavelli Historian, Comic Author, and Tragic Author" [emphases mine].

7. On the Oricellari meetings, see Felix Gilbert, "Bernardo Rucellai and the Orti Oricellari," *Journal of the Warburg and Courtald Institutes* 11–13 (1948–50): 101–31, and Carlo Dionisotti, "Machiavellerie (II)," in *Rivista storica italiana* 83 (1971): 227–63.

8. For the relations of Rucellai and Trissino with the Oricellari and with each other, see Giovanni Rucellai, *Opere,* ed. Guido Mazzoni (Bologna: Zanichelli, 1897), vii–xviii; and Renzo Cremante, ed., *Teatro del Cinquecento, Tomo I: La tragedia* (Milan-Naples: Ricciardi, 1988), 165–76.

9. On Bernardo as historian, see Gilbert, "Bernardo Rucellai," 128, and Dionisotti, "Machiavellerie (II)," 253–55. See also Francesco Guicciardini, *Storia d'Italia* (Milan: Garzanti, 1993), 1:3–80 (in translation, *The History of Italy,* trans. Sidney Alexander [Princeton: Princeton University Press, 1969], 3–49).

10. See Petrarch, *Africa,* trans. T. G. Bergin and A. Wilson (New Haven: Yale University Press, 1977), book 5; *Triumphi,* ed. Marco Ariani (Milan: Mursia, 1988), 2.4–93. For Livy's text, see *The Early History of Rome,* trans. Aubrey de Selincourt (Harmondsworth: Penguin Books), 1.46–49.

11. See Gilbert, "The Orti Oricellari," 122, 128; and Dionisotti, "Machiavellerie (II)," 254–63.

12. For the anti-imperialist reading of Sophonisba, see Beatrice Corrigan's edition in *Two Renaissance Plays* (Manchester: Manchester University Press, 1973), 11–15, and Marco Ariani, *Tra classicismo e manierismo: la tragedia italiana del Cinquecento* (Florence: Olschki, 1974), 15–33; this interpretation is contested by Giulio Ferroni, "*La Sofonisba:* un classicismo senza conflitto," in *Convegno di studi su Giangiorgio Trissino* (Vicenza: Accademia Olimpica, 1980), 111–37.

13. *Tullia* can be read in the series *Teatro italiano antico* (Milan: Classici italiani, 1809), 3:29–112. Martelli's tragedy was perhaps sparked by Livy's remark that the violent Tarquins modeled themselves after royal families in tragedy (therefore Greeks), a passage that also applies to the later account of Lucretia; see *Early History of Rome,* 1.46.

14. Little is known of Martelli, who was captured by the French after the sea battle of

Capo di Orso (April 1528) and died, perhaps by poisoning, in the same year; see Benedetto Croce, *Poeti e scrittori del pieno e tardi rinascimento* (Bari: Laterza, 1945), 1:274–89.

15. See the following essays and lecture, all by Riccardo Bruscagli, "La corte in scena: genesi politica della tragedia ferrarese," in *Il rinascimento nelle corti padane* (Bari: de Donato, 1977), 569–95; "Giovanni Battista Giraldi: comico, tragico, et satirico," in *Teatro del Cinquecento,* ed. Maristella Lorch (Milan: Edizioni di comunita, 1980), 261–84; and "Throne of Blood," a lecture delivered at the University of California, Berkeley, in 1993.

16. For the Senecan influence on Rucellai, see Ettore Paratore, "Nuove prospettive sull'influsso del teatro classico nel '500," in *Il teatro classico,* 9–95, esp. 23, 25, 35–38. Bruscagli downplays Senecan parallels, inconsistently with the known influence of the plays. The chronological difficulties in positing conversations between Rucellai and Machiavelli in the Orti are pointed out by Bruscagli, "Throne of Blood."

17. Translations are mine. Although such summation-schemata are in the cinquecento a common feature of formal rhetoric in both Latin and Italian, the similar dramatic situation would seem to warrant the parallel (translations in the text are mine).

18. See Aristotle, *Poetics* 49b9; for Machiavelli's ostentatious use of the unities, see my "Pharmacy of Machiavelli: Roman Lucretia in *Mandragola,*" *Renaissance Drama* 14 (1983): 1–43, esp. 11; also, my "Benefit of Absence: Machiavellian Valediction in *Clizia,*" in *Machiavelli and the Discourse of Literature,* ed. Albert Russell Ascoli and Victoria Kahn (Ithaca: Cornell University Press, 1993), 117–44.

19. *Ars poetica* 180–88; see Allan H. Gilbert, *Literary Criticism: Plato to Dryden* (Detroit: Wayne State University Press, 1962), 133–34.

20. *Ars poetica* 93–94: "At times, however, even Comedy exalts her voice, and an angry Chremes rants and raves" (Gilbert, *Literary Criticism,* 131).

21. For this aspect, see Martinez, "Pharmacy," 23–28; see also Hanna Fenichel Pitkin, *Fortune Is a Woman: Gender and Politics in the Thought of Niccolò Machiavelli* (Berkeley: University of California Press, 1984), 111–13; and Anne Paolucci, "Livy's Lucretia, Shakespeare's 'Lucrece,' Machiavelli's *Mandragola,*" in *Il teatro italiano del Rinascimento,* ed. M. Lorch (Milan: edizioni di Comunità, 1980), 619–35.

22. See note 13, above.

23. See Martinez, "Benefit of Absence," 119, 132–33.

24. For Machiavelli on a supposed conspiracy of Roman matrons to murder their husbands (Livy, *History* 8.18.1–13), see *Discourses* 3.49; see also Pitkin, *Fortune Is a Woman,* 121–23.

25. On the many connections between the two plays, see Martinez, "Benefit of Absence," 118–22.

26. See Plautus, *Casina,* ed. W. T. McCary and M. M. Willcock (Cambridge: Cambridge University Press, 1976), 170–75.

27. On Boccaccio's tale of Pirro, see Albert Russell Ascoli, "Pyrrhus's Rules: Playing with Power from Boccaccio to Machiavelli," *MLN* 114 (1999): 14–57; for tragic potential in the scapegoating of Nicomaco, see Martinez, "Benefit of Absence," 119. Bernardo Dovizi's *La calandria* (1513), a play that stimulated Machiavelli, touches on the mock-tragic with Santilla's lament for the status of women (act 2, scene 8); see *La commedia del Cinquecento,* ed. Guido Davico Bonino (Turin: Einaudi, 1977), 1:38.

28. For these episodes, see Martinez, "Pharmacy," 41–43.

29. See Lucius Apulieus, *The Golden Ass,* trans. P. G. Walsh (Oxford: Clarendon Press, 1994), chap. 10.11: "You are now to read a tragedy and no mere anecdote; you are to rise from the comic sock to the tragic buskin"—a misleading cue, as all ends happily. On Machiavelli's *The Ass,* see now Maurizio Tarantino, "*L'Asino* e la satira politica," in *Niccolò Machiavelli: Politico storico letterato* (Atti del Convegno di Losanna, 27–30 September 1995), ed. J. J. Marchand (Rome: Salerno, 1997), 131–36.

30. See Ezio Raimondi, "Il veleno della *Mandragola,*" in *Politica e commedia* (Bologna: Il mulino, 1972), 253–64; the reproach aimed at contemporary Florence is explicit in Machiavelli's prologue: "For the present age / entirely diverges / from ancient virtue" (translation mine).

31. Atkinson and Sices, *Machiavelli and His Friends,* 372. For Machiavelli's approval of violent remedies against civic corruption, see *Discourses* 3.49, and Pitkin, *Fortune Is a Woman,* 121–23.

32. In the pseudo-Senecan *Octavia,* with its proto-Machiavellian insights into power, Lucretia is named to arouse the courage lacking in Neronian Rome: Tullia is mentioned in a contiguous passage. See L. Annaei Senecae *Tragoediae,* ed. O. Zwierlein (Oxford: Clarendon Press, 1986), 427 (*Octavia* vv. 291–309). In *Phaedra* Seneca contrasts the rape of Lucretia to the feigned outrage of Phaedra (verses 735 and 892, recalling Livy, *Early History of Rome* 1.58.7).

33. For the extensive lore of the mandrake, see Giovanni Aquilecchia, "*Mandragola* la favola si chiama," in *Collected Essays in Italian Language and Literature Presented to Kathleen Speight* (Manchester: Manchester University Press, 1971), 74–100; and Martinez, "Pharmacy," 33–40, where I also discuss Machiavelli's advocacy of violent "remedies" to political corruption. Such later theorists as Minturno make explicit Aristotle's medical metaphor for tragic catharsis: "A physician will not have greater capacity to expel with poisonous medicine the fiery poison of an illness which afflicts the body, than the tragic poet will to purge the mind of mighty perturbations with the force of the passions charmingly expressed in verses" (quoted in Gilbert, *Literary Criticism,* 290).

34. See Hans Baron, *The Crisis of the Early Italian Renaissance* (Princeton: Princeton University Press, 1966), 114–17; Guy Walton, "The Lucretia Panel in the Gardner Museum," *Essays in Honor of Walter Friedlaender,* ed. Marsyas Institute (New York: New York University Press, 1965), 177–86. Ronald Lightbown, *Sandro Botticelli,* 1:141–5, 2:101–06; Laurence Kanter et al., *Botticelli's Witness: Changing Style in a Changing Florence* (Boston: Isabella Steward Gardner Museum, 1997), 58–60; Paola Tinagli, *Women in Italian Renaissance Art* (Manchester: Manchester University Press, 1997), 40–42. To minimize the political potential of this image (e.g., Kanter et al., Barriault to a degree) is to overlook the close interrelation of the domestic and the political in early modern Florence; see the discussion of *Discourses* 3.26 in Pitkin, *Fortune Is a Woman,* 115–18.

35. The panel is described and interpreted in Walton, "The Lucretia Panel"; Lightbown, *Sandro Botticelli;* Kanter et al., *Botticelli's Witness;* Tinagli, *Women in Italian Renaissance Art;* and Anne Barriault, *Spalliera Painting of Renaissance Tuscany* (University Park: Pennsylvania State University Press, 1994), 124–32, 180–81, with bibliography; for discussion of the tale of Lucretia, see Ian Donaldson, *The Rapes of Lucretia* (Oxford: Clarendon Press, 1982); Martinez, "Pharmacy," 7–33; and Stephanie Jed,

Chaste Thinking: The Rape of Lucretia and the Birth of Humanism (Lincoln: University of Nebraska Press, 1992). For Judith and David as icons of civic resistance to tyranny, see John Pope-Hennessy, *Donatello: Sculptor* (New York: Phaidon Press, 1994), 147–55, 280–89, with bibliography.

36. For the Vitruvian tragic and comic scenes in Renaissance painting, see Robert Krautheimer, "The Tragic and Comic Scenes of the Renaissance: The Baltimore and Urbino Panels," *Gazette des Beaux-Arts* 33 (1948): 327–48; Alessandro Parronchi, "La prima rappresentazione della *Mandragola:* Il modello per l'apparato. L'allegoria," in *La bibliofila* 64 (1962): 37–89; Sebastiano Serlio, *The Book of Architecture* (New York: Benjamin Blom, 1970), 2.3 (fol. 24–27). Ludovico Zorzi, *Il teatro e la città* (Turin: Einaudi, 1977), 170–74, gives a considered refutation of Krautheimer's thesis regarding the Baltimore and Urbino panels, and Krautheimer has since modified his views ("The Panels in Urbino, Baltimore, and Berlin Reconsidered," in *The Renaissance from Brunelleschi to Michelangelo: The Representation of Architecture,* ed. H. A. Millon and V. M. Lampugnani [Milan: Bompiani, 1994], 232–57); see also Hubert Damisch, *The Origin of Renaissance Perspective* [Cambridge: MIT Press, 1994], 201–27). But that the Gardner panel evokes staged representations is inescapable, as the ostentation of Lucretia's body recalls that of martyrs in *sacre rappresentazioni,* a genre vigorous in Florence in the 1490s: *Abramo e Isaco,* representing the near-sacrifice of Isaac, by Feo Belcari, a Medici client, first performed in 1449 and printed in 1485, had eight printed editions by the end of the century (for the possible staging of some of Belcari's plays by Brunelleschi, see Zorzi, *Il teatro e la città,* 154–64). Castelvetro (1571) later discussed Lucretia as potentially tragic (Gilbert, *Literary Criticism,* 333), but the only Lucretia tragedies recorded in the cinquecento are Gabriele Bombace's *Lucrezia Romana* (about 1570) and Paolo Regio's *Lucretia,* printed in 1572; Aretino reportedly planned such a tragedy but never completed it (see Ferdinando Neri, *La tragedia italiana del Cinquecento* [Florence: Galletti e Cocci, 1904], 79, 158, 176).

37. See Ferroni, "Classicismo," 115–18. Horace too noted the power of the visual, *Ars poetica* 178–80 (see Gilbert, *Literary Criticism,* 133).

38. See Giangiorgio Trissino, *La Poetica* (1529), ed. B. Fabian (Munich: Fink Verlag, 1969); Quinta divisione (1532), 9; Ariani, *Tra classicismo,* 35–37; Ferroni, "Classicismo," 121–23.

39. See Ezio Raimondi, "Rittratisticha petrarchesca," in *Metafora e storia* (Florence: Einaudi, 1970), 163–88.

40. For plot compared to drawing (*disegno*) rather than color, see *Poetics* 50a33–50b4 (see also 54b8–54b14, the poet's imitation of character compared to that of the portraitist); Aristotle's typology of recognitions is at *Poetics* 54b19–55a22, while at 54a1–54a10 the "tragic situation" is exemplified with visual recognitions (in Gilbert, *Literary Criticism,* 78, 91, 91–94, 88–89, respectively).

41. Tragic norms of course prevented Trissino from showing the suicidal act, narrated by a messenger. For Isabella's painting of Sophonisba, see Ronald Lightbown, *Mantegna* (Berkeley: University of California Press, 1986), 450–51, although Lightbown's identification of the bigamous Sophonisba as a figure of chastity may be doubted (fortitude would be more likely). In 1502, Isabella had also received from Galeotto del Carretto a previous Sophonisba play; see A. Tissoni Benvenuti, *Teatro padano del Quattrocento* (Turin: UTET, 1983), 559–67.

42. For a census of the borrowings from the *Alcestis,* see Ferroni, "Un classicismo," 129–34.

43. Isabella's interest in examples of fortitude and stoic resistance was known; in the *Ritratti* Trissino affirms that she would choose honorable death over a stain on her reputation; later her temperance is compared to that of Alcestis, Trissino's model for Sophonisba. For the *Ritratti,* see *I ritratti del Trissino* (Rome: Stampata per Lodovico de gli Arrighi Vicentino, e Lautitio Perugino, 1524); also Amedeo Quondam, "La poesia duplicata: imitazione e scrittura," in *Convegno . . . Trissino,* 67–109, esp. 82–84.

44. In *Oreste* (ed. Mazzoni, *Le opere,* 108–229), the accounts of the palace at Aulis and of the painting of Leda at Argos, which stimulate the mutual recognition of Orestes and Electra, are elaborate *ekphraseis* (see 4.396–458). That the painting described is Leonardo's lost "Leda" is proposed by J. A. Bertolini, "Ecphrasis and Dramaturgy: Leonardo's 'Leda' in Rucellai's *Oreste,"* in *Renaissance Drama* 7 (1976): 151–76.

45. The messenger's account is prepared with an echo of Ugolino's narrative; compare *Inferno* 33.4: "You wish me to renew desperate grief that already presses my heart merely thinking, before I speak of it," and *Rosmunda* 3.86–87: "I will tell you of it because just the thought of it, not only the telling, horrifies me." Overlooked by Cremante in Rucellai's play, this same parallel is noted by him of Trissino's tragedy, where Dantesque language is used to describe the foreboding of the queen (*Sophonisba* 5–6, *Inferno* 33.5, 13). Translations of Dante in the text are my own; those in the notes are from Dante Alighieri, *Inferno,* ed. and trans. Robert M. Durling, with introduction and notes by Ronald L. Martinez (New York: Oxford, 1996).

46. See Gianfranco Contini, *Un'idea di Dante* (Turin: Einaudi, 1970), 125–28; and Piero Boitani, *Tragic and Sublime in Medieval Literature* (Cambridge: Cambridge University Press, 1989), 20–55. Dante compares the death of Ugolino to the horrors of the Cadmeids of Thebes, one of the two principal tragic clans (the Argive House of Atreus is the other). In defense of his *Canace,* Sperone Speroni would refer to the tragic scene of Ugolino (see Sperone Speroni, *Canace e scritti in sua difesa,* ed. C. Roaf [Bologna: Commissione per I testi di lingua, 1982]).

47. Cremante notes one allusion to the biblical text of Judith but without recognizing that it furnishes the frame for the whole scene; the other major allusion is to the killing of the Cyclops by Ulysses, *Aeneid* 3.632–33 (Cremante, 256).

48. M. Pieri, "La *Rosmunda* del Rucellai e la tragedia fiorentina del primo Cinquecento," *Quaderni di teatro* 2 (1980): 99, affirms the play's adherence to the Leonine program of universal peace.

49. Machiavelli's phrasing, such as "fece del teschio di Comundo una tazza" (he made the skull of Comundo a cup), suggests acquaintance with Rucellai's text. Translations in texts and notes are mine.

50. Justinian's expulsion of the barbarians furnished Trissino with the subject for *Italia liberata da' Gotti* (1547), the first Italian narrative poem to closely follow classical epic models. Did Trissino find his title reading *Florentine Histories* 1.7 ("come prima fu libera l'Italia da' Gotti, Iustiniano morì")?

51. Machiavelli's proximate source is Paulus Diaconus (*Historia langobardorum* 2.27–31), but the choice offered by Rosmunda is precisely that offered Gyges by the wife of Cambyses, as related in Herodotus (*Histories* 1.6–14). For Herodotus's story and the analysis of tyranny, especially as mediated through Plato's discussion of Gyges, *Republic*

2.359d-360e, see Marc Shell, *The Economy of Literature* (Baltimore: Johns Hopkins University Press, 1978), 11–62. For an application contemporary with Machiavelli, see Ronald L. Martinez, "De-Cephalizing Rinaldo: The Money of Tyranny in Niccolò da Correggio's *Fabula de Cefalo* and in *Orlando furioso* 42–43," *Annali d'italianistica* 12 (1994): 87–114.

52. See *Florentine Histories* 1.9 (quoted below in the text); Guicciardini, *History of Italy,* 3 (1.1), 32; 45; 48–49; 104; 165 (6.1); 175; 191 (8.1); 376 (18.1); 384–85 (the Sack of Rome); Luigi Guicciardini, *The Sack of Rome,* trans. James H. McGregor (New York: Italica Press, 1993), 99. For more examples, see André Chastel, *The Sack of Rome, 1527,* trans. Beth Archer (Princeton: Princeton University Press, 1983), 22–24, 115–48.

53. As much is announced by Machiavelli in his *Histories* 2.2: "The reason of the first division is very well known, because it is celebrated by Dante and many other writers; nevertheless I will briefly recount it"; see *Istorie fiorentine,* ed. F. Gaeta (Milan: Feltrinelli, 1962), 141.

54. See Guicciardini's remarks on Borgia, *History of Italy,* 176: "Thus the power of the Duke Valentino, which had risen, as it were, suddenly by cruelty and fraud as much as by the arms and power of the Church, ended in even more sudden ruin: Cesare now experiencing himself those same tricks and deceits with which his father and himself had tormented so many others." Machiavelli's varying portrayals of Cesare are studied by Carlo Dionisotti in "Machiavelli, Cesare Borgia, e Don Micheletto," *Rivista storica italiana* 79 (1967): 960–75, and in his reply to Gennaro Sasso's criticisms, "Machiavellerie," *Rivista storica italiana* 82 (1970): 308–34. For the gendering of the figure of Fortune in Machiavelli's work, see Pitkin, *Fortune Is a Woman,* esp. 143–69.

55. Geoffrey Chaucer, "The Monk's Tale," in *The Works of Geoffrey Chaucer,* ed. F. N. Robinson (New York: Houghton, 1971); and Boitani, *Tragic and Sublime,* 40–55.

56. See Ezio Raimondi, "Una tragedia del Trecento," in *Metafora e storia,* 147–62. For Senecan tragedy, both in Latin and Italian, in the trecento and quattrocento, see *Il teatro tragico italiano,* ed. Federico Doglio (Bologna: Guanda, 1960), xi–xxix; for Renaissance theorizing of the role of fortune in the cathartic effect of tragedy, see Gilbert, *Literary Criticism,* 289–90 (Minturno).

57. See Giovanni Boccaccio, *On famous women,* trans. Guido Guarino (New Brunswick: Rutgers University Press, 1962); *The Fates of Illustrious Men,* trans. Louis Brewer Hall (New York: Ungar, 1965); *De casibus virorum illustrium,* ed. L. B. Hall (Gainesville: Scholar's Facsimiles, 1962).

58. Boccaccio also discusses the story of Rosmunda at the end of book 8 of the *De casibus:* a closer source than those advanced by Cremante. For the cinquecento theorists on Fortune, see Gilbert, *Literary Criticism,* 289 (Minturno on fortune and purgation).

59. Machiavelli begins by explaining as a device of Fortune the tradition of assigning the birth of great but socially obscure great men to the gods: "I do believe that this arises when, fortune wishing to show the world that it is she, and not prudence, who gives men greatness, she begins to display her force early enough so that prudence can claim no part in it, rather the whole of that greatness must be recognized as coming from Fortune herself" (*The Life of Castruccio Castracani of Lucca,* in *Istorie,* 9). See also 32: "But fortune, the enemy of his glory, took away life from him at the moment she should have offered it, and interrupted his designs"; and 33, his farewell to his son: "If I had believed,

my son, that fortune would have wished to cut me off in the middle of the path toward that glory I had promised myself with all my happy successes . . ."; this recalls Valentino's excuses to Machiavelli himself.

60. The parallel of Castruccio with Borgia is often made; cf. Gaeta's preface, *Istorie,* 3– 5. For a detailed exposition of the heroic agonism of Valentino, see Barberi-Squarotti, *La forma tragica,* 165–89. Alessandro d'Ancona, in his still fundamental *Origini del Teatro Italiano,* 2 vols. (Turin: Loescher, 1891), 2:74, records the Vatican celebrations for the wedding of Lucrezia Borgia with the duke of Ferrara in 1502, during which a masque paired Cesare to Hercules as conquerors of Fortune through Virtue. Such events, along with triumphs celebrated by Borgia during the Roman carnival seasons of 1500–02 (see d'Ancona, *Origini,* 2:73–75), show how quickly Borgia's conquest of Fortuna was recast in theatrical form.

61. See the "Legazione al Valentino," in Niccolò Machiavelli, *Legazioni, Comissarie, Scritti di governo,* ed. Fredi Chiappelli (Naples: Laterza, 1973), 192–401.

62. See *Prince,* chap. 7 ("that he be imitated by all those who through fortune and with the arms of others have risen to power"); but this apparent encomium also identifies the agents of Cesare's downfall.

63. *History of Italy* 6.4 (trans. Alexander, 175). Guicciardini ends the book (6.16) by describing the story of Don Giulio d'Este as "a tragic occurrence similar to those of the ancient Thebans" (the choice of city motivated by the fratricidal hatreds involved and by Ippolito's having had Don Giulio blinded, like Oedipus). See also Bacchelli, "Istorico," 9–11.

64. In *Prince,* chap. 7, Borgia explains his failure to Machiavelli himself, the eyewitness of the crises of Borgia's career. Thus Machiavelli "signs" his opinion that Borgia's career was exemplary but also introduces a note of bathos, Valentino's very excuses indicating he has lost power.

65. *Prince,* chap. 7.

66. Dionisotti, in "Machiavelli . . . e Don Micheletto" and "Machiavellerie," proposed that Machiavelli, after the fall of Cesare, had urged the employment by the Florentine Republic of the vicious Borgia henchman Don Micheletto, even more notorious for cruelty than Don Remirro.

67. For example, Victoria Kahn, "*Virtù* and the Example of Agathocles in Machiavelli's *Prince,*" in *Machiavelli and the Discourse of Literature,* 208–10.

68. See, for example, Minturno and Castelvetro, in Gilbert, *Literary Criticism,* 289– 92, 348–53.

69. See Niccolò Machiavelli, *Opere,* ed. Mario Bonfantini (Milan-Naples: Ricciardi, 1957), 457–64.

70. See d'Ancona, *Origini,* 2:21. The play was described in a contemporary document as "the comedy of the duke Valentino and Pope Alexander VI, when they had the intention of occupying the state of the duke of Urbino; when they sent Lady Lucretia to Ferrara; when they invited the duchess to the wedding; when they came to take away the state; when the duke of Urbino returned the first time, and then left; when they killed Vitellozzo and the other lords; when Pope Alexander died, and the duke of Urbino returned to his state" (my translation).

71. Cf. *Prince,* chap. 18, "How faith should be kept by princes."

72. See Riccardo Bruscagli, "La Corte in Scena," 145, and "Throne of Blood," 22–27.

73. See *Prince,* chap. 7, which concludes with this advice regarding Cesare himself. Trissino also explicitly formulated the principle in his "Quinta divisione," quoted in Gilbert, *Literary Criticism,* 219 ("those who have been injured or think they are going to be injured are dangerous because they are ever watching their opportunity"); his source, Aristotle's *Rhetoric* (2.5), was also available to Machiavelli.

74. This is thus a narrative equivalent of the style of "constriction" Barberi-Squarotti outlines for *The Prince,* one based on close marshaling of options into rigorously causal syntactic structures (*La forma tragica,* 103–22). Although Barberi-Squarotti does not directly consider the *Description,* his stylistic analyses are valid for this brief text, one of the several "rehearsals" for *The Prince.*

75. Near the end of the cinquecento, Tasso, in his fragmentary canzone "O del grand'Apennino" (about 1578), selected the Metauro as the site for melancholy reflections on exile and political helplessness, in sharp contrast to the triumphalist history of the river.

76. See *Sophonisba* 101–16; *Rosmunda* 85–103; after Dantesque beginnings, Sophonisba's dream recalls Ugolino's, while Rosmunda's is Vergilian, recalling Aeneas's sight of Hector, with touches of Boccaccio's Tale of Lisabetta and the Pot of Basil (*Decameron* 4.5). For the Senecan dream in Renaissance drama, see C. Martinez, "Fantōmes, oracles, et malédictions: Figures du temps tragiques," in *Le temps e la durée dans la littérature au Moyen Age et à la Rénaissance,* ed. Y. Bellenger (Paris: Nizet, 1986), 139–51.

77. *History of Italy* 5.11. The pointing of "strangolare" resonates with chapter 8 of *The Prince,* in which Oliverotto da Fermo's death at Valentino's hands is closely linked to Oliverotto's rise to power through the murder of the maternal uncle who had nurtured him; that chapter, too, ends with the rhetorically delayed placement of *strangolato.*

78. See Gilbert, *Literary Criticism,* 292 (Minturno), and 328 (Castelvetro) for discussions of Aristotelian *anagnorisis* (recognition) and *peripeteia* (reversal) as parts of tragedy. For the concept of historical or fictional agents as "daemonic" when possessed of a single obsessive motive, see Angus Fletcher, *Allegory: The Theory of a Symbolic Mode* (Ithaca: Cornell University Press, 1968), 25–69.

79. See the first *Decennale,* vv. 382–402, in Niccolò Machiavelli, *Il teatro e le altre opere letterarie,* ed. Franco Gaeta (Milan: Feltrinelli), 250–51, and Dionisotti, "Machiavelli . . . e Don Micheletto," and "Machiavellerie."

80. See Nicola Grasso, *Eutichia,* ed. Luigina Stefani (Florence-Messina: D'Anna, 1981), esp. 59: "because through the injuries of the insatiable hydra my two children were lost . . . with all my possessions it having been necessary for me to flee to Rimini and from thence to Ferrara"; see also the "Argomento" (53): "Ocheutico, a most noble citizen of Urbino, having lost two children through the assaults of Cesare Valentino . . . fled his country" (translation mine). The play's argument, with its description of Eutichia as part of Valentino's plunder, may have influenced Machiavelli's argument in his *Clizia,* in which Clizia becomes plunder ("intra la preda fatta a Napoli questa fanciulla") during the conquest of Naples by Charles VIII.

81. See Stefani's prefatory essay in Grasso, *Eutichia,* 7–40.

82. Although written in octaves, the standard meter for epic narrative and early Italian drama, Castiglione's seven stanzas form a coherent lyric lament; as many cinquecento tragedians used canzone forms for their choruses, the parallel of lyric lament and tragic

chorus is, formally speaking, a close one. See Stefani's prefatory essay to Grasso, *Eutichia*, 18–23, and her "Le 'Ottave d'Italia' del Castiglione e le feste urbinati del 1513," *Paragone* 28 (1977): 67–83. For tragic canzoni written by Oricellari to lament the state of Italy overrun by barbarians, see Marco Ariani, *Tra classicismo* 19–28 (Trissino); Croce, *Scrittori*, 201–11 (Martelli); for canzoni of lament written on the Sack of Rome by Aretino and others, see Luzio, *Pietro Aretino*, 64–70, and Chastel, *Sack*, 22–25; there is similar language in Machiavelli's "Capitolo sull'Ambizione" to Luigi Guicciardini, probably written in 1509 after Machiavelli had witnessed the carnage of the War of the League of Cambrai (cf. vv. 118–35).

83. For Dante's prophecies spoken by Hugh Capet, see *Purgatorio* 20.35–89. Machiavelli's citation is not exact, as Dante's text reads, "I see the fleur-de-lys enter Alagna." I have provided my own translation of Gaeta's edition here (Machiavelli, *Lettere*, 444) and filled in the second hemistich of verse 87, which Machiavelli explicitly leaves to Guicciardini's memory.

84. Bacchelli, "Istorico," 4, speaks of the "irremediabile fatalità" conferred by the Latin quotation.

85. See Rucellai, *Opere*, ed. G. Mazzoni, lix–lx, and Dionisotti, "Machiavellerie (II)," 256–58, who observes that Giovanni Rucellai's contempt for Clement VII was rooted in an aristocratic disdain for bastards.

86. Reprinted in Croce, "Ludovico Martelli," in *Poeti e Scrittori*, 283–85.

87. See Chastel, *Sack*, 87–90, for the Peruzzi illustration; Chastel notes that the tragedy of Lucretia's suicide was revived for describing the agony of the Sack of Rome (*Sack*, 210). Aretino's laments on the Fall of Rome and his prognostications are reprinted in Alessandro Luzio, *Pietro Aretino nei suoi primi anni a venezia e la corte dei Gonzaga* (Loescher: Turin, 1888), 64–70, 112–15.

88. See *Histories* 1.9: "All the wars that after this time were caused by barbarians, and all the barbarians that inundated that [Italy] were in most cases called by those [popes]. . . . Which manner of proceeding endures still in these our times: which has kept and keeps Italy weak and disunited" (translation mine). And see *Discourses* 1.12.

89. For an analysis of this "sublime rhetoric," see Kahn, "Agathocles' Prince," in *Machiavelli and the Discourse of Literature*, 216–17. For Barberi-Squarotti, the fusion of the heroic and prophetic is essential to Machiavelli's view of political palingenesis as a tragic agon (*La forma tragica*, 263–68). For the utopian and prophetic dimensions of the last chapter in the context of Dante's presence in *The Prince*, see also Albert Rusell Ascoli, "Machiavelli and the Gift of Counsel," in *Machiavelli and the Discourse of Literature*, 245–53.

90. For this figure of lamenting Rome in Dante's *Purgatorio* 6, drawing on the personified Jerusalem of the Lamentations of Jeremiah, see my "Lament and Lamentations in the *Purgatorio* and the Case of Dante's Statius," in *Dante Studies* 115 (1999); quotations from Dante's *Purgatorio* are from Dante Alighieri, *Purgatorio*, ed. and trans. R. M. Durling, with introduction and notes by R. L. Martinez (New York: Oxford; forthcoming). There are more parallels than those quoted in my text; the idea of one who might "heal her [Italy's] wounds" (sani le sue ferite) also echoes Dante, who would have the emperor heal the sores of Italy's cities ("cura lor magagne," 6.110) and who reproaches the inactivity of Rudolf of Hapsburg, who ought to "sanar le piaghe c'hanno Italia

morta" ([heal the wounds that have killed Italy], *Purgatorio* 7.95); of course, these passages were also adapted into Petrarch's poems; cf. "Italia mia," 2 ("le piaghe mortal"), and "Spirto gentil," 104–106 ("Roma . . . ti chier mercè" [Rome . . . asks your mercy]). But Machiavelli had Dante much on his mind during the last months of 1525: in his letter to Guicciardini of 19 December, he implicitly compares his own unrewarded service to the case of Romeo of Villeneuve (*Paradiso* 6.127–43; cf. the letter to Vettori of December 10, 1513, emphasizing Machiavelli's "fede" and its proof, his poverty; for discussion, see Ascoli, "Machiavelli and the Gift of Counsel," in *Machiavelli and the Discourse of Literature,* 245).

91. Dante's texts gave rise not only to Petrarch's lyrics and prose letters on the subject, but also to an extensive literature written by exiled Ghibellines in the trecento (some of which are "lamenti storici," some canzoni of exile, called "disperate"; see Natalino Sapegno, ed., *Poesia del Trecento* (Milan-Naples: Ricciardi, 1961), 3–278. Before and during the *Risorgimento,* the political poems of Dante and Petrarch, sometimes refracted through Machiavelli, inspired the work of Vittorio Alfieri, Vincenzo Monti, Giacomo Leopardi, Ugo Foscolo, and Alessandro Manzoni, among others. Gramsci can also be added to this list; see Ascoli, "Gift," in *Machiavelli and the Discourse of Literature,* 256.

6. Love and Longing in L'Asino

1. *The Prince,* trans. and ed. Harvey C. Mansfield (Chicago: University of Chicago Press, 1985), chap. 7.

2. *Discourses on Livy,* trans. Harvey C. Mansfield and Nathan Tarcov (Chicago: University of Chicago Press, 1996), 3.3.

3. A fine literal treatment of this effort to block out grief with armor is found in Shakespeare's *Macbeth,* when Macbeth faces his wife's madness and his own isolation: "*Macbeth:* 'Give me my armor.' *Seyton:* ' 'Tis not needed yet.' *Macbeth:* 'I'll put it on' " (*Riverside Shakespeare,* 2d ed., ed. G. Blakemore Evans [Boston: Houghton Mifflin, 1997], 5.3.33–34).

4. Charles S. Singleton, "The Perspective of Art," *Kenyon Review* 15 (Spring 1953): 169–89, at 180; quoted in Mark Hulliung, *Citizen Machiavelli* (Princeton: Princeton University Press, 1983), 282n.

5. Sheldon Wolin, *Politics and Vision: Continuity and Innovation in Western Political Thought* (Boston: Little, Brown, 1960), 217.

6. Wolin, *Politics and Vision,* 224.

7. "On Ingratitude," ll. 186–87. Quotations from "On Ingratitude" and *L'Asino* are my own translations from the Italian texts in Machiavelli, *Opere,* 8 vols. (Milan: Feltrinelli, 1965).

8. This will not be evident to readers of *L'Asino* in translation. The only scholarly English translation in print, that of Allan Gilbert (in *Machiavelli: The Chief Works and Others,* trans. and ed. Allan Gilbert, 3 vols. [Durham: Duke University Press, 1965], 2:750–72), renders the eleven occurrences of *virtù* with five different terms (vigor, virtue, strength, ability, and energy). Thus a reader of Gilbert's influential translation will never suspect that *L'Asino* can be read as a meditation on virtù.

9. Mario Martelli, "Per un dittico machiavelliano," 7–42, in Niccolò Machiavelli,

Novella di Belfagor, L'Asino, ed. Maurizio Tarantino (Rome: Salerno, 1990), 14. Martelli's essay is a good overview of the sources and textual status of *L'Asino.*

10. Parallels to the *Inferno* throughout the work have often been noted. Central to both works is a quest for an understanding of human life, tied to the narrator's love for a woman who will serve as a guide and teacher. The climax of *L'Asino,* the narrator's encounter with the man transformed into a pig, recalls the sixth canto of the *Inferno,* in which Dante speaks with a man who because of his gluttony now wallows in mud and who gives the first of the political prophecies which appear in Dante's work. In the pig's speech, Machiavelli also apparently drew on Plutarch and Pliny the Elder.

11. This second-century Latin novel tells of the experiences and education of a young man, Lucius, before and after his transformation into an ass. Its most famous episode is the love story of Cupid and Psyche (books 4–6). At the end of the work the young man is returned to human form, it becomes clear that he is Apuleius himself, and he is initiated by steps into the priesthood of "he that is mightiest of the great gods, the highest of the mightiest, the loftiest of the highest, and the sovereign of the loftiest, Osiris" (Apuleius, *Metamorphoses,* Loeb Classical Library [1989], 11.30). Machiavelli thus modeled his poem on a work that is in one perspective a pagan pilgrim's progress, and whose most evil and condemned character is a Christian (at least that is the plainest way to read Apuleius's text. See 9.14). A good introduction to Apuleius's story is James Tatum, *Apuleius and the Golden Ass* (Ithaca: Cornell University Press, 1979).

12. Here Machiavelli is working alongside a tradition of the epic temptress who emasculates a man by seducing him (besides Circe, other such figures include Dido, Alcina, and Amida). But Machiavelli reworks the tradition by separating the seduction and emasculation and indeed reversing the seduction's sign: here the seduction by a strong woman (who in fact shields the protagonist from Circe) will help restore the man's strength. See John Freccero's thoughtful study of the political sexuality of another strong Machiavellian woman, Caterina Sforza, in "Medusa and the Madonna of Forlì: Political Sexuality in Machiavelli," in *Machiavelli and the Discourse of Literature,* ed. Albert Russell Ascoli and Victoria Kahn (Ithaca: Cornell University Press, 1993), 161–78.

13. John Plamenatz, "In Search of Machiavellian *Virtù,*" in *The Political Calculus,* ed. Anthony Parel (Toronto: University of Toronto Press, 1972), 157–78.

14. Quoted in Hanna Fenichel Pitkin, *Fortune Is a Woman: Gender and Politics in the Thought of Niccolò Machiavelli* (Berkeley: University of California Press, 1984), 25.

15. Ibid.

16. J. G. A. Pocock, *The Machiavellian Moment: Florentine Political Thought and the Atlantic Republican Tradition* (Princeton: Princeton University Press, 1975), 178.

17. Hannah Arendt, *Between Past and Future: Six Exercises in Political Thought* (New York: Viking Press, 1961), 137. For additional interpretations of Machiavellian *virtù,* see Friedrich Meinecke, *Machiavellism: The Doctrine of Raison d'Etat and Its Place in Modern History,* trans. Douglas Scott (New Haven: Yale University Press, 1957); Felix Gilbert, *Machiavelli and Guicciardini: Politics and History in Sixteenth-Century Florence* (New York: W. W. Norton, 1984), 179–200; Neal Wood, "Machiavelli's Concept of *Virtù* Reconsidered," *Political Studies* 15 (1967): 159–72; and J. H. Hexter, *The Vision of Politics on the Eve of the Reformation* (New York: Basic Books, 1973), 188–92.

18. *Prince,* chap. 8.

19. Bernard Crick, in Machiavelli, *The Discourses,* ed. Bernard Crick, trans. Leslie J. Walker (Harmondsworth: Penguin Books, 1970), 535n.

20. Arendt, *Between Past and Future,* 137.

21. Pitkin, *Fortune Is a Woman,* 122.

22. Compare Machiavelli's play *Clizia,* in which the old and weakened Nicomaco eats a special meal to ready himself for lovemaking (4.2), and afterward brags of its effect in hardening him: "I'm the man for doing the proper thing; since I've eaten that food, I feel myself as strong as a sword" (*Clizia,* 4.11, in *Chief Works and Others* 2:856).

23. This scene, from dinner to lovemaking, owes much to the Lucius-Photis affair in Apuleius, one of the more famous erotic passages in classical literature. There are parallels (e.g., Photis is the servant of an enchantress, Lucius's erection is treated explicitly), but also an important difference between Machiavelli and his original: Lucius has not been unmanned, and in fact Photis teases him with martial language: " 'Fight,' she said, 'and fight fiercely. . . . Close in and make a frontal assault, if you are a real man' " (Apuleius, *Metamorphoses* 2.17).

24. *The Literary Works of Machiavelli,* trans. J. R. Hale (London: Oxford University Press, 1961), 142.

25. Arendt, *Between Past and Future,* 137.

26. *Prince,* ded. letter.

27. Here Machiavelli, as he does with Dante, imitates the form but rejects the substance of his model, the Cupid and Psyche love story in Apuleius's *Metamorphoses.* In Apuleius's story, the transcendent power of love leads the soul to heaven.

28. Dante Alighieri, *Inferno* 6.58–63.

29. *Prince,* chap. 19.

30. Mansfield, Introduction to *Prince,* xxiii–xxiv.

31. Antonio Gramsci, *The Modern Prince, and Other Writings,* trans. Louis Marks (New York: International Publishers, 1957), 135.

32. *Chief Works* 2:961–62. On Machiavelli's letters, see John M. Najemy, *Between Friends: Discourses of Power and Desire in the Machiavelli-Vettori Letters of 1513–1515* (Princeton: Princeton University Press, 1993).

33. *Opere* 6:444.

34. Gilbert, *Machiavelli and Guicciardini,* 180.

35. Wolin, *Politics and Vision,* 224.

36. *Chief Works* 2:1006–07.

37. Ibid., 2:994.

38. Albert Russell Ascoli has written evocatively on the unstable but unbridgeable gap in Machiavelli between pragmatism and prophecy, in "Machiavelli's Gift of Counsel," in *Machiavelli and the Discourse of Literature,* 219–57.

7. The Politician as Writer

1. Niccolò Machiavelli, *Legazioni, Commissarie, Scritti di governo,* ed. Fredi Chiappelli (Bari: Laterza, 1973), 2:125. I am borrowing the English translation from Sebastian de Grazia, *Machiavelli in Hell* (Princeton: Princeton University Press, 1989), 303. Hereinafter whenever a printed English translation is not used and cited, translation is mine.

2. Niccolò Machiavelli, *Lettere*, ed. Franco Gaeta (Milan: Feltrinelli, 1961), 82.

3. Machiavelli, *Legazioni* 2:275.

4. For the title and the text of the *Description*, see the introduction to its most recent edition, in Niccolò Machiavelli, *Opere*, ed. Corrado Vivanti (Turin: Einaudi-Gallimard, 1997), 766, and Jean-Jacques Marchand, *Niccolò Machiavelli, I primi scritti politici (1499–1512): Nascita di un pensiero e di uno stile* (Padova: Antenore, 1975).

5. See, for instance, Federico Chabod, *Scritti su Machiavelli* (Turin: Einaudi, 1964), 297–306; and the introductory note to the *Descrizione* in Niccolò Machiavelli, *Arte della guerra e scritti politici minori*, ed. Sergio Bertelli (Milan: Feltrinelli, 1961), 35–37.

6. Niccolò Machiavelli, *Il modo che tenne il duca Valentino per ammazar Vitellozzo, Oliverotto da Fermo, il signor Pagolo et il duca di Gravina Orsini in Senigaglia*, in *Opere*, ed. Vivanti, 17–18.

7. See, for instance, Gennaro Sasso, *Niccolò Machiavelli: Storia del suo pensiero politico* (Naples: Istituto Italiano per gli Studi Storici, 1958), 42–56.

8. Machiavelli, *Il modo*, 21.

9. "Julius placed himself with only a small guard in the hands of his enemy Baglioni. . . . Sagacious men who were with the Pope [that is, Machiavelli] observed his temerity and the cowardice of Baglioni, and could not understand why the latter had not by a single blow rid himself of his enemy" (Niccolò Machiavelli, *The Prince and the Discourses*, trans. Max Richter [New York: Random House, 1950], 185).

10. Carlo Dionisotti, *Geografia e storia della letteratura italiana* (Turin: Einaudi, 1976), 42–44.

11. Niccolò Machiavelli, *The Chief Works and Others*, trans. Allan Gilbert (Durham: Duke University Press, 1989), 3:1453–54.

12. *Chief Works* 3:1448.

13. Ibid., 3:1457.

14. *The Portable Machiavelli*, trans. Peter Bondanella and Mark Musa (Harmondsworth: Penguin Books, 1979), 88.

15. One can think, for instance, of the letters written in 1503 from Constantinople by Gian Giacomo Caroldo, who later will write, not unlike Machiavelli, but without publishing it, an interesting history of Venice (*Historie venete*). See Angelo Ventura, Introduction to the reprint of *Relazioni degli ambasciatori veneti* (Bari: Laterza, 1976), 1:xxxiii–xxxviii.

16. On Machiavelli's activity and early writings about the institution of a Florentine militia (*La cagione dell'ordinanza; Provisione della ordinanza*), see the chapter "Pisa and the Militia: 1504–1506)," admirable for its concision and clarity, in John Hale, *Machiavelli and Renaissance Italy* (New York: Macmillan, 1960), 82–99.

17. *Chief Works* 2:577.

18. Ibid., 2:724.

19. Ibid., 2:572.

20. Machiavelli, *Lettere*, 389.

21. See the text of the "condotta" in Pasquale Villari, *Niccolò Machiavelli e i suoi tempi* (Milan: Hoepli, 1927), 2:344–45.

22. Machiavelli, *Discourse on Reforming the Government of Florence Written at the Request of Pope Leo X*, in *The Prince and Other Works*, trans. Allan H. Gilbert (New York: Hendricks House, 1964), 80.

23. On these other opinions, cf. Rudolf von Albertini, *Das florentinische Staatsbewußtsein im Übergang von the Republik zum Prinzipat,* which I have seen in Italian: *Firenze dalla repubblica al principato,* trans. Cesare Cristofolini (Turin: Einaudi, 1970), 27–31, 113–19, 33–36, respectively.

24. Machiavelli, *Lettere,* 395.

25. *Portable Machiavelli,* 540.

26. Machiavelli, *Prince and Discourses,* 383.

27. On the sources of the *Florentine Histories,* see Anna Maria Cabrini, *Per una valutazione delle "Istorie fiorentine" del Machiavelli: Note sulle fonti del Secondo libro* (Florence: La Nuova Italia, 1985); for Cavalcanti, Eric Cochrane, *Historians and Historiography in the Italian Renaissance* (Chicago: University of Chicago Press, 1985), 22, and essential bibliography 506n78.

28. *Chief Works* 3:1128.

29. Ibid., 3:1061.

30. Ibid., 3:1062.

31. Ibid., 3:1079.

32. Ibid., 3:1337.

33. Ibid., 3:1309.

34. Ibid., 3:1160.

35. Thucydides, *The Peloponnesian War* 5.105.1–4; see especially the Athenians' cynical remark about the Melians' hope (in fact, wishful thinking) in some help from the Spartans: "The Lacedaemonians, when their own interests or their country's laws are in question, are the worthiest men alive; of their conduct towards others much might be said, but no clearer idea of it could be given than by shortly saying that of all the men we know they are most conspicuous in considering *what is agreeable honorable, and what is expedient just*" (trans. John H. Finley [New York: Random House, 1951], 334; emphasis mine).

36. *Chief Works* 3:1230.

37. Ibid., 3:1343.

38. Ibid., 3:1346.

39. Carlo Dionisotti, *Machiavellerie: Storia e fortuna di Machiavelli* (Turin: Einaudi, 1980), 398.

40. *Chief Works* 3:1366.

41. Ibid., 2:978.

42. Ibid., 3:1233.

43. Ibid., 3:1406–07.

44. Ibid., 3:1330.

45. Throughout my notes I have kept bibliographical references to an indispensable minimum. Two collections of essays, however, deserve a specific mention because most of the issues touched upon in the pages above are treated there in greater detail and often very brilliantly: Myron P. Gilmore, ed., *Studies on Machiavelli* (Florence: Sansoni, 1972), including the papers read at a seminar on Machiavelli organized in 1969 by Villa "I Tatti," Harvard University Center for Italian Renaissance Studies; and *Niccolò Machiavelli politico storico letterato: Atti del Convegno di Losanna — 27–30 settembre 1995,* ed. Jean-Jacques Marchand (Rome: Salerno, 1996).

8. Beyond Limits: Time, Space, Language in Machiavelli's Decennali

1. Niccolò Machiavelli, *Lettere,* ed. Franco Gaeta (Milan: Feltrinelli, 1981), 135. My translation. Emphasis added.

2. So, too, is the second *Decennale* (presumably written in 1514), though it stands incomplete, comprised in two hundred and sixteen verses and dealing with events from 1504 to 1509. Terza rima is an Italian form of iambic verse consisting of eleven-syllable lines arranged in tercets, the middle line of each tercet rhyming with the first and last lines of the following tercet.

3. Cf. Carlo Dionisotti, "Machiavelli, Man of Letters," in *Machiavelli and the Discourse of Literature,* ed. Albert Russell Ascoli and Victoria Kahn (Ithaca: Cornell University Press, 1993). Apropos of Machiavelli's choice of poetry over prose in his early literary works and of the Florentine secretary's "unwavering preference for terza rima" over other metrical forms (such as ottava rima), see Dionisotti, "Man of Letters," 35–36.

4. Niccolò Machiavelli, *Machiavelli: Tutte le Opere,* ed. Mario Martelli (Florence: Sansoni, 1971), 1159; my translation.

5. Cf. Dionisotti, "Man of Letters," 38–39. Dionisotti refutes the suggestion that Machiavelli's poetry in terza rima had Petrarchan influences, insisting instead that, in terms of literary history, Machiavelli's poetic allegiance in this matter was exclusively to Dante: "At the beginning of the sixteenth century, a preference for terza rima in narrative works implied fidelity to the tradition of Dante. In spite of the great popularity of Petrarch's *Trionfi* in the fifteenth century, the original opposition between the works of Dante and Petrarch, the two supreme models of Italian poetry, had lately been reduced to a metrical opposition between long poems in terza rima influenced by Dante, and lyric poems influenced by Petrarch. [. . . Machiavelli's] rejection of Petrarchan lyric poetry, on which even Savonarola modeled his verses, represents an attachment to the older Florence and a distrust of the newer style typical of the younger, Medicean Florence and courtly Italy."

6. Raffaele Spongano, *Nozioni ed esempi di metrica italiana* (Bologna: Pàtron, 1974), 43.

7. Cf. W. Th. Elwert, *Versificazione italiana dalle origini ai giorni nostri.* (Florence: Le Monnier, 1983), 143–44: "The tercet soon became one of the preferred metrical schemes of Italian poetry. Thanks to the Dantesque example, it became, in the fourteenth century, the meter of allegorical-didactic poetry . . . , and of chronicle in verse" (my translation).

8. Niccolò Machiavelli, *The Decennali,* in *Machiavelli: The Chief Works and Others,* trans. Allan Gilbert (Durham: Duke University Press, 1965), 3:1444.

9. Both Martelli (*Tutte le opere,* xxxix) and Elwert (*Versificazione italiana,* 144) indicate *Il centiloquio* by Antonio Pucci as a notable example of fourteenth-century *cronaca* written in terza rima. Martelli asserts a direct connection between *Il centiloquio* and the *Decennali* by pointing to the former as a textual forerunner, in certain respects, to the *Decennali.*

10. Cf. Spongano, *Nozioni ed esempi,* 12: Chronicle in terza rima occurred up to the *Decennali* of Machiavelli.

11. Barbara J. Godorecci, *After Machiavelli: "Re-writing" and the "Hermeneutic Attitude"* (West Lafayette, Ind.: Purdue University Press, 1993), 117.

12. Roberto Ridolfi, *Vita di Niccolò Machiavelli* (Rome: Angelo Belardetti Editore, 1954), 126; my translation. Cf. Francesco Guicciardini, *Storie fiorentine,* in *Opere,* ed. Vittorio de Caprariis (Milan, Naples: Riccardo Ricciardi Editore, 1953), 215–33.

13. Gilbert, *Chief Works,* 1444.

14. All citations from the *Decennali* in Italian and Latin are taken from Martelli's edition of *Tutte le Opere.* The page numbers and, where appropriate, the verse numbers appear in the text. English translations of the *Decennali* are taken from the third volume of Gilbert's *Chief Works* unless otherwise specified. The page numbers of this edition appear in the text.

15. Cf. this verse with verses 193–95 in *Decennale II:* "I' non potrei sì presto raccontarve / quanto sì presto poi de' Viniziani, / dopo la rotta, quello stato sparve" (954) [I could not be so quick in telling you of it as after their defeat that Venetian domain was quick in vanishing (1461)]. The poet grapples again with the problem of expressing the swift passing of time in language. In a manner which recalls Petrarch, he declares his inability to accomplish the feat while contemporaneously managing, within the limited space of the terzina, to discover a rhetorical solution to the task. The phrase "sì presto [so quick]," twice repeated, places emphasis on the speed that at first was lacking, ("non potrei [. . .] raccontarve [I could not . . . tell you]") and then so quickly brought the fact to its conclusion ("sparve [vanishing]").

16. Cf. Godorecci, *After Machiavelli,* 114–17, for a detailed analysis of Duke Valentino's betrayal of Vitellozzo Vitelli and others as represented in the *Decennali.*

17. Cf. also vv. 530, 533, 535.

18. In total, Pisa is brought up some sixteen times in *Decennale I* and another five times in *Decennale II.* Machiavelli, it seems, offers some response, apropos of Pisa, to Soderini's letter in his verses, acknowledging Florence's extreme preoccupation with conquering this rival city. The most revealing tercet is perhaps found in *Decennale II:* "In questo voi provvedimenti assai / avevi fatti, *perché verso Pisa / tenevi volti gli occhi sempre mai* (953, vv. 145–47; emphasis added) [Meanwhile you had made full preparations, *because toward Pisa you kept your eyes turned always* (1460)].

19. Cf. Gilbert, *Chief Works,* 1457.

9. The Classical Heritage in Machiavelli's Histories

1. For example, Karl Löwith, *Meaning and History: The Theological Implications of the Philosophy of History* (Chicago: University of Chicago Press, 1949); Hayden White, *Metahistory: The Historical Imagination in Nineteenth-Century Europe* (Baltimore: Johns Hopkins University Press, 1973), 45ff.

2. *Discourses* 2.5. Quotations and citations to Machiavelli are from *Machiavelli: tutte le opere,* ed. Mario Martelli (Florence: Sansoni, 1971). Translations are my own.

3. Alasdair MacIntyre, *After Virtue* (South Bend: University of Notre Dame Press), 1–5.

4. *Discourses* 2.5.

5. One is tempted to say here that, as with so many things, Machiavelli anticipated the modern, or maybe postmodern, idea that language was not merely the way a people described the world but the way they cut out its relevant pieces from the surrounding

chaos. This may, however, read too much into Machiavelli. Still, the Renaissance problem of translation, or rendering into Christian Latin, the pagan concepts of the past was enough to open a corridor of doors about universality. Thus Leonardo Bruni discovered, when trying to use his concepts of Christian virtue to update Aristotle's *Ethics,* that the ancient concepts simply did not fit. It is to give the old Italian expression *traduttore traditore* a deeper meaning.

6. The idea that history was cyclical, that cities rose from barbarism and then became corrupt and returned to chaos was not, of course, new. It had roots in the ancient world in figures like Herodotus, Thucydides, and Polybius and probably underlay the concept of the "rebirth" of civilization we know as the Renaissance after the Dark Ages that followed the fall of Rome.

7. *Discourses* 3.1; see, too, *Discourses* 2, pr.

8. J. G. A. Pocock, *The Machiavellian Moment: Florentine Political Thought and the Atlantic Republican Tradition,* (Princeton: Princeton University Press, 1975), 31.

9. This agreement between Strauss and Pocock is, of course, limited and based on the idea that what characterized modernity was the unprecedented effort to defy the historical cycle that had doomed all previous cultures to final failure through hubris and/or fortune. The idea that moderns could finally "get it right," could eliminate mystery and escape the wheel of fortune by duplicating God's making of the world by making an eternal republic, Strauss first attributed to Hobbes. It was only later that he attributed this idea to Machiavelli's belief in *virtù* understood as the skill or ability *(arete)* to defy history and *fortuna.* That Strauss believed that modern arrogance had, in fact, escaped the cycle, that it had banished mystery, *fortuna,* or the gods, is unlikely. In short, for Strauss, modernity would have the same tragic ending that all other states have had. Modernity, therefore, is a comedy in the sense that the participants do not understand what the ancients understood, namely, that they cannot escape the last tragic act. Thus for Strauss, the Enlightenment "project" was not the engineering that moderns thought they were engaged in, but the "projection" of one more illusion upon the walls of the Platonic cave. By making Machiavelli the author of this great illusion, Strauss found the roots of modernity not in the Enlightenment, but in Machiavellian bravado. Whether Machiavelli himself believed what moderns believe is another issue.

Pocock agrees that modernity, especially in its liberal and hyperindividualistic form is dangerous and presumptuous. But he also thinks that at least in the Anglo-American tradition, this liberalism is a relatively recent arrival and one without very deep roots. Indeed, the true Anglo-American tradition, according to Pocock, is republican and that tradition has roots that extend back to the ancients. Thus where Strauss found a break with the past in the arrogance and insubordination of a modern Machiavellian reason, Pocock found — precisely in Machiavelli — the link with the past and the language of fortune and virtue that moderns had thought long overcome by the Enlightenment "project." For Pocock, however, "virtue" is not *arete* or skill, ability, and technique, but the absence of or, better, the renunciation of self-interest and individualism favored today by republicans and communitarians. For Machiavelli, however, it could well be argued (for example, in *The Prince,* chaps. 3 and 21) that the acquisition of property is normal and legitimate activity and that self-interest and the interest of the community were not incompatible but interdependent. Certainly excluding self-interest from the list of motives that animate citizens seems a more precarious position than Machiavelli would ever have assumed. In any case, who today can deny after two decades or so of the relentless driving of the private out into the public that the results, even for the virtuous, have not been ambiguous?

10. And an art form it remains today, according to figures like Benedetto Croce, Hayden White, Simon Schama, and many others.

11. As illusive as ever, however, Plato, the master of art and rhetoric, composed this perhaps greatest work of art to disparage art and defend truth, or perhaps to defend truth as art.

12. R. G. Collingwood, in fact, remarked on how astonishing it was that the Greeks had any conception of history at all since, for them, only the world of essences had been valuable and permanent: "Ancient Greek thought as a whole has a very definite prevailing tendency not only uncongenial to the growth of historical thought but actually based, one might say, on a rigorously anti-historical metaphysics." Greek thought, Collingwood continued, made "a distinction between two types of thought, knowledge proper and what we translate by 'opinion.'" Because knowledge — science and philosophy — could only be of the permanent and not the changing, it was obvious in Greek thought that one could never have a science of history, which is constant change: "True knowledge . . . holds good not only here and now but everywhere and always." See R. G. Collingwood, *The Idea of History* (Oxford University Press, 1956), 20–21.

13. Though more interested in poetic and dramatic structure certainly than Plato, like Plato (*Republic* 607b; 509b-511e), Aristotle was suspicious of poetry's persuasive power, its ability to escape philosophical tutelage, especially when it teamed up with the sophisticated rhetoric of classical Athens. Philosophy, therefore, said Aristotle, had to constantly chaperon rhetoric lest it take up again with poetry. "It was," he says, "naturally the poets who [had] first set [rhetoric] going. . . . [And] it was because the poets seemed to win fame through their fine language when their thoughts were simple enough, that the language of oratorical prose at first took a poetical color, for example, that of Gorgias. . . . [But today, he says nervously] it is ridiculous to imitate a poetical manner which the poets themselves have dropped" (*Rhetoric* 1404a 9–10).

14. Aristotle, *Poetics,* trans. Richard Janko (Indianapolis: Hackett, 1987), 51b 1–13.

15. And, as Heidegger has pointed out, it has never been lost.

16. As quoted in Michael Grant, in Introduction to *Tacitus: The Annals of Imperial Rome* (New York: Dorset, 1984), 11.

17. Vico, *The New Science of Giambattista Vico,* trans. Thomas Goddard Bergin and Max Harold Fisch (Ithaca: Cornell University Press, 1984), paras. 376, 378–79.

18. Vico, *New Science,* para. 367.

19. As one scholar has warned, it would be worthwhile considering whether our own historians have overcome poetic history before we scorn it. See Harvey Mansfield, Translator's Introduction, the *Florentine Histories,* trans. Harvey C. Mansfield and Laura F. Banfield (Princeton: Princeton University Press, 1988), xi.

20. Cicero, *De Oratore,* trans. J. S. Watson (Carbondale: Southern Illinois University Press, 1970), 2.13. Emphasis added.

21. Cicero, *De Oratore* 2.12.

22. Ernst Breisach, *Historiography: Ancient, Medieval, and Modern* (Chicago: University of Chicago Press, 1944), 53.

23. Thus, in *De Legibus,* after a long discussion about the nature of history, Cicero warned Atticus and his brother Quintus against "inquiring too critically into traditions that are handed down" to the present (Cicero, *De Legibus,* Loeb Classical Library [1928; repr. 1994], 11.4).

24. Cicero, *De Legibus* 11.4.

25. Cicero, *Legibus* 12.4–7. To emphasize the impossibility of a scientific history, Cicero (*De Oratore* 2.14–15) gives an astonishing list of the requirements for such a history: "It is the first law in writing that the historian must not dare to tell any falsehood, and the next, that he must be bold enough to tell the whole truth. Also, that there must be no suspicion of partiality in his writings, or of personal animosity. These fundamental rules are doubtless universally known. The superstructure depends on facts and style. The course of facts requires attention to order of time and descriptions of countries; and since, in great affairs, and such as are worthy of remembrance, first the designs, then the actions, and afterward the results, are expected, it demands also that it should be shown, in regard to the designs, what the writer approves, and that it should be told, in regard to the actions, not only what was done or said, but in what manner; and when the result is stated, that all the causes contributing to it should be set forth, whether arising from accident, wisdom, or temerity; and of the characters concerned, not only their acts, but, at least of those eminent in reputation and dignity, the life and manners of each. The sort of language and character of style to be observed must be regular and continuous, flowing with a kind of equable smoothness, without the roughness of judicial pleadings, and the sharp-pointed sentences used at the bar."

26. Francis Cornford, in 1907, found this poetic-history rather quaint (a result, he said, of the "destitute poverty [of the Greeks] in the apparatus and machinery of thinking"). He excused it because reason was as good as it could be in those days. "What," he asked sympathetically, "were the possible alternatives in an age which lacked the true conception of universal causality? There were two, and only two: Fate and Providence." Cornford's easy use of metaphors like "machinery" and "apparatus" for the thought process shows the way mechanical *ratio* conceived of sound thinking and why it had to dismiss evidently unsophisticated imaginative thought as inappropriate to history. Thucydides, continued Cornford, "had an admirably scientific temper, [but] he lacked the indispensable aid of accumulated and systematic knowledge, and of *the apparatus of scientific conceptions.* . . . Instead of this furniture of thought, to the inheritance of which every modern student is born, Thucydides possessed, in common with his contemporaries at Athens, the cast of mind induced by an early education consisting almost exclusively of the poets. No amount of hard, rational thinking . . . could suffice to break up this mould, in an age when science had as yet provided no alternative system of conception. . . . The principle that forms and connects [*The Peloponnesian Wars*] is the tragic theory of human nature. . . . The Greek historians can be interpreted only by reference to the poets." Thus there is a "broad distinction of type between Thucydides' work" and history as we know it. Modern history "can be described generally as realistic. . . . Thucydides [on the other hand] tried to be scientific . . . [but] ended by choosing those [methods] which were useful for a very different end—a lesson in morality." It is worth wondering, however, whether the Greeks thought that the scientific mentality was itself a moral, or perhaps immoral, lesson. See Francis M. Cornford, *Thucydides Mythistoricus* (1907; repr. Philadelphia: University of Pennsylvania Press, 1971), ix–x, 73, 126–27; emphasis added.

27. In his now mostly lost *Origins*.

28. In *The Conspiracy of Catiline, The War with Jugartha*, and the *Histories*.

29. Livy continues, "For true it is that the less men's wealth was, the less was their greed. Of late, riches have brought in avarice, and excessive pleasures the longing to carry wantonness and licence to the point of ruin for oneself and of universal destruction [Adeo quanto rerum minus, tanto minus cupidatis erat; nuper divitiae avaritiam et abundantes voluptates desiderium per luxum atque libidinem pereundi perdendique omnia invexere]" (Livy, *Ab Urbe Condita*, Loeb Classical Library [1918; repr. 1988], 1.8–13).

30. Breisach notes, for example, that Cremetius Cordus was arraigned in the reign of Cossus and Agrippa (A.D. 25) for having praised Marcus Brutus and Caius Cassius. See *Historiography*, 65–66.

31. The title of his work is itself a trope recalling the (perhaps) less self-conscious religious chronicles begun in the third century B.C. Long before Cato the Censor, the Roman Senate had ordered the publication of these annals, or "Records of the Priests," which were concerned primarily with important religious matters. On the face of it such records were mere chronicles; but because religion was omnipresent, they also involved political issues. So, the "Records" became a kind of history often combined with legend and religious portents. Because they often involved annual patterns of ceremonies, these came to be called annals. See Grant, Introduction to Tacitus, *Annals*, 12ff.

32. Ibid., 11–14.

33. Tacitus's inability to keep his obvious political sympathies out of his *Annals*, however, has caused dismay among modern historians. "This [political] attitude," said Collingwood in despair, "leads Tacitus to distort history systematically by representing it as essentially a clash of characters, exaggeratedly good with exaggeratedly bad." The modern historian, on the other hand, aims at a disinterested and evidently more reliable recovery of the past. Moreover, the modern historian "knows that if only he had the [physical] capacity he could become the interpreter of the whole past of mankind." Thus, according to Collingwood, "what is really wrong with Tacitus is that he has never thought out the fundamental problems of his enterprise. His attitude towards the philosophical groundwork of history is frivolous, and he takes over the current pragmatic view of its purpose in the spirit of a rhetorician rather than that of a serious thinker" (Collingwood, *Idea of History*, 39).

34. Hans Baron, *The Crisis of the Early Italian Renaissance* (Princeton: Princeton University Press, 1966), 7; Eugenio Garin, *Science and Civic Life in the Italian Renaissance*, trans. Peter Munz (Garden City, N.Y.: Doubleday/Anchor, 1969), 4. The reappearance of political history can easily be seen by comparing Dante's medieval fascination with the abstraction of an Imperial Rome that had long since passed away with Bruni's interest in the Roman republic as a model for contemporary life. The concrete, the local, in short, had begun to intrude on the vision of eternal truth, the abstract and out-of-fashion universal empire: "We ought to compare Bruni's position with that of Dante Alighieri, whom he loved. . . . To Dante, the ideal Florence is the Florence of the Cacciaguida, the distant vision of a patriarchal past. This city is enclosed in its old walls, regulated by an austere discipline. Dante's vision is dominated by a rigid moralism, by a rejection of the present, and by an archaic myth which stands in strong contrast to contemporary life, its trade, its wealth, and its culture in all its many aspects. Dante saw

his *Monarchy* as a universal empire which reproduced that of Augustus and represented the myth of Rome." When one compares this to Bruni's history one sees that "Bruni's work is so important because his ideal city, so full of echoes of Plato, is not a work of fantasy, divorced from reality, but tends to identify itself with an actually existing city. He merely idealises and corrects some of its features according to a higher rationality. He is, of course, thinking of [contemporary] Florence." Garin, "The Ideal City," in *Science and Civic Life,* 21–48, quotes from 31 and 32.

35. Victoria Kahn especially noted the significance of rhetorical literature as a source of moral instruction. See *Machiavellian Rhetoric* (Princeton: Princeton University Press, 1994). Likewise, Brian Vickers, rightly rejecting the charge that the Renaissance had *confused* rhetoric and poetry, rhetoric and literature, noted that "the subsuming of poetry with prose or oratory under rhetoric, endorsed by Cicero, Ovid, and Quintilian, continued through the Middle Ages, so that to speak of a 'confusion of rhetoric and poetic' in the Renaissance, is anachronistic." Brian Vickers, *In Defence of Rhetoric* (Oxford: Oxford University Clarendon Press, 1990), 278. How, asked Vickers, in arguing against C. S. Baldwin, *Medieval Rhetoric and Poetic (to 1400)* (New York: Doubleday, 1928), and later Bernard Weinberg, *A History of Literary Criticism in the Italian Renaissance,* 2 vols. (Chicago: University of Chicago Press, 1961), could relating the two fields, so intimately related in origin even in Aristotle, be considered confused?

36. Vickers, *In Defence,* 285–87.

37. Baron's 1955 work on the "crisis" of the Renaissance aimed at showing the emergence of "the major tenets of historical philosophy of the Renaissance as early as 1400" (Baron, *Crisis,* 465). For Baron, such history was, like earlier classical history, civic, humanist, and political. As is well known, for Baron the key work, "the most vigorous and most complete expression of the new complex of political-historical ideas," "the genesis of Quattrocento thought," the "pioneer to which must be traced the development that leads . . . to Machiavelli and other great Florentine historians of the late Renaissance," was Leonardo Bruni's *Laudatio Florentinae urbis (In Praise of the City of Florence)* (c. 1401). The *Laudatio,* written in the political crisis that developed between republican Florence and tyrannical Milan as well as during the growing oligarchic tendencies within the Florentine government itself, pointedly traced the founding of Florence back to the time of the ancient Roman republic, eschewing any contamination from the era of Roman Empire. Written in the style of Thucydides' oration for Pericles and of the *Panegyricus* of Isocrates, the *Laudatio* was, as Baron noted, updated so that it "stemmed from the experiences and trends of his own day" (Baron, *Crisis,* 196). The work was, in effect, a hymn to the virtues of republicanism written in the form of history.

38. Because most Renaissance writers were unfamiliar with Greek culture, the model was Cicero — with his suspicion of speculation and the contemplative life. In effect, for the Renaissance humanists, classical life *meant Roman life* (Vickers, *In Defence,* 286).

39. See Felix Gilbert, *Niccolò Machiavelli e la vita culturale del suo tempo* (Bologna: Il Mulino, 1969), 223–42.

40. *La vita di Castruccio Castracani da Luca,* Machiavelli, *Opere,* 615.

41. December 23, 1502 and December 16, 1502, nos. 76 and 77.

42. See the three legation letters (*Legazioni*) from June 1502 at Urbino, October 1502–January 1503 at Imola, and October–December 1503 at Rome, later refined into the

Decennials of 1504 (*Decennali*) and then into *The Description* (*Descrizione del modo tenuto dal duca Valentino nello ammazzare Vitellozzo Vitelli, Oliverotto da Fermo, il signor Pagolo e il duca Gravina Orsini).* See the fine study by Barbara Godorecci, *After Machiavelli: "Re-writing" and the "Hermeneutic Attitude"* (West Lafayette, Ind.: Purdue University Press, 1993).

43. Peter Bondanella, *Machiavelli and the Art of Renaissance History* (Detroit: Wayne State University Press, 1973), 44. See, too, Peter Burke, *The Renaissance Sense of the Past* (New York: St. Martins, 1970), 106ff.; Felix Gilbert, "The Renaissance Interest in History," in *Art, Science, and History in the Renaissance,* ed. Charles S. Singleton (Baltimore: Johns Hopkins University Press, 1967), 377–78.

44. Cicero uses "Rome" as a hieroglyphic for thought rooted in tradition, *sensus communis,* and topics and "Greece" as a metaphor for critical philosophy. This indicates the difference between the Greek and Roman perspectives. "The streams of learning," said Cicero, "have flowed . . . in different directions, so that the philosophers have passed, as it were, into the Upper or Ionian Sea, a Greek sea . . . but the orators have fallen into the Lower or Tuscan [sea]" (*De Oratore* 3.16). For Cicero, this separation of learning and eloquence was due to his constant intellectual interlocutor, Socrates, who "separated in his discussions the ability of thinking wisely and speaking gracefully, though they are naturally united" (*De Oratore* 3.16. 68ff.). Nonetheless, Cicero knew that Socrates was a master of rhetoric and philosophy who knew that we could not know certain deep things (*Republica* 1.15–16; *De Oratore* 3.16; in *De Officis* 1.108). For "Greece" the *summum bonum* had been to discover truth, whereas for "Rome" the aim was to mobilize truth and opinion in the world.

45. Jacqueline de Romilly, *The Rise and Fall of States According to Greek Authors* (Ann Arbor: University of Michigan Press, 1977), 36ff.

46. *Discourses* 3.1.

47. Such knowledge, of course, could not eliminate *fortuna.* It could, however, suggest the kind of behavior that would provide the best chance of survival when the encounter with *fortuna* came. This acceptance of chance is one of the most difficult things for us to accept about Machiavelli's work. Our concept of knowledge, whether historicist, empirical, or rational, does not accept chance as anything but ignorance. Unexpected consequences are simply off our mental radar screen. For Machiavelli, on the other hand, the world was a tragic drama shot full of chance and mystery; and nothing, certainly not anything as feeble as reason, could hope to tame chance. One of the unexpected consequences of the postmodern revolution that came from Heidegger's exposure of rationality as a mere "framework," however, is that the tidy world of predictable occurrence and steadily increasing knowledge is being eroded by a new appreciation of how little we know. Chaos theory in physics, the work of Stephen J. Gould in evolution and paleontology, the impact of Foucault's *épistémê,* and Derrida's transcendental signifier as well as the work of historians like Hayden White, Simon Schama, Dominick LaCapra, and many other thinkers point to a possible new understanding of the relationship between human and natural things.

48. As Baron pointed out, Bruni's work was to provide a whole new interpretation of the republican era in ancient Roman history, an era that had been ignored by the "historians" who had worked under the medieval ideal of the empire. In Bruni, the classical

history as envisioned by Livy and Cicero was reborn. History showed that the building of new foundations in the present required the aid of history. This left Bruni in an awkward position, for his determination to give Florence a republican foundation required rejecting his beloved Dante, whose imperial sympathies had led him to condemn the republican conspirators, Brutus and Cassius. See Baron, *Crisis,* 50ff. Machiavelli, too, had condemned Dante for his support of the fantasy of the universal empire. But Machiavelli at least had seen clearly what horrors one must commit to preserve a republic. What is interesting, then, in Baron's Bruni — aside from the interesting conflict with Pocock's and Seigel's view of Bruni as caught up not in a political battle but in linguistic problems — is, in other words, the ingenuous political instrumentalism of Bruni's history.

49. Machiavelli worked on his more complete text for about four years until May 1525, when he presented the completed portion to Clement VII. What he presented is the work we have today, the events up to 1494. Though there are some *fragments* which seem to indicate that he intended to continue the history, he never got around to it. See Machiavelli, *Opere,* 23–37.

50. "If every example of a republic is moving, those which one reads concerning one's own move one much more and are much more useful" (*Florentine Histories,* pr).

51. Ibid., 5.1.

52. Ibid., 3.1.

53. Ibid., 2.39.

54. Ibid., 3.1. Emphasis added.

55. Ibid.

56. Ibid.

57. Ibid., 2.42.

58. Ibid.

59. Modern philosophy begins with the assumption of the natural equality of all human beings. Certainly, it makes the case for diversity, but that case rests on the idea that *disturbing* differences are merely apparent, superficial matters to be tolerated or ignored because the binding social and political equality is more important and fundamental. Equality also is fundamental to the modern idea that conflict is abnormal and uncivil. Thus the more perceived qualities or inequalities are subordinated to equality, the less conflict there is and the closer one moves to the natural norm of tranquility. Thus modernity must subordinate so-called natural differences to equality because they are simply irrational barriers raised by the few against the many. In the modern scheme of things, therefore, differences can be tolerated only if they can be made to serve the lowest common denominator or, as one scholar put it, "The higher expectations of those better situated are just if and only if they work as part of a scheme which improves the expectations of the least advantaged members of society." John Rawls, *A Theory of Justice* (Cambridge: Harvard University Press, 1971), 75. One result of such modern and postmodern starting points in current academia is the effort devoted to "outing" the various ways power has been surreptitiously deployed to maintain inequality or, as is said today, in the "construction of the Other." Rooting out such arbitrary construction thus plays the role in the humanities and social sciences today that maintaining *virtù* did in an earlier period. *Outside* the Academy, the results of well-meaning attempts to create inequality can be even more spectacular. For example, Richard Collins noted (in "On Top," *Flying*

[May 1997]: 16), that he found something new at the airport when he leaned from his car to punch in the code to open the gate to the T-hangers where the planes were parked. "Each key," he observed, "had the appropriate Braille characters." He then wondered whether, "when we have to have Braille for someone driving a car to open a gate to get to an airplane to fly away," we have gone too far.

60. See, for example, *Prince,* chap. 15.

61. Sallust, for example, in his *The Conspiracy of Catiline* noted that "when Carthage, the rival of Rome's dominion, had been utterly destroyed, and sea and land lay everywhere open to her sway, Fortune then began to exercise her tyranny, and to introduce universal innovation. To those who had easily endured toils, dangers, and doubtful and difficult circumstances, ease and wealth, the objects of desires to others, became a burden and a trouble. At first the love of money, and then that of power, began to prevail, and these became, as it were, the sources of every evil. For avarice subverted honesty, integrity, and other honorable principles, and, in their stead inculcated pride, inhumanity, contempt of religion, and general venality. Ambition prompted many to become deceitful; to keep one thing concealed in the breast, and another ready on the tongue; to estimate friendships and enmities, not by their worth, but according to interest; and to carry rather a specious countenance than an honest heart. These vices at first advanced very slowly, and were sometimes restrained by correction; but afterward, when their infection had spread like a pestilence, the state was entirely changed, and the government, from being the most equitable and praiseworthy, became rapacious and insupportable" (*Catiline,* trans. Rev. John Selby Watson [Philadelphia: David McKay, 1896], 1.30). The problem of wealth has also attracted the attention of moderns as well, though most seem to think not that it corrupts, but that its unequal distribution corrupts; or, alternatively that wealth, far from being dangerous or malignant, is the only measure of a nation's development. See, for example, Walt Rostow, *The Stages of Economic Growth: A Non-Communist Manifesto,* 3d ed. (Cambridge: Cambridge University Press, 1991).

62. *Florentine Histories* 5.1; see also *Discourses* 1.10.

63. *Ozio* is a difficult word to translate. It is "leisure"; but unlike the Greek idea that wealth gave one the "leisure" to become cultivated, *ozio* was the "idleness" that gave birth to hedonism and slothfulness, as in the old expression "L'ozio e il padre dei vizi" (Idleness is the sire of vices).

64. *Florentine Histories* 5.1.

65. Machiavelli made several charges against Christianity: that it loved the weak and contemplative rather than men of ability; that the Roman Court's constant self-interest had destroyed religion in Italy; that it kept Italy weak and divided because while it was too weak to unite Italy, it was too strong to be eliminated; that it taught contempt for this world so that while others contemplated God, it could seize the earth. In short, it does not believe or practice its own teachings (*Discourses* 1.11, 12; 2.2; 3.1). On the need to go back to the teachings of the original founder, see *Discourses* 1.12.

66. Letter to Vettori, April 14, 1527. Letter 321 in Martelli, *Opere,* 1250.

67. *Florentine Histories* 5.1.

Index